BATTLEGROUND
THE FAMILY

BATTLEGROUND

THE FAMILY

VOLUME 1 (A–G)

Edited by Kimberly P. Brackett

GREENWOOD PRESS
Westport, Connecticut • London

Library of Congress Cataloging-in-Publication Data

Battleground : the family / edited by Kimberly P. Brackett.
    p. cm.
  Includes bibliographical references and index.
    ISBN 978-0-313-34095-6 (set : alk. paper) — ISBN 978-0-313-34096-3 (vol. 1 : alk. paper) — ISBN 978-0-313-34097-0 (vol. 2 : alk. paper)
  1. Family—Encyclopedias.   I. Brackett, Kimberly P.
    HQ515.B38   2009
    306.8503—dc22   2008038759

British Library Cataloguing in Publication Data is available.

Copyright © 2009 by Greenwood Publishing Group, Inc.

All rights reserved. No portion of this book may be reproduced, by any process or technique, without the express written consent of the publisher.

Library of Congress Catalog Card Number: 2008038759
ISBN: 978-0-313-34095-6 (set)
       978-0-313-34096-3 (vol. 1)
       978-0-313-34097-0 (vol. 2)

First published in 2009

Greenwood Press, 88 Post Road West, Westport, CT 06881
An imprint of Greenwood Publishing Group, Inc.
www.greenwood.com

Printed in the United States of America

The paper used in this book complies with the Permanent Paper Standard issued by the National Information Standards Organization (Z39.48–1984).

10 9 8 7 6 5 4 3 2 1

CONTENTS

Guide to Related Topics   ix
Series Foreword   xiii
Preface   xv

Entries:

Abortion	1
Addiction and Family	9
Adversarial and No-Fault Divorce	15
African American Fathers	24
Arranged Marriage	33
Attention Deficit Hyperactivity Disorder (ADHD)	40
Battered Woman Syndrome	49
Benefits of Marriage	56
Biological Privilege	63
Birth Control	67
Birth Order	76
Breastfeeding or Formula Feeding	81
Changing Fertility Patterns	89

Child Abuse	98
Child Care Policy	105
Child Support and Parental Responsibility	112
Childbirth Options	117
Childfree Relationships	125
Children as Caregivers	134
Cohabitation, Effects on Marriage	139
Common Law Marriage	145
Corporal Punishment	152
Cosleeping	157
Covenant Marriage	163
Culture of Poverty	167
Dating	177
Day Care	185
Deadbeat Parents	191
Developmental Disability and Marital Stress	196
Divorce and Children	201
Divorce, as Problem, Symptom, or Solution	206
Domestic Partnerships	215
Domestic Violence Behaviors and Causes	221
Domestic Violence Interventions	228
Elder Abuse	239
Elder Care	247
Employed Mothers	252
Extramarital Sexual Relationships	257
Family and Medical Leave Act (FMLA)	265
Family Roles	269
Fatherhood	279
Fictive Kin	285
Foster Care	289
Gay Parent Adoption	297
Grandparenthood	304

Grandparents as Caregivers	311
Homeschooling	319
Housework Allocation	326
Infertility	333
International Adoption	346
Juvenile Delinquency	355
Mail Order Brides	363
Mandatory Arrest Laws	369
Marital Power	375
Marital Satisfaction	383
Marriage Promotion	394
Mate Selection Alternatives	400
Midwifery and Medicalization	405
Mommy Track	414
Motherhood, Opportunity Costs	418
Nonmarital Cohabitation	423
Only Child	431
Overscheduled Children	436
Parenting Styles	443
Pet Death and the Family	450
Plural Marriage	457
Poverty and Public Assistance	464
Premarital Sexual Relationships	472
Prenuptial Agreements	478
Preparation for Marriage	485
Religion and Families	493
Religion, Women, and Domestic Violence	499
Remarriage	504
Same-Sex Marriage	515
Sibling Violence and Abuse	521
Stay at Home Dads	526
Surrogacy	532

Teen Pregnancy	543
Transition to Parenthood	552
Transracial Adoption	558
Wedding and Eloping	567
White Wedding Industry	572
Bibliography	*579*
About the Editor and Contributors	*617*
Index	*625*

GUIDE TO RELATED TOPICS

DATING AND RELATIONSHIP FORMATION
Cohabitation Effects on Marriage
Dating
Fictive Kin
Mate Selection Alternatives
Nonmarital Cohabitation
Prenuptial Agreements

DOMESTIC VIOLENCE
Battered Woman Syndrome
Child Abuse
Domestic Violence Behaviors and Causes
Domestic Violence Interventions
Elder Abuse
Mandatory Arrest Laws
Religion, Women, and Domestic Violence
Sibling Violence and Abuse

ENDING PERSONAL RELATIONSHIPS
Adversarial and No-Fault Divorce
Divorce and Children
Divorce, as Problem, Symptom, or Solution

FAMILY AND OTHER INSTITUTIONAL CONNECTIONS
Biological Privilege
Child Care Policy

Culture of Poverty
Foster Care
Homeschooling
Marriage Promotion
Poverty and Public Assistance
Religion and Families

FAMILY FORMATION OPTIONS
Changing Fertility Patterns
Childbirth Options
Gay Parent Adoption
International Adoption
Midwifery and Medicalization
Surrogacy
Teen Pregnancy
Transracial Adoption

FAMILY WORK, FAMILY CRISES, AND CAREGIVING
Addiction and Family
Children as Caregivers
Elder Care
Grandparents as Caregivers
Housework Allocation
Juvenile Delinquency
Pet Death and the Family

FERTILITY AND SEXUALITY IN RELATIONSHIPS
Abortion
Birth Control
Extramarital Sexual Relationships
Infertility
Premarital Sexual Relationships

PARENTING AND CHILD REARING ISSUES
African American Fathers
Attention Deficit Hyperactivity Disorder (ADHD)
Birth Order
Breast Feeding or Formula Feeding
Child Support and Parental Responsibility
Corporal Punishment
Cosleeping
Deadbeat Parents
Fatherhood
Grandparenthood

Only Child
Overscheduled Children
Parenting Styles
Transition to Parenthood

RELATIONSHIP AND MARITAL PROCESSES
Benefits of Marriage
Childfree Relationships
Developmental Disability and Marital Stress
Family Roles
Marital Power
Marital Satisfaction

TRADITIONAL MARRIAGE AND ITS ALTERNATIVES
Arranged Marriage
Common Law Marriage
Covenant Marriage
Domestic Partnerships
Mail Order Brides
Plural Marriage
Preparation for Marriage
Remarriage
Same-sex Marriage
Wedding and Eloping
White Wedding Industry

WORK AND FAMILY LINKS
Day Care
Employed Mothers
Family and Medical Leave Acts (FMLA)
Mommy Track
Motherhood, Opportunity Costs
Stay-at-home Dads

SERIES FOREWORD

Students, teachers, and librarians frequently need resources for researching the hot-button issues of contemporary society. Whether for term papers, debates, current-events classes, or to just keep informed, library users need balanced, in-depth tools to serve as a launching pad for obtaining a thorough understanding of all sides of those debates that continue to provoke, anger, challenge, and divide us all.

The sets in Greenwood's *Battleground* series are just such a resource. Each *Battleground* set focuses on one broad area of culture in which the debates and conflicts continue to be fast and furious—for example, religion, sports, popular culture, sexuality and gender, science and technology. Each volume comprises dozens of entries on the most timely and far-reaching controversial topics, such as abortion, capital punishment, drugs, ecology, the economy, immigration, and politics. The entries—all written by scholars with a deep understanding of the issues—provide readers with a nonbiased assessment of these topics. What are the main points of contention? Who holds each position? What are the underlying, unspoken concerns of each side of the debate? What might the future hold? The result is a balanced, thoughtful reference resource that will not only provide students with a solid foundation for understanding the issues, but will challenge them to think more deeply about their own beliefs.

In addition to an in-depth analysis of these issues, sets include sidebars on important events or people that help enliven the discussion, and each entry includes a list of "Further Reading" that help readers find the next step in their research. At the end of volume 2, the readers will find a comprehensive Bibliography and Index.

PREFACE

Families are inherently interesting because we have experiences, positive and negative, of them. But that also means we have lots of baggage that accompanies our consideration of families as well. When we think of something that is a battleground, it implies that there is debate, but beyond that it suggests a moral or ethical stand that is worth fighting for. There is a struggle required to resolve a battle and in family what we quickly learn is that the values and stereotypes that we hold toward how family life should occur may be the ammunition. *Battleground: The Family* recognizes the contentiousness of issues that impact family life and attempts to synthesize the current debates for the reader.

An initial question you might have is why family issues are so contentious. Family life has undergone a radical transformation in the last half century, challenging what most persons thought they knew about how to form a partnered relationship, have and rear children, and grow old together. Among the important trends have been an increase in the numbers of single people in the United States, later ages at first marriage and delayed childbearing in marriage, decreasing family size, more women working for pay, higher rates of divorce, and more participation in remarriages and stepfamilies. Greater openness about sexuality, increased birth control options, higher numbers of nonmarital births, and a push for greater acceptance of homosexuality have left the country in a moral quandary. Despite the expectation that families are private, battles over family issues play out in the public domain. Political ideology and domestic policy have coalesced around various family values camps.

Family is undoubtedly essential in the lives of humans. We begin and generally end our lives within the confines of family. Family, then, has a great deal of power over us and a prominent place in our lives. But what do we individuals mean when we talk about family and what do researchers and politicians mean when they talk about family? The answers might surprise you because they can be so similar and so different all at the same time.

If you were to ask three friends to list who is in their family and provide a definition of family, you would get three different answers. However, the definition would probably sound something like, "a group of people who love and support each other and are related in important ways." That is a reasonable way to approach a family and the majority of people in the United States would define family in a similar manner. In our personal definitions we generally include an affective component, one based on emotional bonds, though we tend to be much less specific about how the partners are related, whether it is by marriage, blood, or some other criteria.

However, if you were to ask those same friends what "the family" or the "ideal family" is all about, their definitions, although quite likely similar to each other, will be a bit different than how they described their own families. While an element of affection is likely to be included, so are more traditional conceptions of family as composed of dad, mom, kids, pet, and white picket fence. This second definition is culturally determined and provides a general guide for the model that families are expected to follow. This is the definition for the family as a social institution. The ideal family for most Americans, what Dorothy Smith calls the Standard North American Family, is a nuclear family composed of a legally married, heterosexual couple and their children. These partners are similar in age, education level, income, religion and racial or ethnic category. They have adequate income and generally divide the labor along gender lines. The resulting pattern is one in which men work away from the home for pay, and women work in the home for no pay.

Clearly, the addition of one little word, "the," to family has a marked influence on the answer provided. This volume is called *Battleground: The Family*. That is important because it draws our attention to one of the primary sources of debate in family life, how families today conform to or diverge from the expected ideal family, and whether this is a positive or negative occurrence. The use of "the family" suggests that families are monolithic, exhibiting the same patterns of membership and function regardless of social circumstances. "The Family" represents normative family life. The battle over preferred family patterns begins when comparisons are drawn between actual families and the cultural ideal. The more divergent from the cultural expectations the family type seems, the more likely it is to generate controversy.

As increasingly diverse family forms have emerged over the last half century, questions over family life have become more common and more challenging. Changing family patterns exist alongside a standard of family life that has not changed. In her work, Stephanie Coontz suggests that Americans get trapped by the cultural ideal. Seeing few families in our personal experience that exactly fit the cultural ideal, we assume that there must have been more families that fit the model in the past, and that family life then was significantly better than it is today. By longing for the so-called good old days we get caught in a nostalgia trap that makes today's families seem like dysfunctional nightmares. When we rely on the family as our standard, there are likely to be many more emerging controversies as families forge new paths to help them compensate for changing social conditions. How one defines family is not just an academic exercise. It has real-life consequences for the types of family associations that are considered valid and those that are likely to be supported by other institutions, such as government and religion. For example, if a particular view of family, one that defines family in terms of two married parents, is the preferred model then more societal support and encouragement will be offered to those types of families, despite the fact that families that do not fit the model are more likely to need outside support.

It is common in our society to talk about the family as if there were only one model, approach, or formula. In other words, as if it is a separate entity quite apart from the individuals who live it. While it is true that there are consistent patterns of interaction that people who are bonded by blood or marriage demonstrate, there is only the idea known as the family. Again, this can demonstrate where many of the controversies in family originate. When we think about family as something beyond ourselves, we fail to recognize that family is something we do everyday as we interact in family-like associations with others. In other words, we take family for granted, assuming that all families work like ours. That is, until someone else's view or experience of family is radically different than our own and causes us to question what we have assumed to be true. In recognition of the increasingly diverse and controversial experiences of family life that have emerged in recent years, the most prestigious academic journal of family research changed its name from *Journal of Marriage and the Family* to *Journal of Marriage and Family*. Not only does the controversy over the way family is defined influence the field of family studies in general, it influences the way that many different constituencies approach family life. Questions over definition inform many of the controversies discussed in *Battleground: The Family,* but there are more practical concerns raised as well.

One of the important things to do before studying the controversies that abound regarding family life in the United States is to ask what your personal definition of family contains. Who is in your family? Who is included and who is excluded? How does this relate to who ought to be in a family? This latter question is of key importance for the debates that rage in the areas of family studies, family relationships, and family policies today. One of the tensions apparent in any exploration of family life is the difference between the way that families are and that way that we might like them to be. The chasm between our ideal image of family life and our reality of family experiences can leave us in turmoil. It is in the challenge of reconciling the realities of family life today with the cultural models of the perfect family that the conflicting viewpoints are most evident. At the societal level common areas of conflict include divorce, unwed motherhood, housework, day care, and public assistance. But these issues of ideal and real are just as important in examining the stress that results on the individual level from, for example, rearing a developmentally disabled child or deciding whether to breast feed or bottle feed.

Families today no longer fit neatly into the models of the past. They are significantly more complex, more likely to be formed outside of a traditional marriage and to end more easily. Additional controversies that inform the debate about family in the United States reflect the links between family and other social institutions. Thinking about the role of intervention and social policy in the lives of families indicates the links between government and family life. How involved should government be in what have been described as private decisions? Also on the institutional level, the links between family and religion are ripe for controversy. With family assigned the role of moral steward for children, debate emerges about whether any group other than a traditional two-parent, married heterosexual family can rear a morally conscientious child. The suggestion is routinely offered that changes to family signal a moral decline in the society.

Controversy in family often revolves around stereotypes. Such is the case with African American fathers or gay parents. One continuing debate emphasizes family form compared to function by asking which types of families are best suited to fulfill the socially assigned tasks of having and rearing children, providing emotional and financial support to the members, and regulating sexual activity. For persons who presume that the two parent family is best, social problems can be seen as resulting from the increasing number of single parent families and the failure of many noncustodial parents to pay child support. For persons who consider alternative family forms equally effective at fulfilling these tasks, the critical issue is one of acceptance and support. One of the hottest family debates among the political establishment is whether marriage would be a viable solution for some social problems, especially those resulting from divorce, single parenting, and teen pregnancy. Other areas where the role of marriage is controversial include covenant marriage and poverty and public assistance.

Additional debates arise over the privileging of biology or society when making decisions about family life. Various groups on each side can be found examining the circumstances under which children should be removed from the care of their biological parents and placed in a foster home, whether surrogacy arrangements should be upheld by the courts, or whether children should only be placed for adoption with parents who are their same race. Given the influence of psychology in our lives today, controversies arise as to the best strategies to accomplish certain parenting or growth and development objectives. What types of families or socialization experiences provide the best paths to rearing well-adjusted adults? Topics such as cosleeping, corporal punishment, and divorce and children draw on psychological traditions to debate outcomes.

A number of different constituencies have a stake in the form, organization, and function of family. Anytime there is rapid and continuing social change there is likely to be ongoing conflict. Family fits these criteria for debate perfectly. There is a great deal of public anxiety that surrounds the state of contemporary families. The themes discussed above emerge throughout the topics chosen for inclusion in *Battleground: The Family*.

The two volumes of the set *Battleground: The Family* are designed to provide extensive coverage of critical issues in U.S. culture concerning family life currently and into the future. The issues raised are not likely to be solved to everyone's satisfaction, and certainly not within the next few years. The goal of this work is to serve as a starting point for those who want to learn more about specific aspects of family life and the controversies that surround family construction, interaction, and processes. Advanced high school students and beginning undergraduates will find the work particularly useful because of the extensive cross references at the end of the entries that indicate the complex interwoven patterns of family life and choices. The lay reader may be intrigued to learn more about the different approaches to family life and the passion with which family is debated. Likewise, at the end of each entry, the accessible "Further Readings" note both academic and popular press sources for additional information and reflection. These further readings represent sources that the author consulted to complete the entry as well as materials that will be helpful as one begins to explore the various sides to the topic's debate on a deeper level. At the end of the work there is a general bibliography that the reader will find contains a variety of sources from traditional research journal articles, to popular self-help books, to Internet sites. The range of sources for more information about family life is intentional and represents the ubiquity of family concerns.

Across the spectrum of family life from family formation, to relationship maintenance, and dissolution of family through death or divorce, there are debates of the who, what, how, and why of family. Broad topics that find detailed coverage in this reference are dating, marriage, parenting, work and family, and divorce. While these are obvious topics for which debate is clearly ongoing and expected, other less popular topics are also included. Some of these are pet death and the family, children as caregivers, and mail order brides. These again highlight the range of issues that families encounter on a daily basis and the differing strategies they may employ to perform their evolving role in the culture. Just like different branches of the family tree, these topics converge at the common ancestor of family life.

One may notice that the authors for this work are very diverse in their educational attainment and background. Some are professors, some are graduate students, some work with families in the community, and most are undergraduates. Each brings to the table a desire to understand more about family life, attempting to share their broad knowledge of a topic with inquiring readers. The sharing of information by these different constituencies makes the work very accessible. It also allows a tremendous diversity of topics and views to emerge. The authors and I invite you to question what you know about family. Do your perspectives come from your actual experiences of family life or what you would like for those experiences to be?

As with any work that tries to be inclusive, there are limitations. Astute readers will find that there are more views on individual controversial issues than just those discussed here. We have attempted to present the most common opposing ideas, but know that we could not possibly have included them all here. Likewise, there are more topics in the broad category of family that are controversial than could be included. I suspect that even four volumes would be insufficient to fully catalog the political and lay disagreements over particular aspects of family life. Again, the goal has been to introduce enough substantive issues to adequately inform the novice family professional.

This work would be incomplete without offering thanks to some of the many people who have contributed to its success. First, thank you to the contributors who worked hard to fully explain sometimes unwieldy arguments and disparate approaches to family topics. Second, groups deserving special recognition are students who were enrolled in my classes in Sociology of the Family and Sociology of Gender Roles during fall 2007. Many of them find their work published here because they took seriously my encouragement to write an article. I am very proud of their efforts. Third, there are several persons who contributed portions of what would become entries. They include Shannon Houvouras, Jessica Akau, Leslie Langston Fussell, Bridget Amerson, and Melisa Quattlebaum. I thank them for their contributions as well. Fourth, thank you to my mentor, Connie Shehan. Fifth, at Greenwood Press Kevin Downing and Lindsay Claire were always available and extremely helpful. On the home front, thank you to my colleagues at Auburn University at Montgomery. Finally, it goes without saying that no work on family would be complete without a special acknowledgment of one's own family; without the love and support of my family this work would not have been possible.

Kimberly P. Brackett, June 2008

Further Reading: Coontz, Stephanie. *The Way We Never Were: American Families and the Nostalgia Trap.* New York: Basic Books, 1992; Coontz, Stephanie. *The Way We Really Are: Coming to Terms with America's Changing Families.* New York: Basic Books, 1997; Gubrium, Jaber F., and James A. Holstein. *What is Family?* Mountain View, CA: Mayfield Publishing Co., 1990; Levin, Irene and Jan Trost. "Understanding the Concept of Family." *Family Relations* 41 (1992): 348–351; Smith, Dorothy E. "The Standard North American Family: SNAF as an Ideological Code." *Journal of Family Issues* 14 (1993): 50–65.

A

ABORTION

Abortion refers to the premature end or termination of a pregnancy after implantation of the fertilized ovum in the uterus and before fetal viability or the point in fetal development at which a fetus can survive outside a woman's womb without life support. The term refers to the expulsion of the fetus, fetal membranes, and the placenta from the uterus, and includes spontaneous miscarriages and medical procedures performed by a licensed physician intended to end pregnancy at any gestational age.

ABORTION PROCEDURES

An early abortion procedure, performed during the first trimester, or the first 12 weeks of pregnancy, is one of the safest types of medical procedures when performed by a trained healthcare professional in a hygienic environment. The risk of abortion complications is minimal, with less than 1 percent of all patients experiencing a serious complication. In the United States the risk of death resulting from abortion is less than 0.6 per 100,000 procedures. The risks associated with abortion are less than those associated with childbirth.

There are two major types of procedures used to terminate a pregnancy. These procedures include both medical abortions and surgical abortions. The type of procedure that will be used is selected by the physician and the patient after determining the stage of pregnancy. Early-term abortions, or those occurring in the first trimester of pregnancy, may be either medical or surgical. Surgical abortions are used in later-stage abortions, or those occurring in the second or third trimester.

Early First-Trimester Abortions

Early first-trimester abortions are defined as those performed within the first eight weeks of pregnancy. Two procedures may be used: medical (nonsurgical) or surgical abortions. Medical abortions include the administration of a combination of one of two oral medications that causes expulsion of the fetus from the uterus (miscarriage). Medical abortions include the use of RU-486, commonly referred to as the abortion pill, as well as the use of other combinations of drugs, depending on the stage of pregnancy. Typically, a combination of methotrexate and misoprostol are used to end pregnancies of up to seven weeks in duration. RU-486, a combination of mifepristone and misoprostol is used to terminate pregnancies between seven and nine weeks in duration. Women opting for a medical abortion are typically administered methotrexate orally or by injection in a physician's office. Misoprostal tablets are administered orally or vaginally during a second office visit that occurs five to seven days later. The procedure is then followed up with a visit to the physician to confirm complete expulsion of the fetus and the absence of any complications. Many women find that medical abortions are more private and more natural than surgical abortions.

A surgical abortion involves the use of suction aspiration to remove the fetus from the uterus. Surgical abortion is generally used to end pregnancies between 6 and 14 weeks duration. Vacuum aspiration uses suction to expel the contents of the uterus through the cervix. Vacuum aspiration is performed in a doctor's office or clinic setting and typically takes less than 15 minutes. Patients receive an injection into the cervix to numb the cervical area. The physician inserts dilators to open the cervix where a sterile cannula is inserted. The cannula, attached to tubing that is attached to a vacuum or manual pump, gently empties the contents of uterus. The procedure is highly effective and is used most often in first-trimester abortions.

Second-Trimester Abortions

Second-trimester abortions refer to abortions performed between the thirteenth and twentieth weeks of pregnancy. In some cases, second-trimester abortions may be performed as late as the twenty-fourth week of pregnancy. Second-trimester abortions include a greater risk of complications due to the later stage of fetal development and are performed under local or general anesthesia. The cervix is dilated and a curette or forceps are inserted through the vagina, and the fetus is separated into pieces and extracted. Second-trimester abortions are typically performed in cases where a woman has not had access to early medical care and has only recently had a pregnancy confirmed, or in cases where a recent diagnosis of genetic or fetal developmental problems has been made.

The available abortion procedures provide many options to women. Pregnancy terminations performed between the sixth and twelfth weeks of pregnancy are safe and include both medical and surgical procedures. Medical abortions, induced by a combination of drugs that induce a miscarriage, provide women with the option of ending a pregnancy in the privacy of her home in a more natural way. Surgical abortion, by using vacuum aspiration, gently removes the fetus from the uterus and includes minimal risks. These risks are usually limited to cramping and bleeding that last from a few hours to several days after the procedure. Most women who abort during the first trimester are able to return to their normal routines the following day. Antibiotics are generally prescribed following a first-trimester abortion to decrease any risk of infection and a follow up visit several weeks later makes first-trimester abortions safer than childbirth.

ABORTION AS A SOCIAL ISSUE

As a contemporary social issue, elective abortion raises important questions about the rights of pregnant women, the meaning of motherhood, and the rights of fetuses. Since the late 1960s, abortion has been a key issue in the contemporary U.S. culture wars. The term "culture wars" refers to ongoing political debates over contemporary social issues, including not only abortion but also homosexuality, the death penalty, and euthanasia. Culture wars arise from conflicting sets of values between conservatives and progressives. The culture war debates, particularly those surrounding the issue of abortion, remain contentious among the American public. The debates have resulted in disparate and strongly held opinions among the American public and have resulted in the emergence of activist groups taking a variety of positions on abortion. Activists include those who support a woman's right to abortion (epitomized in groups such as the National Abortion Rights Action League—NARAL Pro-Choice America) and those who oppose abortion on religious or moral grounds (such as right-to-life organizations).

Researchers suggest that the continuing debates over abortion have called into question traditional beliefs about the relations between men and women, raised vexing issues about the control of women's bodies and women's roles, and brought about changes in the division of labor in the family and in the broader occupational arena. Elective abortion has called into question long-standing beliefs about the moral nature of sexuality. Further, elective abortion has challenged the notion of sexual relations as privileged activities that are symbolic of commitments, responsibilities, and obligations between men and women. Elective abortion also brings to the fore the more personal issue of the meaning of pregnancy.

Historically, the debate over abortion has been one of competing definitions of motherhood. Pro-life activists argue that family, and particularly motherhood, is the cornerstone of society. Pro-choice activists argue that reproductive choice is central to women controlling their own lives. More contemporary debates focus on the ethical and moral nature of personhood and the rights of the fetus. In the last 30 years these debates have become politicized, resulting in the passage of increasingly restrictive laws governing abortion, abortion doctors, and abortion clinics.

EARLY ABORTION LAWS

Laws governing abortion up until the early nineteenth century were modeled after English Common Law, which criminalized abortion after "quickening" or the point in fetal gestational development where a woman could feel fetal movement. Prior to quickening, the fetus was believed to be little more than a mass of undifferentiated cells. Concurrent with the formal organization of the American Medical Association in the mid-1800s, increasingly restrictive abortion laws were enacted. In general, these laws were designed to decrease competition between physicians and mid-wives, as well as other lay practitioners of medicine, including pharmacists. A few short years later, The New York Society for the Suppression of Vice successfully lobbied for passage of the Comstock Laws, a series of laws prohibiting not only pornography but also banning contraceptives and information about abortion. With the formal organization of physicians and the enactment of the Comstock Laws, pregnancy and childbirth shifted from the realm of privacy and control by women to one that was increasing public and under the supervision of the male medical establishment. Specifically, all abortions were prohibited except therapeutic abortions that were necessary in order to save the life of the pregnant woman. These laws remained unchallenged until the early 1920s when Margaret Sanger and her husband were charged with illegally distributing information about birth control. An appeal of Sanger's conviction followed and contraception was legalized, but only for the prevention or cure of disease. It was not until the early 1930s that federal laws were enacted that prohibited government inference in the physician-patient relationship as it related to doctors prescribing contraception for their female patients. Unplanned pregnancies continued to occur and women who had access to medical care and a sympathetic physician were often able to obtain a therapeutic abortion. These therapeutic abortions were often performed under less than sanitary conditions because of the stigma attached to both the physicians performing them and to the women who sought to abort.

By the 1950s, a growing abortion reform movement had gained ground. The movement sought to expand the circumstances under which therapeutic abortions were available; it sought to include circumstances in which childbirth endangered a woman's mental or physical health, where there was a high likelihood of fetal abnormality, or when pregnancy was the result of rape or incest. The abortion reform movement also sought to end the threat of "back-alley abortions" performed by questionable practitioners or performed under unsanitary conditions that posed significant health risks to women and often resulted in death.

By the 1960s, although the abortion reform movement was gaining strength, nontherapeutic abortion remained illegal and therapeutic abortion was largely a privilege of the white middle to upper classes. A growing covert underground abortion rights collective emerged in the Midwest. Known as the Jane Project, the movement included members of the National Organization for Women, student activists, housewives and mothers who believed access to safe, affordable abortion was every woman's right. The Jane Project was an anonymous abortion service manned by volunteers who provided counseling services and acted in an intermediary capacity to link women seeking abortions with physicians who were willing to perform the procedure. Members of the collective, outraged over the exorbitant prices charged by many physicians, learned to perform the abortion procedure themselves. Former members of the Jane Project report providing more than 12,000 safe and affordable abortions for women in the years before abortion was legalized.

Activists involved in the early movement to reform abortion laws experienced their first victory in 1967 when the Colorado legislature enacted less restrictive regulations governing abortion. By 1970, four additional states had revised their criminal penalties for abortions performed in the early stages of pregnancy by licensed physicians, as long as the procedures followed legal procedures and conformed to health regulations. These early challenges to restrictive abortion laws set into motion changes that would pave the way to the legal right to abortion.

THE LEGAL RIGHT TO ABORTION

Two important legal cases reviewed by the U.S. Supreme Court in the 1970s established the legal right to abortion. In the first and more important case, *Roe v. Wade,* the court overturned a Texas law that prohibited abortions in all circumstances except when the pregnant woman's life was endangered. In a second companion case, *Doe v. Bolton,* the high court ruled that denying a woman the right to decide whether to carry a pregnancy to term violated privacy rights guaranteed under the U.S. Constitution's Bill of Rights. These decisions, rendered by a 7 to 2 vote by the Supreme Court justices in 1973, struck down state statutes outlawing abortion and laid the groundwork for one of the most controversial public issues in modern history.

The Supreme Court decisions sparked a dramatic reaction by the American public. Supporters viewed the Court's decision as a victory for women's rights, equality, and empowerment while opponents viewed the decision as a frontal attack on religious and moral values. Both supporters and opponents mobilized, forming local and national coalitions that politicized the issue and propelled abortion to the forefront of the political arena. Opponents of abortion identified themselves as "anti-abortion" activists while those who supported a woman's right to choose whether to carry a pregnancy to term adopted the term "pro-choice" activists. These two groups rallied to sway the opinions of a public that was initially disinterested in the issue.

THE EARLY YEARS POST ROE

Following the Roe decision, anti-abortion activists worked to limit the effects of the Supreme Court decision. Specifically, they sought to prevent federal and state monies from being used for abortion. In 1977, the Hyde Amendment was passed by Congress and limits were enacted that restricted the use of federal funds for abortion. In the ensuing years, the amendment underwent several revisions that limited Medicaid coverage for abortion to cases of rape, incest, and life endangerment. The Hyde Amendment significantly impacted low-income women and women of color. It stigmatized abortion care by limiting federal and state health care program provisions for basic reproductive health care.

As anti-abortion and pro-choice advocates mobilized, their battles increasingly played out in front of abortion clinics throughout the country, with both groups eager to promote their platforms about the legal right to abortion. Abortion clinics around the country became the sites of impassioned protests and angry confrontations between activists on both sides of the issue. Confrontations included both anti-abortionists who pled with women to reconsider their decision to abort, and pro-choice activists working as escorts for those who sought abortions, shielding the women from the other activists who were attempting to intervene in their decision. Many clinics became a battleground for media coverage and 30-second sound bites that further polarized activists on both sides of the issue. Moreover, media coverage victimized women who had privately made a decision to abort by publicly thrusting them into the middle of an increasingly public battle.

By the mid-1980s, following courtroom and congressional defeats to overturn the *Roe v. Wade* decision and a growing public that was supportive of the legal right to abortion, anti-abortion activists broadened their strategies and tactics to focus on shutting down abortion clinics. Moreover, anti-abortionist groups began identifying themselves as "pro-life" activists to publicly demonstrate their emphasis on the sanctity of all human life and to reflect their concern for both the pregnant woman and the fetus. The change in labels was also an attempt to neutralize the negative media attention resulting from a number of radical and militant anti-abortion groups that emerged in the 1980s, many of which advocated the use of intimidation and violence to end the availability of abortion and to close down clinics. For these more radical groups, the use of violence against a fetus was seen as justification for violence that included the bombing and destruction of abortion clinics and included, in some cases, the injury or murder of physicians and staff working at the clinics.

The polarization of activists on both sides of the issue and the increased incidence of violence at abortion clinics resulted in the passage of the Freedom of Access to Clinic Entrance Act (FACEA). FACEA prohibited any person from threatening, assaulting, or vandalizing abortion clinic property, clinic staff, or clinic patients, as well as prohibited blockading abortion clinic entrances to prevent entry by any person providing or receiving reproductive health services. The law also provided both criminal and civil penalties for those breaking the law. Increasingly, activists on both sides of the issue shifted their focus from women seeking to abort and abortion clinics to the interior of courtrooms, where challenges to the legal right to abortion continue to be heard. Meanwhile, increasingly restrictive laws governing abortion and abortion clinics were passed.

THE LATER YEARS POST ROE

With the legal right to abortion established and the battle lines between pro-life and pro-choice activists firmly drawn, key legislative actions impacting the legal right to abortion characterized the changing landscape of the abortion debate. In the 1989 *Webster v. Reproductive Health Services* case, the Supreme Court affirmed a Missouri law that imposed restrictions on the use of state funds, facilities and employees in performing, assisting with, or counseling about abortion. The decision for the first time granted specific powers to states to regulate abortion, and has been interpreted by many as the beginning of a series of decisions that might potentially undermine the rights granted in the *Roe* decision.

Following the *Webster* case, the U.S. Supreme Court reviewed and ruled in *Planned Parenthood of Southeastern Pennsylvania v. Casey*, a case that challenged five separate regulations of the Pennsylvania Abortion Control Act as being unconstitutional under *Roe v. Wade*. Specifically, the Pennsylvania act required doctors to provide women seeking abortion with a list of possible health complications and risks of abortion prior to the procedure, required married women to inform their husbands of an abortion beforehand, required parental or guardian consent for minors having an abortion, imposed a 24-hour waiting period before a woman could have an elective abortion, and mandated specific reporting requirements for clinics where abortions were performed. The court upheld four of the five provisions, striking down the spousal consent rule, which was found to give excessive power to husbands over their wives and possibly exacerbate spousal abuse. Moreover, the Court allowed for waivers for extenuating circumstances in the parental notification requirement. *Casey* was the first direct challenge to *Roe* and the court modified the trimester framework that *Roe* had created. It also restructured the legal standard by which restrictive abortion laws were evaluated. *Casey* gave states the right to regulate abortion during the entire period before fetal viability, and they could do so for reasons other than to protect the health of the mother. The increased legal rights provided to states to impose restrictions on laws governing abortion resulted in a tightening of the requirements for clinics providing abortions and adversely affected many women who sought abortions, particularly low-income women and women who lived in rural areas. As a result of the increased power granted to states to regulate abortion, women were required to attend a preabortion counseling session before the procedure, in which they received information on the possible risks and complications from abortion and they were required to wait at least 24 hours after the counseling session to undergo the procedure. For poor women or for women who lived in states where there were no abortion clinics available, the costs associated with the procedure rose dramatically because of the associated travel and time off from work.

Since *Casey*, the Supreme Court has heard only one case related to abortion. In *Stenberg v. Carhart*, the constitutionality of a Nebraska law prohibiting partial birth abortions was heard by the high court. The Nebraska law prohibited partial birth abortions under any circumstance. Physicians who violated the law were charged with a felony, fined, sentenced to jail time, and automatically had their license to practice medicine revoked. Partial birth abortions are performed between the twentieth and twenty-fourth weeks of pregnancy by using a medical procedure referred to "dilation and extraction." The procedure is generally performed in cases where significant fetal abnormalities have been diagnosed, and represents less than one-half of one percent of all abortions performed. The pregnancy is terminated by partially extracting the fetus from the uterus, collapsing its skull and removing its brain. In the *Stenberg* case, the court ruled that the law was unconstitutional because it did not include a provision for an exception in cases where the pregnant woman's health was at risk. However, in 2007 the decision was reversed in *Gonzales v. Carhart*.

THE SHIFT IN RECENT DEBATES

The differences between activist groups involved in the abortion debates have traditionally crystallized publicly as differences in the meaning of abortion. Pro-life activists define abortion as murder and a violation against the sanctity of human life. Pro-choice activists argue that control of reproduction is paramount to women's empowerment and autonomy. More recently the issues have focused on questions about the beginning of life and the rights associated with personhood. Technological advancements in the field of gynecology and obstetrics are occurring rapidly and influencing how we understand reproduction and pregnancy. Advances in the use of ultra-sound technology, the rise in fetal diagnostic testing to identify genetic abnormalities, and the development of intra-uterine fetal surgical techniques to correct abnormalities in the fetus prior to birth each contribute to defining the fetus as a wholly separate being or person from the woman who is pregnant.

These new constructions of the "fetus as a separate person," coupled with visual technologies that allow for very early detection of pregnancy and images of the developing fetus, give rise to debates about what constitutes "personhood" and the rights, if any, the state of personhood confers upon the entity defined as a person. The issue of viability, defined as the developmental stage at which a fetus can survive without medical intervention, is complicated in many respects by these technological advances. Those who define themselves as pro-life argue that all life begins at the moment of conception and point to technology to affirm their position. Many pro-life activists argue that the fetus is a preborn person with full rights of personhood—full rights that justify all actions to preserve, protect, and defend the person and his rights before and after the birth process. Others who define themselves as pro-choice argue that personhood can only be conferred on born persons and that a developing fetus is neither a born person nor a fully-developed being. These contemporary debates concerning personhood and rights continue to divide the public and are particularly germane to the issue of fetal surgery. Fetal surgery is cost-prohibitive, success rates are very low and some argue that the scarcity of medical resources should be directed toward a greater number of patients or toward the provision of services that have greater success rates.

THE IMPACT OF RESTRICTIVE ABORTION LEGISLATION

Abortion is one of the most common and safest medical procedures that women age 15 to 44 can undergo in the United States. Approximately 1.2 million abortions were performed in the United States in 2005. Among women aged 15 to 44, the abortion rate declined from 27 out of 1000 in 1990 to 19.4 out of 1000 in 2005. The number of abortions and the rate of abortions have declined over the years, partly as a result of improved methods of birth control and partly as a result of decreased access to abortion services.

The number of physicians who provide abortion services has declined by approximately 39 percent, from 2900 in 1982 to less than 1800 in 2000. Although some of the decline is the result of a shift from hospital-based providers to specialized clinics offering abortion procedures, this shift is further exacerbated by the number of clinics that have closed in recent years due to increased regulatory requirements that make remaining open more difficult. Moreover, the decline in providers of abortion services means that some women will experience a more difficult time in locating and affording services. Today, only 13 percent of the counties in the United States provide abortion services to women. Abortion services are unavailable in 87 percent of the counties in the United States.

The Food and Drug Administration's (FDA) approval of Plan B, an emergency contraceptive best known as "the morning after pill" and mifepristone (RU-486) for early medication induced abortions may be shifting the location of abortion procedures away from abortion clinics to other locations such as family planning clinics and physicians' offices. However, neither of these recent FDA approvals eliminates the need for reproductive health care that includes abortion care. While the issue of abortion may spawn disparate opinions about the meaning of motherhood, family values, the changing dynamics of male-female relations, and sexual morality, as well as raise issues about personhood and rights, unintended pregnancies disproportionately impact women and their children. This is especially true of poor women and women of color whose access to reproductive healthcare may be limited or nonexistent. Historically, women from the middle and upper classes have had access to abortion—be that access legal, illegal, therapeutic or nontherapeutic—while women from less privileged backgrounds have often been forced to rely on back-alley abortionists whose lack of training and provision of services cost women their health and, oftentimes, their lives.

See also Birth Control; Changing Fertility Patterns; Premarital Sexual Relationships; Religion and Families; Teen Pregnancy.

Further Reading: Ginsberg, Faye, D. *Contested Lives: The Abortion Debate in an American Community.* Berkeley: University of California Press, 1989; Luker, Kristen. *Abortion and the Politics of Motherhood.* Berkeley: University of California Press, 1984; Maxwell, Carol J. C. *Pro-Life Activists in America: Meaning, Motivation, and Direct Action.* Cambridge: Cambridge University Press, 2002; Riddle, John M. *Eve's Herbs: A History of Contraception and Abortion in the West.* Cambridge: Harvard University Press, 1997; Wedam, Elfriede. "Splitting Interests or Common Causes: Style of Moral Reasoning in Opposing Abortion," in *Contemporary American Religion: An Ethnographic Reader,* ed. Penny Edgell Becker and Nancy Eisland, pp. 147–168. Walnut Creek: Alta Mira Press, 1997.

Jonelle Husain

ADDICTION AND FAMILY

Addiction has become an increasingly large problem in the United States over the past few decades. Jails have become overcrowded with those who are caught selling and using addictive substances. It has become the social norm for celebrities to be in and out of Addiction Rehabilitation Centers every other week, and activities such as gambling and overeating have been labeled, along with substances such as alcohol and cocaine, as potentially addictive.

Once a narrowly defined term, addiction, or dependence, has been expanded to describe behaviors or activities that one wouldn't normally think of as being addictive. Among the more recent uses of the term are food addicts, sex addicts, and Internet addicts. With this expanding definition has come a heightened desire to uncover the causes behind addiction, whether it is to a traditional addictive drug or to a certain behavior. While the use of certain substances and certain activities often become addictions, not everyone that engages in these activities or consumes these substances becomes addicted to them, further complicating the issue. As a result, addiction counselors believe that there are certain reasons why one person becomes addicted more easily than another. Personality and biological factors are among some of the proposed reasons. Research into the topic has produced many debates over the subject of dependency and addiction, including conflicts over the cause and treatment of addiction and whether the term should apply to behavioral issues as well as to mood-altering substances.

Addiction has begun to play a large role in family life in the United States. Conceptions of harmonious family life suggest that serious problems such as addiction exist only in other people's families. As a consequence of this view, many families fail to recognize, deal with, and recover from a problem in their midst. The development, maintenance, and treatment of substance abuse are intimately connected with families. Families that have an addicted individual undergo a large assortment of effects, ranging from children lacking a parent due to addiction, to parents struggling to help their child to overcome an addiction, to divorce of marital partners when the lack of communication inherent with addiction leads to a breakdown of the marriage. Regardless of the stance one takes on the origin of addiction, it is important to remember that all addictions can be managed, and overcoming addiction is often achieved with the help of loved ones. Thus family plays a central role in the recovery process.

BACKGROUND

Addiction is a recurring compulsion or need by an individual to engage in some particular activity, or to consume some specific substance. The activity or substance becomes the sole focus in an addicted individual's life. He or she begins to lose interest in other activities, loses focus on goals that were once important, and will begin to abandon normal behavior in order to gain access to the addictive activity. As the need for the activity or substance grows, the individual will do anything for the substance. In extreme cases the addict even breaks laws in order to continue engaging in the activity or substance. Family is often the target of the illegal activity and may pay stiff penalties in personal and financial security as an addiction (particularly to illicit drugs) escalates.

When the term addiction was first coined it clearly referred to the use of a tolerance-inducing drug. This definition recognizes that humans can become quickly addicted to various drugs. The modern understanding of chemical transmission in the brain, and how substances can lead to addiction, began in the middle 1800s in France. From this initial research by Claude Bernard, scientists began to discover how the body responds to drugs.

Addictions develop because the substance or activity produces a pleasure response in the individual who then wants to receive more of the pleasure. For example, if an individual ingests a substance such as crack cocaine he or she will feel a euphoric "high" feeling. As the drug enters the brain it triggers the body's natural pleasure sensor to release endorphins, which results in a pleasurable sensation. The individual wants to continue to feel this euphoric high, but as the addiction builds the individual's tolerance to the substance grows. Over time, greater dosages of the drug must be used to produce an identical effect.

Over the years, however, as a medical model of behavior gained prominence, addiction began to be defined as a disease. This is in reference to the physiological changes that occur when one becomes addicted to a substance. The influence of both the medical and the psychological communities has been crucial in the area of addiction research. Two different types of addiction, physical dependence and psychological dependence, have been identified through their combined efforts.

Physical Addiction

Physical addiction is determined by the appearance of withdrawal symptoms when the substance is suddenly discontinued. Withdrawal refers to the symptoms that appear when a drug that is regularly used for a long time is suddenly discontinued or decreased in dosage. The symptoms of withdrawal are often the opposite of the drug's direct effect. Sudden withdrawal from addictive drugs can be harmful or even fatal, so the drug should not be discontinued without a doctor's supervision and approval. Part of the rehabilitation process is to wean the addict off of the drugs in a safer and less traumatic manner.

Alcohol, nicotine, and antidepressants are examples of substances that, when abused, can produce physical addiction. The speed at which an individual develops an addiction depends on the substance, the frequency of use, the intensity of the pleasure that the drug induces, the means of ingestion, and the individual person.

Psychological Addiction

Psychological addiction is the dependency of the mind, and leads to psychological withdrawal symptoms such as cravings, insomnia, depression, or irritability. Psychological addiction is believed to be strongly associated with the brain's reward system. It is possible to be both psychologically and physically dependent at the same time. Some doctors make little distinction between the two types of addiction because they both result in substance abuse. The cause and characteristics of the two types of addiction are quite different, as are the types of treatment. Psychological dependence does not have to be limited only to substances; activities and behavioral patterns can be considered addictions within this type of dependency. The popularity of Internet chat rooms, pornography, and social networking sites such as MySpace have all been characterized in this manner.

MEDICAL DEBATES

Not all doctors agree on what constitutes addiction. Traditionally, addiction has been defined as only possible when a substance is ingested that temporarily alters the natural chemical behavior of the brain in order to produce the euphoric "high" associated with these drugs. However, over time people have begun to feel that there should be an alteration of the definition of addiction to include psychological dependency on such things as gambling, food, sex, pornography, computers, work, exercise, cutting, shopping, and so forth. These activities do not alter the natural chemical behavior of the brain when they are preformed, thus they would not fit into the traditional views of addiction despite their impacts on social interactions and family life.

Those who support the contemporary view of addiction show that symptoms mimicking withdrawal occur when the individual stops the addictive behavior, even if it is not a physiologically acting substance. Those who believe in the traditional view purport that these withdrawal-like symptoms are not strictly reflective of an addiction, but rather of a behavioral disorder. Proponents of the traditional view say that the overuse of the term may cause the wrong treatment to be used, thus failing the person with the behavioral problem.

The contemporary view of dependency and addiction acknowledges the possibility that individuals who are addicted to a certain activity feel a sense of euphoria, much like the euphoria received from addictive substances. For example, when a person who is addicted to shopping is satisfying his or her craving by engaging in the behavior, chemicals that produce a "feel-good" effect, called endorphins, are produced and released within the brain, enforcing the person's positive associations with the behavior. Additionally, there could be negative, real-life consequences to participation in the activity including isolation from family and friends, increased debt, and so forth.

DEBATE OVER THE CAUSES OF ADDICTION

The causes behind addiction have been debated for years within the scientific community. There is one school of thought that believes that addiction is a disease that cannot be controlled by the individual. This theory states that addiction is an inherited disease and an individual with the inherited trait of the disease is permanently ill with the addiction located at a genetic level. Even those with long periods of overcoming the addiction will always contain the disease. This belief states that if one's parent was addicted to something, whether a substance or an activity, he or she is predisposed to also develop the addiction. Even if the person avoids the substance or activity he or she still technically has an addiction to it. The idea that "alcoholism runs in families" has a long tradition in the substance abuse field. Studies that compare alcoholism rates of natural and adopted children indicate that the adopted children of alcoholics have significantly lower rates of alcoholism than do their biologically related progeny. Additionally, a family history of alcoholism has been linked to a younger initial age of alcohol consumption.

Another school of thought argues that addiction is a dual problem caused by both a physical and a mental dependency on chemicals along with a preexisting mental disorder. This theory says that addiction isn't caused by one factor alone, but instead by many factors combined. Addiction is caused not just by the fact that a person's family member had the disease of addiction, but because the person's family member had the disease of addiction in addition to being emotionally unstable and prone to finding quick ways to happiness. Clearly, when a parent is "absent" due to his or her use of mood-altering substances, the socialization of the children is affected.

The Social Learning model suggests that the pattern of addiction is learned by watching or modeling the behavior of others. In families where addictive behaviors and substance abuse occur, children see role models of how to participate in addictive activities. This occurs even when parents attempt to hide their addictive behaviors. The fact that persons tend to share addictions over time through the process of assortative mating provides support for the idea that two persons with similar tendencies toward addictive behaviors will likely become partnered. There is scientific research to support all concepts of the causes of addiction. No one theory has emerged as having greater veracity in explaining and predicting dependency.

EFFECTS WITHIN THE FAMILY

Addiction is the number one disease in America with one in three families having at least one addicted member. With the problem of addiction so widespread, the effects on the family have become an important subject. Addiction effects the family in many ways. An addicted individual puts stress on the rest of the family. There is often a stigma of shame associated with addiction; this shame burdens the family and makes it harder for the family to seek help for the individual because of the fear of ridicule from the outside world. There is a substantial fear of discovery, and many families may hide the addiction for years without seeking the medical attention needed to help the addicted person. A significant loss of self-esteem in the addicted individual is noticed and may cause the addiction to get worse and the addicted individual to further deteriorate.

Many families that have an individual who has the disease of addiction are overcome by denial. They try to deny that there is a problem to everyone they know, including themselves. This act of denial will often lead to exaggerated feelings and may result in explosive behavior to which the family can become emotionally exhausted. One of the most concerning aspects of addiction in the family is that most illicit drug users are fairly young, of childbearing age (18 to 35 years), and thus are exposing children to addictive substances, behaviors, and outcomes.

Addiction may sometimes produce physical effects. Domestic violence, whether physical, emotional, or sexual, is increased in families that have an addicted member, particularly alcoholism. Domestic violence can occur in well-educated families as well as families with less professional backgrounds. It is predicted that members of families where abuse due to addiction takes place are more likely to require medical care. Additionally, children of substance abusers who experienced physical or sexual abuse are more likely to experience psychiatric symptoms and marital instability than those persons in whose family there was not addictive behavior.

Typically families experiencing substance abuse witness the allocation of the addict's role to others in the family. Often this "absent parent" cedes his or her responsibilities to a child. The child then must assume duties that are inappropriate to his age, even having to "raise" himself because the parents were unavailable to nurture the child. As one can imagine, this leads to strained relationships even as the child reaches adulthood. Resentment for a lost childhood is not uncommon.

Families with an individual who is an addict often withdraw from their community, are distrustful of others, and have severe financial difficulties. The fear of exposure and subsequent stigma may force the withdrawal. If the addict is engaging in illegal activities it is possible that he or she will be caught and sentenced to jail. Indeed, 80 percent of female inmates are mothers, and the vast majority has children under the age of 18. If the individual has no one to care for the children during the incarceration, the children might be left alone, placed in foster care, or put into state-run childcare facilities.

Another issue that families with an addict must face is the fact that children could be born to an addict and be drug-dependent themselves. In these cases, the infants must go through detoxification and often have a low birth weight or other lingering physical and behavioral manifestations of the addiction. If the mothers remain addicted, they may have tremendous difficulty meeting the care needs of their child. One of the factors most associated with an increase in infants addicted to substances is the wide availability and low-cost of crack cocaine.

FAMILY AND RECOVERY

The family often plays a large role in the recovery process for the family member that is an addict. Because denial is the primary barrier to effective treatment for addiction, the addict must admit that there is a problem. It is usually the family members who help the addict admit their addiction and realize that it is something they must overcome. Wives routinely encourage husbands to seek treatment for alcoholism, for example. Today, most recovery programs involve the family members in counseling and behavior modification, suggesting that fewer relapses occur when family support networks are readily available.

In order for an addict to successfully overcome an addiction he or she must have the support of his or her family. It is very important to find a treatment center or a recovery program that is a good fit for the person. There are now programs available that can easily be adjusted to better suit the person undergoing the treatment. Online programs as well as weekly meetings with other recovering addicts are useful methods. There are also live-in treatment centers that take a drastic approach to help the person recover, though they may be avoided due to the stigma of their "hospital-like" approach.

CONCLUSION

Addiction is only one of many subjects relating to the importance of one's family in the world today. The debate over what specifically constitutes an addiction, its precise causes, and which disease metaphor is the most appropriate will likely continue for some time. The focus of these debates should transition into how to prevent addiction and to diminish the damaging effects that it has on the family. We now live in a society where it is the social norm to associate addiction with a negative stigma. Ideally we would live in a society where those with an addiction were embraced so that the recovery process could happen immediately with no shame or blame given to the family of the addict. When we reach this point, family members will be better able to relate to one another and will be more emotionally stable.

See also Child Abuse; Children as Caregivers; Domestic Violence Behaviors and Causes; Juvenile Delinquency.

Further Reading: Alcohol and Drug Treatment Referrals. http://www.alcohol-drug-treatment.net/causes_of_addiction.html; Dowling, Scott. *The Psychology and Treatment of Addictive Behavior.* Madison, CT: International Universities Press, Inc., 1995; Goldstein, Avram. *Addiction: From Biology to Drug Policy.* New York: Oxford University Press, Inc., 2001; Peele, Stanton. *Seven Tools to Beat Addiction.* New York: Three Rivers Press, 2004; Texas Medical Association. http://www.texmed.org; University of Pennsylvania Health System. http://www.uphs.upenn.edu/addiction/berman/treatment/.

Angela Sparrow

ADVERSARIAL AND NO-FAULT DIVORCE

Divorce, also known as dissolution of marriage, is the ending of a marriage before the death of either spouse. Divorce rates in the United States have increased markedly in the twentieth century making it a commonplace occurrence. A divorce must be certified by a court of law because a legal action is needed to dissolve the prior legal action of marriage. Most often, the terms of a divorce are established by the court and may take into account prenuptial agreements or simply certify terms that the spouses have worked out and agreed upon privately. Often, however, spouses disagree about the terms of divorce, which can lead to stressful and sometimes expensive litigation. Divorce is a difficult situation for all parties involved and can result in hurt feelings, the destruction of a relationship, and the painful issues of assets division and custody battles. Because divorce has become so frequent and can be so destructive, less adversarial approaches to divorce and settlements have emerged.

Today there are two kinds of divorce: (1) contested or adversarial divorces and (2) uncontested or no-fault divorces. In an adversarial divorce, the parties cannot come to a private agreement on issues related to the termination of marriage and the resolution is decided in a court of law. In a no-fault divorce, the marriage parties need not show who or what was at fault in order to obtain a termination of the union. They agree to end the marriage without accusing the other of a violation of the marital contract, or to say that they were both equal in the decision. Both types result in a legal dissolution of marriage. The question for spouses seeking divorce is which process would satisfy their personal settlement outcomes. By examining the history of divorce, one can see how adversarial and no-fault divorces emerged and can compare the economic, emotional and health costs of both adversarial and no-fault divorce proceedings.

BACKGROUND

Divorce existed in antiquity, dating back at least to ancient Mesopotamia. The ancient Athenians allowed divorce but requests had to be submitted to a magistrate who would determine if the reasons for the requested divorce were sufficient. Divorce was rare in early Roman culture but as the Roman Empire grew in power, Roman civil law embraced the concept. Both spouses could renounce the marriage at will; however, Roman social and familial taboos guaranteed that divorce occurred only due to serious circumstances. The Christians restricted grounds for divorce to grave cause, but this was relaxed in the sixth century. After the fall of the Roman Empire, familial life was regulated more by ecclesiastical authority than by civil authority. By the ninth and tenth centuries, the frequency of divorce had been greatly curtailed by the influence of Christianity, largely via the Catholic Church. The Christian church considered marriage a sacrament instituted by God and Christ and was indisoluble by human action.

Divorce, as we know it today, was generally prohibited after the tenth century. An annulment of the marriage could take place where the husband and wife physically separated by not living together, but the marriage did not end and the husband had to continue to support his wife financially. Until the eighteenth century, annulment was the only way a marriage could be dissolved and the grounds for an annulment were solely within the control of ecclesiastical courts. The common-law courts had no power over marriage because it was a status granted by the Church and the circumstances for an annulment were determined by church authority. According to the Church, the Sacrament of Marriage produced one person from two.

Marriage eventually came to be considered a civil contract, and civil authorities gradually asserted their power to grant divorce. Because there were no precedents that defined the circumstances under which marriage could be dissolved, civil authorities relied heavily on the ecclesiastic courts and adopted the requirements set down by those courts. Because marriage could not be dissolved except in the most extreme of circumstances, common-law courts refused to grant a divorce if there was any hint of complicity between the husband and wife, or if they attempted to manufacture the grounds for a divorce. Divorce was granted only because one party to the marriage had violated a sacred vow to his or her innocent spouse. Eventually, the idea that marriage could be dissolved because of a violation of a sacred vow allowed other grounds, such as abandonment, adultery, or extreme cruelty, to be accepted as grounds for granting a divorce.

Before 1970 in the United States, due to the ways that the laws were written, getting a divorce meant proving that one spouse had done something wrong or had acted in a way that caused the breakdown of the marriage. Someone had to be at fault, which meant that grounds had to be established. Such legal and permissible grounds for a divorce petition might include adultery, physical or mental abuse, abandonment, confinement or holding against one's will, insanity, or the inability to be sexually intimate with your spouse. The fault had to be something more than not loving one another. When the proceedings ended in front of a judge, the judge might find that the accusation was not true and find both spouses at fault for the dysfunctional nature of the marriage and would refuse to dissolve the marriage.

These rules presented problems in cases where both spouses were at fault, or where neither one of the spouses had committed a truly sinful act but simply could not get along with the other. Lawyers began to craft creative methods to bypass the rules. Some lawyers went so far as to create a situation that proved adultery. Such as situation could be where one spouse would deliberately come home at a certain time and discover the other spouse committing adultery with a person obtained for the occasion. The cheating spouse would admit to the facts, the judge would convict the spouse of adultery, and the couple would be granted the divorce.

The extent to which a husband and wife might go in order to establish grounds for divorce was alarming to both judges and lawyers. These charades put the couples and their counsels at risk of perjury, fraud, and collusion charges. Judges feared making a decision to grant a divorce based on manufactured grounds and lawyers feared that they might be representing a divorce case based on untruths. Neither judges nor lawyers wanted to jeopardize the integrity of the courts and the divorce laws by making perjury a common and accepted practice for obtaining a divorce. In response to the liberalizing social climate, they realized that something needed to change.

In the early 1960s many in the legal institution recognized that two spouses who were determined to end their marriage would get what they wanted by any means necessary. Therefore, it was argued that the law should adapt by providing straightforward procedures for ending a marriage rather than forcing a couple who just couldn't get along to choose between living together in conflict or lying under oath in open court. Thus began what is commonly known as the Divorce Revolution in the United States. Most states substantially amended their divorce legislation and enacted various forms of no-fault divorce laws. Specifically, no-fault divorce ground laws allowed spouses to initiate divorce proceedings without proof of marital wrongdoing, removing fault as a consideration in the couple's division of assets, property settlements, and alimony awards.

NO-FAULT DIVORCE

No-fault divorce was pioneered in the United States by the State of California with the passage of the Family Law Act of 1969. The Act was signed by then-Governor Ronald Regan and took effect on January 1, 1970. It abolished old common-law action for divorce and replaced it with proceedings for dissolution of a marriage on the grounds of irreconcilable differences. By 1983, every state but South Dakota had adopted some form of no-fault divorce. The revolution was complete when South Dakota finally adopted no-fault divorce in 1985. As conceptualized at the time, no-fault divorce procedures would not only reduce the likelihood of perjury and hypocrisy in the courts on a routine basis, but would permit separated couples to formalize their status, thus allowing them permission to remarry if they so chose.

In a majority of states the no-fault divorce laws are very similar. New York, however, is currently the only state without a true no-fault divorce provision and debate continues about whether it would be advantageous to institute one. Currently, couples can blame one of the partners through finding grounds or can separate for a year and live apart before a divorce will be granted. Southern states such as Tennessee, Alabama, Florida, and Georgia have the most relaxed divorce laws and, interestingly, have the highest divorce rates in the country. A few states, like Louisiana, Arkansas, and Arizona, have laws that give couples the option to choose before they marry, through provisions of covenant marriage, which laws they want to apply to their divorce in the event the marriage ends. No-fault divorce proceedings appear to be a popular process and are accepted across the nation. There are Internet sites that even offer so-called no-fault divorce kits that can be ordered and submitted online, and some even offer free gifts with the order. A divorce, whether granted under an adversarial or no-fault divorce statute, is legally binding. The question for couples and attorneys is when to use which process.

Contemplating a divorce is always difficult. The dissolution of a marriage involves a number of legal and financial issues that must be considered before a settlement is achieved. Before a divorce is granted, the typical issues that must be resolved are alimony, spousal support, property division and, if there are children, custody, visitation, and child support. A couple that agrees in writing on all of those issues will likely be granted an uncontested divorce and avoid adversarial litigation. If there is disagreement on any of the basic issues, an adversarial divorce may be necessary. In either case, divorce is a disruption of the collective interests of the family and marks a marriage that is irretrievably broken.

COSTS AND BENEFITS OF NO-FAULT DIVORCE

The primary benefit of no-fault divorce is that the divorce can be accomplished more quickly and at lower cost than in the adversarial model. Divorces costing as little as $250 are available in some states. For couples who have few assets and no children, no-fault divorce helps them sever ties and move on with their lives. For someone experiencing domestic violence, no-fault divorce may permit a quicker way to escape the control of the partner. Feminist groups in the 1970s touted no-fault divorce as a way for women to gain equality with men, stressing that they would not be seen as victims in the courts. The idea that couples could agree to divorce does have benefits. Under the fault-based system, just discussing the grounds by which one was petitioning for divorce has been known to increase hostilities among couples.

In favor of retaining the option of no-fault divorce, Barbara Dafoe Whitehead suggests that adversarial options invite ongoing legal battles that result in increased hostility. In contested divorces, the establishing of fault is a time-consuming and costly matter. Additionally, Whitehead proposes that if there were no options for no-fault divorces some young people would refuse to get married. She argues that the biggest problem is not with divorce, but with how few people are truly prepared to make a lifelong marital commitment.

Critics of no-fault divorce argue that it has led to the breakdown of the family unit. The critics, made up primarily of religious and right-wing groups, blame the decreasing number of traditional nuclear families on no-fault divorce laws. These groups are advocating a renewed commitment to traditional family values that they believe will reverse society's seemingly wholehearted approval and support of divorce and remarriage. They also believe that by toughening divorce laws to make a divorce harder to get, it will eventually change social and cultural acceptance of divorce, lower the divorce rate, and thereby keep families intact and strengthen family values.

The critics of no-fault divorce also feel that a no-fault divorce gives the spouse who wants out of the marriage the power to end the marriage, while the non-consenting spouse has no recourse. Only three states, Mississippi, New York, and Tennessee, refuse to grant unilateral divorces. Critics argue that no-fault divorce reduces both spouses' commitment to the marriage because a no-fault divorce is so easily obtained and that, as it stands today, marriage carries very little social weight. "Couples can be married today, have a divorce tomorrow, and be remarried the next day" seems to sum up their perspective on the no-fault divorce process. These no-fault divorce opponents suggest that the threat of divorce makes people act selfishly in their personal relationships and contend that more wives would stop working to stay home and care for children if they were more secure that the relationship would last.

Politicians also blame no-fault divorces for the current high divorce rates, even though divorce rates have leveled off in the past 10 years and have even decreased from the rates seen when no-fault divorces first became widely available. Researchers suggest that the reason divorce rates were fairly high around the time no-fault divorce provisions were first introduced was because no-fault divorces merely sped up the pipeline for those who were already planning to and preparing for divorce.

Politicians that seem to be at a loss for solutions to profoundly serious social issues such as the high cost of health care, lack of affordable health insurance for all citizens, or the funding of social security usually find a scapegoat in the high divorce rate. They often suggest that many social problems could be solved if couples renounced their romantic notions and remained married. They also blame the no-fault divorce process for making it easier to obtain a divorce, which creates higher rates of persons seeking divorce as a quick solution. More importantly, divorce breaks up families and contributes to the emotional and the financial stress already faced by all families. The politicians contend that divorce makes family ills worse and that laws should be changed to make divorce harder to come by so that families would stay intact.

Divorce, in general, does seem to make family situations and issues worse. It is hard for some two-parent households to make ends meet today. After a divorce, single parents (especially mothers) and their children are at greater financial disadvantage. One parent is trying to do what two did. Studies suggest that after divorce the average annual income for a household comprised of the custodial mother and her children drops roughly 30 percent while the husband's finances rise by 10 percent. Women often have lower earning potential after a divorce because of their historical role in rearing children. In many cases, the mother has been the primary caregiver for the couple's children and has not had the outside work experience that the father had. This is sometimes referred to as the problem of displaced homemakers.

Likely the costliest aspect of no-fault divorce has been the dramatic reduction in alimony (spousal support) payments. One of the assumptions that undergirds no-fault divorce is the equality between women and men. At the inception of no-fault divorce, the assumption was that the sexes had, or would soon have, equal earning power. Thus, women could support themselves as well as men could support themselves. As a result, fewer than 12 percent of divorces today involve awards of spousal support. Given that mothers have custody of children after the divorce far more often than do fathers, their burden of supporting themselves includes their children and the challenge is often difficult to meet. Caring for children reduces mothers' opportunities and abilities to pursue high-paying employment because the costs of child care are often prohibitive. Likewise, women generally earn about 75 percent as much as comparably trained men do. Divorced women in most cases are not able to achieve the same standard of living they had during marriage.

Lenore Weitzman's findings, published in *The Divorce Revolution*, concluded that the majority of women could not sustain themselves financially after a divorce without assistance. This caused supporters of no-fault divorce and women's independence to rethink the value of no-fault divorce for women. While many had claimed that women gained freedoms and equality under no-fault divorce provisions, consistent with the objectives of the women's movement, they also lost financial standing. Many national and local governments have responded to this issue by providing some kind of assistance for divorced mothers and their children. Most interesting is that such public support for male-headed households is far less common. Divorce is the number one contributor to bankruptcy in the United States. Divorce can have severe financial consequences but there are emotional costs as well.

Divorce is often one of the most traumatic experiences a family can go through. Separation of the family can be filled with emotions, sadness, depression, and anger. Most children of divorce have no choice but to endure the process of their parents' separation and many children may suffer long-lasting emotional consequences. According to a study by the Domestic Policy Studies Department of the Heritage Foundation, over one million American children annually suffer from the divorce of their parents. The study also predicted that half of the children born to parents in 1996 (the year of the study) would experience the divorce of their parents before they are 18 years old. The research also showed that the effects of the divorce on children will continue into adulthood and have an effect in the next generation as well, suggesting that divorce, rather than commitment and working out difficulties, will be the norm. This is a common viewpoint of those who oppose divorce in general and no-fault divorce in particular.

A child of divorce is commonly subjected to abrupt and traumatic changes; loss of a father (in most cases) in the home on a regular and consistent basis, and potentially his replacement by a stepfather or by mother's live-in boyfriend. The absence of the father may leave the children feeling less protected and more vulnerable. These children often perform less well in school and there is a 10 to 15 percent higher rate of delinquency in single-parent homes than in intact homes. Current findings indicate that significant numbers of children of divorce have difficulty in establishing relationships. They are two to three times more likely to dissolve their own marriages than are children whose parents remained married.

The divorce process itself has a profound effect on children. Almost no child wants his or her parents to divorce. It does not take much imagination to determine the damage to a child whose parents are publicly struggling over him or her. The children may have a parental preference but do not want to offend either parent by making a choice. One of the criticisms of no-fault divorce is that while the divorce proceedings have gotten less contentious, divorcing partners who are determined to publicly place blame for problems in the marriage might fight the battle through protracted child-custody suits instead. The more adversarial the process of divorce and family dissolution, the greater chance there is for emotional damage from which the family will have to recover.

COSTS AND BENEFITS OF ADVERSARIAL APPROACHES

Divorce, no matter by what process, is not cost-free. An adversarial divorce can cause resentment, revenge, anger, fear, stress, anxiety, depression, low self esteem, grief, guilt, and hate between people who used to love each other enough to get married and have a family together. Contested proceedings can result in mental and emotional crisis, loss of business, job, and income. Family support can diminish as the process wears on. Most of all, damage to children that may witness screaming and abuse between parents may foretell life-long consequences. When married people are unhappy, their first unhappiness is at the level where they are fighting openly, frequently, and with hostility in front of the children. This conflict between the parents usually moves to the courtroom as the divorce process continues. Becoming completely divorced is an emotional as well as a legal process.

The drama of the adversarial divorce takes its toll on all concerned. It may also cost a lot of money. A significant financial impact of divorce is the actual cost of the divorce itself. Court costs and attorney's fees are high and are often an extreme hardship at a time when the divorcing couple begins to incur expenses in excess of the budget that they had during the marriage. This is particularly common when one of the partners has moved out and has expenses from living elsewhere. Parties to an adversarial divorce must retain litigating divorce lawyers in addition to any support experts, such as accountants, that must become party to the proceedings. Each lawyer's attempt to protect his client's rights can lead to increased conflict with the spouse and to a feeling of a loss of control over the process. Therapists, social workers and psychologists may also be required to assist with custody battles and visitation. All these specialists and expert witnesses are expensive and may leave the divorcing couple with debt and unpaid bills or even bankruptcy. The proceedings and consequences may also result in increased health hazards, from weight loss to increased cigarette and alcohol consumption to lower immune function.

One of the concerns that some persons have about adversarial divorce is the need to assign blame and sue the partner. Revelations about the relationship may become public record and, depending on career or social standing, this could be damaging to someone's future prospects. Not to mention that it might simply be embarrassing to have private matters revealed. These legal battles can be protracted, delaying the healing process. Blaming the partner for past marital problems also makes it hard to co-parent when future issues arise in decisions about shared children.

While adversarial divorces have their share of problems, they do have some benefits relative to no-fault divorces. First and foremost is the issue of spousal support, or alimony, which was more likely to be granted in the past than it is today. When alimony is awarded today, it is usually for a limited time and is a much smaller amount than in the past. Another key loss under the no-fault divorce system involves the idea of equal property division. Today couples often have to sell their joint property and divide the profit. Selling the family home when minor children reside there is difficult because it adds the stressors of moving to a new neighborhood, changing schools, and having to establish new friendship networks. Additionally, new mortgage payments may be higher compared to those for a house purchased some years ago. Under the adversarial system, title to the family home was often given to the dependent wife and children, keeping consistent part of their lives after the divorce.

Given the emotional and financial costs of divorce that have been well established, there are groups that would like to see significant changes in the divorce laws in the United States. They call for the repeal of the no-fault divorce option, suggesting that when divorce is too easy to attain, couples marry before being fully committed. When problems arise later, they don't work very hard to iron out their differences. Maggie Gallagher of the Institute for American Values has routinely taken this position. Other conservative groups would even like changes made to the adversarial or so-called fault divorce. There is support for toughening the divorce laws to include the intervention of trained divorce mediators in the process. Supporters of changes in divorce laws want to give nonconsenting spouses more power to fight for their marriage. They are also looking for ways to protect children from the scars of divorce through more equitable settlements of issues like child support and division of assets. These measures, they suggest, would prevent the emotional battles that cost money and prolong the settlement. For example, in the state of Oklahoma practicing matrimonial lawyers are supporting mediation as a less adversarial way to complete a divorce. Mediation can help marriage partners in the voluntary cooperation that Oklahoma's proposed reform laws would require. Supporters of this divorce law reform feel that there would be support for improving a fragile marriage through marriage counseling and mediation so a divorce may not be necessary. Premarital counseling is already mandated in some states and support is growing for provisions that would require counseling by ministers or therapists to be attempted before a divorce is granted. Couples seeking a divorce sometimes resent being ordered to attend such programs, but most of them eventually realize the emotional effects of divorce and are willing to cooperate with the process.

CONCLUSION

With the advent of no-fault divorce, blame is no longer essential in receiving a divorce. The goal of no-fault divorce legislation was to simplify the divorce process by reducing conflict and cost. Critics argue that no-fault divorce has driven up the divorce rate and shifted the acrimony from the battle over who is to blame for ruining the marriage to battles over child support, visitation, and custody. However, no-fault divorces appear to be less expensive and less stressful to accomplish than adversarial divorces.

In no-fault divorce proceedings, the husband and wife accept that the marriage is broken and have come to terms with how assets and debts should be divided. They also usually agree on the custody of the children, including child support and visitation. In an adversarial proceeding, intervention by an attorney is usually needed to push the divorce process along to the final decree. Attorneys can be expensive and the process can be prolonged by disagreement about the settlement issues. This adversarial proceeding is more likely to cause resentment, revenge, anger, fear, stress, and anxiety. These emotions leave the parties depressed and less reasonable regarding the settlement and getting on with their lives after the divorce is final.

Divorce may not be popular but it is common. In any given year the number of divorces that are finalized are equivalent to about half the numbers of marriages that are contracted. The stigma of divorce may have lessened considerably over time, but the effects can no longer be ignored. Divorce, even if amicable, alters the fundamental unit of American society, the family. The family transmits values, socializes children, and protects us as adults. Trauma, hurt, and physical separation of a family is the result, regardless of the process used to grant a divorce.

There are no easy answers to preventing divorce or to minimizing the costs of a divorce once it is granted. Alternatives like mediation before divorce should be considered to minimize conflict and perhaps save the marriage and family.

Marriage and the collective interests of the family must be invested with at least as much value as the right of spouses to abandon the marriage.

See also Covenant Marriage; Deadbeat Parents; Divorce and Children; Divorce as Problem, Symptom, or Solution; Marital Satisfaction; Preparation for Marriage; Remarriage.

Further Reading: Ahrons, C. *The Good Divorce.* New York: Harper Perennial, 1994; Fagan, P., and R. Rector. "The Effects of Divorce on America," *Heritage Foundation Backgrounder* 1373, June 2000, www.heritage.org/research/family/BG1373.cfm; Gest, Ted. "Divorce: How the Game Is Played Now." *U.S. News and World Report,* November 21, 1983, pp. 39–42; The National Marriage Project, www.marriage.rutgers.edu; www.divorcereform.org; Phillips, R. *Untying the Knot: A Short History of Divorce.* New York: Cambridge University Press, 1991; Wallerstein, J., and J. B. Kelly. *Surviving the Breakup: How Children and Parents Cope With Divorce.* New York: Basic Books, 1980; Wallerstein, J. S., Lewis, J. M., and S. Blakeslee. *The Unexpected Legacy of Divorce: The 25 Year Landmark Study.* New York: Hyperion Books, 2000; Weiztman, L. J. *The Divorce Revolution.* New York: Free Press, 1985; Whitehead, Barbara Dafoe. *The Divorce Culture: Rethinking Our Commitments to Marriage and Family.* New York: Vintage Books, 1998.

Stephanie "Christy" McCalman

AFRICAN AMERICAN FATHERS

The modern-day African American father has come under much scrutiny in recent years. Most notable is the attention given to nonresidential fathers (those who don't live in the same home as their child), or what are sometimes referred to as absentee fathers. From the rise in African American juvenile crime to the increase in single-parented homes headed by black women, the African American male as a father has been consistently labeled and blamed for such occurrences. Statistics affirm that the majority of black children are without the presence of a father. About 70 percent of all African American births occur to unmarried women and over 80 percent of African American children will spend some years of their childhood without a father in the home (Nelson, Clampet-Lundquist, and Edin 2002). With statistics such as these, the black father's role in the family has been closely examined. Although the validity of a number of arguments that blame black male fathering is seemingly legitimate, there are in contrast a number of speculations that are false. As with all fathers, there are those who perform well and those who do not excel at the task of fatherhood. The role of black fathers is one of the strongest and most important traditions in the black community.

BACKGROUND

Historical Influence

There is no question that in their earliest years in the New World enslaved African Americans were concerned about their fathers. Their loyalty to their fathers (and mothers) served as a target in the efforts of their white slaveholders to break their family bonds. In her book *Ain't I a Woman: Black Women and Feminism,* bell hooks asserts that scholars have examined and emphasized the impact that slavery has had on the consciousness of the black male. These scholars argued that black men, more so than black women, were the primary victims of the institution of slavery. She documents the actuality that "chauvinist historians and sociologists" have provided the American public with a perspective on slavery in which the most malicious and dehumanizing impact of slavery on the lives of black people was that black men were stripped of their masculinity. Historians and psychologists have argued that the overall interruption, but particularly the disbanding, of preemancipation black family structure has had an undeniable effect on family life. The fact that the African American father is a viable and resourceful entity in the home in many ways remains undeniable.

Media Influence

The traditional as well as unorthodox depictions of the strong African American father of the late 1970s and early 1980s in such programs as *Goodtimes* (James Evans) and *The Jeffersons* (George Jefferson), provided a glimpse into the more socially predominant view of the black father as strong, stern and often times frustrated due to his status as a black man in America. Although many of these stereotypes would have been true and relevant to the times, they also created a stigma of anger and questionable judgment on behalf of the notable black fathers that were portrayed. One who has viewed the program may recall the countless slurs George Jefferson would aim at his white counterparts as a means of expressing his distrust or dislike of them. Parallel to this was the consistent dejection, anger, and disappointment portrayed through James Evans, a barely-making-ends-meet father of three living in a public housing facility in Chicago. While these portraits and personalities were scripted, they were reflections of a society marked by inequity, social dysfunction, and frustration. However daunting these portrayals may have been, there was an alternate side to the coin. There was strength, resilience, and determination to provide for and keep the family afloat and together through the harshest of times.

This view would, however, shift as times have progressed into a more socially equitable age. As a result, along came *The Cosby Show.* This was the portrayal of the contemporary black father at his best. Here was a family headed by both parents, whose professions were doctor and lawyer. Above all, viewers saw a father that was not angry or frustrated; he was affluent and funny. This portrayal remains utopian and was, neither then nor now, as socially accepted as the aforementioned perspectives. Undeniably, the postemancipation African American father had to be of a stronger and stricter variety, but this was of necessity by his circumstances and not the result of natural inclination. To imply, as some have done, that such experiences as the Cosby's did not exist throughout the course of African American history would be false.

PRESENT CONCERNS

As society has progressed into a more technologically advanced social, economic, and academic age, the multiple uncertainties and social ills surrounding the family unit have come into focus. Likewise, attempts to fix what does not work in today's families have become more common. The black family and its supposed dysfunctions have been a prominent area of inquiry and concern, probably because of the continued higher numbers of such families in poverty. The absence of the black father in the home has been tagged as cause for a myriad of increasing social problems and irritations, including rises in black male juvenile crime, an increased number of black male juveniles with criminal records, an increase in the number of homes parented by single black mothers, increased amounts of illegitimate children, and the increased dependency of black women-headed households on the state. All of these can be attributed to the black fathers' recent absence from the home. In order to determine the effects of father absence it is just as vital to denote the causes or sequential happenings that have lead to the absence.

Possible Causes of Paternal Delinquency

In *The Woes of the Inner-City African-American Father,* renowned social inequality specialist William J. Wilson argues that there are structural and cultural explanations for the lack of black fathers in inner city African American homes. He contends that structural economic forces such as deindustrialization and globalization have decreased the number of high-paying manufacturing jobs in America, which were replaced by lower-pay employment. Wilson argues that low pay and limited education have made it increasingly difficult for black men to marry. Also, the lack of employment and educational opportunities create a cultural environment that allows black men to personally assimilate racist sentiments and negative attitudes about themselves. As a result, these African American men view fatherhood and marriage as burdens that they are unwilling to assume. Wilson also suggests that there needs to be a policy that addresses black men's self-esteem and creates readily available, higher-paying employment opportunities (Wilson 2002).

There is also the issue of divorce or separation that influences absence. Approximately two in three divorces are initiated not by the husbands but by the wives, and the children remain living with their mothers in 93 percent of these cases. Encouraged by the government, family courts have consistently taken the stance that if the mother does not want the child to see the father any more, then that must be what is best for the child. Consequently, following divorce or separation, 60 percent of fathers have no further meaningful relationship with their children. These fathers may be in many ways walking away and exhibiting negligence, but they are also being pushed out of their children's lives.

Black Family Awareness

There is a question of accountability and responsibility that the black male has to answer regarding the present state of many African American families, but as a culture and society there has to be a reciprocal solution. In a 2005 Chicago *Sun-Times* poll, of 11 different response categories to the question "What is the most important thing you do for your children?" the largest response (25 percent of the total responses) was to the category "provide." When asked what the idea of a good father meant, the category of nine possible answers that received the most responses was "being able to provide and protect." When asked about the worst aspect of having and raising children, 26 percent of the fathers responded that it was not being able to provide for them. The issue of basic needs provision was chosen most often in all conditions.

With so many African American fathers desiring to support their children, but finding it difficult to do so, there has to be a strategy to combat the absence of black fathers and the systemic ills that accompany it. As an advocate of strengthening African American families, famous black actor and comedian Bill Cosby has been involved on many occasions in recent years in discussions about the role of black fathers. He has gone on speaking tours, appeared on television news programs, and penned books on the subject. With Harvard Medical School psychiatry professor Alvin Poussaint he coauthored the book *Come On, People: On the Path from Victims to Victors* in which he argues that children in single-parent homes often don't get the guidance they need or deserve. He suggests that if you have this generational, fatherless situation, regardless of whether or not the father was married to the child's mother, where the male is not present the child perceives the situation as abandonment. While his harsh criticism of some black families has not always been well received, he has done a very good job bringing the issue to the public's attention.

Regarding family and personal relationships, today's African American males are no less sensitive than their forefathers. According to black psychologist Marvin Krohn, black men come to the psychiatrist's office in large numbers, in pain and genuinely seeking help. Krohn goes on to assert that African American fathers have little or nothing to say about the statistics, myths, and other sociological indictments so often made about them. Rather, many of them come in speaking of depression, unease, aggravation, fear, shame, esteem issues, and anger that are most often associated with the close, ongoing relations (child's mother) in their lives. This suggests that black males are as frustrated over their absence in their children's live as is the rest of society.

BLACK FATHER ABSENTEEISM

Formal Statistics

Father absenteeism has been explored by examining the physical and financial presence of the father in the home. Eighty percent of all African American children will spend part of their childhood living apart from their fathers. Seventy percent of African American children are born to unmarried mothers and 40 percent of all children regardless of race live in homes without fathers. Further studies of African American fathers do indeed suggest that many young African American fathers are relatively uninvolved in the lives of their children.

INTERVENTION STRATEGIES

Although black father absenteeism is a significant problem, there are a number of individuals and community organizations attempting to limit or even eradicate this phenomenon. Programs like the Academy of Black Fathers in Boston, Massachusetts and the Father Focus program located in Baltimore, Maryland are counseling programs that support, encourage, and help fathers develop and maintain close relationships with their children and families. These organizations also provide a society of men who can talk about the experiences of fatherhood.

There are also many government agencies that aid black fathers. One such office is the National Center for Strategic Nonprofit Planning and Community Leadership. Its mission is to improve the management and administration of nonprofit, tax-exempt organizations and strengthen community leadership through family and neighborhood empowerment.

However the most recognizable and easily accessible institution with programs aimed at helping fathers is the YMCA (Young Men's Christian Association). A very prominent YMCA fatherhood program based in Cleveland, Ohio recently met with a number of public health officials to discuss programs that would help to prevent absenteeism or fatherlessness in the black community. The conference participants developed a three-level preventative solution to this problem. The first level educated black fathers about the positive side of fatherhood. The next level covered the needs of at-risk men who were consistently underemployed or involved in the criminal justice system. The third level counseled about the importance of relationships.

Henry E. Edward, author of *Black Families in Crisis: the Middle Class*, constructed a forum of solutions to possibly alleviate the current strife in the black family as a societal unit. The initial solutions presented were to reach out to black fathers and to offer them support. Religion and spirituality were highlighted as a source of strength that could be used in order to aid in morality and accountability for these men. Because of a false sense of masculinity and manliness, black fathers may not want to acknowledge the need for religion. Indeed, rates of church attendance are significantly higher for black women compared to black men. He also discussed at length the effects that mass media has played in the desecration of the black male image and the African American father. Boycotts of radio stations, talk-show hosts, newspapers, and businesses that slander black fathers were proposed to draw attention to the issues. Ultimately, African American men and women were urged to oppose further cuts in jobs and social service programs, to support those programs and policies that allow black fathers to earn the money necessary to provide for their families, and to encourage full-time dads to join a black men's group, such as those structured in the inner cities. These programs help black men support other black men to be better fathers.

The National Longitudinal Survey of Labor Market Experience of Youth (NLSY) indicated that of African American children with mothers of age 20 to 25, about 40 percent primarily lived with both parents, compared to about 90 percent of non-African American children. Of the nonresident fathers, 20 percent had never visited in the past year or had seen their child only once (Lerman and Sorensen 2003). In a sample of 100 fathers and a comparison group of nonfathers, all but one of whom was African American, 18 months after the child's birth, only about 25 percent of the nonresident fathers reported seeing their children daily. A follow-up study of 110 male children mostly born to African American teen mothers in the Baltimore Parenthood Study revealed that more than half of these young males have never lived with their father, and most of the nonresident fathers had irregular contact with their children. Only 20 percent of young fathers were living with their children 5 years after the child's birth, and an additional 20 percent visited regularly.

As it relates to economic support, there is even less information on child support payments by African American fathers. National studies tend to show that about 50 to 75 percent of fathers paid the full amount of court-ordered support in the preceding year. A study based on the Current Population Survey found that minority group fathers of children born to never-married mothers are less likely, overall, to pay child support.

In short, previous research has generated a rather negative image of young African American fathers. Additionally, the portrayals of these men in the media highlight their struggles and absence as normative. They may even be shown as sexual predators, seeking personal gratification and likely to abandon the child and the child's mother when a better opportunity comes along. This image has found its way into the nation's consciousness about race and family, perhaps to the extent of influencing public policy on public assistance and associated issues. One of the most important limitations of much research on fatherhood is that nonresident fathers are highly underrepresented in household surveys and therefore their perspectives are underrepresented in the literature. Data on young, urban, nonresident African American fathers are particularly thin and the limited research that has focused on them continues to employ generally small, unrepresentative samples.

It is also often the case that African American fathers are seen as deadbeats due to their lack of economic support in the home, but it would be a bit fairer to say that they are dead broke as well. Seventy percent of the child support debts owed in 2003 were accumulated by men earning $10,000 a year or less. Over 2.5 million nonresident or absentee fathers of poor children are poor themselves, thus making it extremely difficult for them to fulfill the father role as it is currently conceived in U.S. society (Furstenberg and Weiss 2000).

Informal Statistics

Statistics that account for father support of children have largely been derived from formal child support payments, however the unaccounted for informal child support, which may constitute a significant percentage of the mother's resources, has been overlooked in many cases. Some researchers have suggested that the nonresident status of the fathers may not forecast their lack of involvement, as was previously believed. Some studies have indeed suggested that the contribution of both financial and nonfinancial support by nonresident African American fathers has exceeded expectations. Many African American men are practically involved in their children's lives and make nonfinancial contributions to their children. Diapers, milk, toys, and baby clothes are only a few of the noncash provisions.

Many have asked why these fathers who provide some basic items do not simply pay child support. There are a number of reasons why they do not. Many of the items a father brings to his children are physical support of his efforts to provide for them, despite his dismal economic conditions. In return, the bits and pieces have greater significance, visibility, and permanence than cash payments. Such cash payments often vanish almost instantaneously as bills are paid, are misused by the custodial parent, or, in the case of children receiving public assistance, used to reimburse the government for necessities it has provided the children.

It is quite likely that black fathers have been assaulted, and their contributions in a number of categories have been unjustifiably denigrated. Research supports many assertions about the positive contributions of African American fathers. African American fathers in two-parent families spend more time with their children than do Hispanic or white fathers. African American fathers and black fathers in the Caribbean are more likely than white fathers to treat boys and girls similarly when they are babies. They also interact just as frequently with their young daughters as they do with their young sons. On the other hand, in the United States, black families have higher divorce, separation, and never-living-together rates than white families. However, a top predictor that a black couple will stay together is the black man's enjoyment of, and interest in, being a father and sharing in the day-to-day care of his children (www.marylandbfa.org 2006).

Rates of nonresident fathers being involved with very young children are surprisingly high among nonresident African American fathers, but father involvement drops off considerably as the children age. Correspondingly, as the time since the father has lived with his child increases, father involvement decreases. Most nonresident African American fathers speak movingly of the meaning of their children in their lives, even if they rarely see them. African American fathers sometimes say that when they cannot contribute financially, they feel too guilty to have ongoing contact with their children. Many times a pregnancy and the ensuing birth provide African American fathers who have been participating in frequent illegal activity a strong motive to leave their hazardous street lives. Because of this, African American fathers often claim that their children have literally saved them (www.marylandbfa.org 2006).

However, low-income African American fathers are more likely than both black and white higher-income fathers to place an equal value on the breadwinning, provider role and on the relational functions of fatherhood. Both structural and behavioral factors, such as unemployment, drug use, criminal activity, and conflicts with their child's mother hinder black fathers from fulfilling the duties they say are necessary to be an adequate or good father.

CONCLUSION

There is a question of accountability and responsibility that black males have to answer regarding the present state of many African American families. At the same time, social and cultural supports could be enacted that would assist black males in more fully meeting their obligations. Given the constraints of living in poverty, many African American fathers are torn between their desires to effectively parent and their need for their own survival. The general public, influenced by the stereotypical portrayals of black males in the media, may not recognize the roles that black men do play in the lives of their children.

Having an involved father has noticeable benefits to children. Fathers are important because they help to teach children values and lessons in solving the problems they may face, and they do so in a way that differs from what mothers contribute. Fathers also serve as role models in their children's lives that affect how well they relate to peers and adults outside the home and in society. When speaking of the benefits of being an involved father, focus is placed on the benefits that children receive from such a relationship. Being an involved father means being actively involved in nearly every aspect of a child's life, from direct contact, play, and accountability for childcare, to making oneself available to the child. Black men's social situations influence how well they may or may not meet these demands.

While the common stance regarding African American fathers today is that their absence results in significant financial and social harm to their offspring, it may not be universally true. Researchers studying the issue of paternal involvement for a substantial amount of time have found concise evidence supporting the importance of paternal participation. Recently, some researchers have found that African American fathers can contribute to the health and well being of their children, even if they do not live in the same household. The results of investigations of the influences of nonresident father involvement on children indicate that positive father involvement relates to better child outcome.

Researchers note that it is the quality rather than quantity of time that youth spend with their fathers that is important for their well being. Research has also shown that children whose fathers are involved in rearing them score higher on cognitive tests (they appear smarter) than those with relatively uninvolved fathers. These improved cognitive abilities are associated with higher educational achievement. In fact, fathers who are involved in their children's schools and academic achievement, regardless of their own educational level, increase the chances that their child will graduate from high school and perhaps go to a vocational school or a college. A father's involvement in his children's school activities protects at-risk children from failing or dropping out.

Research shows that fathers who are more involved with their children tend to raise children who experience more success in their careers. Career success can lead to greater income and greater financial stability. Involved fathering is related to lower rates of teen violence, delinquency, and other problems with the legal system. Furthermore, paternal involvement is associated with positive child characteristics such as understanding, self-esteem, self-control, psychological well-being, social competence, and life skills. Children who grow up in homes with involved fathers are more likely to take an active and positive role in raising their own children. For example, fathers who remember a safe, loving relationship with both parents were more involved in the lives of their children and more supportive of their wives.

Finally, being an involved father brings benefits to the dads themselves. When fathers build strong relationships with their children and others in the family, they receive support and caring in return. Research has shown that healthy family relationships provide the strongest and most important support network a person can have, whether that person is a child or an adult. Being involved in their family members' lives helps fathers to enjoy a secure attachment relationship with their children, cope well with stressful situations and everyday problems, feel as if they can depend on others, feel more comfortable in their occupations, and feel that they can do their parenting job better.

The benefits listed above are in reality only a small portion of what accrues for fathers and children in a healthy relationship. There may be others that the research has yet to uncover. Nevertheless, all of the aforementioned benefits for both fathers and children in the African American community will require hard work, patience, support, and diligence. It seems a more prudent use of resources to determine how African American males can be assisted to be present in their children's lives, rather than denigrated for their absence.

See also Child Support and Parental Responsibility; Family Roles; Fatherhood; Marriage Promotion; Parenting Styles.

Further Reading: Biller, Henry B. "A Note on Father Absence and Masculine Development in Lower-Class Negro and White Boys." *Child Development* 39, no. 3 (1968): 1003–1006; Brott, A. A. *The New Father: A Dad's Guide to the First Year.* New York: Abbeville Press, Inc. 1997; Cosby, Bill, and Alvin F. Poussaint. *Fatherhood.* New York: Penguin Group, 1987; Cosby, Bill, and Alvin F. Poussaint. *Come on People: On the Path from Victims to Victors.* Nashville, TN: Thomas Nelson Publishers, 2007; Furstenberg, Frank E., and Christopher C. Weiss. "Intergenerational Transmission of Fathering Roles in At Risk Families." *Marriage and Family Review* 29 (2000): 181–202; hooks, bell. *Ain't I a Woman: Black Women and Feminism.* Boston: South End Press, 1981; Hossain, Z., and J. L. Roopnarine. "Division of Household Labour and Child Care in Dual-earner African-American Families with Infants." *Sex Roles* 29 (1993): 571–583; Lerman, Robert, and Elaine Sorensen. "Child Support: Interactions Between Private and Public Transfers." In *Means-Tested Transfer Programs in the U.S.,* ed. Robert Moffitt. Chicago: University of Chicago Press, 2003; Marsiglio, W., Day, R. D., and M. E. Lamb. "Exploring Fatherhood Diversity: Implications for Conceptualizing Father Involvement." *Marriage and Family Review* 29 (2000): 269–293; Maryland Black Family Alliance. http://www.marylandbfa.org; Mogey, J. M. "A Century of Declining Paternal Authority." *Marriage and Family Living* 19, no. 3 (1957): 234–239; Nelson, T. J., Clampet-Lundquist, S., and K. Edin. "Sustaining Fragile Fatherhood: Father Involvement among Low-income, Noncustodial African American Fathers in Philadelphia." In *A Handbook of Father Involvement,* ed. Catherine S. Tamis-LeMonda and Natasha Cabrera. Mahwah, NJ: Lawrence Erlbaum Assoc., 2002; Pleck, J. H. "Paternal Involvement: Levels, Sources and Consequences." In *The Role of the Father in Child Development,* 3rd ed., ed. Michael E. Lamb. New York: Wiley, 1997; Smith,

Carolyn A., Marvin D. Krohn, R. Chu, and O. Best. "African American Fathers: Myths and Realities about Their Involvement with Their Firstborn Children." *Journal of Family Issues* 26, no. 7 (2005): 975–1001; Wilson, William J. "The Woes of the Inner-City African-American Father" New York: Cambridge University Press, 2002; Zimmerman, Marc A., Deborah A. Salem, and Paul C. Notaro. "Make Room for Daddy II: The Positive Effects of Fathers' Role in Adolescent Development." In *Resilience across Contexts: Family, Work, Culture, and Community,* ed. R. Taylor and L. Wang. Mahwah, NJ: Lawrence Erlbaum Associates, Inc., 2000.

Aaron D. Franks

ARRANGED MARRIAGE

ARRANGED MARRIAGES, SEMI-ARRANGED MARRIAGES, AND LOVE MARRIAGES

Subject to cultural conventions, partners meet and marry through a variety of traditional and nontraditional means. One that is quite familiar among Indian Americans, second-generation Asian Indians who are born and raised in the United States, is arranged marriage. As an exemplar, this group will be examined to highlight the phenomenon. Arranged marriage is not an antiquated, tyrannical concept, but an ever-evolving one that is constantly being reworked by Indian Americans to suit their changing requirements. These transformations can be explained by examining the various forms marriage takes in this ethnic group: arranged marriages, semi-arranged marriages, and love marriages.

Arranged Marriages. Arranged marriages are those marriages generally organized by parents and elderly kin and, at times, with the young couple having little choice in the matter. Such marriages are not entirely foreign to Western cultures. In the past (and perhaps even today, though rarely acknowledged) families sought to preserve or enhance their financial, political or economic positions with judicious marital alliances. While this motive no doubt plays its part in arranged marriages among Indians and Indian Americans, the demand for such arrangements stems also from a perception that marriage is a covenant and a lifelong commitment. Thus, in the Indian ethos, divorce is regarded as a shameful calamity, casting doubt on the morality and chastity of the couple, especially the woman.

Further, arranged marriages address cultural concerns with the family unity, honor and the preservation of the chastity of women. Indians and Indian Americans recognize that individuals are a part of a larger organism such as a family, tribe or caste, and ethnic group. Ties between the individual and the extended family (uncles, cousins, second cousins) remain strong and are perceived as important among Indians. Marriage is therefore regarded as a joining of not merely the individual partners, but also of their families and kindred. Given this, arranging marriages in the traditional way is considered to be the most effective, as it ensures that potential mates are carefully sought out according to identified criteria. Their individual personalities and family backgrounds are thoroughly investigated to ensure compatibility with the extended family, and the union is sanctified by the gods to assure its permanence and reduce the probability of divorce.

Thus the first step in many (if not most) Indian arranged marriages is the matching of horoscopes. Horoscopes plot the effect that the configuration of the nine planets has on a person's life from birth to death. Ideally, the weaknesses in one horoscope should be compensated by the strengths in the other so that the union, so to speak, has both human and divine approval. This horoscope matching necessarily has to precede the meeting of the two partners and, quite often, takes precedence over personal preferences. While anecdotal evidence seems to indicate that horoscope matching is diminishing in importance (particularly in inter-faith, inter-caste marriages) many Indians and Indian Americans continue to believe in the importance of horoscopes. Many arranged marriages are decided on the basis of horoscopes alone with the personal preferences of the partners coming second.

Parents and extended kin consider a range of criteria when arranging marriages. Some of the most important criteria include the families' religion, caste, social class, and region of India, which serves as a means of ethnic group classification among Indians. Additionally, the attributes of the couple in question, such as their physical appearances, education (including culinary skills, artistic achievements), and occupational background, are also considered. The idea of *endogamy*—marrying within one's caste, sub-caste, social class, religion and ethnic group—is very much emphasized in arranging a marriage. Consequently, arranging marriages outside one's group rarely occurs. As is evident from this list, love does not figure as a criterion in arranging marriages. Rather, it is assumed that love would grow after marriage if the couple is matched on the above-mentioned points. It is important to note that identifying the individual as a component of a larger organism also permits independent verification of her or his character and family background from other sources. This gathering of feedback from family and societal networks is an important part of the arranged marriage process.

Once young Indians and Indian Americans have reached marriageable age, a sort-of all-points bulletin is broadcast through a network of family and friends in the Indian community, announcing the availability of the person for marriage. This involves the circulation of the person's horoscope, a listing of the attributes of the young person along the criteria mentioned above, and is, at times, accompanied by a photograph of the eligible person. This is called a *proposal* and these proposals are exchanged between eligible parties who are interested in marriage. Traditionally, a proposal is advertised in the community by word-of-mouth, a practice that continues today. Proposals are also carried in matrimonial advertisements in Indian and ethnic newspapers. In a traditional arranged marriage, proposals are developed and reviewed by family members who identify a suitable match, sometimes without the input of the prospective partners themselves. At this point, a formal meeting is organized by the family where the prospective partners are introduced to each other, negotiations (about dowry, gifts of jewelry that would be given to the bride by her parents, marriage expenses, *etc.*) are conducted and arrangements for the wedding are made by identifying the most auspicious date, time, and location for the union. In some cases, this formal meeting occurs before deciding upon the marriage, allowing the prospective partners to interact with each other and offer some input on the decision.

Indian parents in the United States experience difficulty in implementing the above form of marriage in the case of their second-generation children. While some Indian Americans continue to prefer this form of marriage for all of the reasons stated earlier, a significant proportion of Indian Americans refuse to marry without their choices being accounted for or without them consenting to it. Thus, while the practice of arranging marriages in the traditional way described here continues to exist, it has been steadily declining. In its place is the more recent version of arranged marriage—the semi-arranged marriage.

Semi-Arranged Marriages. Semi-arranged marriage is the transformed version of the traditional arranged marriage described above. In this form of marriage, men and women who pass the eligibility criteria (matching of horoscopes, background checks by the societal network) are introduced to each other and then allowed a courtship or engagement period during which they decide whether or not they are suitably matched for marriage. This form of marriage is highly popular among Indian Americans as it facilitates the simultaneous retention of parental control in the choice of their children's spouses while accommodating the second-generation's desire to make an independent decision and for love. It is important to note that this form of marriage is not only popular among Indian Americans in the United States, but also among the young, educated, urban, and middle-class in India. Among Indian Americans, semi-arranged marriage reflects their attempts to adapt Indian values and traditions to the Westernized society in which they live, while in India it is an indicator of the rapid social change that is underway.

The method of orchestrating a semi-arranged marriage is very similar to the traditional arranged marriage described above with a few key differences. First is the issue of choice of marriage partner. Semi-arranged marriages also depend on the exchange of proposals between families. However, unlike the traditional arranged marriage, in semi-arranged marriages Indian Americans often develop their proposals themselves or in conjunction with their families and exercise significant control in choosing their spouses. While Indian Americans continue to rely on the criteria identified above, they also place emphasis on the individual attributes of potential spouses rather than only familial ones. Thus, physical attraction, mental and emotional compatibility, and similarity of interests and values between potential partners are becoming more important in semi-arranged marriages.

The second difference concerns the decision to marry. Similar to the traditional arranged marriage, suitable couples that are matched according to proposals are introduced to each other by their families. However, once this occurs, parental involvement in arranging the marriage diminishes. Unlike the traditional arranged marriage, the decision to marry is made by the potential partners themselves and not by their families. Following the introduction, should the partners like each other, a fairly long courtship period, which can be understood as dating, ensues. While in some cases this courtship is supervised, research indicates that most second-generation Indian Americans have the freedom to date or court, as long as it occurs within the semi-arranged framework, without supervision. This courtship period allows the couple to get to know each other on an individual basis and fall in love prior to deciding to marry. Should this not occur, or should the couple decide that they are incompatible as life-partners, the relationship is ended without pressure to marry. Once the couple decides to marry, their families are approached so that arrangements for the engagement and wedding can be made. It is for this reason that semi-arranged marriages are also called *assisted marriages* or *introduced marriages;* familial involvement in arranging the marriage ends after the couple is introduced to each other.

As the structure of arranged marriage continues to be transformed to suit the times, as is evident in semi-arranged marriages, so have the methods of seeking suitable spouses. In addition to the methods described earlier, more modern methods like matrimonial Internet and social networking websites (such as shaadi.com, bharatmatrimonials.com, indianmatrimonials.com, orkut, friendster, Facebook) are being embraced by young, technology-savvy Indians and Indian Americans. Online matrimonial sites serving Indians in India and the diaspora are highly organized. The proposals on these sites are categorized according to caste, Indian ethnic group, religion, educational background, age, and profession, facilitating the use of the traditional criteria in seeking a mate. Social networking sites, in contrast, allow Indian Americans to network among themselves, particularly in professional settings and on university campuses, and thereby seek out their own mates.

Internet matrimonial Web sites are especially appealing because of their wide reach. These can be scanned in any part of the Indian diaspora. Likewise, their easily accessible convenience permits proposals from a wide range of prospective partners by advertising on multiple matrimonial sites. Furthermore, couples who find each other through these sites often communicate electronically via email for a while before progressing to exchanging phone conversations, and eventually to a formal introduction along the lines described earlier, followed by a formal courtship period. Of course, this is all dependent on whether they consider themselves suited for each other based on their early email communications. Should this not occur, email communication is terminated and the following stages do not play out. With its anonymity, the Internet enables young Indian Americans to undertake what was not possible earlier; to screen and communicate with a number of prospective partners, with relatively little risk to their reputations, before encountering the one they would like to meet.

Love Marriages. Love marriages are also known as marriages of choice. This form of marriage involves Indian Americans choosing their own spouses and deciding to marry with little or no parental involvement. This form of marriage makes Indian parents in the United States uneasy as it gives them no opportunity to check potential spouses, and this may increase the probability of divorce. However, these marriages are becoming common among Indian Americans as they are accepted by the larger American society and culture. Additionally, as Indian Americans seek higher education and professional employment, there is an increased probability of meeting their future spouse on university campuses or through their professions. Unlike the traditional arranged or semi-arranged marriage, love marriage involves potential partners seeking each other and dating without disclosure to their parents. Indian Americans who have had love marriages indicate that they disclose their relationship and informal engagement to their parents only after having dated for a couple of years and after having decided to marry. Needless to say, the chances of parental disapproval of the marriage are much higher in these cases, often causing intergenerational conflict over whether the marriage should proceed.

GENDER DIFFERENCES IN SEMI-ARRANGED MARRIAGES

Indian American women encounter a different level of social and familial pressures in marriage. Women enter marriage age before men (21 to 25 years and 26 to 28 years respectively) and encounter greater pressure to make a decision about marriage. The most important reason cited for this disparity includes a fear among families that as the women get older, there is a diminished probability of finding a suitable spouse. Additionally, the expectation among Indian families that men will be the primary providers for their families means they need longer years of study and professional employment in which to build a monetary base for family life.

While a fairly long courtship is accepted among Indian Americans, the average duration of courtship for couples who are introduced to each other through a semi-arranged method is six months to one year. By this time, a decision as to whether or not they will marry needs to be made. Indian American women, however, encounter greater pressure to make this decision in a timely manner as their reputations are on the line with prolonged dating. To a large extent this occurs because the Indian American community continues to prize sexual chastity among second-generation women, embodied in her unblemished social reputation at the time of marriage. Oftentimes women who have courted without the relationship culminating in marriage are, regardless of their actual sexual experience, perceived as unchaste, which considerably reduces their future marriage prospects.

CURRENT CONTROVERSIES

A major point of controversy about arranged marriage is on the issue of imposition of marriage on a couple versus a choice in marriage by Indian Americans. The imposition camp perceives arranged marriage to be imposed on Indian Americans by their parents. Accordingly, young Indian Americans are believed to be powerless, with no choice in determining the direction of their married lives. This camp argues that this imposed parental preference has to be understood in the context of the rationale for arranged marriage described above, and of the challenges of being Indian in the United States.

Indian parents in the United States believe arranged marriages to be a mechanism of preserving Indian culture and ethnicity in the United States while limiting the Americanization of their children. This occurs in two ways. One, arranging marriages ensures that Indian Americans marry endogamously, thereby ensuring ethnic and cultural continuity between generations. Two, parents believe that this prevents Indian Americans from indulging in American-style dating, thereby preventing Americanization. Arranged marriages are particularly preferable for Indian American daughters as it ensures their unblemished reputations. It is important to note that imposition in this case is not synonymous with force as Indian Americans often refuse to be forced into an arranged marriage. However, oftentimes imposition takes the form of parental expectations of an arranged marriage. This translates into subtle pressures to begin the process of arranging a marriage (like developing a proposal, screening eligible candidates, communicating with eligible candidates, etc.), and disapproval of exogamous marriages with which Indian Americans have to contend.

As opposed to the imposition camp that believes Indian Americans are powerless against their parents, the choice camp holds that Indian Americans have the power of choice, and a significant proportion choose arranged marriages. Critical to this choice is the perception of arranged marriage by Indian Americans. Some indicate that their preference for a traditional arranged marriage, as fulfilling familial expectations in marriage, is important to them. However, a significant proportion who choose an arranged marriage define it along the lines of the *semi-arranged marriage*, which is acceptable to them for the reasons above. Additionally, some Indian Americans are ambivalent about American-style dating which they perceive as lacking commitment, and trust the logic of the arranged marriage institution (i.e., prescreened couples being introduced to each other with the goal of marriage and the reliance on the experience and judgment of elder kin) in ensuring their marital happiness. Indian Americans also desire to preserve ethnic culture in their married families and thus choose semi-arranged marriage with its emphasis on, and assurance of, endogamy.

It is important to note here that semi-arranged marriage, even as a choice by Indian Americans, is not without its tensions. Indian Americans are quick to point out that parents do not always get it right when introducing them to eligible parties, in some cases resulting in divorce. Others talk of being frustrated with the process (reading numerous proposals, communicating via email, meeting several candidates) or with pressures they encounter to make a decision, particularly if they have been seeking partners unsuccessfully for a couple of years. Indian American women in particular mention apprehensions, such as the process beginning much earlier for them than for their male counterparts, encountering greater pressure to marry before they move out of the marriage age, and sometimes feeling displayed as goods on the market of marriage.

Another controversy in arranged marriage lies in the question of whether an arranged marriage can be a love match as well. The controversy is contextualized in a tendency to classify arranged and love marriages as being in complete opposition to each other. This is embodied in the *arranged versus love* and *arranged with love* marriage camps. Critical to resolving this controversy is each camp's definition of arranged marriage and accompanying ideas of love.

The arranged versus love marriage camp continues to perceive arranged marriage in its most traditional form without the consent and choices of Indian Americans being accounted for. The argument thus made is that arranged marriages are unemotional business arrangements between families who seek to match Indian Americans along relatively objective criteria (horoscope, family's religion, ethnicity, class, caste, etc.). Love, by contrast, is perceived as a quixotic criterion and not sufficient on which to base a life-long commitment. Hence love marriages are associated with divorce and betrayal of parental expectations. According to this camp, it is only in this form that an arranged marriage is authentic and can thus preserve ethnic culture.

The other side of this debate, referred to here as the arranged with love marriage camp, holds that in its transformed version, that is, a semi-arranged or love marriage, love is an integral component of the arranged marriage system. Falling in love with, and being attracted to one's prospective spouse, is critical to the decision of whether or not to marry. Indian Americans who hold this view argue that they are not willing to settle for the probability of love developing after marriage, and thus often define their semi-arranged marriages as love marriages.

An interesting development in this debate has been the navigation of a love marriage that is undertaken without parental involvement. Indian Americans who have chosen this option attempt to circumvent potential parental disapproval by following very closely the mate selection criteria prized by their parents in choosing with whom to fall in love. Thus, they are careful to fall in love with only the "right" kind of Indian to ensure parental support of their marriage. This camp also argues that Indian parents in the United States are realizing the second generation's desire for love and choice in marriage, and are thus developing methods to orchestrate an arranged with a love marriage. One of the most interesting new methods is the emergence of marriage conventions that are often organized by Indian ethnic groups, facilitating endogamous marriages. A marriage convention is a national, annual event, organized in key cities with the purpose of gathering marriage-minded Indian Americans and their parents in one location to meet prospective candidates and exchange necessary information. Thus, in sum, this side of the debate answers yes to the question of whether an arranged marriage can be a love match as well.

In summary, arranged marriage is being transformed by Indian Americans, taking on the forms of the semi-arranged and love marriage. However, even as these changes occur, the perception of arranged marriage as antiquated, oppressive, and lacking love persists both among Americans and Indian Americans. This generates controversies about whether or not Indian Americans choose these marriages for themselves, and whether love can be integral to these marriages. Indian Americans are choosing arranged marriages but in the form that enables them to be true to both parental and personal expectations of marriage.

See also Dating; Mail Order Brides; Mate Selection Alternatives; Prenuptial Agreements.

Further Reading: Bellafante, Gina. "In the U.S., Assisted Marriages for South Asians." *The International Herald Tribune,* August 24, 2005, News section: 2; Divakaruni, Chitra. "Arranged Marriages Can Provide Couples Stronger Relationships: South Asian Families are Adopting an Updated Version of the Old Custom." *The Standard,* June 23, 2001, Viewpoint section, St. Catherines, Ontario edition: A13; Fidelman, Charlie. "Arranged Marriages Still Very Popular: New Generation Yearns for Their Roots." *The Gazette,* April 27, 2003, News section, Montreal, Quebec edition: A10; Khandelwal, Madhulika S. *Becoming American,*

Being Indian: An Immigrant Community in New York City. Ithaca, NY: Cornell University Press, 2002; Leonard, Karen I. *The South Asian Americans.* Westport, CT: Greenwood Press, 1997; Lessinger, Johanna. *From the Ganges to the Hudson: Indian Immigrants in New York City.* Boston: Allyn and Bacon, 1995; Magnusson, Tony. "What's Love Got to Do With It?" *Sunday Magazine,* February 12, 2006, Magazine section: 20; Netting, Nancy S. "Two-Lives, One Partner: Indo-Canadian Youth Between Love and Arranged Marriages." *Journal of Comparative Family Studies* 37, no. 1 (2006): 129–146; Rangaswamy, Padma. *Namasté America: Indian Immigrants in an American Metropolis.* University Park, PA: The Pennsylvania State University Press, 2000; Sheth, P. *Indians in America: One Stream, Two Waves, Three Generations.* Jaipur, India: Rawat Publications, 2001; Sprecher, Susan, and Rachita Chandak. "Attitudes about Arranged Marriages and Dating among Men and Women From India." *Free Inquiry in Creative Sociology* 20, no. 1 (1992): 59–69; Uddin, Mohammad S. "Arranged Marriage: A Dilemma for Young British Asians." *Diversity in Health and Social Care* 3 (2006): 211–219; Vaidyanathan, Prabha, and Jospehine Naidoo. "Asian Indians in Western Countries: Cultural Identity and the Arranged Marriage." In *Contemporary Issues in Cross-Cultural Psychology,* ed. N. Bleichrodt and P. J. Drenth. Amsterdam: Swets and Zeitlinger, 1990; Zaidi, Arsha U., and Muhammad Shuraydi. "Perceptions of Arranged Marriage by Young Pakistani Muslim Women Living in a Western Society." *Journal of Comparative Family Studies* 33, no. 4 (2002): 495–514.

Namita N. Manohar

ATTENTION DEFICIT HYPERACTIVITY DISORDER (ADHD)

Parents often agonize over a child's behavior, wondering if their child is just unruly or if there might be a medical cause to problems experienced in school and other rigid settings. Increasingly parents are finding a diagnosis, attention deficit hyperactivity disorder (ADHD), to account for some of the behavior issues that make parenting a particularly challenging activity. According to the medical community, ADHD is a neurological disorder primarily characterized by inattentiveness, hyperactivity, and impulsivity. ADHD is generally detected in childhood, but increasing numbers of individuals are being diagnosed in adulthood. The vast majority of identified ADHD sufferers are male. A heated debate centers on the nature of the disorder, including whether a medical label is appropriate and how it should be treated.

ADHD is being given increasing attention in the professional and popular literature. Most sources agree that ADHD diagnoses are on the rise in the United States. Comparing two similar data sources illustrates this increase. According to a 1987 study, the weighted national estimate of children receiving treatment for ADHD was approximately one-half million. A follow-up to this research in 1997 reported a weighted national estimate of children receiving ADHD treatment of more than two million. These figures can be loosely compared to the most recent data available from the Centers for Disease Control and Prevention on the number of United States children ever diagnosed with ADHD. According to this source, this distinction applied to greater than four million youth in 2003. From this illustration emerges a general idea of the rate of change surrounding ADHD diagnoses in the United States.

THREE CONTESTED PERSPECTIVES

A crucial element of the ADHD debate involves its definition. Many physicians and psychologists believe that ADHD is a medical issue with neurological implications and genetic causes. Others, those who favor a more holistic approach to life, or may not have parented, feel that ADHD is a creation of overzealous practitioners and pharmaceutical companies. Still others see the phenomenon as social in origin, arising from changing values and ideals regarding childhood. Thus, three main perspectives exist in the ADHD controversy. The first is the medical perspective that views ADHD as a physiological disease. The second perspective describes ADHD as subject to the medicalization process that transforms many behavioral issues into medical problems. The third perspective portrays ADHD as a social issue arising from changing interpretations of behavior rather than children's physical disabilities.

ADHD As a Disease

The underlying assumption of a medical model of a disorder is that some recognized standard of behavior, one that is displayed by the majority of the populace, is absent in an individual. The absence of the expected behavior is attributed to an illness or disease, which, once properly diagnosed, can be treated to help bring about more desired behavior.

Many psychologists, psychiatrists, physicians, and other clinicians, as well as parents, teachers, and members of the general public, believe this model is appropriate for ADHD. The idea that inattentiveness and hyperactivity in children indicate a disorder originated near the turn of the twentieth century. The condition, then termed "Hyperkinetic reaction of childhood" was officially recognized by the American Psychiatric Association in the second edition of its *Diagnostic and Statistical Manual of Mental Disorders* (DSM-II) in 1968. For the DSM-III, the label was revised to attention deficit disorder (ADD). The terminology changed again for the revision of the third addition, the DSM-III-R, when the disorder was given the more inclusive title of ADHD.

The current DSM-IV lists inattentiveness, hyperactivity, and impulsivity as the three primary characteristics of ADHD. The manual also indicates that an ADHD diagnosis is not appropriate unless symptoms have been present for at least six months, these symptoms occur to a degree that is developmentally deviant, and these symptoms were developed by the time the individual was seven years old.

The medical community has been searching for a verifiable physiological cause of ADHD for some time. Although no exact biological origin has been determined, researchers and clinicians have focused their efforts on the brain for answers to the root of the disorder. Among the proposed possibilities are chemical imbalances and brain deficiencies that may arise from low birth weight or premature birth. Some notable investigation has also been done on the frontal lobe, the area of the brain responsible for behavioral and emotional regulation. As this area matures, individuals gain the ability to plan before acting, and, when necessary, to ignore the desire to act. Scientists have observed a difference in the size and shape of the frontal lobe in ADHD individuals compared to non-ADHD individuals. These variations may indicate a diminished capacity for self-control in people with the disorder. Yet this research has also proven inconclusive, even leading some who accept the medical view of ADHD to admit that no irrefutable biological cause has been discovered to explain it; a point that critics and skeptics are quick to point out.

In addition to the argument for neurological markers of ADHD, researchers have also proposed a genetic factor for the disorder. As science learns and understands more about human DNA, the quest to locate particular genetic sources for illnesses has expanded beyond physiological disease to behavioral disorders like ADHD. No one has yet pinpointed an ADHD gene, but many believe it will be discovered eventually. Other proponents of the medical understanding of ADHD see it as more complicated than that, feeling that a single ADHD gene is not likely to be identified. These claimants point out that science is beginning to realize that mental disorders originate from complex interactions of genes, chemicals, and other neurological components, meaning that the isolation of a specific ADHD gene is not likely.

Strong arguments asserting that ADHD is a disease come from individuals, or from the relatives of individuals, who have ADHD. According to many of these advocates, ADHD causes much pain for those it touches, especially when not diagnosed and medical treatment can bring relief. ADHD literature contains a large number of personal stories by individuals dealing with the disorder. Many of these report that they were considered stupid, lazy, and unmotivated as children. They also describe deep feelings of guilt and isolation because they were unable to meet academic and social expectations. For these individuals who found relief and understanding after being diagnosed with ADHD, the validity of the medical model is unquestionable. The stories of ADHD sufferers can often be found alongside reports from family members who describe distress over not knowing how to relate to or help their ADHD loved one. These personal accounts available in the literature give human voices to an issue that is dismissed by some critics as a myth and others as invention.

The Medicalization of ADHD

Another perspective on ADHD is that it, like a number of other social issues, has been subjected to the process of medicalization. Prominent medicalization researchers, along with others, cite as key elements of the medicalizing of ADHD the changing views of children in the United States, the unprecedented power of the medical profession, and the clout of pharmaceutical companies offering so-called miracle drugs to fix behavioral problems.

Prior to the Industrial Revolution, children were seen as miniature adults rather than members of a special life stage prior to adulthood. These children were considered responsible and were expected to become productive members of society at early ages, for most this meant joining the labor force or helping on the family farm. At this time, the realms of childcare and management rested squarely within the family.

But with urbanization came a decreased need for child labor and a greater emphasis on education. Eventually society came to see children's proper place as in the classroom and compulsory education arose. At the same time, youth were being thrust into schools, their parents were coming to view them as innocent creatures with little social power, dependent on the protection and care of adults. Over time, as people began to place more stock in the word of professionals and specialists over the teachings of folkways and tradition, parents more often sought out these specialized groups for ideas about how to properly rear children. This view of youth as innocent and dependent coupled with a loss of authority in the family is described by claimants as a prime contributor to the medicalization of untoward child behavior. Furthermore, as children are not considered mature enough to be culpable, their unacceptable actions cannot be labeled crimes, leaving only illness labels to explain their deviant conduct.

Before medicine gained respect as a scientific field, bad children were thought to be under the devil's influence, morally lacking, or subject to poor parenting. Those were times when religion and the family had the main responsibility for shaping society's views on appropriate and inappropriate behavior. However, once physicians began to make medical breakthroughs, including the advent of vaccinations, the profession began to build expert power. Over the last century or so, the medical field has acquired great authority and now has almost absolute control over how U.S. society defines disease, illness, and treatment. Due to this, when physicians approach behavioral difficulties, such as those displayed with ADHD, as medical issues requiring medical treatment, most people accept this definition without question.

The makers of pharmaceuticals have also been gaining influence in society. Some now see these companies as a driving force behind the medicalization of a host of issues, including ADHD. Many people believe that if a drug exists that treats symptoms then it proves disease is present. Such is often the case with ADHD. Psychostimulants, such as Ritalin and Adderall, have been shown to be very effective at helping children calm down and pay attention. Because of this success, despite the positive effects found for alternative treatments such as parent training programs, medications are considered the most useful method of curbing ADHD difficulties. Critics contend, however, that the efficacy of psychostimulants for adjusting the behavior of children diagnosed with ADHD is not valid evidence of a biological deficit because these drugs produce similar results in non-ADHD children as well.

Following the view of some proponents, one primary reason aspects of human behavior are being increasingly tied to genetic explanations is because this is financially beneficial for drug manufacturers who are supposedly able to offer the only solutions to medical defects. Supporting this argument is the fact that, in the 1960s, pharmaceutical companies began to aggressively market psychostimulants for ADHD children by using print advertisements in medical journals, direct mailing, and skilled representatives who promoted their products to doctors. These tactics proved effective as more doctors and clinicians looked to psychostimulant medications as solutions for problematic behavior in children. Today, millions of people in the United States take these medications, causing some to fear that drugging children has become a new form of social control or that doctors are handing out prescriptions haphazardly to anyone claiming to have trouble concentrating or sitting still.

ADHD as Social Construction

In addition to the perspectives of ADHD as disease and the medicalization of ADHD is the view of ADHD as social construction. According to social psychology, humans are driven by the desire to make sense of the world around them. Individuals observe one another's behavior, interact in situations, and perform acts all to which they constantly try to attach definitions to help them understand the world and their place in it. This process is social and varies based on situational, historical, and other factors, which means that society's understandings can change over time. Several authors believe this has occurred with the interpretation of youthful conduct.

Ideas about desirable and undesirable child behavior vary within and between cultures. Thus, no universal definitions of good and bad conduct exist. Some claim that, in the United States, children's actions have not changed so much as society's interpretations of them. United States society used to be more understanding of variations in children's behavior and allowed them outlets for excess energy, such as time for recess and physical education built into the school day. Recently, however, following the No Child Left Behind Act of 2001 and the thrust to improve standardized test scores, most schools have done away with these sanctioned play times.

In a scholastic atmosphere now calling for more productivity from even the youngest students, inattentiveness and hyperactivity are being considered more of a problem than they were formerly. Some critics of this social development, such as Armstrong (2005), are troubled by the demands that they believe society places on children to be more like machines than human beings. Following this and some others' views, society, with pressure from experts, no longer sees disruptive students as exuberant or eccentric but rather as sick and in need of medication to put them back on the path to success, almost as if these children are broken and in need of repair.

The emergence of the field of developmental psychology may have also engendered a change in the social definitions of childhood conduct (Timimi 2005). Developmental psychology offers standardized ideals for child development. Milestones are prescribed based on age, and deviation from these standards is considered cause for alarm and is often approached from a medical standpoint. This discipline promotes developmental markers not only for areas such as physical growth, language use, and motor skills but for maturity, ability to attend to stimuli, and social interaction.

Some argue that due to the prescriptions of developmental psychology parents, teachers, and physicians are now more likely to view behaviors that are not deemed age-appropriate or acceptable as highly problematic. What may have once been considered simply a difficult personality is often pathologized today. Authors who hold this view seem to apply a version of the Thomas Theorem to the issue, the basic idea of which is that anything perceived as real is real in its consequences. Following this, it appears to some that people, accurately or not, view ADHD as a real disorder and thus look for symptoms confirming it, causing real consequences for children who are given the resulting pathological label.

A final illustration of society's changing definitions surrounding this issue deals with the locus of blame for children's misbehavior. Some researchers today support the view that poor home environments can impact children such that they display symptoms of ADHD. According to these authors chaos, disharmony, hostility, and dysfunction at home can cause children to have trouble focusing in class or to act out irrationally. Claimants supporting this view, however, are in the minority. Furthermore, prior to the medical diagnosis, behavioral difficulties characterizing ADHD were frequently thought to result from poor parenting, especially by mothers. Today, however, the general professional feeling is that mothering behaviors are a consequence, not a cause, of children's behaviors. Thus, less desirable actions and reactions on the part of parents are now seen as a consequence of stress that builds up from dealing with a troubled child, rather than a poorly behaved child being seen as a symptom of poor parenting. The emphasis on biology over parenting has taken responsibility away from parents and placed it on intangible sources deep within the child's brain.

PARENTS AND ADHD CHILDREN

While the debate rages on about the proper conceptualization of ADHD behaviors, parents and children are caught in the middle. Much research has found that actions consistent with ADHD in a child have negative implications for that child's relationship with his or her parents. In general, households with ADHD children are characterized by higher parental stress and distress and more parent-child conflict than households without ADHD youth. Studies of parents' self-reports find that mothers and fathers of these children have trouble relating to their offspring, often lack a sense of closeness with the child, and view themselves as less skilled and competent as parents. Commonly, these parents experience feelings of hopelessness and desperation to find help. In efforts to address the challenges they face, some parents display negative reactions to their children, including being excessively controlling, viewing the youths less positively, and resorting to more authoritarian discipline styles.

In addition to these joint concerns, studies have found issues unique to mothers and to fathers regarding their ADHD children. For example, research has found a correlation between depression in mothers and parenting ADHD children. Following a social tradition of disproportionate responsibility for rearing children, many mothers internalize the notion that they are to blame when their sons or daughters misbehave. This history of mother blaming has been somewhat relieved by the rise of the medical model for ADHD which takes the liability away from mothers and places it on the child's internal defects that are outside their control. Despite this, a number of mothers today are still deeply troubled when their children behave negatively, both out of concern for the quality of life of the child and for others' potentially hurtful perceptions about their parenting.

A DEBATE WITHIN THE DEBATE

Millions of children in the United States are currently taking Ritalin, Adderall, or some other psychostimulant used to treat attention deficit hyperactivity disorder (ADHD). While other treatment methods exist, medication is by far the most often used. This rise in psychostimulant prescriptions, which has corresponded with the rapid increase in ADHD diagnoses, has sparked a strong debate within the overall ADHD controversy.

Although the conceptualization of a disorder called ADHD was decades in the future, a scientist in 1937 was the first to test the results of stimulants on children with behavioral problems. He was surprised to discover the seemingly illogical effect these drugs had of subduing unruly children. The number one prescribed ADHD drug, Ritalin, was created in the 1950s and was approved by the federal Food and Drug Administration (FDA) for use in children in 1961. Since then, innumerable studies have been conducted to test the effects of psychostimulants on ADHD children. The majority of this research has reported these drugs as successful at calming children down, helping them concentrate, and improving their short-term memory. Supporters of psychostimulant use see this as evidence of the medications' appropriateness and usefulness. They also report the extended effects of helping children learn and socialize better with peers, both of which improve self-esteem. Additionally, they claim that medications improve outcomes of other therapies when they are used in combination.

Critics of psychostimulant use point to the negative effects these drugs can have, some of which are rare. These include lethargy, compulsiveness, slight growth inhibition, appetite loss, dry mouth, seizures, and tics. They also note that the drugs' benefits are short-term. Once patients stop taking them, their ADHD difficulties return. This means that children, once placed on medication, have little hope of ever getting off of it and functioning effectively. Skeptics also point out that psychostimulants have been found to have similar calming and attention-focusing effects on people not considered to have ADHD as they have on those diagnosed with the disorder. They believe this disproves the belief that a disease is present if medications can successfully treat it.

Many fathers of ADHD children experience their role differently from mothers. For example, one study found that fathers were much less willing to accept the medical view of their children's difficulties than were mothers. Additionally, this research noted that a high number of fathers were not active in the diagnostic and treatment process of their children's disorder, but they did not stand in the way of it either. Often they were sidelined during this progression, some by choice and others in an effort to avoid conflict in the marital relationship.

One notable finding by researchers, such as psychiatrist Ilina Singh, is that a number of fathers feel guilt in connection to their sons' ADHD. The medical model for this behavioral disorder proposes a genetic linkage that passes ADHD from father to son. Due to this, some fathers blame themselves for causing their sons' problems. One consequence of acknowledging their possible responsibility is that men think back to their own childhoods, in which they behaved similarly to their sons, and question whether they should have been given the same diagnosis.

Finally, discord can arise between a husband and wife as they struggle to deal with their ADHD child for a number of reasons. One example is a disagreement over the true nature of their offspring's problems. Also, trouble can emerge simply from the general stress of the environment. Partners who are feeling upset about issues with their child may take their emotions out on one another. Another source of conflict might be a husband's opinion that his wife is at least somewhat responsible for their child's unruly behavior because she is too indulgent, a sentiment some fathers report they have.

Critics of the medical model and of the medicalization of ADHD sometimes condemn parents for their willingness to accept such a label for their children. Some of these critics believe that parents today take the easy way out, choosing to take their children to a doctor for medication rather than altering their parenting styles to address more difficult behavior. Contrary to this perception, however, many parents report experiencing great worry over the decision to seek treatment for their children. Many would likely report that these actions were a last resort. A great number of ADHD diagnoses are initiated at school. Parents are often called to school repeatedly to address a child's unruly behavior, and eventually a teacher or administrator suggests an ADHD evaluation. If a parent is reluctant, this suggestion may continue to be made until he or she gives in. Whether they feel the ADHD label is appropriate or not, if a practitioner tells a parent that a son or daughter has ADHD, that parent has additional pressure to take steps to address it. Many parents, who may see themselves as grossly unqualified to determine the nature of their children's problems, eventually defer to the opinion of the experts (teachers, doctors, psychologists) and accept the ADHD diagnosis and treatment. Despite critics' claims, these parents would surely report that this decision is anything but easy.

IS ADHD HERE TO STAY?

ADHD is an issue touching more and more lives in the United States each day. Extensive research has been done on this topic, ranging from medical investigation to social interpretation, yet it remains an area ripe for exploration and debate. Science continues to seek definitive proof that a deficiency or imbalance in the brain, transmittable by DNA, causes recognizable unwanted behaviors that can be labeled and treated as a disease. At the same time, those opposed to this view continue to study and question the social factors surrounding this issue and disprove any biological basis. Neither side has had absolute success, so the controversy continues.

Regardless of where one stands in the debate, it is hard to deny that an increasing number of parents and children are being faced with the ADHD label. Those parents who hear competing information from various sources in the controversy often feel torn over the right thing to do and experience negative feelings, regardless of their decision. Perhaps one day an irrefutable medical discovery will be made to mark ADHD as a disease. Perhaps social opinion on children's behavior will shift, and more rambunctious or unruly behavior will not be considered as problematic as it is today. Either of these events could result in an end to the debate surrounding ADHD. However, at this point there is no indication that either type of solution will occur any time soon. Thus, ADHD diagnoses are sure to continue, with proponents' blessings and critics' curses.

See also Child Abuse; Developmental Disability and Marital Stress; Homeschooling; Juvenile Delinquency; Parenting Styles.

Further Reading: Armstrong, Thomas. "ADD: Does It Really Exist?" In *Taking Sides: Clashing Views on Controversial Issue in Abnormal Psychology,* 3rd ed., ed. Richard P. Halgin. Dubuque, IA: McGraw-Hill/Duskin, 2005; Barkley, Russell A. *Attention-Deficit Hyperactivity Disorder: A Handbook for Diagnosis and Treatment,* 3rd ed. New York: The Guilford Press, 2006; Centers for Disease Control and Prevention. "Mental Health in the United States: Prevalence of Diagnosis and Medication Treatment of Attention-Deficit/Hyperactivity Disorder—United States," 2003. http://www.cdc.gov/mmwr/preview/mmwrhtml/mm5434a2.htm (accessed April 2008); Conrad, Peter, and Joseph W. Schneider. *Deviance and Medicalization: From Badness to Sickness.* Philadelphia: Temple University Press, 1992; Corkum, Penny V., M. Margaret McKinnon, and Jennifer C. Mullane. "The Effect of Involving Classroom Teachers in a Parent Training Program for Families of Children with ADHD." *Child and Family Behavior Therapy* 27 (2005): 29–49; Detweiler, Robert E., Andrew P. Hicks, and Mack R. Hicks. "A Multi-Modal Approach to the Assessment and Management of ADHD." In *ADHD: Research, Practice and Opinion,* ed. Paul Cooper and Katherine Bilton. London: Whurr Publishers, 1999; Douglas, Anne. "A Mother's Story—Beyond the Debate: Living with the Reality of ADHD." In *ADHD: Research, Practice and Opinion,* ed. Paul Cooper and Katherine Bilton. London: Whurr Publishers, 1999; Hallowell, Edward M. "What I've Learned from ADD." In *Taking Sides: Clashing Views on Controversial Issue in Abnormal Psychology,* 3rd ed., ed. Richard P. Halgin. Dubuque, IA: McGraw-Hill/Duskin, 2005; Leo, Jonathan. "American Preschoolers on Ritalin." *Society* 39 (2002): 52–60; Malacrida, Claudia. "Alternative Therapies and Attention Deficit Disorder: Discourses of Maternal Responsibility and Risk." *Gender and Society* 16 (2002): 366–383; Mattox, Renee, and Jeanette Harder. "Attention Deficit Hyperactivity Disorder (ADHD) and Diverse Populations." *Child and Adolescent Social Work Journal* 24 (2007): 195–207; Olfson, Mark, Marc J. Gameroff, Steven C. Marcus, and Peter S. Jensen. "National Trends in the Treatment of Attention Deficit Hyperactivity Disorder." *The American Journal of Psychiatry* 160 (2003): 1071–1076; Panksepp, Jaak. "Attention Deficit Hyperactivity Disorders, Psychostimulants, and Intolerance of Childhood Playfulness: A Tragedy in the Making?" *Current Directions in Psychological Science* 7 (1998): 91–98; Purdie, Nola, John Hattie, and Annemaree Carroll. "A *Review of the Research* on Interventions for Attention Deficit Hyperactivity Disorder: What Works Best?" Review of Education Research 72 (2002): 61–99; Singh, Ilina. "Boys Will Be Boys: Fathers' Perspectives on ADHD Symptoms, Diagnosis, and Drug Treatment." *Harvard Review of Psychiatry* 11 (2003): 308–316; Thomas, William I., and Dorothy S. Thomas. *The Child in America: Behavior Problems and Programs.* New York: Alfred A. Knopf, 1928; Timimi, Sami. *Naughty Boys: Anti-Social Behavior, ADHD and the Role of Culture.* New York: Palgrave Macmillan, 2005; Wegandt, Lisa L. *An ADHD Primer,* 2nd ed. Mahwah, NJ: Laurence Erlbaum Associates, 2007.

Nicole D. Garrett

B

BATTERED WOMAN SYNDROME

While few people would say that it is acceptable to abuse women, and while most would say that a woman who is being victimized has a right to defend herself, there is considerable controversy over women using past victimization as a justification for retaliation. Claims of battered woman syndrome are often derided as an attempt to get out of legal punishment. These claims may appear false as persons are skeptical of the battered woman defense.

BACKGROUND

Females, throughout history, have been seen as the subordinate of the two sexes, making them an easier target for abuse. While laws against physical violence toward women have been around for centuries, they have not been necessarily vigorously enforced. Stereotypically, females have also seemed needy and ultimately dependent on the "stronger" sex, thus allowing the men in power to make laws that contribute to the victimization of women. Women have dealt with this victimization in many different ways, from fighting against it to accepting it and therefore conforming to the stereotype. Women are more likely to be victimized by family members than strangers.

Spousal abuse used to be looked at as a private matter, and one that should be taken care of in the home. As late as the 1980s, some police officers were looking at spousal abuse as a necessary way to, so to speak, keep wives in line. Thus, they were slow to intervene on domestic disturbance calls. The crime of spousal abuse used to be classified as a misdemeanor offense, meaning that a police officer would need to see a crime in progress in order to make an arrest. Because most domestic violence crimes occur within the home, the police were unable to see the crimes, and this made it very hard to convict an abuser in domestic violence cases. In the early 1980s, there was a domestic violence police experiment in Minneapolis, Minnesota. The police used a lottery system that determined how they would treat domestic violence cases that were called in to dispatch. The results of this study showed that when the offender was arrested at the scene, there was a significant decrease in repeat offences. Since this study, there has been a major shift in classifying domestic violence from a misdemeanor to a felony, and also including mandatory arrests of offenders.

While the law has changed to help battered women in an immediately threatening situation, a lot of the stereotypes of battered women and personal feelings of employees within the justice system have been slow to change. Some legal professionals, including lawyers and judges, based on their past experiences feel that a battered woman will not help in the prosecution's case against an offender, so they are reluctant to prosecute any domestic violence cases. The legal system is trying to bridge the gap between the mandatory arrests required of police officers and the reluctance of prosecuting lawyers and judges to charge the offenders by introducing a so-called no drop policy in some states. The no drop policy means that when a domestic violence case comes before a prosecutor, he must prosecute the offender regardless of the victim's willingness to testify. Another way the legal system is trying to help battered women is by increasingly allowing experts to testify about the phenomenon of battered woman syndrome, sometimes known as the battered-woman defense, as an explanation for why women stay in an abusive relationship or why they themselves may become abusive in self-defense.

BATTERED WOMAN SYNDROME

The so-called mother of the term battered woman syndrome (BWS) is psychologist Lenore Walker. She specializes in the psychological treatment of victims, specifically victims of spousal abuse. In 1979, Walker wanted to examine the different factors in the psychological responses of domestic violence victims. She interviewed 1,500 women and found that there were some similar experiences among the victims. She found that a lot of these women go through three different stages of abuse. These stages have come to be known as the battering cycle. Before discussing the controversies with BWS, the result of long-term physical or psychological abuse, we first need to look at the patterns of the battering cycle, and definition and causes of BWS.

The Battering Cycle

Walker contends that there are three cycles or phases of abuse that a victimized woman experiences. Repeated exposure to the cycle may result in the condition of BWS. The first phase consists of minor battering incidents where the victim is complacent, and hoping to appease the batterer so there is no more battering. The first beating in a relationship often occurs for minor offences, like burning dinner, or not having beer in the home when the partner would like one. When these minor wrongdoings set the batterer off and he hits the woman, if she stays, she will make sure not to burn dinner next time, and will ensure that the beer is constantly stocked. This starts the complacency on the part of the victim and increases the power that the batterer has over the victim.

The second phase is generally an escalation in tensions, capped of with an acute battering incident during which the woman feels helpless and isolated. An example of this would be when following an outing in which they both participated, they return home and the victim is beaten for supposed flirting, even though she never left the batterer's side. This second phase is also accompanied with threats against her family and friends, and controlling to whom the victim talks and for what length of time. Threats may also be made and enacted against any children that are part of the household.

The third and final phase is called a conciliation period (also know as a "honeymoon" phase), where the batterer shows remorse for the beatings and the woman is forgiving and understanding. Often he promises the abuse will never happen again and may be solicitous and fawning in his attempts to regain her trust. Following this last element of the cycle, the abused woman believes that she may have misjudged the offender and will take him back, for one more attempt at a harmonious relationship without seeking outside help.

Shelter-Seeking

It was not until the late 1980s that the United States Surgeon General classified family violence and violence against women as an epidemic and one that should be looked at as a health problem. It was then that many community programs, interventions, and prevention programs were founded or expanded to try to combat the problem. These programs tended to examine factors related to women's risk of victimization as well as their resilience to abuse rather than illness and cure factors. Giving girls and women the strength and training to spot domestic violence, or an abusive spouse, is a good policy in the short run, but it is a strategy that is unlikely to stop abuse in the long run. These initial attempts to monitor and educate were targeted at particular groups of women, but they did little beyond that. Without going to the source of the problem and examining the reasons that men batter and women stay, this strategy was equated with putting a band-aid on a severed limb. One just has to hope it holds and everything works out.

Noticeable in the prevention and intervention of domestic violence has been the shelter movement. In the whole United States in 1976 there were only six shelters or safe houses. But thanks to the awareness raised by the Surgeon General and others, by 1994 at the time of the passage of the federal Violence Against Women Act (VAWA) there were over 1000. Shelters are a wonderful option when available; however, they have a hidden problem in that women can not stay there indefinitely.

BWS Patterns

When the batterer starts to control the female victim, and starts to isolate the woman from her friends, she feels there is no one left to turn to. The battered woman starts to feel extremely isolated and as if the only person that can understand her is the batterer, with whom she lives and of whom she is in constant fear. Women also start to exhibit feelings of so-called learned helplessness. This is where the psychological pressures of living in constant fear make the woman cope with the abuse rather than finding a way out. The man's efforts to isolate the abused woman from her family, finances, and friends make it extremely difficult for the woman to request any outside help from anyone else. Unusually low self-esteem interacts with fear, depression, confusion, powerful anxiety, feelings of self-blame, and a general sense of helplessness to create BWS, in which an abused woman feels incapable of making any positive changes in her life, not the least of which is leaving her batterer.

Another contributing factor to the woman staying might be the tendency of women to invest themselves deeply into the relationship, as well as for family or religious beliefs. For example, if the abused woman was raised Catholic, a religion that frowns on getting divorced, she would be less inclined to seek help, not wanting to go against her religion or her family if they held a similar belief. This can also contribute to the syndrome.

BATTERED WOMEN AND THE LEGAL SYSTEM

The first time most battered women go to a courthouse it is to obtain a restraining order against an abusive partner. Often this is done with the help of advocates from a domestic abuse shelter. The language of the restraining order, however, leads some to believe that it may actually be harder to obtain one than ever before. Some of the court officials, judges included, claim that women make up stories, or exaggerate the beatings to win custody hearings and divorce cases. Some judges have indicated they believe that it is the women causing the problems and the men are being falsely charged to get them out of the home so that the wife can do what she wants. Within the restraining order wording, the victim must talk about the abuser's tactics and strategies used in the attacks against her. This can lead to problems if the woman doesn't know her abuser's intent, or the reasons he attacks her, or feels that she deserved the beating.

The next step is the court system's response to the information that the battered woman provides about her attacker. Despite numerous medical records, police reports, and court proceedings, courts have occasionally found that the woman is the aggressor and the male was only trying to defend himself. Prosecutors are wary of trying an abusive spouse, many times because of the stereotypes they hold about the battered woman. If a woman who has decided to press charges against her attacker decides later, maybe as a result of pressure from the abuser, that she does not want to testify, she could be charged with contempt of court and thrown in jail. Once she gets out, an arrest record will make it that much harder for her to be believed or even subsequently listened to because of her lack of follow-through the first time.

It is not just the prosecutors that have a stereotype against battered women; judges have them as well. Some judges feel that proceedings where battered women come into the courtroom to get protective orders against their significant others are trivial and not worth the taxpayers' time. It is common for the judge to blame the victim for the incident in order to justify dismissing the charges against the abuser and sending him back into the home. The problem with sending the abuser back into the home is that researchers can predict with almost certainty that there will be extreme violence or retaliation from the abuser for the victim's bold action of seeking legal recourse. Judges have also been known to threaten the abused wife with jail if she returns with a similar claim, or to admonish her to be an adult and handle it on her own. Such an admonishment had disastrous consequences when a judge scolded a woman who, after receiving an order of protection, asked for a police escort to remove her belongings from her home. The judge scolded her and her victim advocate, citing that this matter was trivial and that there were bigger cases out there that needed the taxpayer's attention. Five months after the judge made that statement, the woman was found stabbed, beaten, and strangled in the city dump; killed by the husband from whom she tried so desperately to get away.

BATTERED WOMAN SYNDROME AS A LEGAL DEFENSE

Given the historical lack of support from the legal system, it is no wonder that many women are reluctant to press charges. The shelters that are available are usually temporary measures that allow women to stay for a finite time before seeking alternative living arrangements. Additionally, the private nature of family life ensures that many women keep their victimization hidden from others. These situations leave some women feeling desperate and helpless and often push them to make difficult choices about how to end the abuse. Some women choose violence against their abuser. Lenore Walker has said that a battered woman who kills does not do so for malice, but rather because the woman can take no more beatings. After repeated losses to her self-worth, she perceives no other way out of her desperate situation. The statement a battered woman makes by stopping her attacker is "I've had it and realize that you can not or will not change. You can't beat, hurt, or control me any more." The use of battered woman syndrome as a defense in court is quite controversial.

Beginning in the late 1970s and early 1980s, as a greater awareness of domestic violence was occurring in the United States, lawyers began to explore the possibility of being a victim of battering as a defense for some women's illegal actions. What has become known as the battered-woman defense is nothing more than a woman claiming self-defense in the context of her experience as a battered woman. This means that BWS helps to account for the woman's actions and assists in providing a justification for her behaviors. It was first employed in domestic homicide cases, but has since been used in some assault cases as well.

Opposition to the Battered-Woman Defense

There are some negatives to using BWS as a legal defense. There are some who believe that the battered-woman defense is actually hurting the victim rather than helping her by cutting off other avenues of defense, simply by resting all her hopes on this one defense. A big problem with BWS is it relies heavily on the victim being the stereotypical battered woman. This includes a woman who was either abused as a young child or witnessed abuse as a young child, thus making that part of her upbringing and leading her to look for a controlling person to fit that model as an intimate partner.

Skeptics abound among persons who have never been abused, leading some to even suggest that women fabricate stories of abuse to terminate unsatisfactory relationships and avoid future punishment. To combat this stereotype lawyers attempt to get as much evidence and expert testimony in support of their clients' claims of BWS as possible. Additionally, skeptics charge that the crime may not have been done in self-defense, but women have the advantage over men in having BWS as an option in defense. They suggest that the problem of men who are victims of domestic violence is hidden when BWS cases receive media attention. Research data does suggest, however, that more than 90 percent of spousal or partner assaults are committed by men.

Among the criticism of the battered-woman defense is that BWS is a constellation of psychological symptoms that can not be diagnosed definitively. This leads to questions over its legitimacy. While BWS is not listed in the *Diagnostic and Statistical Manual of Mental Disorders IV* (the definitive guide for psychological illness) as a separate ailment, it is mentioned in conjunction with Post-Traumatic Stress Disorder (PTSD).

Some legal scholars have argued that the self-defense provision that already exists in the legal system should be enough to support these women's cases, although others suggest that there is a gender bias in favor of males in the way that most self-defense statutes are worded.

Support for the Battered-Woman Defense

Many feminists believe that the self-defense law is male-biased, and leaves battered women out of the equation. Because a fair amount of abused women who kill their spouses kill them when they are not being harmed or threatened, some feminists believe that without introducing the battered-woman defense into the trial, the abused woman is almost certainly condemned to death.

The law of self-defense itself, some argue, is a male biased law and doesn't take into consideration the battered woman. The self-defense law states that a person has the right to defend themselves only if they are in imminent danger, and can only use deadly force when all other avenues of escape are exhausted. Ideally one has a witness that can corroborate the account, something battered women can virtually never produce. When an opponent outweighs a victim by 200 pounds, and she is seriously afraid of retaliation, it is no wonder that most women who kill their abusers do so in non-confrontational situations. A woman in jail awaiting trial for shooting and killing her husband while he was sitting down claimed that she was afraid that he would get up and beat her for causing a mess on the carpet. Such psychological abuse battered women suffer at the hands of their attacker is comparable to that of a prisoner of war. With this type of abuse, coming at the woman from all angles, a woman could break at anytime, finding the window of opportunity when the abuser is docile.

Even BWS researcher Lenore Walker says that not all abused women should have a right to kill their attackers. A battered woman, however, lives in fear and is always in danger of a future attack. It is important that the woman feel her life is in danger. Walker suggests that courts have to consider if it is a reasonable perception of danger from the viewpoint of the battered woman.

Advocates for abused women suggest that the battered-woman defense, although not perfect, provides at least some footing for women in a legal system that has neither treated domestic violence as a serious problem nor responded to it appropriately. Police and courts have been inconsistent in their responses, although some courts permit civil law suits against police failure to protect. There is good evidence that while not all women who claim BWS in their defense are exonerated of their crimes, they can have charges and sentences reduced in recognition of the extreme circumstances.

CONCLUSION

There are many stereotypes about abused women, and how they will handle themselves in the courtroom. It's the lack of support many battered women feel that leads them not to outside legal help, but to take matters into their own hands. Societal response to domestic violence has improved, but many more improvements are needed as even today there are fewer than 2000 domestic violence shelters in the United States. Those that are available might only have a few rooms in which to house victims and, less often, their children.

There is a continuing need to examine self-defense law and to definitively determine if the advent of the battered-woman defense has helped or hurt the battered woman. There has been talk that BWS targets those women who were predisposed to familial violence, and therefore are easier to fit into the cycle in a neat package for a jury. As we all know, not everyone fits the same kind of mold. One could argue that being in an abusive relationship is like a long term self-defense law in action. Women try everything to get away from their attacker, whether it is police reports, orders of protection, or prosecution. When using BWS as a legal defense, the defendant must recognize and accept the idea of helplessness as the reason that they couldn't get out of the situation without killing the abuser. This too causes problems because it places the blame on the abused for not getting out of the situation, rather than placing the blame on the legal system for not standing up for the battered woman or on the perpetrator of the abuse.

Community views of battered women also follow the same injustices that await the woman in the courtroom. The community, more importantly the jury, brings stereotyped notions of abused women to their jury work. Some lawyers have indicated that the most important step in using the BWS as a legal defense is to carefully vet the jury to determine their receptivity to such claims. Unfortunately, the long tradition of domestic violence has meant that some in the community view these offenses as trivial, and not worthy of their time. There are both positive and negative outcomes of using the battered-woman defense within a legal context.

See also Domestic Violence Behaviors and Causes; Domestic Violence Interventions; Mandatory Arrest Laws; Marital Power; Religion, Women, and Domestic Violence.

Further Reading: Downs, Donald Alexander. *More Than Victims: Battered Women, The Syndrome Society, and the Law.* Chicago: The University of Chicago Press, 1996; Dutton, Donald G. *Rethinking Domestic Violence.* Vancouver, BC: UBC Press, 2006; Gillespie, Cynthia K. *Justifiable Homicide: Battered Women, Self-Defense and the Law.* Columbus: Ohio State University Press, 1989; Maschke, Karen J. *The Legal Response to Violence Against Women.* New York: Garland Publishing, 1997; Ptacek, James. *Battered Women in the Courtroom: The Power of Judicial Responses.* Boston: Northeastern University Press, 1999; Walker, Lenore E. A. *The Battered Woman Syndrome,* 2nd ed. New York: Springer Publishing Company, 2000; Walker, Lenore E. *Terrifying Love: Why Battered Women Kill and How Society Responds.* New York: Harper and Row, Publishers, Inc., 1989.

Njeri Kershaw

BENEFITS OF MARRIAGE

The climate surrounding marriage in contemporary America is one of great debate. Many feel that a so-called marriage war is taking place between those who say marriage is a fundamental, irreplaceable institution of American society and those who feel that it is just one of many possibilities for family formation, and not necessarily the best one. The former group sees the rising divorce, cohabitation, and unmarried parent rates in the United States as detrimental to individuals, family, and society as a whole. They stress marriage as a beneficial institution that can improve people's lives in a variety of ways. The latter group is less concerned with the actual form of relationships and families than they are with the content of them (what the environment is like). Some with this viewpoint also say marriage can actually be harmful to those involved, especially women.

Those holding the pro-marriage position cite copious amounts of research that concludes that marriage is beneficial to those involved, and that these benefits span many areas. They point to studies showing that married people are generally physically and mentally healthier, do better financially, and rear happier and healthier children than their unmarried counterparts. They support the marriage protection effects stance that claims that marriage is good for one's health. Prominent voices for this argument include Linda J. Waite and Maggie Gallagher, James Dobson and the Family Research Council, and the Institute for American Values. Another strong force for this side of the debate is the current administration of the U.S. government under George W. Bush.

With the opposing view is the pro-alternative relationships side. These individuals disagree with the notion that American society will crumble if the more traditional family structure is not upheld. In fact, they point to studies showing that, while marriage does appear to benefit men greatly, it does not have equal advantages for women. Moreover, some research has found that marriage can be harmful to women. This group also raises the argument that the financial and societal benefits afforded to married couples are discriminatory toward other couple and family types. They contend that the seemingly better lives of married people are not a direct result of the act of getting married but that those who marry are generally healthier, happier, and better off to start with. This is known as the marriage selection effects stance, which holds that healthy people are more likely to get and stay married. Some proponents of this perspective are Jessie Bernard, Susan Maushart, Delma Heyn, the Council on Contemporary Families, and Thomas Coleman with Unmarried America.

THE PRO-MARRIAGE ARGUMENT

Physical Benefits

Does getting married improve one's health? This is a question that has been widely researched. Many positive correlations between tying the knot and good health have been found. One finding that marriage advocates point to is that married people have a longer life expectancy than unmarried people, and that they are less likely to die of all causes. Although true for women to a degree, the greatest health advantages are for men. This is often explained with one of two considerations. First, while living the bachelor life, men often take risks with themselves. Single men are more likely to have a poor diet, to drink to excess, to smoke, to speed, to have multiple sexual partners, and to engage in other behaviors that, while they may be pleasurable at the time, can have dire consequences for both the immediate and long-term futures of these men. But marriage seems to turn this around for a lot of males. Research has shown that as the wedding date approaches, men become more responsible with their behavior, and once the rice has been thrown, they settle into a much safer lifestyle. Researchers often accredit this change to a realization of responsibility on the part of the husbands and the realization that someone else now has a stake in their lives. Also contributing to this is the fact that married men often spend much more time at work than do unmarried men.

A second factor of married life that helps husbands improve health is the involvement of their wives. Besides discouraging risky bachelor behaviors such as drinking and smoking, wives often take an active part in the maintenance of their husband's health. As the majority of women have primary responsibility for planning and preparing the family's meals, wives can impact the amount of fruits and vegetables their mates eat and they can cook overall healthier meals. Wives also may encourage their husbands to adopt better sleeping habits. Possibly the most influential things wives do for their spouses' health is to "nag" them about seeing the doctor. They often take an active part in scheduling doctors' visits and following up on doctors' orders. Some even accompany their mates to appointments and many act as liaisons with medical bureaucracies.

Although not as great as for men, marriage has been found to improve the physical health of married women over unmarried women. This is often attributed to women's improved financial resources and the availability of better insurance and healthcare that comes with access to their husband's income. It has been found that men do not take as active a role in their wives' physical health as their wives take in theirs.

Psychological Benefits

Pro-marriage individuals assert that not only are married people healthier, but they are happier too. Evidence shows that married men and women are less depressed, stressed, and prone to other psychological disorders than are their unmarried peers. One study found that married women reported a greater purpose and meaning in life and several other studies indicate that married men and women self-report higher levels of happiness.

One theory behind these findings says that the support and understanding of a loving and intimate partner improves their spouses' mental health. Acts of self-disclosure, developing deep trust, and cultivating a strong bond with a mate can all improve an individual's peace of mind. Self-esteem and feelings of acceptance that come from such a relationship also enhance men and women's psychological well-being.

The better mental health of married people can also be attributed to societal factors. Although less so than in past eras, cohabitation, divorce, unwed pregnancies, and the choice to live life alone are still stigmatized in American society, while marriage is praised. The decrease in stress that comes with the acceptance of society for their chosen lifestyle can better a married couple's outlook on life.

Financial Benefits

Although they don't claim that getting married will necessarily make a person rich, marriage advocates do say that matrimony leads to firmer financial footing. These monetary rewards are reaped in a few different ways. One is the pooling of resources. Two people can often live as cheaply, if not more so, than one. Frequently, prior to marriage the man and woman are handling separate rent or mortgage payments, utility payments, grocery bills, and other costs of living with only one income. Once they take up a household together, the bills associated with the two separate lives are consolidated into one, generally with two incomes to support it.

Another financial advantage comes from the government and employers to married people. For starters, the tax advantages are numerous. These include the option to file joint tax returns, the ability to divide business income among family members, and exemptions from estate and gift taxes for property transferred to a spouse. Men and women can also receive Social Security, Medicare, disability, veterans', and military benefits for spouses. Employers tend to favor married employees as well. For instance, it is commonly recognized that married men earn a so-called marriage premium that places their salaries between 10 and 40 percent higher than single men doing the same work. A study in the mid-

1990s by Robert Schoeni put the number at 30 percent. Besides this, marriage allows family rates on insurance and makes a husband or wife's wages, workers' compensation, and retirement plans available to surviving spouses should the employee pass away.

For women, who regularly earn less at work than men, most economic gains come from access to their husband's earnings. This is especially true for those wives who cut back or choose not to work at all upon marriage or the birth of a child.

Benefits for Children

In addition to the myriad improvements marriage can make in a couple's lives, marriage supporters also claim that wedding bells are good for children too. This group points to investigations that find two married parents in a home has a positive correlation with numerous measures of child wellbeing. Children of these families are said to have less physical and psychological ailments, better behavior, and less involvement in crime and promiscuity as youngsters and as adults. They are also said to go on to have better educational outcomes, higher occupational statuses, and more stable marriages themselves. A reason for this is that having two parents in the home has been found to give children more supervision, support, and help with school, and to improve the youths' ability to form strong bonds with others because they first experience such a relationship with their parents and their parents' marriage. Faith-based groups, such as Focus on the Family, the Family Research Council, and others of the pro-marriage opinion feel that providing children with anything but this type of environment is setting them up for failure in many areas of life.

A point advocates make is that children are more likely to experience abuse in a home including a stepfather or mother's boyfriend than they are in a home with their biological parents living together. Proponents of marriage will cite facts such as this when arguing that an unhappily married couple with children will do less harm to their offspring by staying together than by divorcing and possibly remarrying. Another point is that never-married or divorced mothers who do not remarry are likely to live below the poverty line. This socioeconomic status can have dire consequences for the educational, behavioral, and other outcomes of their sons and daughters. Overall the pro-marriage perspective says that a home headed by a married mother and father is the ideal environment that produces happy and healthy children.

Marriage Protection Effects

An idea that weaves together many of the aspects of the pro-marriage argument is the notion that marriage provides protection effects to husbands and wives. This presents marriage as an insulator to the outside world that bonds two people together who can provide companionship, intimacy, emotional fulfillment, and support to one another in a way that is not achieved by other relationships. In sum, matrimony becomes a buffer against physical, mental, and emotional pathology for the man and the woman involved.

MARRIAGE WARNING LABELS

In the past decade and a half several states have proposed, and some have passed, legislation requiring the presence of a marriage warning label of sorts to all marriage applications. Among these states are Washington, Massachusetts, and South Dakota. The language of the warning on South Dakota's application reads:

> The laws of this state affirm your right to enter into this marriage and at the same time to live within the marriage free from violence and abuse. Neither of you is the property of the other. Physical abuse, sexual abuse, battery, and assault of a spouse or other family member, as well as other provisions of the criminal laws of this state, are applicable to spouses and other family members and violations thereof are punishable by law.

All the labels generally include a statement regarding neither partner owning the other upon marriage and against either partner physically abusing the other.

THE PRO-ALTERNATIVE RELATIONSHIPS ARGUMENT

The group that opposes many of the pro-marriage camp's viewpoints can not accurately be described as "anti-marriage." Although some may feel that marriage is an outdated institution that no longer serves a viable purpose in society, the majority is not against marriage as a rule. In general, these individuals desire society to embrace relationships and families in all the myriad forms they come in today; to accept that traditional ideas about marriage and family are no longer the norm, and to adapt to meet the needs of these types of relationships as they exist today. Therefore, a more correct label for those with opposing arguments is pro-alternative relationships.

Unequal Benefits

Alternatives advocates often accept research that shows the positive results marriage can bring to husbands. It is the wives, however, that they say are at risk. Originally proposed was the idea that a marriage is actually two separate relationships, a his and a hers, that are experienced very differently by the man and the woman involved. While the husband gets a companion who will take on the majority of housework and child rearing responsibilities, be a guardian over his health, and tend to basic relationship maintenance, the wife gets to be all these things to her husband without receiving equal reciprocity in these areas in return. They give as evidence for this the fact that women initiate divorce at much higher rates than do men and then remarry at much lower rates.

Others say that marriage limits women's opportunities, especially once children are added, because many put their careers on hold to take care of the family. In the United States, single women are often found to have higher educational attainment, a higher occupational status, and a higher median income than married women. Some also claim the marriage convention crushes women's emerging identities as they assume the behavior society expects of one in the role of wife and mother. These expectations are born out of some major assumptions found in American marriage laws, which include the following: the husband is the head of the household, the husband is responsible for the economic support of his wife and children, and the wife is responsible for domestic services and child care.

Some research has found that married women are more likely to be depressed than are unmarried women, and that they are up to twice as likely to be depressed than are married men, indicating that marriage has negative psychological and emotional effects for females. Others would agree with this standpoint and explain that women experience a gradual and subtle suppression of individuality after marriage, which is a contributing factor to their unhappiness. Others of this opinion would say that these findings also come from the added stress and burden of a disproportionate amount of family responsibilities assumed by the wife in comparison to her husband. In addition to psychological testing, some physical testing indicates that marriage can be disadvantageous to women's health as well. Despite the generally accepted fact that a wife will likely outlive her husband by a number of years, married women experience more chronic conditions and seek more medical attention than do married men.

Some proponents of this view would say that the only advantage women acquire from getting married is access to their husband's financial resources. But this too, they often warn, can hurt many wives in the long run should the marriage end in divorce or the husband pass away. The loss of a mate by either method can be financially devastating for a woman, especially if she has children, and many women end up in poverty. One recent research study found that divorced women are five times more likely to be below the poverty line than other women. Although in contemporary America the majority of wives work outside the home, it is still commonplace for the husband to be the primary wage earner. The alternatives advocates argue that during marriage women may work only part-time or put their careers on hold altogether in order to take care of a family, or they may specialize in ways that leave them worse off if the marriage ends due to death or divorce. The alternatives advocates also point out that another strain on women following the dissolution of a marriage is the inadequate legal protection available to them under no-fault divorce.

Another area of concern involving wives is that being married puts them at risk for violence perpetrated by their husbands. Domestic violence is a major area of concern for American society, with the majority of victims being women. In fact, women are much more likely to be abused or murdered by a male with whom they are intimately involved, including husbands, than they are by a stranger. It has been written that marriage as an institution is still structured in such a way as to encourage male dominance, and such dominance makes high rates of battering inevitable. Whatever the explanations behind it, some people warn that becoming a wife can be a very dangerous status for a woman to take on.

Marriage Rights are Discriminatory

Another case made by those who favor the pro-alternative relationship perspective is that federal and state laws and employment policies that encourage marriage—cited as some of the institution's benefits by pro-marriage advocates—are discriminatory to single adults, homosexual couples, and their children. This group resents the societal implication that married people are better, more productive citizens and better parents and are thus more deserving of legal and financial consideration than are unmarried people or those in alternative relationship styles.

Entities like the American Association for Single People and individuals like Arlene Skolnick claim that it is not family composition but rather family dynamics and relationship environments that affect the lives and futures of family members, especially children. They point to poverty and inadequate income as major threats to children's well-being and development, not having unwed parents or not living in a two-parent household. Therefore, denying single parents, homosexual couples, or individuals in other alternative relationship structures the same rights as married people is discriminatory and has no justifiable basis as a part of American society in the twenty-first century.

Marriage Selection Effects

In all the areas that advocates cite the positive influences of marriage protection effects (physical, psychological, financial, and child rearing), pro-alternative relationship advocates refer to evidence that the benefits are actually a result of marriage selection effects. It makes sense, they argue, that healthier, happier, more financially secure people, and those with better parenting skills, would be more likely to attract, wed, and keep a mate than their peers who do not posses attractive traits in these crucial areas. Members of the opposing perspective have even had to give some ground and admit that selection effects do likely contribute to some of the benefits they find to marriage. Linda J. Waite and Maggie Gallagher write that some of the advantages married people have is undoubtedly due to selection, and the Center for Marriage and Families admits that selection effects exist, but claim they do not tell the whole story themselves.

One criticism the alternative relationships group has of studies ruling out selection effects and boasting protection effects is that these studies are too often performed cross-sectionally as opposed to longitudinally. Due to this, the research often includes a disproportionate number of newly married couples that may initially report various gains from marriage because the so-called honeymoon phase is not over and they have yet to set the long-term patterns of their wedded partnering.

THE DEBATE CONTINUES

Although pro-marriage advocates are worried about its downfall, marriage remains an important institution in American society. Surveys find that most Americans plan to marry and count having a happy marriage among their crucial life goals. Yet, a high number of marriages and remarriages eventually end in divorce, and the idealized traditional family form, if it ever really existed, has died a death from which it almost surely will not be resurrected. In its wake, many different relationship structures have emerged, reflecting the diversity that is present in so many other aspects of American culture. As change occurs, there are always some who want to halt it and others who want to further it, and it is no different for the issue of marriage. The pro-marriage versus pro-alternative relationships debate will likely continue into the unforeseeable future. The marriage war has dedicated soldiers on each side continuously seeking researched ammunition to help their cause. Whether common ground will ever be acknowledged and compromises reached, only time will tell.

See also Cohabitation, Effects on Marriage; Divorce, as Problem, Symptom, or Solution; Marital Satisfaction.

Further Reading: Baxter, Janeen, and Edith Gray. "For Richer or Poorer: Women, Men and Marriage." http://lifecourse.anu.edu.au/publications/Discussion_papers/NLCDP012.pdf (accessed September 1, 2006); Burton, Russell P. D. "Global Integrative Meaning as a Mediating Factor in the Relationship Between Social Roles and Psychological Distress." *Journal of Health and Social Behavior* 39 (1998): 201–215; Jacobson, Neil, and John Gottman. *When Men Batter Women: New Insights into Ending Abusive Relationships.* New York: Simon and Schuster, 1998; Lamb, Kathleen A., Gary R. Lee, and Alfred DeMaris. "Union Formation and Depression: Selection and Relationship Effects." *Journal of Marriage and Family* 65, no. 4 (2003): 953–962; Maushart, Susan. *Wifework: What Marriage Really Means for Women.* New York: Bloomsbury, 2001; Shehan, Constance L. *Through the Eyes of a Child.* Greenwich, CT: JAI Press, 1999; Waite, Linda J., and Maggie Gallagher. *The Case for Marriage: Why Married People are Happier, Healthier, and Better Off Financially.* New York: Broadway Books, 2000; Wilson, Chris M., and Andrew J. Oswald. *How Does Marriage Affect Physical and Psychological Health? A Survey of the Longitudinal Evidence.* http://papers.ssrn.com/sol3/papers.cfm?abstract_id=735205 (accessed September 19, 2006).

Nicole D. Garrett

BIOLOGICAL PRIVILEGE

Biological privilege refers to the commonly held idea that children are inherently better off when raised by their biological parents. Many current social policies endorse this perspective, particularly those that are designed to maintain the family unit despite problems that may be present. Suggesting more restrictive divorce laws when children are present in the marriage is one indication of the sway of biological privilege. In those instances where families are divided it is the presumed closer biological link between mother and child that is privileged, resulting in the greater likelihood of mothers receiving primary custody, for example.

However, there are voices and initiatives starting to question the extreme emphasis placed on biology. In some situations, it is not in the child's best interests to remain with his or her biological parents, such as when the environment is highly abusive or drug use is present. Given the increasingly flexible way that

Americans define family, reflected in the notion of fictive kin, overemphasizing biology has become problematic. Areas in which questions of biological primacy have been raised include adoption, surrogacy, child custody, and foster care. Recently critics of biologically based social policies have highlighted their discriminatory nature, noticing that they privilege the relationships of heterosexual couples who can conceive and give birth.

SOCIAL POLICY

Social policies related to family life can be of two types, those that focus on social relationships and those that focus on biological relationships. A common phrase employed in favor of the former is what is in the "best interests of child," regardless of whether that is with a blood relative or not, married or not. The emphasis on birth or biological ties is often couched in terms of what is most natural. Consequently, as a result of biological ties, the birth parent is defined as the one most suited to raise a child.

In the United States today, most legal policies related to family place greater emphasis on biological ties. This suggests that birth ties are more powerful, as well as more appropriate, than other bonds and therefore they must be stronger. This legal emphasis on biology is clearly seen in child custody decisions where mothers are overwhelmingly the primary custodial parent. A woman would have to be proven particularly unfit to parent or had to have abandoned the child for the pattern to waiver. Part of this preference for mothers relates to the ways that motherhood has been viewed in the culture.

VIEWS OF MOTHERHOOD

Mothering is viewed in many instances as natural, universal, and unchanging as women's biology sets them up for this expectation. The biological imperatives for women are to conceive, birth, and nurse the infant. Males can not biologically do these things, but can do all of the other tasks that have historically been defined as mothering. However, most persons are not comfortable with men in the caregiving role and insist that women are somehow biologically programmed to do these tasks, which they will enjoy more than will men, and will be better at when compared to men. Increasingly, motherhood researchers stress that mothering and what is considered good mothering is culturally determined.

Our culture views the bond between mother and child as inviolable. However, our culture divides mothers into four different types. In order of cultural acceptability, these are married and financially secure women, single or lesbian women, welfare mothers, and then teen mothers. While every woman has a fundamental right to raise her own child, how acceptable this is depends on into which category she falls. Married, heterosexual women with sufficient resources are certainly seen as having the right, even the obligation, to raise their own children. When these financial resources are not available to the mother, however, the situation is often seen much differently. This is especially true with regard to teen mothers. In these circumstances, material well-being takes priority over the connection between biological mother and child. The same is true under other conditions, such as addiction, mental illness, rape, or if the mother is not married. Thus, in such cases, a woman defined as a good mother would not choose to keep her child, but would place it for adoption instead. To raise the child on her own would likely be seen as selfishness on her part; a trait seen as unforgivable in a mother. Society is quick to ask where her maternal instinct is and if she wants the best for her child.

These expectations for motherhood result in different attitudes toward behaviors when a mother, compared with a father, participates. For example, social stigma is much greater for a mother who abandons her child than for a father. Because the mother is presumed to be tied to the child through the biological pull to nurture him, witnesses ask how she could be so cruel as to cede her parental right. Likewise, when a mother voluntarily relinquishes custody of her child to a former spouse, she faces much more negative attentions than does a father who has relinquished custody to an ex-wife.

CHILD CUSTODY

Child custody decisions in the United States provide clear evidence of the privilege afforded to biological ties. Children are most frequently placed with the mother. In nearly 90 percent of divorce cases involving children, it is the mother who receives primary residential custody. This preference for the mother suggests that she is somehow better for the child. The link implies that her biological ties to the child are closer as a result of her birth experience and the presumption of strong maternal instincts. Additionally the concept of "tender years doctrine" supports the granting of custody to mothers. Again supporting the supposed closer biological tie between mothers and children than between fathers and children, the assumption is that when children are in their tender, formative years they benefit more from the nurturing that only their mother presumably can provide. She is therefore seen by the legal system as the superior parent for younger children.

The second most likely person to be granted custody for a child is the biological father, followed by another relative by birth or marriage. This pattern of privileging biology has been particularly distressing for grandparents, who often do not have any contact with grandchildren if sole custody after divorce has been granted to the parent that is not their child. When attempting to gain visitation rights, the vast majority of these grandparents find their requests denied. On the agenda of many men's organizations is a request for states to revisit child custody criteria to give fathers a greater chance to be granted primary custody of minor children.

FOSTER CARE AND ADOPTION

Foster care is designed to provide a family-like environment for children who must be removed from their parents' custody due to mistreatment. While claims of child abuse are being investigated, for example, children may be placed with a temporary foster family. There must be reasonably strong evidence for a child to be removed from the home initially. While most people put the safety of the child above other concerns, there is the suggestion from the biological family preservation camp that social workers and children's advocates find it easier to remove a child from the home than to find ways to support the family so that the child can stay. Therefore, they argue, more children are placed in state custody than should be, leading to a backlog of cases and an overcrowded foster care system. Social workers counter that their interests are with the child first, but ideally remaining in the home with the parents would be the outcome. The one consistent exception across all sides is in cases of severe abuse or neglect of the child. In these situations alone, the family preservationists argue, would it be in a child's best interest to be removed from his or her parents and placed elsewhere.

Once a child has been removed to foster care as a result of neglect or abuse, there are two schools of thought as to where he or she should be permanently placed. Family preservationists argue that, in all but the most severe cases, the child should not be removed from his family home at all; rather, intensive counseling with the family as a whole is called for. They purport that it is less stressful for the family if the children remain at home (NCCPR 2006), and any support provided through counseling is therefore likely to be much more effective. Others claim that this is potentially dangerous for the child. Because time spent in foster care is certain to have detrimental effects on a child's happiness and well-being, the child should thus be placed for adoption as soon as it has become reasonably obvious that their present circumstances are unlikely to provide them with all they need in order to thrive and grow into productive, well adjusted adults. This should be done as soon as possible because children are not only more likely to be adopted at younger ages, but studies have shown that the earlier a child is placed in a stable and nurturing environment the better off they are. In response, Robinson (2000) has argued that in fact there are no circumstances which would ever call for a child to be placed for adoption and raised by someone genetically unrelated.

Adoption out of the foster care system is not the only situation in which biology is at issue. In several cases, most notably the 1993 case in Michigan of Baby Jessica, the birth parents' rights have been given more weight in adoption proceedings. At any point prior to an adoption becoming final birth parents can contest the adoption and will likely regain custody of the child they surrendered for adoption. Given that many times the adoptive parents are the only parents the child has ever known, favoring the role of psychological parent over biological parent may be in the best interest of the child.

LOOKING TO THE FUTURE

Arlene Skolnick has argued that a new biologism is emerging in which biological ties are given privilege over social ties, even when evidence to support social influences is present. This is of great concern to family professionals who focus on the role of persons in the family rather than their biological ties to one another. One of the primary limitations of privileging biology is that it limits the persons who are seen as appropriate to care for children and establish a loving, effective home life.

As alternative family forms become more visible in the culture, through media presentation and individual awareness, it remains to be seen if public policy with lean more toward relationships and away from biology as the most important criteria for children's care. Expanding definitions of family, including cohabitation and gay marriage, force policy makers to reconsider the utility of a strictly biological model of kinship. It will be interesting to see if wider knowledge of alternative family forms will challenge expectations of biological privilege in the laws and lives of individual Americans.

See also Fictive Kin; Foster Care; International Adoption; Surrogacy; Transracial Adoption.

Further Reading: Bartholet, Elizabeth. *Nobody's Children: Abuse, Neglect, Foster Drift, and the Adoption Alternative.* Boston: Beacon Press, 2000; Hall, Beth, and Gail Steinberg. "Adoptism: A Definition." Pact, an Adoption Alliance, http://www.pactadopt.org; Lowe, Heather. "What You Should Know If You're Considering Adoption for Your Baby." Concerned United Birthparents, http://www.cubirthparents.org; March, Karen, and Charlene E. Miall. "Reinforcing the Motherhood Ideal: Public Perceptions of Biological Mothers Who Make an Adoption Plan." *The Canadian Review of Sociology and Anthropology* 43 (2006): 367–386; Marshner, Connie. "Reform the Nation's Foster Care System Now." Family Research Council. http://www.frc.org; Mason, Mary Ann, Arlene Skolnick, and Stephen D. Sugarman. *All Our Families: New Policies for a New Century.* New York: Oxford University Press, 1998; National Coalition for Child Protection Reform. "Foster Care vs. Keeping Families Together: The Definitive Study." National Coalition for Child Protection Reform. http://www.nccpr.org; National Coalition for Child Protection Reform. "What is 'Family Preservation'?" National Coalition for Child Protection Reform. http://www.nccpr.org; Robinson, Evelyn Burns. *Adoption and Loss: The Hidden Grief.* Christies Beach, Australia: Clova Publications, 2000; Smith, Susan. "Safeguarding the Rights and Well-being of Birthparents in the Adoption Process." Evan B. Donaldson Adoption Institute. http://www.adoptioninstitute.org.

Kimberly P. Brackett

BIRTH CONTROL

Birth control is the control of fertility, or the prevention of pregnancy, through one of several methods. Another common name for birth control is contraception, because that is precisely what the various birth control methods do; they prevent the viable sperm and egg from uniting to form a fertilized embryo. Though discussing birth control is no longer likely to lead to an arrest, as in the days of birth control pioneer Margaret Sanger, public debates remain. Some debates address which methods of birth control are the most effective at attaining one's reproductive goals, while others address whether insurance benefits should include the cost of birth control, the likely long- and short-term effects of their use, how to increase the use of birth control among sexually active young people, and questions over why there are still so many more methods that focus on female fertility compared with those that focus on male fertility.

INTRODUCTION

Controlling fertility affects the well-being of women, men, children, families, and society by providing methods and strategies to prevent unplanned pregnancies. Planned fertility positively impacts the health of children, maternal longevity and the empowerment of women. Access to birth control provides women and men with choices regarding family size, timing between pregnancies, and spacing of children. Additionally, controlling fertility reduces the prevalence of chronic illness and maternal death from pregnancy-related conditions.

Globally, approximately 210 million women become pregnant each year. Of these pregnancies, nearly 40 percent are unplanned. In the United States, 49 percent of pregnancies are estimated to be unplanned. Research shows that unintended pregnancies can have devastating impacts on not only women but also children and families. An unintended pregnancy places a woman at risk for depression, physical abuse, and the normal risks associated with pregnancy, including maternal death. Pregnancies that are spaced closely together present risks to children including low birth weight, increased likelihood of death in the first year, and decreased access to resources necessary for healthy development. Unintended pregnancies can have devastating impacts on the well-being of the family unit. An unplanned pregnancy often pushes families with limited economic resources into a cycle of poverty that further limits their opportunities for success.

Although control of fertility spans approximately 30 years of the male and female reproductive life, preferences for birth control methods and strategies vary among individuals, across the life course, and are influenced by multiple social factors. These factors may include socioeconomic status, religious or moral beliefs, purpose for using birth control (permanent pregnancy prevention, delay of pregnancy, or spacing between births), availability of birth control products, access to medical care, willingness to use birth control consistently, concern over side effects, and variability in the failure rates of different types of birth control products. Although the primary purpose of birth control is to control fertility, increases in the prevalence of sexually transmitted infections (STIs) and the human immunodeficiency virus (HIV), which causes acquired immunodeficiency syndrome (AIDS), have created pressures to develop new pregnancy prevention options that combine contraception and STI prevention. The availability of contraceptive options allows women and men the opportunity to maximize the benefits of birth control while minimizing the risks of contraceptive use according to their needs.

The availability of birth control has raised important questions about reproductive control and the relationships between men and women. Traditionalists argue that pregnancy and childrearing are the natural or biologically-determined roles of women, given their capacity to become pregnant and give birth. Opponents of this view argue that reproduction and motherhood are one of many choices available to women. Providing options to women and men that allow them to control their fertility has shifted pregnancy and motherhood from a position of duty to one of choice. This shift is a consequence of changes to the work force, increased opportunities for women, and changes in the economic structure of contemporary families. These changes, along with ongoing developments in fertility control research, provide women and men today with many innovative choices concerning birth control. These choices allow women and men to tailor birth control to their individual needs and life circumstances.

Today, birth control debates focus on the advantages and disadvantages of different birth control methods. The most common debates focus on the merits of temporary versus permanent methods of pregnancy prevention. Other debates examine the benefits of natural versus barrier methods of controlling reproduction. Still other debates examine the advantages and disadvantages of male and female contraception. With the growing pandemic of AIDS in sub-Saharan Africa and Asia and the increasing prevalence of sexually transmitted diseases that threaten world health, contemporary debates about birth control focus on the feasibility and practicality of combining STI prevention and contraception.

BRIEF HISTORY OF CONTRACEPTION

Although women have sought to control their fertility since ancient times, safe and effective contraception was not developed until this past century. The large influx of immigrants in the 1900s and the emergence of feminist groups working for women's rights helped bring to the forefront large-scale birth control movements in the United States and abroad. Ancient forms of birth control included potions, magic charms, chants, and herbal recipes. Ancient recipes often featured leaves, hawthorn bark, ivy, willow, and poplar, believed to contain sterilizing agents. During the Middle Ages, potions containing lead, arsenic, or strychnine caused death to many women seeking to control their fertility. Additionally, crude barrier methods were used in which the genitals were covered with cedar gum or alum was applied to the uterus. Later, pessary mixtures of elephant dung, lime (mineral), and pomegranate seeds were inserted into a woman's vagina to prevent pregnancy. Other barrier methods believed to prevent pregnancy included sicklewort leaves, wool tampons soaked in wine, and crudely fashioned vaginal sponges.

Later birth control developments were based on more accurate information concerning conception. Condoms were developed in the early 1700s by the physician to King Charles II. By the early 1800s, a contraceptive sponge and a contraceptive syringe were available. By the mid-1800s, a number of more modern barrier methods to control conception were available to women. However, it was illegal to advertise these options and most were available only through physicians and only in cases that were clinically indicated. Thus, early modern conception was limited to health reasons.

Modern contraceptive devices such as the condom, diaphragm, cervical cap and intrauterine device (IUD), developed in the twentieth century, and represented a marked advance in medical technology. Effectiveness was largely dependent on user compliance. While these methods represented a significant improvement over more archaic methods, contraceptive safety remained an issue. Other modern methods included the insertion of various substances (some toxic) into the vagina, resulting in inflammation or irritation of the vaginal walls, while other devices often caused discomfort.

The birth control pill, developed in the 1950s by biologist Dr. Charles Pincus, represented a major advance in fertility control. Pincus is credited with the discovery of the effects of combining estrogen and progesterone in an oral contraceptive that would prevent pregnancy. The development and mass-marketing of the birth control pill not only provided women with a way to control their fertility but also to control their lives.

OVERVIEW OF TRADITIONAL CONTRACEPTIVE METHODS

Traditional contraception includes both temporary and permanent methods of controlling fertility. Temporary contraception provides temporary or time-limited protection from becoming pregnant. Permanent contraception refers to surgical procedures that result in a lasting or permanent inability to become pregnant. The choice of contraception takes into consideration several biological and social factors, including age, lifestyle (frequency of sexual activity, monogamy or multiple partners), religious or moral beliefs, legal issues, family planning objectives, as well as medical history and concerns. These factors vary among individuals and across the life span.

Traditional Contraceptive Methods

Traditional contraceptive methods provide varying degrees of protection from becoming pregnant and protection from STIs. While some of these methods provide non-contraceptive benefits, they require consistent and appropriate use and are associated with varying degrees of risks. Traditional contraception includes both hormonal and non-hormonal methods of preventing pregnancy and sexually transmitted diseases. These methods provide protection as long as they are used correctly but their effects are temporary and reversible once discontinued. Traditional contraceptive methods include sexual abstinence, coitus interruptus, rhythm method, barrier methods, spermicides, male or female condoms, IUDs, and oral contraceptive pills.

Sexual abstinence refers to the voluntary practice of refraining from all forms of sexual activity that could result in pregnancy or the transmission of sexually transmitted diseases. Abstinence is commonly referred to as the only form of birth control that is 100 percent effective in preventing pregnancy and STIs; however, failed abstinence results in unprotected sex which increases the risks of unintended pregnancy and transmission of STIs.

Coitus interruptus is the oldest method of contraception and requires the man to withdraw his penis from the vagina just prior to ejaculation. Often referred to as a so-called natural method of birth control, coitus interruptus is highly unreliable because a small amount of seminal fluid, containing sperm, is secreted from the penis prior to ejaculation and can result in conception. This method offers no protection from sexually transmitted diseases.

The *rhythm method* of birth control developed in response to research on the timing of ovulation. Research findings indicate that women ovulate approximately 14 days before the onset of their menstrual cycle. The rhythm method assumes that a woman is the most fertile during ovulation. To determine an individual cycle of ovulation, this method requires a woman to count backward 14 days from the first day of her menstrual period. During this time period, a woman should abstain from sexual activity or use another form of birth control (such as condoms) to avoid pregnancy. The rhythm method is another natural form of birth control that is highly risky. Few women ovulate at the exact same time from month to month, making accurate calculations of ovulation difficult. Additionally, sperm can live inside a woman for up to seven days, further complicating the calculations of safe periods for sex. Finally, the rhythm method does not provide protection from sexually transmitted diseases.

Barrier methods of contraception prevent sperm from reaching the fallopian tubes and fertilizing an egg. Barrier methods include both male and female condoms, diaphragms, cervical caps, and vaginal sponges. With the exception of the male condom, these methods are exclusively used by women. Barrier contraception is most often used with a spermicide to increase effectiveness. Spermicides contain nonoxynol-9, a chemical that immobilizes sperm to prevent them from joining and fertilizing an egg. Barrier methods of contraception and spermicides provide moderate protection from pregnancy and sexually transmitted diseases although failure rates (incidence of pregnancy resulting from use) vary from 20 to 30 percent.

Condoms, a popular and non-prescription form of barrier contraception available to both men and women, provides moderate protection from pregnancy and STIs. The male condom is a latex, polyurethane, or natural skin sheath that covers the erect penis and traps semen before it enters the vagina. The female condom is a soft, loosely fitting polyurethane tube-like sheath that lines the vagina during sex. Female condoms have a closed end with rings at each end. The ring at the closed end is inserted deep into the vagina over the cervix to secure the tube in place. Female condoms protect against pregnancy by trapping sperm in the sheath and preventing entry into the vagina. Used correctly, condoms are between 80 and 85 percent effective in preventing pregnancy and the transmission of STIs. Risks that decrease the effectiveness of condoms include incorrect usage, slippage during sexual activity, and breakage. Natural skin condoms used by some males do not protect against the transmission of HIV and other STIs.

The female diaphragm is a shallow, dome-shaped, flexible rubber disk that fits inside the vagina to cover the cervix. The diaphragm prevents sperm from entering the uterus. Diaphragms are used with spermicide to immobilize or kill sperm and to prevent fertilization of the female egg. Diaphragms may be left inside the vagina for up to 24 hours but a spermicide should be used with each intercourse encounter. To be fully effective, the diaphragm should be left in place for six hours after intercourse before removal. Approximately 80 to 95 percent effective in preventing pregnancy and the transmission of gonorrhea and

Chlamydia, the diaphragm does not protect against the transmission of herpes or HIV.

Cervical caps are small, soft rubber, thimble-shaped caps that are fitted inside the woman's cervix. Cervical caps prevent pregnancy by blocking the entrance of the uterus. Approximately 80 to 95 percent effective when used alone, effectiveness is increased when used with spermicides. Unlike the diaphragm, the cervical cap may be left in place for up to 48 hours. Similar to the diaphragm, the cervical cap provides protection against gonorrhea and chlamydia but does not provide protection against herpes or HIV.

Vaginal sponges, removed from the market in 1995 due to concerns about possible contaminants, are round, donut-shaped polyurethane devices containing spermicides and a loop that hangs down in the vagina allowing for easy removal. Sponges prevent pregnancy by blocking the uterus and preventing fertilization of the egg. Vaginal sponges are approximately 70 to 80 percent effective in preventing pregnancy but provide no protection against STIs. Risks include toxic shock syndrome if left inside the vagina for more than 24 hours.

Barrier methods of birth control provide moderate protection from pregnancy and STIs but are not fail-safe. Effectiveness is dependent on consistency and proper use. Advantages include lower cost, availability without a prescription, and ease of use (with the exception of the diaphragm). Disadvantages include lowered effectiveness as compared to other forms of birth control and little or no protection against certain STIs.

Non-Barrier Contraceptive Methods

Two other traditional contraceptive methods are the IUD and oral contraceptive pills. Both of these methods are characterized by increased effectiveness if used properly. The IUD is a T-shaped device inserted into a woman's vagina by a health professional. Inserted into the wall of the uterus, the IUD prevents pregnancy by changing the motility (movement) of the sperm and egg and by altering the lining of the uterus to prevent egg implantation. The effectiveness of IUDs in preventing pregnancy is approximately 98 percent, however, IUDs do not provide protection from STIs. Oral contraceptive pills are taken daily for 21 days each month. Oral contraceptives prevent pregnancy by preventing ovulation, the monthly release of an egg. This form of contraception does not interfere with the monthly menstrual cycle. Many birth control pills combine progesterone and estrogen, however, newer oral contraceptives contain progesterone only. Taken regularly, oral contraceptives are approximately 98 percent effective in preventing pregnancy but do not provide STI protection.

NEW CONTRACEPTIVE TECHNOLOGIES

In spite of the availability of a broad range of contraceptive methods, the effectiveness of traditional contraceptive methods is largely dependent on user consistency and proper use. Even with consistent and proper use, each method is associated with varying degrees of risk. Risks include the likelihood of pregnancy, side effects, and possible STI transmission. New developments in contraceptive technology focus on improvement of side effects and the development of contraceptives that do not require users to adhere to a daily regiment. These new technologies are designed to make use simpler and more suitable to users' lives. Additionally, many of the new technologies seek to combine fertility control with protection from STIs.

The *vaginal contraceptive ring* is inserted into a woman's vagina for a period of three weeks and removed for one week. During the three week period, the ring releases small doses of progestin and estrogen, providing month-long contraception. The release of progestin and estrogen prevents the ovaries from releasing an egg and increases cervical mucus that helps to prevent sperm from entering the uterus. Fully effective after seven days, supplementary contraceptive methods should be used during the first week after insertion. Benefits include a high effectiveness rate, ease of use, shorter and lighter menstrual periods, and protection from ovarian cysts and from ovarian and uterine cancer. Disadvantages include spotting between menstrual periods for the first several months and no protection against STIs.

Hormonal implants provide highly effective, long-term, but reversible, protection from pregnancy. Particularly suitable for users who find it difficult to consistently take daily contraceptives, hormonal implants deliver progesterone by using a rod system inserted underneath the skin. Closely related to implants are hormonal injections that are administered monthly. Both hormonal implants and injections are highly effective in preventing pregnancy but may cause breakthrough bleeding. Neither provides protection from STIs at this stage of development.

Contraceptive patches deliver a combination of progestin and estrogen through an adhesive patch located on the upper arm, buttocks, lower abdomen or upper torso. Applied weekly for three weeks, followed by one week without, the contraceptive patch is highly effective in preventing pregnancy but does not protect against the transmission of STIs. The use of the patch is associated with withdrawal bleeding during the week that it is not worn. Compliance is reported to be higher than with oral contraceptive pills.

Levonorgestrel intrauterine systems provide long-term birth control without sterilization by delivering small amounts of the progestin levonorgestrel directly to the lining of the uterus to prevent pregnancy. Delivered through a small T-shaped intrauterine plastic device implanted by a health professional, the levonorgestrel system provides protection from pregnancy for up to five years. It does not currently offer protection from STIs.

New contraceptive technologies are designed to provide longer-term protection from pregnancy and to remove compliance obstacles that decrease effectiveness and increase the likelihood of unintended pregnancies. The availability of contraceptive options provides users with choices that assess not only fertility purposes but also variations in sexual activity. However, until new contraceptive technologies that combine pregnancy and STI prevention are readily available, proper use of male and female condoms provides the most effective strategy for prevention of sexually transmitted diseases and HIV.

ABORTION

Abortion, defined as the intentional termination of a pregnancy, was legally established in 1973 with the Supreme Court decision in *Roe v. Wade* (*Roe v. Wade* 410 U.S. 113). The decision spawned disparate and strongly held opinions among the American public and the emergence of activist groups taking a variety of positions on abortion. The availability of elective abortion has called into question traditional beliefs about the relations between men and women, has raised vexing issues about the control of women's bodies, and has intensified contentious debates about women's roles and brought about changes in the division of labor, both in the family and in the broader occupational arena. Elective abortion has called into question long-standing beliefs about the moral nature of sexuality. Further, elective abortion has challenged the notion of sexual relations as privileged activities that are symbolic of commitments, responsibilities, and obligations between men and women. Elective abortion also brings to the fore the more personal issue of the meaning of pregnancy.

Historically, the debate over abortion has been one of competing definitions of motherhood. Pro-life activists argue that family, and particularly motherhood, is the cornerstone of society. Pro-choice activists argue that reproductive choice is central to women controlling their lives. More contemporary debates focus on the ethical and moral nature of personhood and the rights of the fetus. In the last 30 years, these debates have become politicized, resulting in the passage of increasingly restrictive laws governing abortion, abortion doctors, and abortion clinics. Currently, South Dakota is the only state that has passed laws making abortions illegal except in cases in which the woman's life is endangered. Other states are considering passage of similarly restrictive legislation.

The consequences of unintended pregnancy are well documented and contribute to the need for the continued development of contraceptive options that will meet the needs and goals of diverse populations whose reproductive needs change throughout their life course. By definition abortion is not a type of contraception but is an option when contraceptive efforts did not prevent pregnancy.

PERMANENT CONTRACEPTION

Permanent contraception refers to sterilization techniques that permanently prevent pregnancy. Frequently referred to as sterilization, permanent contraception prevents males from impregnating females and prevents females from becoming pregnant.

Tubal ligation refers to surgery to tie a woman's fallopian tubes, preventing the movement of eggs from the ovaries to the uterus. The procedure is considered permanent and involves the cauterization of the fallopian tubes. However, some women who later choose to become pregnant have successfully had the procedure reversed. The reversal of tubal ligation procedures are successful in 50 to 80 percent of cases.

Hysterectomy refers to the complete removal of a woman's uterus or the uterus and cervix, depending on the type of procedure performed, and results in permanent sterility. Hysterectomies may be performed through an incision in the abdominal wall, vaginally, or by using laparoscopic incisions on the abdomen.

Vasectomy refers to a surgical procedure for males in which the vas deferens are tied off and cut apart to prevent sperm from moving out of the testes. The procedure results in permanent sterility although the procedure may be reversed under certain conditions.

Permanent contraception is generally recommended only in cases in which there is no desire for children, family size is complete, or in cases where medical concerns necessitate permanent prevention of pregnancy.

EMERGENCY CONTRACEPTION

Emergency contraception, commonly referred to as post coital contraception or the so-called morning after pill, encompasses a number of therapies designed to prevent pregnancy following unprotected sexual intercourse. Emergency contraception is also indicated when a condom slips or breaks, a diaphragm dislodges, two or more oral contraceptives are missed or the monthly regimen of birth control pills are begun two or more days late, a hormonal injection is two weeks overdue, or a woman has been raped. Emergency contraception prevents pregnancy by preventing the release of an egg from the ovary, by preventing fertilization, or by preventing attachment of an egg to the uterine wall. Most effective when used within 72 hours of unprotected sex, emergency contraception does not affect a fertilized egg already attached to the uterine wall. Emergency contraception does not induce an abortion or disrupt an existing pregnancy; it prevents a pregnancy from occurring following unprotected sexual intercourse.

CONCLUSION

Ideally, birth control should be a shared responsibility between a woman and her partner. In the U.S., approximately 1.6 million pregnancies each year are unplanned. Unplanned pregnancies position women, men, and families in a precarious situation that has social, economic, personal and health consequences. An unintended pregnancy leaves a woman and her partner facing pregnancy termination, adoption, or raising an unplanned child—often times under less-than-ideal conditions. Contraceptive technologies and research developments in the transmission of sexually transmitted diseases represent increased opportunities for not only controlling fertility but also improving safe sex practices.

See also Abortion; Breastfeeding or Formula Feeding; Changing Fertility Patterns; Only Child; Premarital Sexual Relationships; Teen Pregnancy; Transition to Parenthood.

Further Reading: Connell, Elizabeth B. *The Contraception Sourcebook.* New York: McGraw-Hill, 2002; Ginsberg, Faye, D. *Contested Lives: The Abortion Debate in an American Community.* Berkeley: University of California Press, 1989; Luker, Kristen. *Abortion and the*

Politics of Motherhood. Berkeley: University of California Press, 1984; Maxwell, Carol J. C. *Pro-Life Activists in America: Meaning, Motivation, and Direct Action.* Cambridge: Cambridge University Press, 2002; Weschler, Toni. *Taking Charge of Your Fertility.* New York: Harper Collins, 2006.

Jonelle Husain

BIRTH ORDER

One of the many things that can affect who we are and how we relate to the people in our family is birth order. Birth order refers to the numerical place of a person in the order of births in his or her family. Birth order is determined by the order in which a child is born into the family. For centuries people have supposed that the order in which a child is born into a family changes the way others relate to the child as well as how the child sees himself or herself. Though some evidence exists to suggest that siblings develop particular characteristics based on their status as the oldest, middle, or youngest child, questions remain about the predictability of these findings. Birth order remains a popular topic on most parenting websites and in most childrearing manuals.

BACKGROUND

One of the first modern psychologists to address the influence of birth order was Alfred Adler in the 1920s. He argued that birth order could leave an indelible impression on the individual's style of life. Style of life is a habitual way of dealing with the tasks of friendship, love, and work. There are five basic positions and accompanying personalities associated with birth order: the first-born, the middle child, the later-born, the youngest, and the only child. Adler thought that birth order played a significant role in people's lives. Psychologists have continued to be interested in birth order studies, even incorporating the ideas into clinical practice with clients. Where a child places in the birth order can have an effect on how he sees himself, as well as how others view him. Research on birth order, sometimes referred to as ordinal position, shows that first-born children are more likely to go to college than children in any other position in the family. The middle child often seems to have the most negative impressions of her lot in life. Younger children always want to be able to do the things that older siblings are allowed to do, while older siblings may feel that the younger children get away with all the things that they were not able to when they were the same age. Data suggest that these may be more than just casual coincidences and sibling observances.

Each birth order personality is distinct. In very large families the behaviors associated with different ordinal positions repeat first- through fourth-born. Exceptions do occur so that personality may not match birth order position in the family, but trends can be observed. Psychologists suggest that birth order personality is established by the age of two for most children. The most plausible explanation for the influence of birth order is that its effects result from coping with life situations, and not from programming by parents, that differ signifi cantly from one child to the next. Birth order personality affects every area of life and includes strengths and weaknesses.

FIRST-BORN CHILDREN

The life of a first-born child is characterized by the existence of a period of being an only child, by a transition phase as siblings are born, by the fact of being the oldest sibling, and by a lack of having any older siblings. Anything a first-born child does is a big deal because it is a first for their family. Family and friends usually shower the first-born with attention until the second child comes along, when this behavior may be curtailed somewhat. As a result of this attention, many first-born children develop a great deal of confidence in their abilities and worth. More first-borns are perfectionists and are often described as conscientious and responsible. It is true that parents often rely on the first-born when a task needs to be done.

One of the characteristics of first-born children is their desire to always be right. The competition for attention drives most first-borns' desire for success in their education and occupation. They tend to advance farther in their education and to stay in school longer. This birth position generally has higher incomes and IQs than later-born children. First-born children are more likely to join social organizations and generally try to avoid conflict. Because first-borns are favored by their parents and achieve more in their professional lives, they are often considered the most fortunate birth position. However, depression and anxiety patterns tend to be higher in first-borns than in their siblings. Their moods range from highly sensitive to extremely serious.

More than half of the U.S. presidents have been first-born children, including Jimmy Carter, George W. Bush, and Bill Clinton. More than 50 percent of the CEOs of the Fortune 500 companies are first-born, and more Nobel Prize winners have been first-born than any other birth order ranking. Other well-known first-born children include: Winston Churchill, Josef Stalin, Hillary Clinton, Oprah Winfrey and J. K. Rowling.

MIDDLE-BORN CHILDREN

The middle-child position is considered the most difficult of all birth positions. Being stuck in the middle can make that child very competitive as they try to keep up with the accomplishments of the oldest child and garner some of the attention usually reserved for their younger sibling; the so-called baby of the family. The addition of any sibling results in significant changes in the family's environment and interaction. Middle children are thought to struggle with finding their place in the family, and sometimes feel as if they are invisible. This is known as middle child syndrome. They also have a diverse range of personalities. Birth order theorists suggest that the middle child tends to be more excitable, demanding, attention getting, and undependable than the older and younger siblings are. Middle children are the least likely position to attend college or to attain high academic degrees. They are, however, reported to be the most monogamous birth position and are motivated to make their marriages and families work successfully. Middle-born children are thought to be the least likely group to procrastinate.

Middle-born children are likely to look outside of the family for significant relationships, forming close associations within peer groups that can be especially influential during adolescence. Parents, who themselves have stereotyped expectations of what their children will be like, may have fewer expectations for who the middle child will become, leaving her the freedom to create her own place in the family. Because middle children often see themselves as underdogs compared to their older sibling, they are more likely to develop a genuine interest in others and demonstrate more empathy for those who are less fortunate.

Like other children who are born later, parents are less strict on the children after the oldest. While middle-born children receive less of their parents' attention than the oldest child, like other later-born children they may enjoy the benefits of being born when the family is well-established, has more money, resides in a larger house, or has worked out some of the challenges of being in a young family. Some famous second-born children include: George Washington, Cindy Crawford, Donald Trump, Madonna, and Barbara Walters.

YOUNGEST CHILDREN

The youngest child is sometimes referred to as the baby of the family and has been stereotyped as the spoiled child. Youngest children tend to be charming, people-oriented, tenacious, affectionate, and attention seeking. By the time the youngest child is born, parents tend to be more relaxed and less strict. So it is true that they allow the youngest to get away with more than the older siblings. Unlike their first-born siblings, youngest children tend to lack concern for academic achievement and struggle to excel further in school. They tend to be viewed as more popular and accepted by their peers than are their older siblings. The youngest child is the so-called party animal and entertainer, who is not afraid to test his or her luck with parents and others in authority. They are more likely than their older siblings to take risks and be adventurous. This is reflected in their higher high school drop-out rates. If teased, the youngest may become irritable, extremely aggressive, and prone to escalate to violence more quickly than her older siblings. While not true of all youngest children, proponents of birth order theory state that the youngest in a family is an endearing and delightful friend.

Among the famous rule-breaking youngest children was Copernicus, who in 1530 said that the earth revolves around the sun. His theory was in direct opposition to the popular thinking at that time, so much so that those who followed his work were punished for supporting his ideas. Another well-know rebel youngest child was Harriet Tubman. Thanks to her father's training as a scout, at the age of 30 she escaped slavery by traveling alone and navigating via the North Star. Her underground railroad was responsible for ferrying numerous escaping slaves to safety in the northern United States.

Many actors, entertainers, and comedians are the youngest children in their families. Some famous "babies" include: Mark Twain, Drew Carey, Jim Carrey, Stephen Colbert, Eddie Murphy, and Whoopi Goldberg.

BIRTH ORDER DEBATE

From the examples of each birth position mentioned above, one's place in the family does seem to have an influence on the type of person one becomes and the type of activities that one pursues. While Alfred Adler was among the first to recognize and consider birth order as a significant factor in personality, Walter Toman is a more recent theorist of birth order. His book, *Family Constellation*, discusses 11 birth positions instead of four. Many therapists and psychologists have been interested in birth order studies because of the idea that different familial positions are subject to different experiences and pressures, brought by both the family and society as a whole.

There are many studies involving birth order that indicate no significant results, but theories abound about a connection between birth order and many other facets of life including achievement, interpersonal relations, self-esteem, risk-taking, conformity, and so forth. While the effects of birth order are generally small, it is important to keep in mind that families themselves are smaller today than in the past. As a consequence of smaller family size, the effects of birth order may be less robust. With the tendency of most American families to have two children, the effects of birth order may be mediated. It also seems to be the case that total family income mediates the effects, with children from wealthy families demonstrating less influences related to birth order than do children from low-income families.

There are some aspects of ordinal position that are well documented. More recent examinations of birth order suggest that changes in parenting from one child to the next have the greatest effect on the differing birth order personalities. One of the aspects of parenting that is noticeably different from the first child to subsequent children is discipline. It seems that parents want to set the example with the oldest child by punishing him more harshly. The oldest bears the brunt of the parental strictness, while the younger siblings generally coast on through. Perhaps parents are just practicing on the first child, or perhaps they get tired of the following through with the discipline.

This tendency of parents to be stricter with the first-born is reflected in the finding that first-born children are typically more rule-abiding and responsible than their later-born siblings. They are less likely to drop out of school and less likely to experience a premarital pregnancy than is the youngest in a family. One study found that those first-born children who dropped out of school were 20 percent less likely than their younger siblings in the same situation to be getting most of their income from their parents. Among daughters who were pregnant as teens, first-born girls were 30 percent less likely to be getting money from their parents than were later birth order girls.

While it may seem that all of the parenting directed at first-born children is strict, there are benefits to being the oldest in the family. Leman (1998) indicates that first-born children get more time with and attention from their parents than do later-born children. At the same ages, oldest children get 30 percent more time with their parents. This adds up to at least three thousand more hours, indicating that the difference in attention continues even after subsequent children are born.

There may not yet be enough hard evidence to support that birth order really does matter in one's future outcomes. Dalton Conley, sociologist at New York University, suggests that birth order is of most significance in very large families (four siblings or more) which constitute only a small percentage of American families today. Anecdotally, parents often indicate that their children follow the patterns predicted by their birth order. Perhaps some of this is due to their expectations for their children and the roles that they encourage them to play. Some of the debate may come from the belief that most people have about their uniqueness and desire to be seen as individuals, not positions. Thus, more importance is given to personal choices rather than predetermined factors attached to one's hierarchy of birth in a family.

CONCLUSION

Birth order personalities are formed early in life as each child has to solve particular problems by using a set of coping skills at her disposal. Psychologists suggest that first-born children come to feel unloved initially following the birth of a younger sibling because there is a perceived redirection of mother's love from them to the new baby. The child mentally trades love for attention in the forms of respect, admiration, and approval.

The second-born child must cope with the oldest child taking away attention by outperforming him or her. The child feels inadequate and tries to overcome the feeling by choosing perfectionism in some area of life. The second born feels that nobody cares about how she feels; the oldest child clearly does not care. Consequently, in an attempt to avoid emotional pain, the middle child tries to suppress her own feelings.

The third-born, often the youngest child, must cope with the second-born picking on him to pass on the feelings of inadequacy. The persecution by the middle child makes the youngest feel vulnerable, as if anyone can get to him anytime they want. The youngest decides to cope by being strong. The third-born child who succeeds at being strong becomes fearless; the child who fails becomes fearful.

While birth order does not predict the future, it can help to explain why people are drawn down certain paths. Because the dynamics of the family differ at the time of each child's birth, the personalities each develops and the opportunities available to each will necessarily differ.

See also Only Child; Parenting Styles; Transition to Parenthood.

Further Reading: Adams, Leslie. "The Effects of Birth Order on Procrastination." Missouri Western State University. http://clearinghouse.missouriwestern.edu/manuscripts/14.asp; Guastello, Denise D., and Stephen J. Guastello. "Birth Category Effects on the Gordon Personal Profile Variables." Reyson Group. http://www.jasnh.com/a1.htm;

Leman, Kevin. *The New Birth Order Book: Why You Are the Way You Are*. Grand Rapids, MI: Revell Books, 1998; Putter, Philip. "The Effects of Birth Order on Depressive Symptoms in Early Adolescence." *Perspectives in Psychology* (2003): 9–18. http://bespin.stwing.upenn.edu/~upsych/Perspectives/2003/Putter.pdf; Schilling, Renee M. "The Effects of Birth Order on Interpersonal Relationships." McKendree University. http://faculty.mckendree.edu/scholars/2001/Schilling.htm; Sulloway, Frank J. *Born to Rebel: Birth Order, Family Dynamics, and Creative Lives*. New York: Vintage Books, 1997; Toman, Walter. *Family Constellation: It's Effects on Personality and Social Behavior*. New York: Springer Publishing Group, 1992.

Britten Allison Brooks

BREASTFEEDING OR FORMULA FEEDING

Every so often, news stories circulate in the media about women who breastfeed in public. A breastfeeding woman is escorted off a plane, another is asked to leave a restaurant, a woman in a shopping mall is asked to nurse her infant in the public bathroom. These stories raise many questions. Why is breastfeeding widely unaccepted in American culture? Why don't the women just give the infant a bottle? Why is it such a big deal? Not all of these questions can be addressed in this entry, but the advantages and disadvantages of bottle feeding and breastfeeding will be discussed, along with areas that will need to be addressed as this debate continues. It's important to note that the debate about breastfeeding is multifaceted—part of it deals with health issues and the medical field, part of it deals with formula companies and marketing techniques, and other parts of it deal with aspects of social support. The issue of breastfeeding is quite complicated, but it's useful to begin with an overview of current recommendations regarding infant feeding.

EXPRESSING BREAST MILK AND TERMINOLOGY

It is important to recognize that many women use a breast-pump to express breast milk. Many women combine work and breastfeeding in this way, and it also allows the father to be more involved in the feeding of young infants. However, expressing milk is also challenging—it requires time to pump, careful cleaning of the components, and attention to storage details. Additionally, pumps can be quite expensive. Because pumping milk and then giving breast milk in a bottle is common, it is important to distinguish between bottle feeding and formula feeding. Bottle feeding can be used to refer to either breast milk or formula, but formula feeding refers only to feeding an infant formula.

BREASTFEEDING IN THE UNITED STATES

The American Academy of Pediatrics and the Centers for Disease Control and Prevention, among other organizations, recommend that infants are breastfed. The current recommendation is to include only breast milk in a baby's diet for the first six months and to begin offering supplements such as baby cereal at six months. Breast milk should remain in the baby's diet for at least a year, and it is beneficial to continue to breastfeed as long as it is mutually desired by both the mother and the infant.

These recommendations are based on an abundance of literature about the health benefits of breastfeeding. Breastfed babies tend to have fewer ear infections, fewer hospital admissions, and fewer cases of diarrhea than formula-fed infants. Human milk is designed specifically for humans, and therefore it contains the nutritional properties that babies need and that babies can digest. Breastfeeding may also offer some protection against sudden infant death syndrome, diabetes, and obesity.

In addition to the benefits for infants, breastfeeding can also be beneficial for the mother. It seems to reduce the risk of ovarian cancer, breast cancer, and osteoporosis. While those are somewhat long-term advantages, there are also short-term health benefits for women. Breastfeeding helps the uterus contract after giving birth, and it generally seems to help women lose more of their pregnancy weight faster because of the calories expended to create the milk. Another important health aspect to breastfeeding is the psychological bond that is developed between the mother and the infant.

Breastfeeding is recommended for all of the above reasons, but few women in the United States are breastfeeding as suggested. According to the Centers for Disease Control and Prevention, approximately 74 percent of women in the U.S. will breastfeed during the early postpartum period. Approximately 42 percent are breastfeeding at six months, and 21 percent are breastfeeding at a year. When looking at rates of exclusive breastfeeding, the rates drop to only about 30 percent at three months and 12 percent at six months. Exclusive breastfeeding refers to not offering the baby any supplemental foods or liquids, however one limitation of research in this area is that the term "exclusive" is often not well defined.

Breastfeeding rates also vary by mother's age, educational attainment, race, income level, and the mother's geographic location within the United States. Women are more likely to breastfeed if they are older when the child is born; women under age 20 are the least likely to breastfeed whereas women over age 30 are the most likely. As far as educational attainment, women who have a high school degree are the least likely to breastfeed while women who have graduated from college are the most likely to do so. Asian women are the most likely to breastfeed, and African American women are the least likely to do so. Women in lower income brackets are less likely to breastfeed than wealthier women. Lastly, when geographic location is taken into consideration, women in rural areas are less likely to breastfeed than those in more suburban areas. Additionally, women in the south-central United States have the lowest rates of breastfeeding (CDC 2007).

CHALLENGES OF BREASTFEEDING

There are many reasons why women stop breastfeeding before it is recommended to do so, and reasons for stopping vary with the infant's age. According to the Pregnancy Risk Assessment and Monitoring System, when women stop breastfeeding within the baby's first week, 34 percent of women experienced sore, cracked, or bleeding nipples, and 48 percent cited the baby having difficulty nursing as a reason for stopping. When women stopped nursing the baby between one and four weeks old, the most common response was because they weren't producing enough milk. Lastly, when women stopped nursing after the baby was four weeks old, the most common response was because the baby wasn't satisfied with breast milk. In addition to sore nipples and difficulties with the baby getting enough milk, many women stop breastfeeding because of work or school responsibilities.

Another difficulty women have with breastfeeding is the limitations it places on them as far as what they can eat and drink. Everything that is in a mother's system could be passed on to the infant through the breast milk, so mothers must be careful about what they consume. Some say that breastfed babies will eat a wider variety of food because they were exposed to more flavors through the mother's breast milk, but this situation can also cause a great deal of stress for a mother. Babies can have allergies to things in the mother's diet, such as dairy, and sometimes foods such as broccoli cause an infant to have painful gas. Some women will go on elimination diets and keep food diaries while they are breastfeeding to try to find the source of the infant's discomfort. In addition to everyday foods such as green vegetables and dairy, women are restricted in the amount of caffeine they should consume and the amount of alcohol they can drink. Breastfeeding mothers can drink alcohol, but it is recommended that they drink one drink for every two hours the baby won't nurse. If a baby won't nurse again for four hours, it is generally considered safe for the mother to drink two alcoholic beverages. These limits placed on a mother's consumption can frustrate some women and can be seen as a disadvantage to breastfeeding.

Another important aspect to consider when looking at breastfeeding rates in the United States is the acceptability of breastfeeding in public. According to the Healthstyles 2000 national mail survey, 31 percent of respondents felt that one-year-old children should not be breastfed, and 27 percent felt it was embarrassing for a mother to breastfeed in front of others. More negative attitudes toward breastfeeding were held by people with lower household incomes and less education, and by those who were non-white and who were under 30 years old or over 65 years old (Li 2002). Many women do not feel comfortable nursing in public because of other people's reactions and will instead go to public restrooms, to their cars, carefully time trips out, or give the baby a bottle when they are in public. Women who nurse older children in public are even more likely to experience a feeling of inappropriateness based on other's looks, comments, or body posture, and women have said that their experiences nursing in public have lessened the enjoyment of breastfeeding.

Overall, breastfeeding is the recommended way to feed an infant because of its numerous health benefits. However, many variables, such as mother's age, race, and income level influence the decision to breastfeed. Many women stop breastfeeding because of sore or cracked nipples, milk supply concerns, and returning to work, and restrictive diets and nursing in public also complicate the breastfeeding experience.

Formula Feeding

While some women breastfeed successfully, and others turn to formula feeding after breastfeeding fails, others choose to formula feed from the beginning. Before looking at the disadvantages and advantages of bottle feeding, it is important to recognize that the sources of breast milk and formula are fundamentally different. Part of this breastfeeding or bottle feeding debate focuses on the fact that formula companies are inclined to sell a product and that their primary goal is to make money. Some claim that for every dollar charged for formula, only 16 cents is used to cover the costs of production. Another concern with the business side of formula is that free gifts are often given to obstetricians, birthing units in hospitals, and pediatrician offices. Having these free samples makes it easier for women to supplement with formula in the very beginning, which reduces rates for both the exclusivity and duration of breastfeeding.

REGULATING FORMULA COMPANIES

The Infant Formula Act was created as an amendment to the federal Food, Drug, and Cosmetic Act in 1980. It named infant formula as a separate category of food and was the first in a series of major legislative and regulatory steps taken to ensure the safety of infant formulas. The act requires that infant formulas meet specified standards of quality and safety. Another interesting aspect of regulation is that formula companies are required to state that breast milk is the optimal source of nutrition for infants on their products.

Source: Food and Drug Administration. http://www.cfsan.fda.gov/~dms/inf-toc.html.

Advantages of Bottle Feeding

Despite the official recommendations regarding and the health benefits of breastfeeding, there are also advantages to bottle feeding an infant. Newborn babies usually need to breastfeed every two hours, and this can be overwhelming for mothers. Formula is digested more slowly by infants, and therefore feedings can be spaced farther apart than with breastfed infants. Additionally, bottle feeding offers the possibility of someone else giving the baby a bottle, allowing the mother to rest. Some couples are concerned about the father's role in a breastfeeding relationship and worry that he might be excluded from bonding with the child. If a father wants to be an active caregiver, bottle feeding offers one avenue for such action and can give the mother some respite at the same time.

Another benefit of bottle feeding is that caregivers can know exactly how much an infant is receiving. Many women experience anxiety about whether or not their baby is receiving enough breast milk because there is not an exact way to know at every feeding. Many lactation consultants will help women with this by inviting them to nurse while at an office visit. The baby is weighed before nursing and again after, and this can give an estimate to how much milk the baby received. However, there is concern that some mothers may mistakenly believe that the baby is receiving enough milk when in fact the baby is not. This is a serious concern because infants become dehydrated very quickly and their ability to thrive is negatively impacted. Thus bottle feeding can help mothers with this anxiety and can allow caregivers certainty in knowing the baby is receiving enough.

In addition to women who want to bottle feed, some women are advised against breastfeeding. For instance, women who are taking some medications should not breastfeed because amounts of the medication are transferred to the baby through the breast milk. Likewise, women who use drugs or drink a lot of alcohol should not breastfeed. In the United States, it is recommended that women who are HIV positive not breastfeed because the virus could be transmitted through the breast milk. Additionally, studies have shown that women who have received breast implants often have more difficulty with breastfeeding and with levels of milk production.

Disadvantages of Bottle Feeding

There are also some disadvantages to bottle feeding. Regardless of whether breast milk or formula is used, careful attention must be given to how it is stored and the cleaning of equipment and bottles. There are strict guidelines as to how long prepared bottles can be stored in the refrigerator or kept at room temperature. If bottles are being heated, this too, must be done carefully to ensure the liquid does not become too hot. Sanitizing bottles and equipment can be time consuming but must be done thoroughly to ensure the quality of the baby's food.

Summary

Overall, then, there are advantages and disadvantages to bottle feeding. Disadvantages include not offering the infant the health benefits of breastfeeding, or if breast milk is being expressed, the time and effort required to do so can be seen as a disadvantage. Formula can be quite expensive (several hundred dollars a month) whereas breast milk is free, and if the baby is nursed at the breast, no cleaning or sterilization of bottles is necessary. Advantages of bottle feeding include being able to involve other caregivers, especially fathers. Each woman will ultimately need to decide what is best for her and her family in each situation, but there are additional structural factors that need to be addressed as the breast or formula feeding debate continues.

Structural Factors

It seems that while there is stigma associated with breastfeeding in public, there is also stigma associated with formula feeding. The messages promoting breastfeeding as the optimal way of feeding an infant are quite widespread, and many people today are aware that breastfeeding is medically recommended. Many women feel that being a good mother is synonymous with breastfeeding, and when they encounter difficulty with breastfeeding and turn to formula, they feel guilty that they were not able to give their baby the "best." It is important to keep in mind that almost every mother wants what is best for her child, and that formula feeding is sometimes necessary.

Another issue relevant to the debate about breast or bottle feeding is the extent to which people are knowledgeable and comfortable talking about breasts and breastfeeding. Often children learn things from their parents, even as adult children. When a woman first has a child, it is not uncommon for one of the grandmothers to come and stay with the new mom. This serves several functions—being there to help the mom during the recovery period after childbirth, as well as to teach the new mom about caring for a baby. An issue here is that many women did not breastfeed because the previously accepted message was that formula feeding was better than breastfeeding. Thus, there is a gap in knowledge and because it is missing, it can't be passed on to the next generation. In addition, breasts are highly sexualized in American culture, and because of this, many women might be uncomfortable talking with other women or men about breastfeeding. Both of these factors lead to the idea that breastfeeding is something that must be figured out without much social support, and this could lead to more frustration with the situation.

A third issue worth discussing is the work-family combination that many women face. In the United States, the Family and Medical Leave Act allows for 12 weeks of unpaid leave after a child is born. While some companies might offer some paid time off, overall, women feel pressured to re-enter the workforce quickly because they can't afford the loss of income. It is possible to combine work and breastfeeding through pumping, but not every workplace will offer women a quiet and private place to express her milk. Onsite childcare could also help with combining work and family in that the mother could take breaks to go and feed the baby. This, too, is left up to workplaces to develop and trying to combine breastfeeding and work is stressful for many women.

All three of these issues point to important policy recommendations if breastfeeding is to be promoted. For one, perhaps a more nuanced view of exclusive breastfeeding is called for. Many women give up completely because they are experiencing difficulties or because they have to return to work. However, wouldn't even including some breast milk in the baby's diet be beneficial? This might allow the baby to get at least some of the health benefits, and it would also allow the mother a little bit of a break and space for the father to become more involved. Additionally, something must be done to open up the discussion of breastfeeding beyond lactation consultants and small groups of female friends. Socially, it must become acceptable to breastfeed in public and to have conversations about breastfeeding. These changes might happen slowly, with each of us doing our part to promote a breastfeeding-friendly environment. Lastly, we should examine how family-friendly some of our policies are and see if changes should be made. Offering paid time off would greatly influence many women's lives, and more on-site childcare programs might support an increase in breastfeeding duration.

CONCLUSION

Many people tend to think of breastfeeding as a very personal decision, and there are many influences on a mother's decision. Ultimately, each woman must decide what she feels is best for her and her family in their situation, but many things, both individual and societal, influence that decision.

See also Birth Control; Cosleeping; Midwifery and Medicalization; Transition to Parenthood.

Further Reading: Ahluwalia, I., B. Morrow, and J. Hsia. "Why Do Women Stop Breastfeeding? Findings From the Pregnancy Risk Assessment and Monitoring System." *Pediatrics* 116, no. 6 (2005): 1408–1412. http://pediatrics.aappublications.org/cgi/reprint/116/6/1408 (accessed April 2007); American Academy of Pediatrics. "Children's Health Topics: Breastfeeding." http://www.aap.org/healthtopics/breastfeeding.cfm; Baumslag, N., and D. Michels. *Milk, Money, and Madness: The Culture and Politics of Breastfeeding.* Westport, CT: Bergin and Garvey, 1995; Blum, L. *At the Breast: Ideologies of Breastfeeding and Motherhood in the Contemporary United States.* Boston: Beacon Press, 1999; Centers for Disease Control and Prevention. "Breastfeeding Practices—Results from the National Immunization Survey." http://www.cdc.gov/breastfeeding/data/NIS_data/data_2004.htm (accessed November 2007); Hausman, Bernice. *Mother's Milk: Breastfeeding Controversies in American Culture.* New York: Routledge, 2003; Homeier, Barbara P., "Breastfeeding vs. Formula Feeding," *Kids Health,* 2005. http://www.kidshealth.org/parent/food/infants/breast_bottle_feeding.html; Kellymom. "Pumping & Bottle Feeding." http://www.kellymom.com/bf/pumping/index.html; La Lache League International. http://www.llli.org/; Li, R., F. Fridinger, and L. Grummer-Strwn. "Public Perceptions on Breastfeeding Constraints." *Journal of Human Lactation* 18, no. 3 (2002): 227–235; Sears, W., and M. Sears. *The Breastfeeding Book.* New York: Little, Brown and Company, 2002; Simpson, Kathleen. "Formula Companies and their 'Free' Gifts." http://www.breastfeedingonline.com/free.shtml (accessed November 2007); Stearns, Cindy A. "Breastfeeding and the Good Maternal Body." *Gender and Society* 13, no. 3 (1999): 308–325; World Health Organization. "Breastfeeding." http://www.who.int/topics/breastfeeding/en/.

Jeanne Holcomb

C

CHANGING FERTILITY PATTERNS

Patterns of family life are not just the result of choices that individuals make, but they reflect changes and trends on a societal level. During the past century two family fertility patterns have had significant impacts on social life. They are the baby boom and the birth dearth. As the names suggest, the baby boom was an unexpected increase in birth rates and birth dearth was a greater than anticipated decrease in birth rates. While the effects of the baby boom generation (sometimes referred to as boomers) have been occurring for some time, the consequences of and for the birth dearth generation (occasionally referred to as the baby bust) are still being examined. There are debates about which cohort will ultimately have the greatest effects on United States population patterns.

THE BABY BOOM

In twentieth-century America fertility hit an all time high during the years 1946 to 1964, when approximately 75 million babies were born. In fact, this period was an anomaly in a century-long decline in fertility rates. Persons born during this time period make up the baby boom. This time in America focused on the birth and development of children, how they were reared and the way that they continued to progress in the rest of their lives. Thus, familism, placing a high value on family, was a hallmark of this generation. In 1955, near the peak of the baby boom, the birthrate was 25 births per one thousand people.

Though this cohort was born after World War II, the war is considered a critical historical event impacting their lives. When the War started, many women whose husbands were called to military service had to take charge and become the head of the household. They entered the work force to do their patriotic duty, some even raising children alone while their husbands were overseas. As a result of the flurry of weddings at the start of the war, many newlywed women had to make the best of their situations as not only wives whose husbands were unavailable, but some as soon-to-be mothers. The war was a difficult time for the whole country, with shortages of some key products, such as gasoline, having an effect on how people lived their lives.

Following World War II, birth rates rose sharply. Some of this rise has been linked to a desire for a more peaceful, simple lifestyle following the sacrifices of war. Other factors included readily available jobs and government benefits. Fueled by a strong economy, young men and women married early and could afford to start families. It was reasonable for a high school graduate to get a high-paying manufacturing job right out of school because of the demand for products that had been unavailable during the war time economy. Coupled with the strong economic prospects, a number of government initiatives were aimed at creating normalcy, with its reliance on family as its cornerstone, in postwar America. Not only were most veterans eligible for educational benefits under the GI Bill, but federal housing loans, low interest rate mortgages, and increased income tax credits for dependent children fed young families' dreams of a harmonious home life.

The post–World War II era also ushered in the planned subdivision development, the bastion of family living. The idea behind this type of housing was a family-friendly location that could provide more space for the larger families. Though some were reasonably priced, low interest Veteran's Administration loans for former GIs certainly helped families acquire these new properties. Additionally, when men returned from military service, they moved back into the jobs they had held prior to their military duty. Because many women had held those jobs while the men were away, they were displaced by the men's return and many women found themselves back home. With this move home, there was social pressure on women to have children. Some of this pressure was generated by the government, by Hollywood, and by the women themselves. Content analyses of popular women' magazines at the time revel that a primary cultural goal was family, particularly traditional motherhood. However, women increasingly expected the men to help in rearing the children, just as women had helped maintain the economy while the men were away fighting the war.

The Baby Boom Family

Marriage was more important for women in the 1940s and 1950s than it has become today. Most conservative pundits consider the 1950s the "golden age" of family life and suggest America would be better off if more families today looked and acted like families in the baby boom era. At the time, most young people wanted and expected to marry. Likewise, early marriage was expected. The average age at first marriage for females marrying in the 1950s and 1960s was 20; for males it was 22.5 years of age. These couples would marry young and become part of the "American Dream" that included several children in a family operating under a traditional gender role model. Males were the breadwinners, away from the home working to earn a living while women stayed home as housewives. Given the low reliability of birth control (the birth control pill was not available until 1960), families also tended to be larger than families today, with the majority having more than 2 children.

While this pattern characterized much of middle class white America at the time, it was not a universal experience. Women, who seemed to have everything such as children, homes, and marriages, were sometimes unhappy with this arrangement and their discontent would sow the seeds for the Modern Women's Movement. This conflict between utopia and reality pushed family to center stage. Families were supposed to be the dream that everyone wanted and the unhappiness and disharmony that some families faced was not supposed to be occurring. Families struggled with the issues of child rearing and who held the power in the family. Betty Friedan discussed these issues in her classic work *The Feminine Mystique*.

Childhood for the Baby Boom

The childhood experience of the baby boom generation was different than the experiences of children today. The children were often expected to contribute work to whatever the family did for a living. In the Depression of the 1930s many children had worked in the fields with their families. When these children became parents they wanted their children to go to school and receive an education. The psychological effect of growing up during the Great Depression has been linked to the increase in nurturing parenting styles and a greater desire to experience normative family life.

After the school day, children were expected to help their family in whatever way that the family needed. They were to do their chores and their homework. At this time many families had radios in their homes and the children were likely allowed to listen to the radio before they went to bed. In the 1950s some families had television sets and the children were allowed to watch some shows during the day and after the chores were completed. The television shows that were popular during this time were *Queen for a Day, Dragnet, Leave It to Beaver, Father Knows Best,* and *Man against Crime.*

Given that so many children were born in such a short time period, and parents were in favor of their children receiving a good education to prepare them for a good career, it became a top priority and necessity for America to build more schools. Elementary schools were full of students during the 1950s and 1960s. Children were taught the basic subjects such as reading writing, and arithmetic. As the baby boomers aged they continued to be a challenge for society because there were so many of them. When they left the overcrowded elementary schools, they moved on to crowded junior and senior high schools.

Adolescence for the Baby Boom

The baby boomers entered adolescence in the 1960s. During this time the United States experienced difficult times dealing with social and cultural changes such as the Vietnam War, the Modern Women's Movement, and the Civil Rights struggle. Many of these changes helped define the baby boomers.

One of the major events was the Civil Rights struggle. As a result of institutionalized segregation, blacks were not allowed to use the same restaurants, schools, or bathrooms as whites. African Americans wanted to be treated as the equals of whites; after all, they had fought as bravely as whites in World War II and many had died for America. They also wanted permission for their children to attend the same schools as white children, thereby receiving the same opportunities for success. Boomer children were exposed to freedom marches, violent protests, Martin Luther King, Jr., and police responses through the medium of television.

However, in contrast to the events that were occurring in the larger society, television during this time was fixated on the stereotypical family shows such as *Leave it to Beaver* and *Lassie*. As Hollywood tried to show Americans how families were supposed to be and encouraged shared family values and morals, families that did not fit the stereotype were left to assume they had somehow failed at providing a perfect family life.

Another major event affecting the generation of baby boomers was the death of President John F. Kennedy. Boomers recall this event in different ways. Most were shocked about what happened and others watched in disbelief. With the death of the president many boomers began to wonder what kind of world they were living in and to question their own safety.

The turbulence of the 1960s and the wide range of social changes that occurred paved the way for a questioning of ideology and the status quo. This resulted in young people having a lot of influence in the culture. The large numbers of teenagers meant that there was a market for products and entertainment directed specifically at them. Enter rock and roll music and the Beatles. The Beatles, Bob Dylan, the Rolling Stones, and Elvis Presley all proved challenging for parents as young people's interests began to diverge significantly from those of their parents. Drug experimentation was more widespread during this period as an attempt to remove oneself from what was happening in the world.

The classic activity of American courtship, the date, was also prominent during this time period. With male adolescents getting jobs in the strong economy, many had money to spend on leisure. They had greater access to automobiles than had previous generations and they found many more activities geared toward daters. Drive-in movies, concerts, local soda shops, and community activities all served the function of getting young people involved in relationships that would hopefully lead to marriage and a continuation of the American Dream. While the activities in which young people participated were fairly scripted along gender lines, there was more freedom in partner selection and opportunities for social interaction.

This carried over into the high schools. There the boomers were able to continue to develop close friendships and participate in acceptable activities. Organized by gender, boys were able to participate in football and basketball and many girls were cheerleaders. As was the case with their earlier schooling, the numbers of young people reaching high school age simultaneously meant that schools were often crowded and communities had to build new schools rapidly to account for the large population. After high school many boomers went straight into the workforce. The economy was strong, particularly for the oldest boomers, and they could earn money to make a solid middle class living through factory and skilled labor positions. Trade school and college were also viable options for a number of boomers, many of whose fathers had attended universities under the provisions of the GI Bill. Just as had been the case when they began elementary school, the large number of people in this birth cohort necessitated an increase in the number of colleges and universities, and class sizes also increased.

Adult Baby Boomers

As the majority of boomers moved into adulthood, they pushed for a new type of society. The social movements for peace, women, and racial equality ushered in more job and educational opportunities for a wider cross-section of the population. Women, in particular, began to push for equal rights. They wanted to earn the same wages as their male counterparts for the same work and to be treated fairly. The traditional model that mothers of the baby boom cohort experienced, where men received the better jobs while women were supposed to take the less important occupations, was unsatisfactory for baby boom women. All of the talk about equality in the larger society resulted in similar discussions about equality in family life. Many men decided that they wanted more from life than just work. Some had seen their fathers only rarely due to the long hours often needed to maintain a family with only one earner; others may have been involved with a fledgling men's movement that encouraged men to devote themselves to caring for their children in more ways than just financially. Even the women's movement and the feminist rhetoric encouraged men to take a more active role in the lives of their children.

Although many mothers still continued to be stay-at-home mothers and homemakers, employment was a more viable option. For those women who did work, their options for what to do with their preschool-age children during the workday brought forth the issue of day care. People began to use facilities that specialized in childcare. Recognizing that providing their children with the best care possible would help women feel more comfortable with the decision to work, the National Organization for Women included a strong statement about the need for quality child care in its Bill of Rights. These changing patterns would influence the Birth Dearth.

THE BIRTH DEARTH

Changes in society that began in the 1960s and picked up steam in the 1970s and 1980s began to influence family size and there was a noticeable decline in the numbers of births. This lower-than-anticipated birth rate is known as the birth dearth or baby bust. As more women were choosing to attend college and move into careers, marrying young was no longer seen as the ideal, nor were families with large numbers of children highly desirable. The total fertility rate, or the number of births that a woman is likely to experience over her reproductive lifetime, fell from a high of 3.8 in 1957 to 1.7 in 1976. Like with the prior baby boom, this precipitous decline in births was not anticipated.

Reasons for the Birth Dearth

Demographers have suggested several reasons for the drastic decline in and continued low numbers of births in the United States. One important change came from more women in the workforce. Resulting from the political strides of the women's movement, attitudes regarding the place of women in society and the family were changing. More women were attending graduate and professional schools. Additionally, these educated women were moving into new career fields that went beyond the traditionally female occupations of nursing and teaching. As newcomers to the professions, many women sensed that they would not be taken seriously as professionals if their family life was to impinge upon their work responsibilities. This contributed to a greater likelihood of postponing marriage until a later age, although postponement was not as large a contributor to changing fertility patterns then as it is today. Unlike in previous generations where women who worked outside the home were usually single, it was married women who increasingly moved into the labor force in the 1970s. Because fewer women were choosing to be stay-at-home mothers, families were generally smaller.

Fertility and sexuality options were enhanced in the post baby boom era. Abortion has been hypothesized as playing a role in the lowered fertility rate. In 1973 the Supreme Court case of *Roe v. Wade* dealt with a woman's legal right to choose a safe abortion. This increased acceptability and access to abortion helped some women end an unplanned pregnancy and permitted a greater level of control over motherhood. Contraception options were also increasing during this time, with the birth control pill being introduced in 1960 which made it possible for women to participate in sexual encounters with less threat of an unintended pregnancy. Other contraceptive methods were enhanced and perfected, and better manufacturing techniques meant that condoms and diaphragms were more reliable. There was also an increase in sterilization as vasectomy and tubal ligation procedures received more attention. These options gave couples more direct control over parenthood timing and family size.

As cohabitation, or living together in a marriage-like relationship without being legally married, became more of an option, it had impacts on fertility. Couples that are not married, but just living together, may decide not to bring children into the relationship because they fear that the relationship may not be permanent. There is another social trend regarding permanency that should be considered: divorce. At the time that birth rates were declining, divorce rates were increasing. Because marriages were of shorter duration, families were smaller.

The late 1960s through the 1980s witnessed a slowing of the economy in the United States. When economic times are hard, couples may carefully consider the financial costs of having additional children. Today, few Americans live on farms where the labor of children can enhance the productive capabilities of the family and where large numbers of children are assets. Children are liabilities today because they do not contribute appreciably to the family economy until well into their teenage years, and the modern standards of childhood push families to acquire many additional goods and services directed solely at the children.

Finally, due to enhanced medical technology, the infant mortality rate has declined. Even compared with the baby boom generation, the likelihood that an infant will survive the first year of life has increased.

THE EFFECTS OF FLUCTUATIONS IN FERTILITY

Both the baby boom and birth dearth have had effects on American social life, although which will ultimately have the greatest influence remains to be seen. The baby boom changed the social landscape because of the sheer numbers within the age cohort. Everywhere they have gone, at each life stage, there have been too many of them. From a dramatic need to increase educational facilities when they started school to the projections regarding the bankrupting of Social Security when they retire, there is little doubt that their influence has been high. For example, one of the reasons that the 1960s were so turbulent may be linked to the age of the baby boom cohort at that time. Historians Bidwell and Vander Mey suggest that there is a correlation between high numbers of young adults in a society and high degrees of social change. Young adults are old enough to be aware of the economic and social injustices that exist in the world and perhaps translate their knowledge into social action. Older persons often have more preoccupations with issues directly influencing their daily lives, such as work and family obligations, which prevent activist activities.

The baby boomers make up approximately one-fourth of the current United States population. Most of the baby boomers are now in their middle-age years and the first boomers will reach age 65 in the year 2011. This occurrence will have a huge impact on the Social Security program. Social Security payments are funded by taxes collected from employers and employees. This money represents a percentage of one's earnings and is based in the idea that the people who are currently working can help to support those who are not working. The expectation is that population increases will mean that there will always be workers whose taxes can pay for the support of the older generation. Social Security is a major source of income for approximately 80 percent of the elderly persons in the U.S. and serves as the only source of income for about one-half of the nation's retirees. As the number of retirees expecting to receive payments increases as the boomers retire, the baby bust generation will still be in the work place; there will be fewer people paying into the system yet payments will be made to a greater number of people than now. Some agencies, such as the Government Accountability Office, and many economists predict that there will not be enough funds to go around, leading them to wonder where the money to pay basic benefits will come from. Medicare will also face pressures from the baby boomers' retirement. Medicare is a program that helps older people who do not have enough insurance or money to pay for their medical costs. With medical costs increasing by double-digit percentages each year, any increase in the number of beneficiaries will strap the system. Thus, persons who are still in the employment sector will likely see an increase in the payroll taxes that support medical benefits.

Boomers themselves wonder if there will be any money left for them when they reach their golden years. They have paid taxes into the programs during the years that they worked and want to count on the program to help them when they need it most. With life expectancy increasing over time, and currently being higher than at any other prior time, people realize that they are going to need some help with medial treatments and medications in the future. This has prompted the introduction of individual retirement investments and options such as individual retirement accounts (IRAs and Roth IRAs) and medical savings accounts.

Boomers have been prominent in shaping the social agenda for many years and currently hold many of the most important positions in the economy and government. The past two presidents, Bill Clinton and George W. Bush, are both baby boomers, as are many people in Congress. As these and other folks retire, there are concerns that there will not be enough highly trained workers to take their places.

The birth dearth is affecting, and will continue to affect, America as well. Sociologists have been discussing the changing patterns of social life through the phrase "the graying of the United States." This is a reference to the increasing average age of the population. Rather than being a youth-centered society, we are a middle-age-centered society. As the boomers retire, we will be an older-age centered society, with already powerful lobbying groups such as the American Association for Retired Persons (AARP) continuing to influence social and governmental policy. The need for increased medical intervention, daily elder care, and financial support for the elderly will impact the lives of the baby bust cohort. Many will find that as their aging parents live longer, they will have the responsibility of caring for their parents as well as for their own children, many of whom are living at home for longer periods than in the past. These birth dearth children will do double-duty caregiving.

The birth dearth is currently affecting America in a shortage of skilled workers. Unemployment rates have remained fairly low in recent years and many work places have to rely on one person to do the work of two or three people. The decline in population has meant that corporate America has sought other solutions to an undersupply of workers, including outsourcing and overseas expansion. Americans are realizing the great effect that the birth dearth has had on our economy. More families today follow the precedent established during the birth dearth and decide to only have only one or two children or to remain childless.

Among the issues that demographers consider concerning changing fertility patterns is zero population growth, and replacement level. Zero population growth refers to the situation where the number of births and deaths are approximately equal, so that the total change in population in the society is negligible. Replacement level indicates what the total childbearing rate would need to be to fully replace the population as older persons die. The generally accepted replacement level is a total fertility rate of 2.1. In 2004 the total fertility rate was 1.9, or below the rate needed for population replacement. In principle, then, the United States population as a whole should be declining. However, the numbers of immigrants to the U.S. in any given year are enough to increase the total size of the U.S. population. The current birthrate, on the other hand, is not leading to an increase in population.

Following the period of declining fertility known as the baby bust, there was a slight increase in the birth rate in the early 1990s. Researchers were immediately intrigued. Was another baby boom about to happen? The consensus at the present time is no. This birth rate increase, dubbed the so-called baby boomlet or baby echo, resulted from the fact that there were so many persons in the baby boom generation. When even a small number of these women had children or had more than the expected number of children, it over-inflated the birth rates. Perhaps this increase was due to an upturn in the economy, but the total fertility rate has hovered just below replacement level since the 1970s. According to the experts, it is not likely to change much in the coming years.

CONCLUSIONS

Choices that persons make regarding child bearing are often driven by factors outside of the couple. As World War II ended and the U.S. experienced a pronounced period of economic stability, having a large family seemed affordable. In today's economic climate, partners may be less likely to opt for large families due to the cost of items in the desired lifestyle. The baby boom and birth dearth cohorts represent adaptations to the larger social world in which persons find themselves. The final influences of these very different fertility patterns have yet to occur, but one must include both of them when exploring the current population characteristics and influences on American social life.

See also Abortion; Birth Control; Elder Care; Grandparenthood; Grandparents as Caregivers; Only Child.

Further Reading: Bidwell, Lee D. Millar, and Brenda J. Vander Mey. *Sociology of the Family: Investigating Family Issues.* Boston: Allyn and Bacon, 2000; Coontz, Stephanie. *The Way We Never Were: American Families and the Nostalgia Trap.* New York: Basic Books, 1992; Coontz, Stephanie. *The Way We Really Are: Coming to Terms with America's Changing Families.* New York: Basic Books, 1997; Friedan, Betty. *The Feminine Mystique.* New York: W.W. Norton and Company, 1963; Gross, Michael. *The More Things Change: Why the Baby Boom Won't Fade Away.* New York: Harper Collins Publishers, Inc., 2000; Harris, Leslie M. *After Fifty: How the Baby Boom will Redefine the Mature Market.* Ithaca, NY: Paramount Market Publishing, Inc., 2003; Harris, Fred R. *The Baby Bust: Who Will Do the Work? Who Will Pay the Taxes?* Lanham, MD: Rowman and Littlefield Publishers, Inc., 2005; Smith, J. Walker, and Ann Clurman. *Generation Ageless: How Baby Boomers are Changing the Way We Live Today . . . And They're Just Getting Started.* New York: HarperCollins, 2007; Wattenberg, Ben J. *The Birth Dearth: What Happens When People* in *Free Countries Don't Have Enough Babies.* New York: Ballantine Books, 1987; Weiss, Jessica. *To Have and To Hold: Marriage, the Baby Boom and Social Change.* Chicago: The University of Chicago Press, 2000.

Jessica Sexton

CHILD ABUSE

Child abuse is generally defined in two ways. One is the nonaccidental injury to a child that requires medical attention. These are acts of commission. The second part of the definition is neglect, acts of omission where parents and other adults fail to meet the basic needs of the child. Nearly all experts concur that neglect is far more likely than other forms of abuse. The U.S. Department of Health and Human Services reported that in 2004 there were approximately 872,000 victims of child abuse and neglect; 1500 of whom died as a result of the abuse. Sixty-two percent of the total victims experienced neglect, 18 percent were physically abused, sexual abuse harmed 10 percent, 7 percent were psychologically mistreated, and medical neglect accounted for 2 percent.

As with any abuse situation, the child abuse may be physical, psychological, emotional, sexual, or some combination. Clearly these are broad categorizations for what constitutes the complex phenomenon of abuse and this has made the whole domain of child abuse controversial. The societal expectation that parents are nearly exclusively in charge of the care and rearing of their children, has meant that interventions into the private family setting have only been likely when abuse is very serious and can be documented.

The controversies surrounding child abuse are grounded in the question, "Does the child stay in the home or get removed from the home?" Society has made it known that abuse of a child is horrific. The problem is in how to stop the abuse with a solution that will best benefit the child. Specifically the concern is over whether a child should be completely removed from the home or whether attempts should be made to maintain the family unit. When considering the solutions to child abuse, among the primary controversies are questions about exactly what constitutes abuse, particularly with regard to physical discipline, and how do other forms of domestic violence complicate the scene.

CAUSES OF CHILD ABUSE

The causes of child abuse are many and not all are found in all cases. Child abuse is mainly perpetrated by an adult who wields physical and emotional control over a child. Many factors can relate to someone's risk to abuse children. Some of the factors at work in child abuse are cultural, social, and personal. In very early studies of child abuse, the assumptions were that abusers must be mentally ill. While that is an easy supposition, the evidence suggests that only around 10 percent of abusers have psychoses or severe personality disorders. Reliance on mental illness as an explanation has hindered a more complete understanding of child abuse. This has lead recent researchers, such as Richard

Gelles, to broaden the discussion to include other factors that might make one prone to abuse a child.

Personal psychological factors in parents can play a significant role in the risk of abuse. However, these factors usually relate to the stressors that parents might experience. Stress can arise from many sources, not the least of which is the task of parenting itself. It is a permanent status that at times can seem overwhelming, particularly for persons with inadequate support networks. Some children with special needs require additional care that heightens caregiving stress. Not all babies are equally easy-going and those that seem more prone to crying can lead parents to question their skills. Stress is increased when one is a single parent, has lower income or is unemployed, is ill, or experiences conflict with a romantic partner. Furthermore, environmental stressors such as the family ideal, work, finances, and even health issues can cause a large amount of stress.

The use of alcohol or drugs reduces inhibitions and heightens the abusers' awareness of personal insecurities. Both alcohol and drugs can, through aggravating stress and impairing judgment, cause an abuser to verbally or physically attack a child for some perceived wrong. If an individual is a victim of prior abuse, he or she is more likely to become an abuser, too, although the individual is not destined to be abusive. Estimates are that 30 percent of abused children will grow up to be abusers, in contrast to 3 percent of persons who were not abused. Low self-esteem and feelings of inadequacy have also been linked to a greater tendency to abuse when compared with persons with higher levels of self-esteem. After prolonged exposure to negative opinions, an individual may become violent as a way of venting the built-up pressure and anxiety caused by low self-esteem.

Abuse is also used as a method to gain control over a child. A person who has a poor self-concept, low self-esteem, or has been a victim of prior abuse has a stronger need for control and power because it is the ability to gain power and control that validates the abuser. This cyclical pattern is difficult to break. Often parents have very little preparation for the tasks of parenting, have unrealistic expectations about what it entails, and have little understanding of how children can be expected to behave at various stages of development. While the images of babies in most parenting magazines show a smiling, cooing cherubic face, they don't show the child crying with a runny nose, messy diaper, or other distasteful daily occurrences of child rearing. Abuse may occur as an attempt to gain conformity from unruly children. For whatever reason, studies suggest that abusive parents tend to be much more demanding than nonabusive parents.

Society's focus on the ideal family creates stress when an individual realizes that he or she is not living up to society's standard of the modern family, be it by not making enough income, not living in the right neighborhood, or having to have a two income household in order to get by. Also, pressure from a boss at work may cause tension that adds to the build-up of stress. These stressors may create a volatile home life where abuse is the outlet for a massive release of pent-up stresses. And unfortunately, children are likely to be the targets for the abusive release.

This inclusion of economic status in the likelihood of abuse is important. A number of studies suggest that child abuse is more likely in families from low socioeconomic backgrounds, although they differ on the reasons for why this is so. One explanation posits that it only appears that the rates are higher in poor families because they seek treatment in settings, such as public hospitals, in which the suspicion of abuse is likely to be reported. Wealthy families may seek care from a private physician who may be more reluctant to label a suspicious injury as abuse. So, wealthier families may be better able to hide abuse. Another explanation for the link between poverty and abuse is the stress that accompanies poverty. Additionally, low-income parents have less education, inadequate support systems, higher rates of substance abuse, and are more likely to be young. Compounded, these risk factors make being a lower-class child a potentially harmful position. Low-income parents tend to be single parents. The risk of neglect among low income children is an astounding 44 times higher than among middle- and upper-income children.

Contrary to the stereotype of women's constant nurturing, evidence indicates that in cases of child abuse women are as likely as men to be the perpetrators. The majority of low-income families are mother-only families. Some of these women are no doubt forced into the mothering role by a lack of well-paying or fulfilling employment, as well as by unplanned pregnancies. Unwanted children are an added mental and economic burden, making them prone to abuse.

CHILD ABUSE ADVOCACY GROUPS

Child abuse prevention and advocacy websites have proliferated in recent years. Some are the websites of well established nonprofit organizations and others are solely cyberspace creations. Nearly all encourage visitors to the site to donate money to help the cause of education and advocacy. Because child abuse is an issue that commands attention and garners sympathy, particularly from those who identify with the child, it is a cause that persons are likely to donate toward. The so-called innocence of childhood is a strong cultural image and it is easy to sell abuse as violating that innocence. This model of innocence is used as a contrast for data on abuse.

Some particularly useful websites and organizations devoted to child welfare include www.childhelp.org and www.cwla.org. Childhelp is a large nonprofit organization that uses celebrity ambassadors, product partnerships, and media outlets to spread the word about child abuse. Their hotline 1–800–4-A-Child is a well publicized reporting mechanism. The Child Welfare League of America is the oldest and largest child abuse information and prevention organization in the country. In contrast to these long-standing organizations (Childhelp was founded in 1959; the Child Welfare League in 1920), www.childabuse.com is purely an online venture and promotes prevention through education and awareness.

CONSEQUENCES OF CHILD ABUSE

Because the causes of abuse are many, it follows that the consequences of abuse are just as numerous. While statistics can not tell the whole story of the consequences of child abuse, they can give insight into the frequency and severity of the problem. However, statistics about child abuse have to be viewed with caution. Given the unacceptability of harming a child, parents are often inaccurate in their reporting of such behaviors, fearing legal reprisal and social condemnation. A lot of the statistics, then, come from the reports of teachers, physicians, social workers, and others who must make assumptions about the origin of injuries.

There are nearly three million reports of child abuse made each year, suggesting that awareness of the issue is resulting in some action. However, estimates are that the actual rates of child abuse are at least three times what are reported. According to Childhelp, one of the largest and oldest nonprofit organizations dedicated to the issue of child abuse, children between birth and age three are the most likely group to experience abuse. They are victimized at a rate of 16.4 per 1,000 children, compared with a rate of 12.3 per 1000 children for all children under age 18. This means that for every 1000 infants and toddlers, more than 16 of them will be abused. Around four children die everyday from abuse or neglect and 79 percent of these juvenile homicide victims are children younger than four years old.

Consequences also encompass the likely future outcomes for the victims of abuse. According to data compiled by the U.S. Department of Health and Human Services, there can be many long-term consequences for children who are abused. Among them is a 25 percent greater likelihood of teen pregnancy, abused teens being three times less likely than nonabused teens to practice safe sex, increasing their risks of STDs and AIDS. Abused children are nearly 30 percent more likely to abuse their own children.

Victimization through child abuse is also correlated with more contact with the criminal justice system. Children who experience child abuse and neglect are 59 percent more likely to be arrested as juveniles, 28 percent more likely to be arrested as adults, and 30 percent more likely to commit violent crime than are nonabused persons. Data indicate that among the prison population, 36.7 percent of female inmates were abused as children, while 14.4 percent of male inmates were.

Psychological and psychiatric outcomes also are linked with child abuse. Eighty percent of young adults who had been abused met the diagnostic criteria for at least one psychiatric disorder at the age of 21. Common disorders among this group included depression, anxiety, eating disorders, and posttraumatic stress disorder (PTSD). Sexual abuse compounds these issues. Children who are victims of sexual abuse are 2.5 times more likely to abuse alcohol and 3.8 times more likely to become addicted to drugs than their nonabused peers. In fact, nearly two-thirds of those persons in drug abuse treatment programs report having been abused as children.

CONTROVERSIES

Controversies have surfaced when determining healthy solutions for child abuse victims. The key controversies concerning child abuse are the definition of abuse, the presence of other risk behaviors and factors, and whether the child should remain in or be removed from the home. Solutions to child abuse are difficult to create because each child abuse case is different and the solution that works for one child may harm another child even more. When handling child abuse cases, caseworkers must do their absolute best not to add to the child's trauma. It is this desire to minimize an abused child's trauma that makes finding solutions to these controversies difficult.

Defining Abuse

The definitions of child abuse have changed significantly over time. No longer do parents have rights of life and death over children, as was common in the days of the Roman Empire where children not blessed by their fathers were left to die through neglect. Nor can parents in the United States turn their children into commodities by selling them to the highest bidder. Today the question of abuse is focused on the point of where a parent crosses the fine line between acceptable use of force and unacceptable abuse, and with what frequency. At what point should a neighbor, teacher, physician, or social worker intervene? Extreme cases, such as burning, imprisoning, or beating are easy to define as child abuse. However, there is much grey area in what is acceptable behavior of a parent toward a child.

Definitions that focus only on physically hurting the child might be too broadly interpreted. The result is that any physical act, such as tightly holding a toddler during a tantrum, becomes defined as abuse by some. The legal standard recognizes that it is not always easy to distinguish between physical discipline and abuse. The former condition is the result of what is considered reasonable by the cultural context. While 90 percent of parents of three- and four-year-olds have used spankings on their child and nearly that many consider it acceptable to do so, does that mean 90 percent of parents are abusive? This question is not easily answered, but is important because the definition of abuse that is applied by social workers, courts, and so on can determine whether children are permitted to remain with the parent or whether they are taken in by the state. In fact the American Bar Association has no universally recognized definition of child abuse to use in court settings.

As difficult as defining physical abuse is in practice, defining neglect is even more difficult. While abandonment or gross failure to provide for the basic needs of a child are clear, statutes that define parental negligence in broad ways may mean that different parenting models than the community norm, or failure to instill morals, or even permitting truancy are seen as negligent. In the early days of the homeschool movement some parents were considered neglectful for not sending their children for standard classroom instruction.

Defining Abusers and Settings

For many years there have been concerns over who is most likely to abuse a child. Stereotypes hold that the particularly likely culprit is a stepfather. While it seems easy to place the blame on a male, nonbiological family member because of the expectation that males are more violent than females, and the supposition that biological ties are stronger than social ties, this is inaccurate. Biological parents are more likely than other persons to abuse a child and it is the mother who is most likely to do so. This pattern is particularly true for African American families that have a greater proportion of single parent homes. Does this then mean that single black mothers are profiled as child abusers?

Police who are called to homes to investigate domestic disturbance calls are taught to pay attention to any children who are present for signs of abuse. Statistics indicate that when women are abused in a domestic setting, their children have a higher likelihood of being abused as well. This might be abuse from the woman's abuser, or paradoxically abuse from the woman herself. It is often extremely difficult to determine who in a household is abusing whom.

Interventions

Since the 1950s both private and public agencies have dedicated themselves to helping children. One of the primary tasks of the agencies involves educating the public about the issues surrounding child abuse and proposing specific solutions. It has only been recently that laws have been developed to aid children, such as the Child Abuse Prevention and Treatment Act of 1974. The goal of this act was to encourage states to develop their own laws and strategies to protect children from maltreatment and neglect. While every state handles child abuse cases in a slightly different way and relies on slightly different administrative structures, they have been fairly successful in their assault on child abuse and neglect.

One of the most traumatic aspects of child abuse and neglect is the decision to remove the child from the home, even on a temporary basis. This is granted under the states' rights to protect the interest of the child, but the question that is raised is what to then do with the child. Options are limited. For infants and young children, the foster care system is their destination, at least on a temporary basis while abuse claims are investigated. For adolescents and severely disabled children, the care is frequently provided in a group home where a small number of similar children are tended by a staff of child care workers. These decisions to remove children from the care of their biological parents are controversial for several reasons.

First, the expanding definitions of child abuse mean that children can be removed with far less proof than was needed in the past. Additionally, the numbers of cases that social workers and child advocates are saddled with mean that it takes some time for the data regarding each case to be gathered, leaving the child in foster care for longer periods of time than most state regulations initially intended. Second, parents may be encouraged not to contest the child's removal in order to avoid damaging allegations of abuse. After an assessment, the child may be sent back home, sometimes with court supervision and follow-up services, but sometimes without.

When individuals hear about a case of child abuse, they automatically want the child removed from the home. It is true that removing the child from the home the most effective way to stop the abuse. But is tearing a child away from the only home he or she has known really helping the child? Young children are particularly prone to be victims of violence, but there is a common cultural idea that very young children need their parents (particularly their mothers) more than at any other age. Indeed, federal laws governing foster care encourage states to work vigorously to reunite children with their parents. Unfortunately, the frequent court reviews of the cases often just mean moving the child to a new foster placement.

In extreme cases of child abuse where the child's life is at risk, removal is the only option. However, temporary removal or family counseling might be more productive in the end if the abuser is taught alternative ways of managing anger and stress, instead of using abusive measures. These types of interventions require a great deal of time, effort, and energy on the part of the abuser and the state counseling agencies, and are often something that cash-strapped states are unable to provide.

Critics of the foster care system suggest that the system is broken and badly needs repair. Children are moved from one foster family to another on a frequent basis. Due to an overwhelming need for foster care providers, many foster families receive little training for their role, and may be caring for too many children. One of the great concerns is what happens to children who age out of the foster care system. At age 18 they are no longer under state care, but may be poorly prepared to live as independent adults.

In some cases parents must give up their rights to a child when the abuse has been determined to be too severe to attempt reuniting the family. However, it is extremely difficult for this to happen because there is a high legal burden of proof for the court to terminate parental rights. Sometimes, the threat of criminal charges will push parents to voluntarily terminate their rights. When a child cannot be returned to the biological family and parental rights are terminated, adoption becomes available to the child. Adoption is another area of controversy. The majority of individuals in society see being adopted by a blood relative as the most beneficial for the child. However, abuse is a learned behavior. If a child's parent is the abuser, the assumption is that the parent's parent was probably abusive as well. In such a case, being adopted by a blood relative may be placing the child back in a potentially abusive situation. The underlying problem of these controversies remains, and until abuse can be prevented no amount of intervention will be adequate.

See also Addiction and Family; Attention Deficit Hyperactivity Disorder (ADHD); Corporal Punishment; Developmental Disability and Marital Stress; Domestic Violence Behaviors and Causes; Domestic Violence Interventions; Foster Care; Parenting Styles; Sibling Violence and Abuse.

Further Reading: Child Welfare Information Gateway. http://www.childwelfare.gov; Child Welfare League of America. http://www.cwla.org; Childhelp USA Foundation. http://www.childhelpusa.org; Crosson-Tower, Cynthia. *Understanding Child Abuse and Neglect.* Boston: Allyn and Bacon, 2007; Farmer, Steven. *Adult Children of Abusive Parents: A Healing Program for Those Who Have Been Physically, Sexually, or Emotionally Abused.*

New York: Ballantine Books, 1989; Flowers, R. Barri. *Domestic Crimes, Family Violence and Child Abuse: A Study of Contemporary American Society.* Jefferson, NC: McFarland and Company, 2000; Gelles, Richard J. *Intimate Violence in Families.* Thousand Oaks, CA: Sage, 1997; Kurst-Swanger, Karel, and Jacqueline L. Petcosky. *Violence in the Home: Multidisciplinary Perspectives.* New York: Oxford University Press, 2003; Monteleone, James A. *A Parent's and Teacher's Handbook on Identifying and Preventing Child Abuse.* St. Louis, MO: G. W. Medical Publishing, Inc., 1998; National Association to Protect Children. http://www.protect.org; The National Children's Advocacy Center. http://www.nationalcac.org; Prevent Child Abuse America. http://www.preventchildabuse.org.

Amanda Singletary

CHILD CARE POLICY

Child care policy provides an excellent venue for understanding the intersection of multiple institutions, social structures, and organizations in the lives of individuals. The institutions of race, class, gender, family, education, the state, and the economy intersect in the decision to work or not to work, the parameters of that decision for a given family, and the subsequent choices regarding care for children in the absence of a parent. For many families, the public policies surrounding child care determine whether they can work and shape the child care choices before them. Child care decisions are deeply personal choices, but for many, the decision to work requires access to child care.

Debates surrounding child care policy tap deeply rooted ideologies about gender, family, work, and public and private responsibility. These discussions often evoke deep-seated race and class ideologies because child care choices reflect labor market and income inequalities that are linked to long-standing race and class inequalities. Critics of public support for child care suggest that child care is a private issue in which the state should play no role beyond regulation for public health and welfare. Others posit that the same arguments that undergird compulsory public education for kindergarten through twelfth grade should lead us to universally available, publicly funded child care from birth to age five. Between these two extremes lies the discussion of the role of states and markets and the intersections of race, class, and gender in educational attainment, labor force participation, and child care choices.

RACE, CLASS, AND GENDER

The last 40 years have seen a dramatic increase in women's labor force participation. For many women the move to paid labor was a matter of choice; an opportunity won by hard-fought battles of the women's movement of the 1970s. But for poor, working class, and lower-middle-class families, the move was often borne of necessity. Stagnant wages, the decline of the family wage (a wage intended to cover the costs for a family with one working parent and one stay-at-home parent), and employment instability brought about by major economic shifts mean that, for many families, electing to stay home is a luxury of the past. For parents, the decision to work is accompanied by the need for child care, at least for children under the age of six. In the low-to-middle wage sector of the labor market, the economic tradeoff that child care costs present leads women to opt out of the labor force until their children reach school age. One low-to-middle wage income is insufficient to comfortably support a family, but low-skilled occupations simply do not pay enough to cover the cost of child care and still contribute meaningfully to the household budget. In other words, it simply does not pay to work. At the other end of the labor market, professional women can choose to work and pay for the child care option of their choice.

In the case of poor women with limited skills, the decision to opt out of the labor market is a rational economic choice. Because African American women are disproportionately represented among poor women and among single-parent householders, they are more likely to be faced with both the low-wage work child care dilemma and to rely on state assistance if they opt out of the paid labor force. Despite the logic of these choices and the reality of the larger structural factors that leave a disproportionate number of black women at the low end of the labor market, politicians and citizens often see the over-representation of black women on the welfare rolls as an indicator of racial inferiority. This over-representation is the result of a complex set of social and economic factors that create a stratified labor market and shape both perceptions and policy debate. Race and class ideologies are present in discussions of child care policy, but gender may be the primary axis on which the issue turns.

It has been argued that the historical absence of aggressive child care policies in community economic development movements is a function of the failure to include gender as a primary axis for analysis in community economic development circles. It has been suggested that race and class consistently trump gender in community economic development discussions, masking the potential impacts of policies that can fundamentally shift women's relationships to and roles in both the public and private spheres. The failure to fully appreciate the role of gender inequality in hampering development is embedded in long-standing gender ideologies that maintain that the economy is either a male sphere or is gender-neutral. Early Childhood Education and Care (ECEC) has the potential to reduce gender inequality because it may reduce or eliminate the child and family penalties that women pay in the labor market. Greater labor force attachment among mothers could help close the wage gap. Improved funding for child care also affects women's wages by increasing the earnings of child care workers who are mostly women. Moreover, public ECEC can reduce family income and human capital inequalities as poor parents are able to move into the labor force and provide their children and themselves with greater opportunities to acquire experience and education.

In addition to obscuring the significant impact of child care policy on women's participation and performance in the economy, traditional gender ideologies suggest that the debate has the potential to disrupt treasured images of motherhood. In several European social democracies, the state provides high-quality child care to all families or provides an allowance to support a stay-at-home parent's decision not to work. In the liberal democratic United States the state provides assistance, but the lowest paid workers are still only able to access the lowest quality care. The subsidy does not level the playing field by ensuring that all children, regardless of family income, have access to high-quality, safe, and reliable care that prepares them for productive futures. Rather, it simply gives low-income families access to the market and may well contribute to depressed wages in that market. Low-income families face multiple disadvantages that may reproduce themselves in their children if they are unable to access better opportunities. Race, class, and gender intersect at all income levels to fundamentally shape workers' labor market participation and child care options. The child care choices and employment decisions faced by professional women are fundamentally different than those faced by low-level service workers.

THE GENDER OF CHILD CARE

Child care is a family issue, not a women's issue. However, the entire discussion surrounding child care revolves around the notion that women are responsible for children, and child care decisions that result from a woman's decision to work are therefore her responsibility. While increasing numbers of men now stay home to care for children, debates surrounding child care policy continue to employ gendered language. The gendered nature of the discussion is problematic, but it also reflects three important realities: (1) the gender gap in pay often means that women's wages are seen as supplemental to the family's income and therefore women's work is seen as optional, (2) the cultural reality that women are seen as primary care givers and are therefore held responsible for child care decisions and for any negative impacts that parental employment may have on children, and (3) the statistical prevalence of female-headed households among single parent households means that more women than men are solely responsible for child care decisions.

FAMILIES, STATES, AND MARKETS

Child care is a public good; it provides diffuse benefits to society as a whole. Child care provides early childhood education and socialization that produces social stability as children learn to interact and function in social groups. Quality child care programs can lower demand for special education as children move into school, lower juvenile delinquency and crime rates, produce a more stable and productive work-force, and produce higher educational attainment. The benefits of early childhood education and high-quality child care are innumerable, but the cultural and political debates that surround it create an atmosphere of tension.

Cultural values and images of the ideal mother and of the ideal childhood are challenged by images of young children spending much of their time in day care centers. After all, if the first three to five years of a child's life are the most important, parents should be with their children during those formative years. Research indicates, however, that children from low-income families that are able to access high-quality child care experience better outcomes in health and educational attainment than low-income children who are cared for at home during their preschool years. The assumption that a stay-at-home parent is always best does not hold. High-quality center-based care provides opportunities for socialization, education, and artistic stimulation that are difficult to replicate at home.

In addition to being a private family benefit and a public good with huge future returns, the child care industry is a key element in sustainable economic development as child care providers not only assist workers, but they are workers. Child care generates income for providers and thus spurs both institutional and individual spending in communities. Estimates of the economic impacts of quality child care vary, but recent economic models suggest that the development impact on a local economy for each dollar spent on child care is significant.

Despite the potential positive impacts of quality child care, the U.S. child care industry operates in a dysfunctional market. Market competition should create an environment where people will pay for quality and where supply and demand will intersect at a logical threshold price that meets the needs of buyers and sellers. This does not happen in child care. The problem is not a lack of demand, but rather the lack of *effective* demand. For many professional women with long work schedules and possible travel, private nannies present an option that best approximates the alternate reality of a stay-at-home mother. Because those who can afford to pay for high quality often choose this private, individualized route, their participation in the child care market does little to help build a viable market in high-quality center-based child care. The opportunity for high-earning families to cross-subsidize and demand quality care is lost. Those relying on center-based care are those most likely to face economic pressure to seek out the cheapest option rather than be discriminating buyers. They are unable to use their consumer dollars to effectively demand high-quality care.

One solution to a dysfunctional market is state support. In the United States public spending for anything thought to be personal in nature is not usually supported. We believe in personal responsibility, both for rearing our children and for paying others to help us rear our children. But child care is not simply a family dilemma. The private choices of families may revolve around personal values and individual needs, but these choices are also facilitated or constrained by market conditions because a family's location in the socioeconomic structure determines the choices available to them. Furthermore, decisions that families make are of great consequence to both the current and future economy.

Arguments in favor of increased government supports for quality child care need not look far for examples of how the state might play a role in the child care market. During World War II the federal government encouraged American women to support the war and keep the U.S. economy going by entering the labor force. The U.S. government offered state-sponsored child care and encouraged women to use it as an act of patriotism. When the war ended the state discontinued their extensive child care programs and encouraged women to return to their households so that veterans could reclaim their place in the labor market. The women who remained in the labor force after the war were primarily working-class or African American women; women whose needs and interests were not well-represented in state decision-making or in the women's movement that would follow just two decades later.

The social upheaval of the 1960s increased awareness of gender inequality and developed leadership and social movement skills among college women who were involved in the labor and civil rights movements of the time, and helped bring about the women's movement of the 1970s. Economic stagnation and rising inflation marked the late 1970s and early 1980s and working and middle-class families, feminist or not, found they needed two incomes to make ends meet and to ensure some measure of protection against unexpected layoffs. The women who made the greatest strides in the professions either made the decision to forego family for the liberation of career success or were earning enough money to hire full-time nannies to support their work outside the home. In the early days, the former was far more common than the latter. But poor families were not left in the dust. Head Start emerged as part of the war on poverty and served to offer a preschool option that would better prepare poor children to enter kindergarten on an even playing field, but it did not, and still does not, provide full-time child care. Moreover, access to Head Start requires that a family meet a low-income ceiling and space is limited. Between the extremes, high-earning women either with no children or with full-time nannies, poor women able to qualify for Head Start, and a remaining contingent of stay-at-home moms, a broad-based child care policy never gained significant traction. But child care did not simply suffer as a policy issue; the failure of business and political leaders to recognize the importance and necessity of quality child care for working families contributed to the creation of the dysfunctional market in child care.

CURRENT POLICY, DEBATES, AND FUTURE PROSPECTS

Ideological discussions of motherhood, childhood, gender, and family will continue, but working families, in both single-parent and two-parent households, are the current norm. Families that are able to and choose to have one parent stay home with their children during the early years may well enjoy great benefits for both parents and children. But under our current economic and policy structure, not all families have or can even make that choice and continue to maintain a decent standard of living. Child care policy will have to contend with this reality.

State support for child care currently takes the form of federal block grants to the states combined with state money, which the states disperse according to their child care subsidy, welfare, and grant-making policies. Federal grants focus on availability and quality. Private child care providers are able to package funds made available through a variety of programs including Temporary Aid to Needy Families, Community Development Block Grants, Head Start funds and federal food programs. Criteria for access to and use of these funds may vary by state, depending on the program. Subsidy rates are based on market analyses of the cost of child care. In some states, inconsistent updates to market studies mean that subsidies fall short of the basic costs to provide care. Subsidy shortfalls mean that centers are less likely to serve low-income families and those that do serve poor families bear the costs when parents cannot pay. In an industry with a dysfunctional market that already reaps low returns for the goods provided, child care centers whose primary clientele are low-income families are unable to maintain quality standards and in some cases are forced to close.

Policy discussions surrounding child care include a variety of options that accommodate a range of parenting and labor market choices. Some of these policies focus on building a functional market in child care through refundable tax credits for parents, increased state subsidies to better fund quality care, tying subsidies to quality standards to ensure that public dollars are spent on programs that will improve children's future performance in school and in their adult lives, and support for child care center operators in the form of small business planning and development programs. In order for the market for child care to be functional, there must be effective demand for quality.

In addition to supporting the demand for quality and the capacity for centers to provide quality care, public policy can provide incentives for improving the quality of the child care labor force. Because the market for child care is dysfunctional, pay is low and turnover is high. Under these conditions, the industry attracts an under-qualified low-skilled labor force. Several states currently support continuing education through licensing requirements and provide grants for child care staff to earn certification. The rewards are often too small to provide any significant incentive beyond personal improvement, and if child care centers and parents are unable to pay more for workers with more education and experience then there is little impetus to build either.

Some countries offer child allowances that acknowledge the public goods provided by those who choose to have children and to offset the costs of quality parenting regardless of child care choices. Under such programs, the allowance may be used to allow a family to forego one income for a year, or the family may use the allowance to purchase quality child care and continue to work. Such policies meet criticism from those who argue that parenthood is a personal choice and financial responsibility lies solely in the hands of those who choose to have children.

One current movement that has the capacity to fundamentally shift public policy, in favor of high-quality child care, is the pre-kindergarten movement for high-quality, universally available programs for four-year-olds. The so-called formative years rationale behind these programs requires that we think carefully about integrating our approach to infants and toddlers with our approach to four-year-old preschoolers and school-age kids. The period from birth to age three is the most important to human brain development. This scientific fact combined with market demand and current policy debates suggests that the time is right for major advancements in public support for our child care system. This shift brings its own set of debates around states and markets as policy makers, advocates, and child care providers wrestle over whether expanded services will be delivered through public schools, private child care providers, or some combination of the two.

CHILD CARE PROVIDES PUBLIC GOODS

Public goods have two properties: nonexcludability and nonrivalness. Nonexcludability means that there is no way to direct the goods exclusively to those who have paid for them. The problem of nonexcludability opens the door to free riders—people who enjoy the benefits of the goods without paying for them. Nonrivalness means that as one person consumes the goods, their use does not limit anyone else's use of the goods. "Many people share in the benefits when children are brought up to be responsible, skilled, and loving adults who treat each other with courtesy and respect" (England and Folbre 1999). To be clear, the public goods provided by child care include such things as a more highly educated workforce and citizenry, lower crime rates and a more reliable and productive workforce.

CONCLUSION

The social structures, institutions, organizations, and cultural ideologies that feed debates about child care policy in the twenty-first century provide an excellent example for understanding how history and biography intersect in the decisions and experiences of individuals. Child care does not fall neatly into either the public or the private sphere. The factors that shape individual family decisions are social and structural, as are the consequences of those family choices. Current child care policy seeks to address issues of access and quality, but fails to sufficiently support a market in quality child care. Proposals for supporting the child care market include a range of policies from per-child subsidies to system-wide extensions of our public education system to include the first five years of life. The decisions we make as a society will affect the lives of individuals, institutions, the labor market, and the social and cultural landscape of the United States.

As a society, we are responsible for the next generation of parents, partners, workers, and citizens; as an economy, we need a well-trained, healthy, and reliable workforce; and as a polity, we need strong and healthy citizens and future leaders. What we choose to do about child care may be one of the most important policy decisions we make as we plan for and manage economic development and democracy in the twenty-first century.

See also Day Care; Employed Mothers; Family and Medical Leave Act (FMLA); Mommy Track.

Further Reading: Blades, Joan, and Kristin Rowe-Finkbeiner. *The Motherhood Manifesto.* New York: Nation Books, 2006; Blau, David M. *The Child Care Problem: An Economic Analysis.* New York: Russell Sage Foundation, 2001; Caporaso, James A., and David P. Levine. *Theories of Political Economy.* New York: Cambridge University Press, 1992; Crittenden, Ann. *The Price of Motherhood: Why the Most Important Job in the World is Still the Least Valued.* New York: Henry Holt and Company, LLC, 2001; England, Paula and Nancy Folbre. "The Cost of Caring." *The Annals of the American Academy of Political and Social Sciences* 561 (1999): 39–51; Folbre, Nancy. "Rethinking the Child Care Sector." *Community Development* 37 (2006): 38–53; Fry Konty, Melissa, and

Jonathan Harrison. *Child Care in Appalachian Kentucky: Financial Sustainability in a Low-income Market.* Berea, KY: Mountain Association for Community Economic Development, 2007; Helburn, Suzanne Wiggons, and Barbara Bergmann. *America's Child Care Problem: The Way Out.* New York: Palgrave Macmillan, 2003; Kelly, Erin. "The Strange History of Employer-Sponsored Child Care: Interested Actors, Uncertainty, and the Transformation of Law in Organizational Fields." *American Journal of Sociology* 109 (2003): 606–649; Leavitt, Jacqueline. "Where's the Gender in Community Development?" *Journal of Women in Culture and Society* 29 (2003): 207–231; Meyers, Marcia K., and Janet C. Gornick. "Public or Private Responsibility? Early Childhood Education and Care, Inequality, and the Welfare State." *Journal of Comparative Family Studies* 34 (2003): 379–406; Peisner-Feinberg, E. S., M. R. Burchinal, R. M. Clifford, M. L. Culkin, C. Howes, S. L. Kagan, N. Yazehian, P. Byler, J. Rustici, and J. Zelazo. *The Children of the Cost, Quality, and Outcomes Study Go to School: Executive Summary.* Chapel Hill: University of North Carolina at Chapel Hill, Frank Porter Graham Child Development Center, 1999; Polakow, Valerie. *Who Cares for Our Children?* New York: Teachers College Press, 2007; Warner, Mildred. "Overview: Articulating the Economic Importance of Child Care for Community Development." *Community Development* 37 (2006): 1–6; Warner, Mildred, Shira Adriance, Nikita Barai, Jenna Hallas, Bjorn Markeson, Taryn Morrissey, and Wendy Soref. *Economic Development Strategies to Promote Quality Child Care.* Ithaca, NY: Cornell Cooperative Extension, 2004.

Melissa Fry Konty

CHILD SUPPORT AND PARENTAL RESPONSIBILITY

Over the past few decades America's thought and behavior toward so-called deadbeat parents has become more aggressive. Deadbeat parent is a pejorative term to describe parents who fail to take responsibility for their children's basic needs. Despite the broad definition of deadbeat, the use of the term has been limited to noncustodial parents, mainly fathers, who fail to take financial responsibility for their children, placing a heavy burden on the custodial parent. Parental responsibility, that is, caring for your children, is an important value in America. In fact, it is so important that President Clinton signed two major pieces of legislation regarding parental responsibility—the Personal Responsibility and Work Opportunity Reconciliation Act (PRWORA) of 1996 and the Deadbeat Parents Punishment Act (DPPA) of 1998. Both pieces of legislation seek to make parents more financially responsible for their children by setting strict child support enforcement rules and consequences, including imprisonment.

ENCOURAGING PARENTAL RESPONSIBILITY

Parental responsibility has a long history in the United States. Since the arrival of settlers in America, parental responsibility has always been at the heart of child support collections, having its foundations in the Elizabethan Poor Laws of 1601, sometimes referred to as the English Poor Laws. The English Poor Laws were a system of relief to the poor that was financed and administered at the local level.

Under the English Poor Laws, a father had a nonenforceable duty to support his children; child support was considered a civil matter. Although desertion was rare, when a man did desert his family, the local community would provide for the mother and child to prevent destitution. In return, local communities would attempt to recover from the father those monies spent in support of the mother and their child. The money collected from the father was put back into the poor relief system's reserves to be used for the next needy child.

However, the revolutionary changes brought about by the industrialization and urbanization of the nineteenth century also disrupted family processes. This move to greater mechanization in production and concentration of work in cities changed family life dramatically. For instance, many fathers were working in cities away from their families for long periods of time. Some scholars suggest that exposure to the city life, coupled with the relief from domestic duties of family life, may have played a role in some men abandoning their families, leaving many mothers and their children dependent on the state for survival. Therefore, it became necessary for courts to strengthen the child support system by formally making fathers financially responsible for the children they abandoned. States began to make child support a criminal matter by establishing a legally enforceable child support duty. Desertion and nonsupport statutes were passed that criminalized and punished fathers for refusing to support their child, especially if the mother and child were recipients of public child support.

Although states improved their efforts to enforce child support obligations and to reduce public child support expenditures, parental irresponsibility continued to be problematic. A host of destitute mothers and children were overwhelming the public welfare services as some fathers and husbands moved from one state to another to avoid their parental responsibility for child support. In the mid-twentieth century, the Uniform Reciprocal Enforcement of Support Act implemented federal guidelines that made fathers who moved from state to state to avoid child support still responsible for their children through both civil and criminal enforcement. Yet, the confusion between states regarding the jurisdiction of child support provided irresponsible fathers with a means to continue avoiding their child support obligations.

States, the federal government, and children's rights advocates persisted in their effort to make parental responsibility a national initiative. Consequently, PRWORA emphasized parental responsibility for the financial support of their children as well as implemented more aggressive enforcement techniques and some additional provisions that unified state collection efforts. DPPA made it a federal offense for a noncustodial parent to willfully fail to pay a past-due child support obligation due to a child residing in another state.

FATHER'S CONCERNS

Many Americans have reservations about the punitive nature of child support enforcement legislation. These critics argue that the legislation assumes that these deadbeat dads are able to pay the court ordered child support, when in fact many of them are unable to pay their child support, especially when it is coupled with steep interest charges for falling behind. In addition, some ask the question, "How does it benefit the child or the state to throw the father in jail for defaulting on child support they cannot pay?" Each incarceration for child support noncompliance lessens the father's chances of obtaining gainful employment that can be to the benefit of the child. Moreover, incarcerating these fathers adds to jail overcrowding. In addition to questioning the wisdom of incarcerating parents for failure to pay child support, fathers' rights activists suggest that child support enforcement is not distributed equally. While there is little data on the incidence of deadbeat dad incarceration, activists contend that fathers are incarcerated disproportionately more than are mothers.

Another issue of concern, especially among fathers' rights activists, is that the national initiative to make parents, especially fathers, pay is limited in its focus. Because maternal custody is awarded more often than paternal custody in this nation, it is fathers who would be the most affected by the recent parental responsibility legislation. However, some activists insist that any discussion of parental responsibility must take into account other ways of demonstrating parental irresponsibility, to which mothers are more susceptible; yet mothers are not incarcerated, to a large degree, for these behaviors. In fact, activists argue that the laws that govern these irresponsible behaviors seek to work with families by providing support in various forms to keep the family together.

One irresponsible behavior that activists identify is baby abandonment. Baby abandonment is when an infant under the age of 12 months is discarded or left alone for an extended period of time in a public or private setting with the intention of disposing of the baby. In 1998, 30,800 babies were abandoned in hospitals, a 43 percent increase from 1991. That same year, 105 babies were abandoned in public settings, a 62 percent increase from 1991. While all states have laws that prohibit leaving babies unsupervised and unprotected, there are only 28 states that have baby abandonment laws. Baby abandonment laws tend to focus on providing a process for legally abandoning a child, with the intent of giving parents an avenue to safely turn over their child to a third party. States hope that such laws will encourage responsible behavior among those individuals not willing or able to care for their babies by assuring that the child is left safely in the hands of caretakers who can provide appropriate care. Yet, fathers' rights activists suggest that this response to parental irresponsibility gives mothers a legitimate way out of being responsible for their children, while no such law exists for fathers who owe child support.

Child neglect is another form of parental irresponsibility that is not treated as punitively as is defaulting on child support payments. It is the most common form of child maltreatment reported to child protective services. Child neglect is a type of maltreatment that refers to the failure to provide needed age-appropriate care, such as shelter, food, clothing, education, supervision, medical care, and other basic necessities for the development of physical, intellectual, and emotional capacities. Child neglect is closely correlated with poverty, with the majority of cases of child maltreatment occurring at the hands of mother. A major assumption underlying the child protection law governing child neglect is that living in a permanent family relationship is in the best interest of children. Therefore, the law seeks to promote and protect that kind of living situation for all children. In seeking to simultaneously protect children and support families, mothers are offered a variety of services to assist in developing their parenting skills. In addition, other services are offered to help lift the family out of poverty. Fathers' rights advocates argue that men are offered limited services to assist them in finding gainful employment, and when those services are offered, fines and penalties still accrue to the amount of support owed, thus making it difficult to catch up on child support obligations.

Finally, some activists have pointed to infanticide as another form of a mother failing to take responsibility for her children. Homicide is the fifteenth leading cause of infant death in the United States, with the most homicides occurring during the first four months of life. With little ability to abort an unwanted pregnancy safely, some troubled parents may have little choice but to wait until full-term delivery before disposing of the conception. In these cases, the overwhelming majority of the perpetrators were mothers, many of whom were later criminally convicted. However, activists have pointed out that millions of unwanted pregnancies result in abortions each year. The focus is not on the issue of abortion itself, but that mothers have the right to choose not to be responsible for their child, without fear of penalty, while fathers are penalized for their inability to pay child support obligations.

POVERTY AND PARENTAL IRRESPONSIBILITY

Parental irresponsibility is a social problem that, in many cases, is linked to other more persistent social issues. Infanticide, child neglect, baby abandonment, and noncompliance with child support have been found to be related to factors such as poverty, unemployment, low educational attainment, and drug or alcohol abuse. What's more, despite the controversy over how to define poverty in either absolute or relative terms, strong correlations exist between all of the above factors and poverty. In fact, unemployment, low educational attainment, and drug or alcohol abuse can be both the cause and effect of poverty. Absolute poverty refers to the numbers of persons below a specified income level where they cannot meet their basic needs. Relative poverty refers to how a group compares to the median income of the society.

The issue of poverty in the United States has been debated for decades. There has been debate over how poverty is defined. Because poverty measures can be either absolute or relative, advocates for a relative measure of poverty believe that poverty statistics are overstated, while proponents for an absolute measure of poverty argue that statistics are often understated. Despite the definition of poverty, the effect of poverty in the lives of millions of Americans, including their ability to successfully parent their children, is real. Hence, America has to come to terms with how we will handle poverty, so that American citizens, especially children, will have better life chances and life choices.

PARENTAL RESPONSIBILITY: ANOTHER VIEW

Fathers' rights activists' concern for equal treatment in child support enforcement as well as the expansion of deadbeat to include mothers whose behaviors can be considered irresponsible spawns much debate. However, child advocates are mainly concerned with ensuring the health and well-being of children and thus parental behaviors that promote the well-being of children are seen as good. Like fathers' rights activists, child rights advocates do hold our social institutions partly responsible for creating an environment that is conducive to healthy parenting and parental responsibility.

Shared Parenting

Recognizing that divorce does occur, child advocates support shared parenting, which has been shown to have significant benefits for children. Shared parenting helps provide emotional stability for children by promoting the involvement of both parents. There are two aspects to shared parenting in divorce: joint legal custody, which refers to shared decision-making responsibility between divorced parents, and joint physical custody, which provides children with a more balanced living arrangement than was allowed under sole custody. With joint physical custody, children spend at least 33 percent of their time with each parent. Presently, about 30 states have case law statutes that are compatible with shared parenting.

Child Neglect

Although the full extent of child maltreatment is not known, based on information from child protective services, child maltreatment is a serious problem for some families. Of reported cases of child maltreatment, the majority are child neglect cases. Child advocates support child abuse prevention and education programs that work directly with parents and community leaders to strengthen and hold families together. In addition, efforts are focused on support legislation that is in the best interests of the children and the families. Child advocates argue that through prevention, education, and research families will receive the services needed to navigate the challenges of family life. Moreover, if at-risk parents can be identified, we will reduce the need to remove children from their homes or to place parents in jail for violent behavior.

Baby Abandonment

Child advocates agree that baby abandonment is a problem in the United States based on the data we do have available. Child advocates argue that mothers who abandon babies are often experiencing social, economic, and psychological difficulties that interfere with their ability to adequately provide for a child. With a focus on the health and well-being of children, advocates support so-called safe haven laws that allow a parent to anonymously leave an unwanted newborn baby in a safe place, such as a hospital, emergency medical services, police station, or fire station, and not have to worry about getting in trouble with law enforcement. The baby is then given to the state's child welfare department to find a loving family environment for the child.

Unfortunately, young mothers who typically abandon babies are not very well informed about safe haven laws; therefore, the evidence available suggests that such laws have not impacted the number of babies being abandoned in unsafe places. Child advocates are in favor of increased publicity, so that people are aware of this option to help ensure that unwanted babies are left in a safe place and not abandoned where they may not be found until it is too late.

Infanticide

Unwanted pregnancies and unwanted births are particularly difficult for mothers. Child advocates note the correlation between infanticide and a host of social problems, such as poverty, alienation (living in rural areas), low level of education and employment, alcoholism, drug abuse, or other criminal behavior. Infanticide is classified as a homicide. Depending on state laws, those who commit infanticide may be eligible for the death penalty. Most of the mothers convicted are granted suspended sentences or probation; however, fathers are generally not afforded the same leniency.

Prevention of infanticide is difficult. Several scholars argue that the legalization of abortion has resulted in decreased rates of infanticide. Yet pro-life supporters contend that abortion is infanticide. Given that many abortions are available but not utilized, some suggest that the best form of prevention for young women most at risk for neonaticide (killing of a newborn) is abstinence or effective contraceptive use.

See also African American Fathers; Deadbeat Parents; Divorce and Children; Foster Care; Poverty and Public Assistance.

Further Reading: Alliance for Non-custodial Parents' Rights. http://www.ancpr.org; Chichetti, Dante, and Vicki Carlson. *Child Maltreatment: Theory and Research on the Causes and Consequences of Child Abuse and Neglect.* New York: Cambridge University Press, 1997; Child Welfare League of America. http://www.cwla.org; Downs, Susan Whitelaw, Ernestine Moore, Emily Jean McFadden, and Susan Michaud. *Child Welfare and Family Services: Policies and Practices,* 7th ed. Boston: Allyn-Bacon, 2003; Father's Rights. http://www.fathersrightsinc.com; Gross, James J. *Fathers' Rights: A Legal Guide to Protecting the Best Interests of Your Children.* Naperville, IL: Sphinx Legal Publishing, 2004; Spinelli, Margaret G. *Infanticide: Psychosocial and Legal Perspectives on Mothers Who Kill.* Arlington, VA: American Psychiatric Publishing, 2002.

Annice Yarber

CHILDBIRTH OPTIONS

Among women in the United States there is increasing talk about the choices that they have and would like to have regarding childbirth. U.S. women have many options for how to give birth. Women can decide to give birth in a hospital, birth center, or at home. They can choose to have a doctor or a midwife as their primary healthcare provider. They can decide to give birth naturally, meaning without the use of pain-relief medications, or they can choose to use medications to reduce pain. Beyond these considerations about medical issues, women face increasing choices about the details of the birth, from whom they would like to attend the birth to whether the newborn stays with the mother or in the hospital nursery. As mothers have started to demand more control over the birthing setting and process, a childbirth industry has started to emerge to accommodate their wishes. One of the most important decisions a woman can make that determines the type of birth she will have is selecting a healthcare provider.

CHOICES OF CHILDBIRTH HEALTH CARE PROVIDERS

The choice of healthcare provider is important because there are certain assumptions that each provider brings to the birth event. The philosophy of birth followed by the health care provider can be an important part of a woman's overall plan for how she would like the birth to proceed. One of the critical elements in how much choice the woman has, however, is whether her pregnancy is considered low- or high-risk. A pregnancy is defined as low-risk when the mother is pregnant with only one child (no twins or multiple births) and the mother does not have any serious illnesses that will interfere with her ability to give birth. For a birth to qualify as low-risk, the mother must begin labor when she is between 37 and 43 weeks gestation. Women who do not meet the qualifications of low-risk must seek care from a physician.

For most women in the United States, their first choice for care is from an obstetrician, a medical doctor who specializes in providing care for pregnant, laboring, birthing, and postpartum women. Obstetricians usually provide healthcare for women birthing in hospitals, so most women who chose an obstetrician will give birth in a hospital or other clinical setting. Some internal medicine and family medicine physicians also attend to birthing women, although their ranks are declining due to the push to specialize and the increasing malpractice insurance premiums for those who assist at births.

Some women in the United States choose to give birth with a midwife. Midwives are healthcare providers who are trained to assist women while they are pregnant, in labor, giving birth, and postpartum, but they are not medical doctors. There are two types of midwives: nurse midwives and certified professional midwives. Nurse midwives are trained as nurses first and then obtain additional training in midwifery. They are required by law to work under the supervision of a medical doctor. Most nurse midwives work in hospitals or birth centers that are affiliated with hospitals. Some nurse midwives work in free-standing birth centers that are not affiliated with hospitals. Very few nurse midwives work in home-birth practices. Certified professional midwives are also called professional midwives, direct-entry midwives, or licensed midwives, and are trained only in midwifery. They are not required to work under the supervision of a doctor, and generally work in free-standing birth centers and home-birth practices rather than in hospitals. Only women who have low-risk pregnancies are allowed by law to give birth in an out-of-hospital setting with a midwife. Some hospitals may allow women with high-risk pregnancies to be cared for by both a nurse midwife and an obstetrician. This option depends on the availability of nurse midwives and the routine practices of the hospital. A high risk pregnancy is one in which there is a better than average chance that medical intervention in the birth will be necessary.

DIFFERING BIRTH EXPERIENCES

One of the most significant differences between the medical and midwifery models of care is the experiences women have when they are in labor and giving birth. When a woman is admitted to a hospital in labor, one of the first occurrences is that she is given an intravenous infusion (IV). The purpose of the IV is to provide the woman with adequate nutrients and hydration throughout her labor and birth. The medical model of care uses IV because food and water can negatively interact with anesthesia that may be used in the event of a cesarean section. Most women who give birth within the medical model are not allowed to eat or drink during labor and birth. Midwives encourage women to eat and drink during labor, comparing labor to a marathon during which one needs sustenance.

Laboring women in hospitals are usually also connected to an electronic fetal monitor, a device that measures the baby's heart rate, and a device that measures the strength and length of contractions. Both the baby's heart rate and the woman's contractions are visible on a screen in the hospital room. Midwives typically use fetal monitors to measure the baby's heart rate only at certain times throughout labor rather than continuously. Midwives do not use contraction monitors because they believe that they can tell the strength and length of a woman's contractions by paying attention to the woman's verbal and nonverbal cues (e.g., facial expressions, sounds, movements, etc.). Midwives also say monitors can distract people's attention to the screen instead of focusing on the laboring woman.

Women laboring in hospitals are usually confined to a hospital bed. Because women are hooked up to an IV, fetal monitor, and contraction monitor, it is difficult for them to move around. Midwives typically encourage their clients to move around during labor. They encourage women to walk, bathe, and move in any way that they want. Because midwifery clients are not attached to any devices, they can move about freely.

The medical model of care suggests that women should be in labor for a total of 12 hours. They believe that a woman's cervix should dilate at least one centimeter each hour (full dilation is ten centimeters), and the woman should push for no more than two hours. If a woman does not labor according to this timeframe (called the Freedman's Curve), medical technologies are often used to speed up the labor. The most common medical technologies used to speed the pace of labor are synthetic hormones, such as pitocin, commonly administered through an IV. The midwifery model, however, believes that each woman's body is different and uses a different timeframe to labor and give birth. As long as both the woman and her baby are healthy, midwives typically will not interfere with the pace of labor or birth.

Medical and midwifery models of care also differ in their pain management techniques. Women who give birth in the medical model are typically offered medication to relieve the pain of labor contractions. The most common pain relief medication is epidural anesthesia, a continuous anesthesia that is administered through a needle inserted between two vertebrae in the lower part of the woman's spine. Epidural anesthesia numbs the woman from her waist down, which reduces or eliminates the pain she feels from uterine contractions. Midwives encourage women to use nonmedical forms of pain relief. Women who give birth with midwives often use water, such as a bath, shower, or heated massage bath, to reduce pain. Other pain relieving techniques midwives encourage include physical movement (such as walking or rocking), heating pads, massage, aromatherapy, homeopathy, herbal remedies, or teas. Some midwives even use acupuncture, acupressure, or hypnosis.

Women in hospitals typically give birth in the supine position—lying on their back with their feet in stirrups. Midwives allow women to give birth in whatever position they feel is most comfortable, typically encouraging women to try giving birth in a position that works with gravity, such as standing, squatting or sitting. Some midwives have special stools or birth balls that women can sit on or lean against when giving birth. Some midwives also encourage women to give birth in water, such as in a bathtub. As interest in these methods has increased, some hospitals have begun to offer water births for their low-risk patients.

A procedure commonly used in hospitals is episiotomy. An episiotomy is a small incision that is cut through the skin and muscle tissue between the vagina and anus, or perineum, to enlarge the space through which babies exit women's bodies. Some doctors perform episiotomies as a regular part of all childbirths, although this as a routine practice is decreasing. Midwives argue that because women's bodies were created to stretch during childbirth, episiotomies are not necessary for most women. Midwives perform episiotomies only in the rare circumstance that a woman's perineum is not stretching adequately to release the baby from her body.

Women who give birth within the medical model are more likely to have their babies extracted from their bodies by the use of forceps, vacuum extraction, or cesarean section than women who give birth within the midwifery model of care. The fact that more high-risk pregnancies are attended by obstetricians might also play a role in the use of these medical interventions. Forceps are metal devices shaped like salad tongs that are enclosed around a baby's head and used to help pull the baby out of the birth canal. Vacuum extraction is when a suction device is attached to a baby's head to help suction the baby out of the birth canal. A cesarean section is a surgical procedure where a baby is removed from a woman's body through an incision that is cut through the woman's abdomen and uterus. While women do not generally expect to have these types of procedures, with the notable exception in elective cesarean sections, it is important that they consider what options they would like used first in the event intervention becomes necessary. Women birthing in hospitals are more likely to need these technologies to help them give birth because they are more likely to use epidural anesthesia. Epidural anesthesia numbs a woman's body from the waist down, which makes it more difficult for her to push a baby out of her body. Women who give birth with midwives rely on their own physical strength to push the baby through the birth canal. Because women who give birth within the midwifery model of care do not use pain relief medications, they are able to use their whole bodies to give birth.

After women weigh the above information, they must decide what the right combination of provider and birth setting is for them. About eight percent of births today are attended by a midwife, but this has significantly increased since the early 1970s when only one percent of women were attended by a midwife. Women who use a midwife tend to feel more knowledgeable about and more in control of their choices and more satisfied with their delivery decisions.

CHOICES OF PAIN CONTROL

One of the most ubiquitous ideas about childbirth in the United States is that it is a painful experience. Many women fear having children because of the pain associated with labor contractions and giving birth. The choice to intervene in pain is, however, quite controversial. Some in the natural childbirth and midwifery camp would go so far as to suggest that pain medication dampens the whole birth experience making for a second-rate delivery. They are critical of women who have pain medication in all but the most extreme circumstances. On the other hand, physician Gilbert Grant at New York University Medical Center has argued that opposition to women receiving pain medication, specifically epidurals, in child birth is misogynistic because there is no other situation in medicine where pain relief is routinely withheld.

Medical Pain Control

Physicians and pharmacists have been able to develop methods of pain relief that permit the laboring woman to be awake and aware, but to not feel pain. This has been one of the most attractive elements of hospital birth. The availability of medical technologies that reduce pain from labor and birth help some women feel comfortable and confident about the childbearing process. Many women today, however, are seeking even greater choices in pain relief. The most common strategy today, epidural anesthesia is very effective at reducing pain, but does not permit mobility, often for some time after the birth.

Prepared Childbirth

Prepared childbirth, also known as natural childbirth was popularized by Grantly Dick-Read in the 1970s. Dick-Read suggested that fear, a common element in childbirth, would cause a woman's muscles to tense, thus increasing the pain and stress experienced during childbirth. He argued that the more informed women were about the process of birth and the more they were educated on the stages and likely experiences the more likely they would be to control the stress responses. Thus, teaching women relaxation techniques and tension-reducing exercises would make labor and birth less painful. A predecessor of Dick-Read, Ferdinand Lamaze, focused on the idea of conditioned reflexes as an element of labor and delivery pain. He suggested that teaching women to mentally separate the physical stimulus of uterine contractions from the conditioned response of pain would make labor and birth much less uncomfortable. The breathing exercises that Lamaze developed have been incorporated into more modern prepared childbirth classes. These classes, often attended by both partners, do help laboring women handle pain more successfully in that those who have had the courses use less medication and express more satisfaction with the birth process. Another pioneer in this area, Robert Bradley, is know for the Bradley Method in which fathers take a pivotal role as child birth coaches for their laboring partners.

WITNESSES TO THE BIRTH

Among the choices arising in recent years involves who should be present at the birth. While home births have been attended by whomever the laboring woman wished to have present, hospital births have been limited by who was permitted to attend. Obviously medical staff would be present, but what about the woman's partner, or the children she had previously birthed, family members, or hired help?

As part of the natural childbirth movement of the 1970s, fathers were encouraged to be in the delivery room with their wives. Some physicians were at first reluctant to permit this because the delivery room was a sterile environment that might be contaminated by the father's presence. It has become standard practice in the United States for fathers to be in attendance, even at cesarean births. This was historically not the case. When most women were sedated for delivery, fathers were isolated in a waiting area while they anticipated the physician's pronouncement of the child's sex and safe arrival. The presence of fathers can be particularly helpful to laboring mothers and establish a positive tone to parenting. When fathers are nervous about being present, however, they can increase the mother's stress.

There is an increasing movement to provide paid assistance to mothers during labor and birth. Doulas are birthing assistants, sometimes referred to as labor coaches. However, they are present in addition to a woman's partner, not in place of the partner. They are not physicians, nurses, nor midwives, but women who act as private labor assistants, tending to the comfort of the mother. The doula, a Greek word that means in support of, provides encouragement and support that can extend even after the birth. An international organization for doulas, Doulas of North America (DONA), indicates that the women are trained as resources for pregnant and laboring women, providing information on choices during labor and delivery on a whole host of topics. Movement, relaxation, breathing, and positioning are just a few of the pieces of advice that doulas might provide. DONA also certifies doulas through a 16-hour course.

One of the tasks of a doula is to provide continuous emotional support and encouragement. This means that unlike nursing staff that might change shift during the course of a woman's labor, the doula stays with the laboring woman for as long as the process takes. While the practice of having women attend birth in a supportive capacity is centuries old, it is enjoying a heightened interest in the United States. While only a few hospitals provide doulas, nearly all permit them to attend births, though there is some resistance. Doula fees range from $200 to $800 depending on region and demand. The price is well worth the service when one considers that births attended by doulas have lower rates of medication use, cesarean sections, and other minor complications.

ROLE OF HEALTH INSURANCE IN CHILDBIRTH OPTIONS

The United States is the only developed country in the world that does not have a nationwide health care system. Health insurance is mainly provided by a citizen's employer. The average American, however, has three to five careers and from 10 to 12 jobs. Americans' fluctuating careers and the dozen different jobs they are expected to hold in a lifetime lead to a dizzying number of different insurance plans, providers, benefits and deductibles. As of 2005 over 46.6 million Americans lacked health insurance. This figure is especially surprising because the United States has the priciest healthcare in the world. Health care expense is due to the rising cost of medical technology, prescriptions, and high administrative costs. The uninsured also contribute to these costs because they often refuse to seek care at the start of illness and then are forced to use emergency services that cost more than routine care. Even those middle-class Americans with HMOs (health maintenance organizations) have limited choices in which doctors they can see or what treatments are allowed. HMOs have been accused of influencing doctor decisions in treatment plans and even initial diagnosis if it would mean greater cost.

America's healthcare system has a great impact on post- and prematernity care. Those who are uninsured or on strict managed health care plans rarely, if ever, have a choice in the obstetricians they see or in the clinics or hospitals in which they can give birth. Very few private health insurance companies will pay for births that take place in out-of-hospital settings. Only 9 of 24 states where professional midwifery is legal and regulated will allow women to pay for professional midwife-assisted births with Medicaid funds. Thus, many women who choose to give birth with professional midwives must pay out of their own pockets for their healthcare. Because not all women can afford to pay for healthcare expenses, a woman's financial status limits her childbirth options. Upper-class women are afforded more attention and greater freedom in choosing their providers when giving birth.

MEDIATING THE CHOICES: THE BIRTH PLAN

Many pregnancy guides and Internet parenting sites encourage pregnant women to create a birth plan. It is a document that allows a woman to express her wishes for an ideal birth experience and includes useful data that can help the physician or midwife determine the best care for the laboring woman. The primary benefit of a birth plan is in discussing the options and contingencies in advance. Given the range of options in childbirth today, considering one's preferences is probably a very smart thing to do. Not only can the woman and her partner consider how they would like the birth to go, the birth attendant can discuss with them what is most likely to occur. It is recommended that a copy of the birth plan go to the physician or midwife, to the hospital or birth center, and kept with the woman's partner.

Topics commonly covered in a birth plan include who the woman would like to have present at the birth and who she would not like to have attend, which might include students and interns if it is a teaching institution. Provisions for photography, music, lighting, food, and other environmental elements are usually included. Additionally, there are places to specify one's preferred medical treatment, such as no IV fluids, intermittent fetal monitoring, permission to labor as long as neither the mother nor baby are experiencing distress, and so forth. These plans also discuss attitudes toward pain management, attitudes toward episiotomy, and contingencies for a cesarean section. Issues related to the baby are also likely to be included, such as viewing the birth with a mirror, breastfeeding, rooming in, and, in the case of a male child, circumcision.

A criticism of birth plans is that they give the woman a sense of control that realistically may not exist in most pregnancies. There has yet to be a birth that proceeded exactly according to plan. However, some women may feel quite troubled if their labor and delivery does not proceed according to the map that they have created. Rather than enjoying the birth, they focus on how things went awry. This is why they are encouraged to focus on the end product, their amazing new baby, rather than the path to get there.

FUTURE OF CHILDBIRTH OPTIONS

In recent years families have demanded that hospitals reconsider their policies regarding birth as well as the environment in which the birth occurs. Hospitals have been quick to respond, making birthing rooms more homelike, comfortable, and attractive. Additionally they have loosened restrictions about who can be present in the room for the birth. Many options for low-risk births include laboring in water, alternative positions for delivery, and staying in one room for the whole labor, delivery, and postpartum time. Hospital nurseries and neonatal services have also been revamped in line with the increasing demands of mothers. Increased security measures have been instituted after media reports of strangers and even some nurses walking out of hospitals with patients' newborns. New mothers often have the option of keeping their infants in the room with them, rather than having to call the nursery for visits with their own child. The practice of rooming-in allows the mother and child ready access for breastfeeding and starts the bonding process. These patterns of choice are likely to be expanded as older first-time mothers, who have a clearer image of their desired experience of childbirth, demand the services, and constitute a significant percentage of those giving birth in American hospitals.

For women who might choose to use a midwife instead of an obstetrician, the legal status of midwifery might limit their options. While nurse midwifery is legal in every state, certified midwifery is not. Certified midwifery is legal and regulated by the government in 24 states. Fourteen states either have laws that are interpreted to mean that midwifery is legal but not governmentally regulated, or have no laws defining midwifery as either legal or illegal. Two states have laws that say midwifery is legal with a specific state licensure that is not actually available. Ten states and the District of Columbia have laws that specifically prohibit the practice of professional midwifery. This means that women must live in a state that allows the practice of professional midwifery in order to give birth with a professional midwife. Even in states where professional midwifery is legal, midwifery services are not offered in all communities. As more women pursue care in this format, laws regarding midwifery will likely be challenged.

Given the suggestion by some choice advocates that childbirth is at a crossroads in the United States today, American women are demanding more options and choices of services in conjunction with the birth event. Women want the technological interventions when medically necessary, but want to maintain as much autonomy as possible about deciding when to employ them. Of increasing concern to women is the decline in physicians who are willing to deliver babies. As a result of costly malpractice suits and hefty insurance premiums, many physicians have decided to no longer delivery babies, resulting in few options for women when they select an obstetrician.

See also Midwifery and Medicalization; Transition to Parenthood.

Further Reading: American Pregnancy Association. http://www.americanpregnancy.org; Baby Center. www.babycenter.com; Davis-Floyd, Robbie E. *Birth as an American Rite of Passage.* Berkeley, CA: University of California Press, 2004; Doulas of North America. http://www.dona.org; Goer, Henci. *Obstetric Myths Versus Research Realities: A Guide to the Medical Literature.* Westport, CT: Bergin and Garvey, 1995; Goer, Henci. *The Thinking Woman's Guide to a Better Birth.* New York: Perigee, 1999; Grant, Gilbert. *Enjoy Your Labor: A New Approach to Pain Relief for Childbirth.* White Plains, NY: Russell Hastings Press, Ltd., 2005; Kitzinger, Sheila. *The Complete Book of Pregnancy and Childbirth,* 4th ed. New York: Knopf, 2003; Mitford, Jessica. *The American Way of Birth.* New York: Penguin, 1992; Rooks, Judith Pence. *Midwifery and Childbirth in America.* Philadelphia: Temple University Press, 1997; Sears, William, and Martha Sears. *The Birth Book: Everything You Need to Know to Have a Safe and Satisfying Birth.* New York: Little, Brown, and Co., 1994; Sears, William, and Martha Sears. *The Pregnancy Book: A Month-by-Month Guide.* New York: Little, Brown, and Co., 1997; Simkin, Penny. *Pregnancy, Childbirth and the Newborn, Revised and Updated: The Complete Guide.* Minnetonka, MN: Meadowbrook Press, 2001.

Kimberly P. Brackett

CHILDFREE RELATIONSHIPS

In today's society there are many diverse options a person can choose in life. A lifestyle choice that is quickly gaining popularity and attention is the childfree lifestyle. Childfree is a social movement that includes men and women who do not want children, either biologically or through adoption. There are many issues childfree individuals deal with on personal and societal levels. The childfree movement is becoming a more accepted lifestyle choice, although many who choose to remain voluntarily childless must still face misunderstanding and criticism from some within society.

WHAT IS CHILDFREE?

The term childfree was coined by Leslie Lafayette in the 1990s and is used to describe a person who does not ever want to have children, whether biologically or through adoption. Lafayette created the Childfree Network, which was formed to be a group for childfree individuals. Childfree individuals distinguish themselves from those who are considered childless because the childfree feel that the term childless denotes that something is missing, whereas those who consider themselves to be childfree are voluntarily without children and feel no sense of loss. Childfree individuals feel that their lives are just as fulfilling and rewarding as the lives of parents.

There are many different reasons why individuals choose to be childfree. Medical, personal, environmental, financial, and religious explanations are commonly given as reasons by the childfree when asked about their choice to not have children. Most childfree individuals do not have only one reason for their decision, because deciding whether or not to have children is a complex one. There are also many issues that are of great concern to childfree men and women worldwide, including reproduction, contraception, inequalities within the workplace, and social issues that affect them on a daily basis.

There is no cookie-cutter mold of what a childfree person is or is not. Some childfree individuals are well educated and have lucrative careers, while others may have less formal education and modest career aspirations. Some childfree men and women are rich, while others are poor. Some who consider themselves to be childfree know early in their lives that they do not wish to have children, while others may decide later in life that they do not want to become parents.

Probably the most important point about a childfree lifestyle is that not all childfree individuals dislike children. Today's society has a very negative perception of persons who are childfree as being child-haters who disdain all children. Many times it is actually the bad behavior of children that childfree people feel frustrated with, not the children themselves. The reality is that some more militant childfree people do not like children, but there are also many childfree people who do like children and enjoy being around them. The choice to remain childfree is a complex one with many different variations.

The common denominator among the childfree is the desire to never have children. Although there are many distinctions among the childfree, statistics and studies have shown that men and women who choose to be childfree are generally well educated people who live in urban areas of the United States. Childfree women are often very career-oriented and may hold professional positions in their workplace. According to a report published in June 2002 by the Fertility of American Women, 44 percent of women 15 to 44 years of age were childless and 71 percent of those childless women were members of the labor force. These numbers, while they do not distinguishing childless from childfree, show that many women without children are entering and participating in the workforce.

WHAT IS CHILDLESS?

Childless individuals are those who do not currently have children, but would like to in the future. The term childless includes those who wish to have biological children at some later point in life and also those who choose to adopt. Childfree men and women make a point to distinguish themselves from those who are considered childless and do not consider themselves to be in the same situation as childless individuals.

WHAT IS A FENCE SITTER?

A fence sitter is a person who has not decided whether or not he or she wants to have children. Fence sitters are not considered childfree because they have not made the decision to not ever have children. Fence sitters are also not considered childless, because childless individuals eventually want children.

REASONS FOR REMAINING CHILDFREE

There are many reasons cited by childfree individuals explaining their choice to remain childless by choice. Some individuals know from an early age that they want to be parents and conversely many childfree individuals know from a very early age that they do not want to have children. Other men and women decide later in life that they do not want to be parents. The reasons are numerous and varied but they are all valid explanations for choosing to remain childfree.

Medical Reasons

The first reason given by childfree individuals when asked why they do not want children deals with medical problems. Childfree people who have hereditary diseases or mental disorders do not want to pass on their disorders to any child. Those childfree individuals who have lived through the pain of hereditary disorders of any kind realize that they could pass on the same pain to a child. Some common medical disorders are diabetes, depression, and other hereditary diseases.

There are also childfree men and women who are unable to have children for various reasons and choose not to adopt. Women who are unable to carry a pregnancy to term may choose to become childfree because of their medical condition. For other childfree women, pregnancy may be an option but due to risks and complications caused by various health problems it is recommended that these women not become pregnant. Some childfree women are simply incapable of becoming pregnant. Some childfree men are also sterile and are unable to impregnate their significant other.

Another physical reason given by childfree individuals as to why they do not want children has to do with pregnancy itself. The damage that can be done to a woman's body during pregnancy is a deterrent to having children for many women within the childfree community. The distended stomach of the pregnant woman, stretch marks, changes in the breasts, and damage done to the reproductive system during childbirth are all reasons that some childfree women cite. There are also childfree individuals who are disgusted by the whole pregnancy and childbirth experience. While some people may see pregnancy and childbirth as a beautiful and natural experience there are those who do not share the same feelings about the process of becoming a parent.

Personal Reasons

Some childfree persons are also concerned that they will not enjoy being a parent, which is an irreversible decision. The idea of not enjoying children may seem strange to some people, but childfree individuals feel that it is better to realize their feelings before a child is born than to decide later that they do not wish to be a parent. Childfree individuals may feel that they cannot be effective and responsible parents and decide to remain childless. There are also childfree men and women who feel that their relationship with their significant other could suffer if children were introduced into the relationship. Many childfree individuals value the intimate relationship with their partner and do no want to jeopardize their relationship.

The desire to concentrate on careers is another reason cited by childfree individuals when explaining why they do not want to have children. Many childfree individuals feel that having a child would reduce their ability to advance within their career field. Because many childfree individuals are well-educated they can be very focused on their work and do not want to jeopardize any future career opportunities. Childfree individuals have the ability to change their career or their city of residence easily because they are not tied to any one area. This can become an important factor for career-oriented individuals because many jobs require frequent moves and business trips.

The long hours required for many careers also play into the decision not to have children. Men and women who are fully committed to their career feel that they do not have time to be a devoted parent so they opt not to have children. Parents often have to take time off work because of their children and childfree workers do not want to do this. A time constraint due to work obligations is an important factor that is taken into consideration by those deciding whether or not they truly want to become a parent.

Volunteering with organizations that give the individual a rewarding sense of accomplishment have also been cited as a reason for remaining childfree. Childfree men and women who choose to devote their lives to philanthropic pursuits often feel that they are fulfilled by helping others. There are childfree individuals who volunteer with many charitable organizations and use their energy, time, and resources to help those in their communities.

Childfree men and women also value their independence and carefree lifestyle. Many childfree people do not wish to change the way their life is structured in order to have children. Having a child takes sacrifice that many childfree do not feel is worth the reward. Some childfree individuals also prefer the company of adults to the company of children; therefore, they do not feel that children would fit into their lifestyle.

Travel and spontaneity are also valued by many childfree men and women and they feel that this would end if they had children. Many in the childfree community feel that their current way of life would be drastically altered if they were to have children. Because most childfree people enjoy their lives so much, they do not want to have children and take the risk of decreasing their quality of life.

Another reason for choosing the childfree lifestyle is a dislike of children. There are childfree individuals who do not feel comfortable around children. Some childfree women have even described a lack of maternal instinct or the lack of a biological clock as reasons why they choose to remain childfree. The dislike of children is the reason the childfree are labeled as child-haters, by some, though many childfree individuals do not openly express their dislike of children.

Even though there are some childfree men and women who do not like children, there are also many childfree individuals who do. Childfree people do not automatically hate children just because they choose not to have any of their own. Many childfree men and women are happy to be god-parents, mentors, aunts or uncles, or educators to children instead of having their own children. Many childfree do not dislike all children, but do not like the behavior of some children. Most childfree individuals admit that it is bad parenting that they hate, not necessarily the children exhibiting the bad behavior.

Environmental Reasons

An additional reason given by some childfree individuals when questioned about their decision to not have children is that the world is already overpopulated. This line of reasoning has been described as an environmental reason for being childfree. Those childfree individuals who feel that the world is overpopulated feel that it is unfair to put a strain on the environment in order to reproduce. Diminished natural resources, pollution, global warming, and other environmental factors that affect our world today can also be considered environmental reasons for not having children.

Financial Reasons

There are also financial reasons that are taken into consideration when deciding whether or not to have children. The U.S. Department of Agriculture estimated in 2005 that families making $70,200 a year or more will spend $279,450 to raise a child born in 2005 to age 17. Families earning $41,700 to $70,200 will spend $190,980 and families earning less than $41,700 will spend $139,110. The cost of raising a child is significant and there are childfree individuals who take into account the financial responsibilities involved when making their decision to not have children.

Religious Reasons

The final reason some men and women choose to be childfree is for religious reasons. Nuns and priests are not allowed to have children because of their commitment to their faith. There are other people who choose to remain celibate, whether for personal or religious reasons. For nuns, priests, and any others who might choose celibacy, remaining childfree is done so because of their calling to that path in life.

THE CHILDFREE MOVEMENT

The childfree movement is a social movement that has gained strength and popularity in recent years. The formation of childfree organizations has helped provide the general public with a better understanding of what being childfree really means. There are also numerous groups that are accessible through the Internet that provide a social outlet for childfree men and women. Internet resources also offer a wealth of information regarding the childfree lifestyle.

Childfree Organizations

There are numerous organizations that have been formed to offer information and support to childfree men and women worldwide. Support networks have been developed in recent year to connect childfree people all over the world. These networks help bring childfree people together and also help childfree men and women see that they are not alone in their decision. A few childfree organizations are: No Kidding!, The World Childfree Association, and Kidding Aside.

Childfree Slang Terms

The childfree community has an entire vocabulary of slang terms that are used in communication with other childfree individuals and with non-childfree people. The slang terms used by childfree individuals are used to discuss parents, children, and even remarks the childfree receive about their lifestyle choice. The terms that childfree men and women use in conversation can be found widely on Internet communities and are also used in everyday conversation with other childfree individuals. The term childfree is generally abbreviated as CF and is distinguished from childless, which is abbreviated as CL.

There are terms that distinguish between parents and what childfree call "breeders," which are people who do not effectively parent their children. In childfree slang terminology parents are good and are referred to as PNBs

(Parents, Not Breeders) and breeders or BNPs (Breeders, Not Parents) are bad. There are also terms that differentiate between male and female breeders. In childfree slang terminology a female breeder is referred to as a "moo" and a male breeder is called a "duh." The term "baby rabies" is a childfree term used to describe women who continually have children, talk about children, or want to have children.

There is also terminology used to discuss children. A common term used by childfree men and women to describe children is "sprog." There are many other more derogatory terms used to distinguish children who misbehave and are considered annoyances from those who are well behaved. In general, most childfree individuals have no problem with children and parents, but they do dislike breeders and their offspring. The child-hater term that is usually attached to childfree individuals can be attributed to the reaction by the childfree to poor parenting and the results of that parenting that become evident in their children.

CHILDFREE SLANG TERMS

Baby Rabies—Used to describe women who continually have children or want to have children. Also, women who continually talk about children can be said to have the "baby rabies."

Bingo—Commonly heard phrases made by non-childfree individuals regarding childfree choices not to have children. Examples include: "You'll want children when you meet the right person", "It's different when they're your own," "Who will take care of you when you get old?" "You were a child once too!" "It is the most important job in the world" and "People who don't want kids are selfish."

BNP (*Breeder, Not Parent*)—Individuals who are not active in parenting and who do not discipline their children; in other words bad parents.

Breeder—Bad parents.

CF—Abbreviation for the term childfree.

CL—Abbreviation for childless.

DINK—An abbreviation for Dual Income No Kids. This term is used by many married childfree to describe their status.

Duh—A male breeder (father).

Fence Sitter—A person who has not decided whether or not they want children.

Moo—A female breeder (mother).

PNB (*Parent, Not Breeder*)—Individuals who take an active role in parenting and discipline their children; in other words good parents.

SINK—An abbreviation for Single Income No Kids. This term is used to describe childfree individuals or couples who only have one source of income.

Sprog—A child.

SUV Stroller—Any large, oversized stroller.

IMPORTANT CHILDFREE ISSUES

Reproductive Issues

Childfree individuals are concerned with many issues that affect different people throughout the United States, not only those within the childfree community. The issue of sterilization is one of growing concern among the childfree. Many childfree men and women want to be able to be rendered permanently unable to have children, but there is hesitation and resistance among many in the medical field. Many doctors refuse to perform tubal ligations or chemical sterilization procedures on women who have not had children, who are considered too young, or who are unmarried. Some doctors also fear that women will change their minds after the procedure and will sue the physician who performed the operation.

Childfree individuals who have been denied sterilization argue that it is their choice and their bodies and they should be able to have sterilization procedures if they request it. Many childfree women feel patronized and belittled by doctors who are unwilling to perform sterilization procedures. Childfree men also seek permanent sterilization in the form of vasectomies. The ability to take control of one's own reproductive life is an important issue among childfree men and women.

Many childfree people are also very interested in contraception and abortion issues. Like many around the world, childfree individuals feel that safe, effective contraception options should be available to all who need them. Opinions on abortion vary, but there is a strong pro-choice voice among the childfree community. Issues dealing with sterilization, contraception, and abortion are all heavily debated by and at the heart of many childfree individuals.

Workplace Issues

Childfree men and women within the American workforce are also campaigning for changes in the treatment of the childfree compared to the treatment of parents in many businesses. Childfree men and women who feel that they are treated unequally in the workplace want to be able to have the flex time and comparable benefits that are offered to many workers with children. Childfree workers believe strongly in equal work for equal pay, but many feel that pay is not currently equivalent in many respects. Childfree individuals may be asked to take on a heavier workload because working parents have to take more time off from work. Childfree workers may have to work longer hours, take on extra responsibilities, and travel more than those who have children.

Childfree individuals also want to be afforded some tax breaks that are comparable to those available to couples who have a child or children. There are certain tax breaks, such as a dependent exemption and the child tax credit, that are only available to those with children. Parents also have access to public education for their children from kindergarten through twelfth grade that is paid for with taxpayer dollars. Parents may also receive other incentives from the government or from their employers for having children. Many workers who do not have children but who have the responsibility of taking care of sick family members feel that they should be offered similar benefits for their dependents as parents receive for their children.

Social Issues

Another set of issues that affect childfree men and women are the remarks made by non-childfree people concerning their childfree status. Many people feel that becoming a parent is an important part of life and do not understand why some choose to remain voluntarily childless. Childfree men and women deal with comments and questions frequently regarding their decision to remain childfree. Questions and remarks made by non-childfree people are used very often in an attempt to change the minds of the childfree, but they are heard so often that they become frustrating.

There are religious groups who disagree with childfree individuals because they feel that those who choose not to have children are rebelling against God. There are those in the religious community who feel that people should not have the option to remain childless if they are capable of becoming parents. Opposition to the childfree lifestyle by religious groups causes Christian childfree individuals to feel the need to justify their choices in light of their religious beliefs. Married childfree couples who are members of the Christian faith especially feel pressured to procreate because of the teachings of the church.

Childfree men and women are frequently called selfish for their decision not to have children. Childfree people are many times labeled as immature, unhappy, unnatural, unfeminine, abnormal, child-haters, and so on. Childfree individuals, on the other hand, do not feel that children are an obligation that all people must fulfill. Childfree individuals see their contribution to society as being through their volunteer efforts, their career, or their other interests and talents that can improve society as a whole.

Many childfree individuals are devoted to their careers and philanthropic work, and while they do not wish to have children of their own, they may enjoy other people's children. Other childfree individuals choose to work with children as mentors, teachers, or caregivers while choosing to remain voluntarily childless in their personal lives. In today's society, deviating from the norm of having children, whether they are biological or adopted, is seen as abnormal no matter what reasons are given to justify the action.

SUMMARY

The term childfree is used to describe a social movement of men and women who do not want children, either biologically or through adoption. Childfree individuals distinguish themselves from those who are considered to be childless because the term "less" implies that something is missing, when childfree individuals do not feel they are missing out on anything. Childless differs from childfree in that childless men and women do not presently have children, but they want to in the future.

Childfree individuals deal with issues on many levels and are many times viewed negatively by others in society. There are numerous reasons for an individual to choose to be childfree, including medical, personal, environmental, financial, and religious reasons. Being childfree is a personal choice that is not reached without much thought and consideration. Men and women who are childfree have made a choice and want to live their lives as they wish, without being pressured to have children they do not want.

See also Infertility; Transition to Parenthood.

Further Reading: Bartlett, Jane. *Will You Be Mother? Women Who Choose to Say No.* New York: New York University Press, 1995; Burkett, Elinor. *The Baby Boon: How Family-Friendly America Cheats the Childless.* New York: The Free Press, 2000; Cain, Madelyn. *The Childless Revolution.* Boston: Perseus Publishing, 2001; Defago, Nicki. *Childfree and Loving It!* London: Vision, 2005; Lisle, Laurie. *Without Child: Challenging the Stigma of Childlessness.* New York: Ballantine Books, 1996; Safer, Jennifer. *Beyond Motherhood: Choosing Life Without Children.* New York: Pocket Books, 1996; Shawne, Jennifer L. *Baby Not on Board: A Celebration of Life without Kids.* San Francisco: Chronicle Book, LLC, 2005.

Anne Strickland

CHILDREN AS CAREGIVERS

When thinking about the role of children in society, one rarely expects that children will be caring for others. The cultural model supposes that children are the ones in need of care. However, an estimated 1.4 children in the United States provide care for a parent or other adult. They may help a grandparent with dressing and feeding or help a parent with household chores and meal preparation. For some children, the experience is stressful, isolating, and its negative effects may persist into adulthood. For other children, the experience can be an opportunity to build life skills, to help a family member, and to feel useful and important. The duration of the caregiving experience and the support and recognition provided to the child can help to determine whether the caregiving experience is a positive or a negative one.

CHILD CAREGIVERS AND PARENTIFICATION

The National Alliance on Caregiving and the United Hospital Fund define a child caregiver as anyone aged 8 to 18 "who provides unpaid help or care to anyone in the household or any relative, whether or not the relative lives with the caregiver" (National Alliance on Caregiving 2005). Caregiving activities can include helping with meals, personal needs, household chores, shopping, transportation, medicine, and emotional support.

The concept of parentification is related to the experience of child caregiving. Parentification involves a reversal of roles in which children set aside their own needs to address the emotional or physical needs of a parent or sibling. Parentification can take different forms—children can experience instrumental, emotional, and destructive parentification. Instrumental parentification refers to the experience of children who assume household duties such as completing chores, preparing meals, and paying bills. Children who experience emotional parentification respond to the emotional needs of family members and may take responsibility for resolving conflicts in the home. Finally, destructive parentification occurs when there is a lack of boundaries between family members, and children assume a disproportionate amount of caretaking responsibilities.

PREVALENCE OF CHILD CAREGIVING

The National Alliance on Caregiving and the United Hospital Fund estimate that as many as 1.4 million children in the United States provide care to a relative. About three percent of all U.S. households with children have a child carer as a member (National Alliance on Caregiving 2005).

A variety of factors contribute to the need for child caregiving. Longer life expectancies and increases in the prevalence of chronic diseases have led more adults to live longer but to require more care as they age. This trend is likely to continue and warrants greater involvement of children in caring for older family members. Shifts in the health care system, including shorter hospitalizations and rising nursing home costs, have increased the need for home care. Based in the notion that persons are more comfortable recuperating at home and consequently will heal more quickly there, patients are unlikely to spend protracted time in a medical facility. As medical costs and insurance premiums have increased, a cost saving measure has been to decrease the number of hospital days covered by insurance, thus forcing some persons home early when their ability to pay for treatment ends. At the same time, increases in the prevalence of single-parent families and the number of adults working outside the home have decreased the number of adults who can assume caregiving responsibilities. Traditionally an adult daughter would be caring for aging relatives, but as these women are increasingly in the labor force, the task may be assigned to her child.

CHARACTERISTICS OF CHILD CAREGIVERS

Children of all ages offer caregiving assistance. Nearly one-third of child caregivers in the United States are between the ages of 8 and 11. Close to 40 percent are aged 12 to 15, and 31 percent are between the ages of 16 and 18 (National Alliance on Caregiving 2005). Contrary to the findings regarding adult caregivers, nearly equal numbers of child caregivers are female and male.

Child caregivers tend to live in homes with more children than do noncaregiving children. However, over one-third of child caregivers are the only child under 18 in their household, and over 60 percent are the only children providing care in their home. Child caregivers also are more likely to live in a home with a single parent and are more likely to live in households that earn less than $25,000 per year, compared to noncaregiving children (National Alliance on Caregiving 2005).

CHARACTERISTICS OF CARE RECEIVERS

Most child caregivers care for a parent or grandparent. Of these, children usually care for a female relative—a mother or grandmother—and usually care for someone who lives in their home. Child caregivers who are part of a minority racial or ethnic group are more likely to provide care for their mother than nonminority child caregivers. Nearly one in nine child caregivers care for a sibling and fewer numbers provide care for other relatives or nonrelatives (National Alliance on Caregiving 2005).

Child caregivers provide assistance to adults with a wide range of physical, mental, and emotional needs. According to one survey, children are most likely to provide assistance to adults who have Alzheimer's Disease or dementia; heart, lung or kidney disease; arthritis; and diabetes. Physical conditions for which children provide care also include the functional decline of older adults who cannot complete certain tasks due to old age; back, bone, or joint injuries; paralysis or spine injury; stroke; fibromyalgia; cancer; and mental retardation. Other children provide care to family members with HIV and alcoholism.

Over one-half of child caregivers assist with at least one activity of daily living (National Alliance on Caregiving 2005). These include feeding, dressing, bathing, and helping the care recipient get into and out of beds and chairs. In addition to assisting with physical activities, many child caregivers also provide emotional support to the care receiver. Children may serve as the peacemaker in the family or spend time listening to the ill family member.

YOUNG CARERS PROJECTS

Young caregivers in the United Kingdom (UK) can find support and resources through the Young Carers Projects, local organizations that were created to provide child-centered support to young caregivers and their families. There are approximately 100 Young Carers Projects in the UK (The Young Carers Initiative 2008). These organizations provide opportunities for young caregivers to meet other children who are caring for an older relative and provide much-needed free time for young caregivers. The projects sponsor activities, such as evening clubs, day and weekend trips, and some even provide respite care. In addition, the projects provide a place where children can access information about the caregiving process as well as learn about available government services and benefits. Some projects have a befriending component, where adults volunteer to mentor and provide respite activities for young caregivers.

Several of the organizations have their own kid-friendly websites. Among them are the Gloucestershire Young Carers Project (http://www.glosyoungcarers.org.uk/) and the Dundee Young Carers Project (http://www.youngcarers.co.uk/).

EFFECTS OF CAREGIVING ON CHILDREN

Effects of child caregiving are varied and are just beginning to be studied. Early research on child caregiving did not occur until the late 1980s and focused on assessing the extent of child caregiving and child caregivers' needs in the United Kingdom. Subsequent studies have focused on quantifying the number and characteristics of child caregivers in the United States and describing the experiences and effects of child caregiving. Research into the phenomenon in the United States has demonstrated that caregiving experiences can have both positive and negative effects for child caregivers.

Positive Effects

Caregiving can provide children with a sense of responsibility, help them feel like they are contributing to their family, and allow them to gain important life skills. When adults who had cared for family members with chronic physical illnesses as children were asked what they liked about caregiving, they said that the experience gave them opportunities "to be part of the family" and to feel "appreciated," "important," and "useful" (Lackey and Gates 2001). Many of the adults currently were employed in careers that involved caregiving, such as nursing or teaching, suggesting that their caregiving experience may have had an influence on their career choice.

Children who helped to care for grandparents with Alzheimer's Disease also reported feeling that their caregiving activities were helpful and beneficial. Some grandchildren also said that they developed closer relationships with grandparents during the caregiving period. They described the coping skills they gained from their experience, and several offered advice to families facing a similar situation.

Negative Effects

The experience of caregiving is a stressful one for many children. Many child caregivers feel helpless because they lack information about the family member's illness. Others describe increased stress and tension due to the combination of providing care and adjusting to their family member's illness. Anxiety and fear about aging was common among those children who care for grandparents with Alzheimer's Disease. As a result of their experiences, some child caregivers suffer from chronic psychological problems, such as depression and separation anxiety.

The effects of caregiving on school and social life are profound for some child caregivers. Care responsibilities leave children with less time for after school activities and homework. In some cases, adults have reported that they dropped out of high school as teenagers to care for a family member with a chronic physical illness. Other child caregivers have expressed that school provided a needed break from caregiving responsibilities and that the ill family member encouraged them and helped them with schoolwork.

Some child caregivers choose not to tell their friends about their caregiving experience or their ill family member, while others find that their friends are supportive. Child caregivers who are of dating age may choose not to date or date early to "get out of the home." The negative effects and burden of caring for another person when one is at a young age can be difficult. One child caring for an adult with a chronic physical illness reported that she "married the first person I dated to escape" (Lackey and Gates 2001).

For some children, the negative effects of child caregiving can persist into adulthood. Fear of developing a chronic or terminal illness themselves and unresolved feelings of anger and guilt over the task can remain with child caregivers long after the caregiving experience has ended. In addition, some young caregivers show symptoms of depression in adulthood.

WHEN DOES CAREGIVING BECOME A NEGATIVE EXPERIENCE?

In general, the longer the duration of the caregiving experience, the more likely child caregivers are to experience negative outcomes. Child caregivers who are female, live in single parent families, and care for their nonworking mothers are more likely to have long-term or disproportionate care responsibilities. In addition, children who care for an adult with unpleasant symptoms and who lack adequate information about the disease are more likely to report negative effects of caregiving, suggesting that at minimum child caregivers should be given useful knowledge about the person for whom they are caring and the basic facts about their condition.

Child caregivers' relationships with their parents are associated with adult mental health outcomes. Adults who cared for a parent or adult relative as a child received less warmth and caring from their parents than did noncaregiving adults. Children who cared for alcoholic parents and experienced destructive parentification were more likely to develop a negative self-concept than were children who cared for alcoholic parents and whose contributions were supported and recognized.

Constructive caregiving experiences usually occur when children have clearly defined tasks, provide care under adult supervision, and receive assurance that they are not solely responsible for providing care. In addition, receiving recognition for their contributions and participating in supportive services also help children have positive caregiving experiences that can have benefits in their adult lives.

See also Addiction and Family; Elder Abuse; Elder Care; Grandparenthood; Grandparents as Caregivers; Housework Allocation; Pet Death and the Family.

Further Reading: Akerman, Sherri. "Young Caregivers Face Many Challenges." *Tampa Tribune,* January 29, 2007; Aldridge, Jo. "The Experiences of Children Living with and Caring for Parents with Mental Illness." *Child Abuse Review* 15, no. 2 (2006): 79–88; Aldridge, Jo, and Saul Becker. "Befriending Young Carers: A Pilot Study." Loughboro University. http://www.lboro.ac.uk/departments/ss/centres/YCRG/youngCarersDownload/pilot%20study.pdf; Aldridge, Jo, and Saul Becker. "Inside the World of Young Carers." Loughboro University. http://www.lboro.ac.uk/departments/ss/centres/YCRG/youngCarersDownload/ Children%20who%20care.pdf; Austin, LeAne. "Children as Caregivers." Caregiver.com. http://www.caregiver.com/articles/children/children_as_caregivers.htm; Bauman, Laurie J., Ellen J. Silver, Barbara H. Draimin, and Jan Hudis. "Children of Mothers With HIV/AIDS: Unmet Needs for Mental Health Services."

Pediatrics 120, no. 5 (2007): 1141–1147; Becker, Saul. "Young Carers in Europe: An Exploratory Cross-National Study. Young Carers Research Group." Loughboro University. http://www.lboro.ac.uk/departments/ss/centres/YCRG/youngCarersDownload/Young%20Carers%20in%20Europe1.pdf; Blum, Jonathan. "Caring for Dad." *Scholastic Action* 30, no. 1 (2006): 14–16; Chideya, Farai. "When Children Must Care for Others." *NPR News and Notes,* October 12, 2006; Dearden, Chris, and Becker, Saul. "Young Carers and Education." Carers UK. http://www.lboro.ac.uk/departments/ss/centres/YCRG/youngCarersDownload/yceduc[1].pdf; Godsall, Robert E., Gregory J. Jurkovic, James Emshoff, Louis Anderson, and Douglas Stanwyck. "Why Some Kids Do Well in Bad Situations: Relation of Parental Alcohol Misuse and Parentification to Children's Self-Concept." *Substance Use and Misuse* 39, no. 5 (2004): 789–809; Hooper, Lisa. M. "Expanding the Discussion Regarding Parentification and Its Varied Outcomes: Implications for Mental Health Research and Practice." *Journal of Mental Health Counseling* 29, no. 4 (2007): 322–337; Kornblum, Janet. "When Child Cares for Parent." *USA Today,* September, 14, 2005; Lackey, Nancy R., and Marie F. Gates. "Adults' Recollections of their Experiences as Young Caregivers of Family Members with Chronic Physical Illnesses." *Journal of Advanced Nursing* 34, no. 3 (2001): 320–328; National Alliance on Caregiving and the United Hospital Fund. "Young Caregivers in the U.S." http://www.caregiving.org/data/youngcaregivers.pdf; Newton, Betty, and Saul Becker. "The Capital Carers: An Evaluation of the Capital Carers Young Carers Project." Loughboro University. http://www.lboro.ac.uk/departments/ss/centres/YCRG/youngCarersDownload/capital%20carers.pdf; Orel, Nancy A., and Paula Dupuy. "Grandchildren as Auxiliary Caregivers for Grandparents with Cognitive and/or Physical Limitations: Coping Strategies and Ramifications." *Child Study Journal* 32, no. 4 (2002): 193–213; Pollack, Eunice G. "The Children We Have Lost: When Siblings were Caregivers, 1900–1970." *Journal of Social History* 36, no. 1 (2002): 31; The Princess Royal Trust for Carers. "Who Does What?: Young Carers Projects," 2004–2007. http://www.youngcarers.net/who_can_help_me/86/92; Shifren, Kim, and Lauren V. Kachorek. "Does Early Caregiving Matter? The Effects on Young Caregivers' Adult Mental Health." *International Journal of Behavioral Development* 27, no. 4 (2003): 338–346; Social Care Institute for Excellence. "The Health and Well-Being of Young Carers." *Research Briefing Number* 11 (2005). http://www.scie.org.uk/publications/briefings/briefing11/index.asp; The Young Carers Initiative. "Projects A–Z Index." http://www.youngcarer.com/showPage.php?file=projects.htm.

Katie Kerstetter

COHABITATION, EFFECTS ON MARRIAGE

Cohabitation literally means living together. In our society this term is most often used to refer to persons who are in a romantic or sexual relationship, reside at the same residence, but are not legally married. The influence of nonmarital cohabitation on a subsequent marriage continues to be hotly debated. Does cohabiting with one's partner prior to marriage lead to a decrease in marital quality and a greater likelihood of divorce? Or does cohabiting allow partners to determine if they will be good spouses prior to committing to marriage, and therefore decrease their chances of marital dissolution? Not only is there concern about divorce being greater for couples that cohabited prior to marriage, but there is a concern that all aspects of the marriage might be altered by the cohabitation experience.

Beginning in the 1970s, as cohabitation rates increased in the United States, researchers began to examine the effects that cohabitation might have on marriage. This examination considered how cohabitation might have an impact on the institution of marriage as well as how individual marriages might be different if partners cohabited prior to their marriage. The assumption that under-girds this research is that cohabitation and marriage are qualitatively different experiences. In other words, marriage can not be completely replaced by cohabitation because marriage is somehow unique. Therefore, comparisons of cohabitors and married couples would support the notion that the two statuses differ in significant ways, beyond the obvious legal difference.

COMPARISONS OF MARRIED AND NONMARRIED COHABITANTS

As options for conducting a personal relationship, marriage and cohabitation share many similarities. They are both expected to be sexual relationships, partners have some idea that their obligations are drawn along gender lines, and there is the presumption of some stability and attachment among the partners. However, cohabitation and marriage hold different status in the culture. While cohabitation has gained in acceptability as more persons have experienced it as a lifestyle in recent decades, it has neither the legal status nor moral acceptability of marriage. As a result, the legality of the status is in doubt in some states and the morality of the choice continues to be debated. The rise in cohabitation among persons claiming a religious affiliation, particularly among Protestants, has led to an emphasis on evaluating how Christian principles disagree with cohabitation. The book *Living Together* by Jeff VanGoethem is a good example of the pastoral approach to cohabitation. In marriage, the obligations of the partners to each other are prescribed in tradition as well as the law. Cohabitors do not have such an institutionalized set of roles, so they often must make things up as they go along. Because couples are most familiar with them, expected marital roles might sometimes guide a cohabiting relationship.

While persons recognize that marriage is a relationship designed to last forever, many ambiguities surround cohabitation. For some partners, cohabitation will lead to marriage, for others it is only likely to last as long as both partners are benefiting from the arrangement. Thus, cohabiting relationships often begin and end in rapid fashion, as there are no legal requirements to get into or out of them.

As a group, cohabiting partners have less traditional attitudes toward gender roles than do married partners. This means that they are more likely to be egalitarian about the roles of males and females. Most cohabiting partners are both employed outside the home, but just as in a marriage, women do more of the domestic labor. Despite having two earners, cohabitors tend to have lower incomes and more economic instability when compared with married couples. Cohabitants tend to keep their financial lives separate from each other and are less likely to own their residence than are married partners.

Questions about differences in the quality of marital and cohabiting relationships indicate that married persons are happier overall and express more relationship satisfaction than do cohabitors. Both married and cohabiting partners experience health benefits from being in a partnered relationship, but cohabitors have higher overall rates of domestic violence. Spouses claim higher levels of commitment to the partner and the relationship than do cohabitants, resulting in higher rates of dissolution for cohabiting relationships compared with marriages.

Most persons who cohabit are not doing so as a lifelong alternative to marriage. Many are doing it as a prelude to marriage or an extension of a dating relationship. Cohabiting relationships are fairly short-term relationships overall, with the average length of a relationship being 1.5 years. Many cohabiting partners never intend to marry; they may simply be in the relationship because it is convenient. In fact, within three years of their beginning to live together, only half of the couples that expect that their cohabitation will lead to marriage actually end up married to each other. Cohabiting couples have a rate of separation that is five times that of married couples, and in the event of separation, cohabitors have a rate of reconciliation that is only 33 percent as high as that of married couples.

COHABITATION STRENGTHENS MARRIAGE

While few experts would argue that cohabitation strengthens subsequent marriages, lay persons often provide anecdotal evidence of cohabitation as being the right choice for them. Consistent with the testing model, persons who choose to cohabit often say that they are doing so to weed out any potential problems with the partner before the marriage occurs. In this way they might hope to save themselves from future divorce. If couples wish to try out the partner as a spouse before marriage, it may indicate that they place a strong value on marriage and do not want to enter a marriage unwisely. Thus, the motive is to strengthen the subsequent marriage.

The directors of the Alternatives to Marriage Project have suggested that cohabitation can be helpful for subsequent marriages provided that partners enter cohabitation with the right approach. Essentially, cohabitation must be undertaken thoughtfully rather than casually. Partners need to clarify their motives for cohabiting and have a date in mind to re-evaluate the choice or set a marriage date. Partners are encouraged to talk about how their relationship might change after marriage and to even write a living together agreement that outlines the expectations for each partner.

There is a growing body of evidence that under certain circumstances prior cohabitation has little, if any, discernable effect on subsequent marriages. In a recent study published in the well respected *Journal of Marriage and the Family*, when a woman's cohabiting relationship or premarital sexual relationship was limited to the future husband, there seemed to be no effects of cohabitation on likelihood of divorce. This finding points toward the circumstances of the cohabitation itself being a far more critical consideration than whether or not the cohabitation occurred. When partners who cohabited prior to engagement were compared with those who cohabited postengagement, the group that cohabited after a specific commitment to marry were positive, committed, confident and experiencing as high of a quality relationship as a control group that had not cohabited. This lends further support to those persons who say that the motives for cohabitation and circumstances surrounding it are critical in whether it strengthens or weakens a subsequent marriage.

Due to the fact that cohabitation is often a stage in courtship, one must be wary of comparisons between cohabitors and noncohabitors. For example, some researchers have suggested that the most accurate comparisons would be between persons who are married and those who have selected cohabitation as a permanent alternative to marriage. A researcher wishing to uncover any benefits that cohabitation provides for marriage would be best served by studying only cohabitors in a trial marriage or testing relationship.

TRIAL MARRIAGE

One of the more controversial suggestions for determining compatibility over the last century was proposed by anthropologist Margaret Mead. She suggested that society would be best served by two distinct stages or steps in marriage. In the first step, partners would be committed to each other, but would not be permitted to have children. In other words, they would agree to make sure their bonds would be permanent first. Mead called this first step individual marriage.

After demonstrating their commitment to each other and the relationship, partners could move to the second stage, parental marriage. In the second step, partners indicated their intent to have children. This new component to the marriage would be marked by a formal ceremony and an expectation for permanence. In some limited ways it could be argued that we have a de facto two-stage marriage system now with the high numbers of persons who cohabit prior to marrying. Persons who do cohabit often postpone having children until after being legally married, or marrying once a pregnancy has occurred.

COHABITATION WEAKENS MARRIAGE

One of the arguments on the institutional level of society suggests that marriage is suffering as a result of cohabitation. As rates of cohabitation have increased steadily during the last 30 to 40 years, rates of marriage have gone down. It is accurate to say that nearly as many young people are partnered today as in the past. They are, however, marrying at lower rates and postponing marriage until later ages. The alternative behavior that they are engaging in is cohabitation. The concern among those most critical of the increases in cohabitation, particularly conservative religious and political groups such as the Institute for American Values, Focus on the Family, or the Moral Majority, is that persons are rejecting a traditional legal marriage in favor of a fad in relationships. Persons who are more liberal on family issues agree that young people are cohabiting in greater numbers rather than marrying. They argue, however, that the young people are concerned over the high rates of divorce and lack confidence in the institution of marriage.

The link between marriage and childrearing has been the most fruitful for critics to pursue. Marriage is touted as the best environment in which to protect and rear children in U.S. society. Most cohabiting persons who desire to bring children into their relationship will marry before the child is born. This pattern does not, however, hold true for African Americans who are less likely than other racial or ethnic groups to marry following a nonmarital conception.

Studies conducted in the United States and elsewhere with both small and large samples have found evidence that cohabitors report being less happy when compared with married couples and that cohabitation leads to lower-quality marriages. Perhaps this is a result of what some conservative advice columnists assert, that cohabitation takes the mystery away from marriage. You don't get to learn all those special things about the partner after marriage. It short-changes the partners.

Most religiously conservative groups equate cohabitation with a cheapening of the sexual bond that is supposed to develop between couples after the marriage in a traditional model of family life. The saying "why buy the cow when you can get the milk for free" reminds couples that there is potential for sexual exploitation in a cohabiting relationship. Additionally, partners who cohabit are more likely to be unfaithful at some point during the marriage.

Rates of divorce for partners who cohabited prior to marriage are higher than for partners who did not live together before the wedding. This pattern holds true even after taking age at marriage and education level, factors that are known to be associated with divorce, into account. However, there does seem to be a decrease in the difference between cohabiting and noncohabiting groups in more recent studies. While the pattern was clearly established for those who cohabited in the 1970s and 1980s, persons who have cohabited more recently have not shown as dramatic a difference with regard to likelihood of divorce. It is suggested that this decreasing of the effect of divorce has resulted not from any major changes to marriage, but to the greater acceptance of cohabitation as a lifestyle choice. The group for whom the divorce rate remains high is a subgroup that has experienced multiple cohabiting relationships prior to marrying. This group is referred to as serial cohabitors because when one cohabiting relationship ends, they move right into another.

Selection Effect or Experience Effect?

Is the slightly greater chance of divorce for couples who cohabit prior to marriage linked to the selection effect—the suggestion that those who cohabit hold unique characteristics compared with those who do not cohabit—or to the effect of the experience of the cohabitation relationship itself? The selection idea that persons who choose to cohabit are somehow different than those who do not cohabit has merit.

Selection effects that make data on cohabitation particularly hard to interpret are of two types. First, persons in the cohabiting group may have background characteristics that make them less likely to have positive relationships. Persons who cohabit are more likely than those who marry without cohabiting to have lower economic standing, less education, and a greater likelihood of a premarital conception. All are factors that can lead to fewer resources and greater stress in relationships. These persons may have difficulty maintaining any relationship, a fact that might actually push them to choose cohabitation. Second, persons who choose cohabitation are less conventional in their beliefs and might, therefore, hold attitudes that would be counterproductive in marriage. For example, if a couple is liberal enough in their attitude toward marriage and family to be willing to cohabit, then if things do not work out as they would like, they may be liberal enough to select divorce as a way to end an unsatisfactory marriage.

The experience effect, on the other hand, posits that there is something about cohabiting relationships that changes the participants and makes couples behave differently in the marriage or be more likely to seek divorce. One theory of how the experience effect might work suggests that because of the relatively commitment-free nature of cohabitation couples do not work to stay together in a cohabiting relationship. Persons who cohabit learn that if things are not working out, the partner should just leave and go on to a new relationship. Therefore, if these partners marry they are less likely to try to work through any problems that arise in their relationship. The interaction styles learned through cohabitation influence how the couple will relate to each other when a marriage is contracted.

Additionally, because cohabitation is still viewed by many as a deviant relationship, the partners may view themselves as more deviant and take on other behaviors that are unconventional. Another way in which future marriage may be influenced by prior cohabitation is through the social support that couples receive. Studies suggest that cohabitors have more distant relationships with their families, thus reducing the support network that might be available if problems arise in a subsequent marriage. When thinking about the likelihood of divorce following cohabitation it is particularly relevant that cohabitation is more common before a remarriage than it is before a first marriage. In this instance selection and experience effects are both involved.

FUTURE OF MARRIAGE

Whether marriage is strengthened or weakened by cohabitation continues to be debated on moral, practical, and legal grounds. What is difficult to dispute is the fact that cohabitation is a part of most persons' relationship experiences today and the trends suggest that this will continue. Estimates are that 60 percent of marriages begun in the 1990s were preceded by cohabitation. Most of these data were gathered by examining the addresses couples used when they applied for a marriage license. If the address was the same, researchers assumed that the couple was cohabiting. Some researchers predict that more than 70 percent of couples that marry during this first decade of the twenty-first century will cohabit prior to marriage.

See also Benefits of Marriage; Common Law Marriage; Family Roles; Nonmarital Cohabitation.

Further Reading: Alternatives to Marriage Project. http://www.unmarried.org; Ambert, Anne-Marie. *Cohabitation and Marriage: How Are They Related?* Ottawa, Ont.: The Vanier Institute of the Family, 2005; Casper, Lynne M., and Suzanne M. Bianchi. *Continuity and Change in the American Family.* Thousand Oaks, CA: Sage, 2001; Kamp Dush, Claire M., Catherine L. Cohan, and Paul Amato. "The Relationship Between Cohabitation and Marital Quality and Stability: Change Across Cohorts." *Journal of Marriage and Family* 63 (2003): 539–549; National Marriage Project. http://www.marriage.rutgers.edu; Popenoe, David, and Barbara Defoe Whitehead. *Should We Live Together? What Young Adults Need to Know About Cohabitation Before Marriage—A Comprehensive Review of Recent Research,* 2nd ed. New Brunswick, NJ: The National Marriage Project, Rutgers University, 2002; Solot, Dorian, and Marshall Miller. *Unmarried to Each Other: The Essential Guide to Living Together as an Unmarried Couple.* New York: Marlowe and Company, 2002; VanGoethem, Jeff. *Living Together: A Guide to Counseling Unmarried Couples.* Grand Rapids, MI: Kregel Publications, 2005; Waite, Linda, and Maggie Gallagher. *The Case for Marriage: Why Married People are Happier, Healthier, and Better-off Financially.* New York: Broadway Books, 2001; Wilson, James Q. *The Marriage Problem.* New York: HarperCollins, 2002.

Kimberly P. Brackett

COMMON LAW MARRIAGE

A common law marriage is a marriage without a state recognized ceremony for the purpose of establishing the relationship of husband and wife. These marriage are not formalized by traditional ceremonies, but are entered into with "a positive mutual agreement, permanent and exclusive of all others, to enter into a marriage relationship, cohabitation sufficient to warrant a fulfillment of necessary relationship of man and wife, and an assumption of marital duties and obligations" (*Black's Law Dictionary* 1991). In a limited number of states, heterosexual couples can become legally married without a license or ceremony. Common law marriage is also known as an informal marriage or, in legal terms, "marriage by habit and repute."

Why people enter into legal marriages as opposed to common law marriages varies with social and personal perceptions. Marriage is regarded by some as a publicly sanctioned institution that should be documented in the same public fashion. Others consider marriage a civil contract which requires registration in order to settle legal issues and formalize familial obligations. Marriage is a personal relationship between a man and a woman with governmental, social, or religious recognition, and is created as a contract or through a civil process. Such marriages are also called statutory or civil marriages because they use the statutory law system in which a license is required prior to the lawful rite of the marriage.

When people consider common law marriage, they often include domestic partnerships and cohabitation. Domestic partnerships are relationships between individuals who live together and share a common domestic life, but are not joined in a traditional civil marriage. This type of arrangement includes same-sex couples as well as opposite-sex couples. Domestic partnerships in the United States are determined by each state or local jurisdiction, so there is no nationwide consistency on the rights, responsibilities, and benefits for these couples. The terminology for such unions is still evolving, and the exact level of rights and responsibilities granted by a domestic partnership varies widely from place to place.

Cohabitation is two people living together as husband and wife. This arrangement is an emotional and physical relationship which includes a common living place and usually exists without any legal or religious sanction. According to *Black's Law Dictionary*, cohabitation includes the mutual assumption of marital duties and obligations that occur with married people, including, but not necessarily dependent on, sexual relations. In the social science literature, cohabitation is generally referred to as a marriage-like relationship. Some couples prefer cohabitation because it does not legally commit them for an extended period of time, and because it is easier to establish and dissolve than a legal marriage. Partners often use this arrangement to test the likelihood of future marital success with the partner.

Today the most commonly accepted method of marriage is to acquire a state civil marriage license. Modern American society has changed in its social attitudes toward both common law marriage and civil marriage with regards to gender, age, religion, and social class which add to the ever-changing posture of relationships. Supporters of common law marriage may see requirements of a state license as surrendering personal independence to the government. Opponents feel that any method short of legal marriage will neither support family stability nor afford couples legal protection.

BACKGROUND

The idea of common law marriage began in medieval England, where couples got married by methods that had developed from local customs. Clerics and justices who performed ceremonial marriages were not always able to travel to rural locations where some couples lived, so couples established a marriage by habit and reputation. This marriage by "habit and repute" was seen as legal under England's Common Law. In the mid-1500s, the Council of Trent outlawed common law marriages and established the necessity of a Roman Catholic priest to witness a legal marriage ceremony. This law was not accepted in the Protestant nations of Europe, Protestant colonies in the Americas, nor by Eastern Orthodox Christians. Nevertheless, all Protestant and Eastern Orthodox countries in Europe eventually abolished marriage by habit and repute, with Scotland being the last to do so, in 2006.

At present all 50 states in the United States have marriage licensing laws, but not all of the state's laws are the same. In 1923, the federal government established the Uniform Marriage and Marriage License Act and later established the Uniform Marriage and Divorce Act. By 1929, every state in the Union had adopted marriage license laws. In the United States, the theory of common law marriage is one of estoppel—meaning that parties who have told the world they are married should not be allowed to claim that they are not married in a dispute between the parties themselves.

Common Law States

Currently, only 10 states (Alabama, Colorado, Iowa, Kansas, Montana, Pennsylvania, Rhode Island, South Carolina, Texas, and Utah) and the District of Columbia recognize common law marriages contracted in their respective states. In addition, The National Conferences of State Legislatures (www.ncsl.org) has listed five states that have "grandfathered" common law marriage, allowing those unions established before a certain date to be recognized. These states include Georgia (if began before January 1, 1997), Idaho (if began before January 1, 1996), Ohio (if began before October 10, 1991), Oklahoma (if began before November 1, 1998), and New Hampshire (only at death). Common law marriage can no longer be contracted in the following states, as of the dates given: Alaska (1917), Arizona (1913), California (1895), Florida (1968), Georgia (1997), Hawaii (1920), Idaho (1996), Illinois (1905), Indiana (1958), Kentucky (1852), Maine (1652, when it became part of Massachusetts; then as a state, 1820), Massachusetts (1646), Michigan (1957), Minnesota (1941), Mississippi (1956), Missouri (1921), Nebraska (1923), Nevada (1943), New Mexico (1860), New York (1933, also 1902–1908), New Jersey (1939), North Dakota (1890), Ohio (1991), Pennsylvania (2005), South Dakota (1959), and Wisconsin (1917). Some states have never actually permitted common law marriage. They are Arkansas, Connecticut, Delaware, Louisiana, Maryland, North Carolina, Oregon, Tennessee, Vermont, Virginia, Washington, West Virginia, and Wyoming.

Individual states have also amended the local laws to specify conditions to regulate the conditions of common law marriages. New Hampshire recognizes common law marriage only for purposes of probate after death (N.H. Rev. Stat. Ann 457:39), and Utah recognizes common law marriages only if they have been validated by a court or administrative order (Utah Code Ann. 30-1-4.5). Alabama amended its state constitution to specify all marriages (including common law marriages and transferring out-of-state marriages) must be between a man and a woman, therefore excluding same-sex marriages (Alabama Constitutional Amendment #774). In 2002, Kansas law prohibited recognition of common law marriage if either party was less than 18 years of age (Kansas Session Laws, SB 486, §23–101).

Law

The elements of a common law marriage vary only slightly from state to state among those states that permit common law marriage. The elements are capacity (age, mental health, and no prior contract requirements), cohabitation, and that the parties tell the world that they are husband and wife. The couple tells the world that they are husband and wife through their conduct, such as the woman using the man's surname, and the couple filing a joint federal income tax return. A statutory or civil marriage is the result of a man and a woman applying for a state marriage license. Through that license the parties enter into a three party contract, which includes the husband, the wife, and the specific state. Each specific state, because of contract record keeping, knows of the marriage's existence. In common law marriage, the state has no record of the marriage so the marriage is not invalid or illegal; it simply is not known to exist, therefore, is not recognized even if the couple has created a private written contract.

Contrary to popular belief, two people simply living together for a certain number of years does not constitute a common law marriage. Of course, many disputes arise when facts, such as intentions of the parties or statements made to third parties, are in controversy. State laws do not interfere with a common law marriage or any other marriage unless there is a problem or until the validity of the union is challenged in a court of law. If the union is presented to the state, the court will use the English common law standards that are recommended to decide if the specific common law marriage was actually established. The key requirement is cohabitation while acting as a married couple, so simply living together without holding themselves out to the community as a married couple does not constitute marriage.

Once a common law marriage is established between two people in court, the state officially recognizes the union and the couple receives the same legal treatment as a married couple. Whether recognized by the court or not, if a couple wishes to end their common law marriage they must obtain a legal divorce. There is no such thing as a common law divorce. Once parties are married, regardless of the manner in which they were married, they can only be divorced by appropriate methods. In all 50 states of the United States, that means only in a court of law. People who marry in the common law tradition must petition the correct court in their state for termination of marriage.

CONTROVERSY OVER COMMON LAW MARRIAGE

Common law marriage supporters are often more concerned with the extensive government control on their personal conduct than with the conduct itself. These allies of alternative marriages see a common law marriage as a private contract between two parties and as binding and legal as a civil marriage even when the state is not involved. They do not want to surrender their personal independence to the State. Therefore, supporters have been known to quote from the decision of the United States Supreme Court in *Meister v. Moore* 96 U.S. 76 (1877). In the *Meister v. Moore* case, it is remarked that any directions to render invalid marriages illegal are simply suggestions, and not law because "marriage is a thing of common right." According to this argument, individual states can only direct suggestion or instruction with no obligatory force because marriage is a common right that is not subject to interference by the government. Supporters have warned that once a common law marriage issue goes to court, whether family law court or local jurisdiction court, couples are bound by the decisions of the court just like entering into a statutory marriage, because the state is afterward the superior party of interest.

Supporters of alternative marriages see marriage as a God-given right that has existed since before the formation of state or national government. Therefore, it should be beyond the government's control to alter, abolish, or interfere with such a right. No state can show that common law marriage is unlawful, only that it is not recognized by the state. Any law to make common law marriage illegal would be hard to uphold, considering the *Meister v. Moore* case in the United States Supreme Court. *Meister v. Moore* has never been overturned or revised and is still considered in case law relating to the fundamental right to marry without state interference. *Meister v. Moore* did establish that states do have the right to ban or restrict common law marriage. However, unless the state in question does not explicitly ban common law marriage, then there is a general presumption that such marriages are not illegal. The issues of this case differ between the actual state case law and the recommendations of the judges involved. These comments were added after the rendered case decision by the judges and are the judge's personal opinions' about the legal direction and intent of the specific laws.

Opposition to common law marriage comes mainly from conservative religious and family ethics groups. According to their argument, the total and absolute commitment of marriage strengthens a couple's relationship and makes the partners feel more secure, relaxed, and happier than those who choose not to marry. Data from the U.S. Division of Vital Statistics show that both characteristics of individuals and the communities in which they live are often important factors in understanding cohabitation and types of marriage. The community around a couple, including religious and family ethic groups, relate not only to a couple's success rate but also the true benefits to be gained from being married as opposed to being unmarried.

People tend to stay away from common law marriage today because they feel it is nothing more than so-called shacking-up covered by common law respectability. Those in opposition to cohabitation of any kind usually argue that living together, as opposed to legal marriage, is more unstable and harmful for both partners, as well as for any children from the union. Statistics show that couples who have lived together, whether by common law or by cohabitation, before legally marrying are more likely to divorce after the first 10 years. Unhappiness, bad health, poverty, and violence are more common in cohabiting unmarried couples than in married ones. According to The National Center for Health Statistics, unmarried and divorced couples exhibit lower levels of well-being, more health problems, more social isolation, less satisfying sex lives, more negative expectation of life, greater levels of depression, higher alcohol use, and lower levels of happiness and self-acceptance. Supporters of cohabitation cite research claims that these statistical differences are due to factors other than living together, such as race, ethnicity, age, poverty, education, employment, and income. Common law marriage advocates, however, do not often include their marriage type with the cohabitation statistics because they view themselves as husband and wife regardless of the government's analysis of their marriage.

Common law marriage affords no legal protection concerning property rights and child custody issues until settled through long and costly court disputes.

For example, the state of Alabama's constitution declares that marriage is a sacred covenant, which is inherently a unique relationship between a man and a woman. As a matter of public policy, the state of Alabama has a "special interest in encouraging, supporting, and protecting this unique relationship in order to promote, among other goals, the stability and welfare of society and its children" (State of Alabama Sanctity of Marriage Amendment #744). The National Conference of State Legislatures maintains that "many states have abolished common law marriage by statute, because common law marriage was seen as encouraging fraud and condoning vice, debasing conventional marriage, and as no longer necessary with increased access to clergy and justices of the peace" (www.ncsl.org/programs/cyf/commonlaw.htm).

Common law marriage is controversial; even religious figures will disagree, sometimes drastically, about the virtues of common law marriage. Rev. William J. McRae in his book, *Preparing for Your Marriage,* states that "Parent/child relationships are temporary; husband/wife relationship is enduring. Cleave to your wife *legally* [author's emphasis]—Common law marriages are sin!" (p. 80). Pastor Matt Trewhella gives a very different viewpoint with his brochure "5 Reasons Why Christians should not obtain a State Marriage License." Pastor Trewhella suggests that when Christian parents "give" their children to be married, a pastor of God unites the couple, the marriage is recorded, as simply as recording their names in the family Bible, and the two individuals are a married couple by contract. Trewhella leads his followers to create a bond with God and not with any state. This is done not only for religious freedom but also to allow parents to dictate the education and discipline of their children. This, in specific states, is a common law marriage.

If one considers common law marriage a type of personal contract marriage by reputation and habit then some feminists favor this arrangement. In the book *Marriage Proposals: Questioning a Legal Status,* Martha Albertson Fineman writes about the feminists' point of view concerning out-of-date relations between husbands and wives and the resulting dependency of the wives. Wives are no longer totally dependent on their husbands in modern American society, and so there is no longer any appropriate rationale for the state's involvement in marriage. Given modern society's and the government's aspirations of gender equality, which assumes that couples are capable of creating marital terms, it should be the couples, not the states, who make determinations about contracted relationships.

When it comes to issues like child custody, hospital visitation, inheritance, immigration, owning property, taxes, survivors' benefits, and Social Security, legal marital status does matter. In general, married people receive legal rights and protections that unmarried people don't get automatically. These and other issues not only affect those couples who consider themselves married by common law but those persons who live together and wish not to be considered married.

If a couple lives in one of the common law states and does not want their relationship to become a common law marriage, they must be clear with their intention not to marry. Attorneys recommend a written agreement, signed and dated by both partners indicating whether a couple intends to remain unmarried or to become married by common law. For example, couples who wish to remain as unmarried might approve the following statement: "We have been and plan to continue living together as two free, independent people and that neither has ever intended to enter into any form of marriage, common law or otherwise." For a couple that desires to be considered married under common law status, a simple certification of marriage signed by the couple and witnesses is recommended.

Due to the greater acceptance of cohabitation in society today, senior citizens, as well as younger adults, opt for less formal living arrangements. For many seniors, any type of marriage is not financially or emotionally practical. Older couples might choose living together rather than marriage because of financial reasons including tax disincentives, loss of military and pension benefits, fear of incurring liability for the partner's medical expenses, or credit rating protection. Additionally, cohabiting provides ability to share expenses, to retain Social Security benefits, and to control asset protection, and also prevents the loss of alimony and health benefits. Personal reasons seniors are cohabiting may include lack of concern about what others think, love and friendship, and their children's inheritance concerns.

Many people simply use the principles of common law marriage as a socially acceptable and convenient cover for cohabiting without any intention of entering into a legal marriage. It is also true, that the state courts have been filled with people alleging to be the spouse of a deceased person in order to get the decedent's property. These conditions and others have led our nation's courts to begin creating specific standard measures for establishing common law marriages, a pattern that will likely continue.

See also Cohabitation, Effects on Marriage; Domestic Partnerships; Fictive Kin; Nonmarital Cohabitation.

Further Reading: Alternatives to Marriage Project. http://www.unmarried.org; Anonymous. *The American Bar Association Legal Guide for Women: What Every Woman Needs to Know about the Law and Marriage, Health Care, Divorce, Discrimination, Retirement, and More.* New York: Random House Reference, 2004; Bible Based Marriages, 2000. www.bible.ca/marriage; Black, Henry Campbell. *Black's Law Dictionary,* abridged 6th ed. St. Paul, MN: West Publishing Co., 1991; Bride to Be.Com. http://www.1800bride2b.com/articles/marriagelaws_chart.htm; Constitution of Alabama 1901, "State of Alabama Sanctity of Marriage Amendment #744." http://alisdb.legislature.state.al.us/acas/CodeOfAlabama/Constitution/1901/Constitution1901_toc.htm; Divorce Net. Family Law Information, Solutions, News, and Community. http://www.divorcenet.com; Fineman, Martha Albertson. *Marriage Proposals; Questioning a Legal Status.* New York University Press, 2006; Justia.com. "United States Supreme Court *Meister v. Moore,* 1877." http://supreme.justia.com/us/96/76/index.html; Krause, Harry D., and David D. Meyer. *Family Law: In a Nutshell,* 4th ed. Stamford, CT: Thomson West, 2003; McRae, William J. *Preparing for Your Marriage.* Grand Rapids, MI: The Zondervan Corporation, 1980; National Center for Health Statistics. http://www.cdc.gov/nchs/fastats/divorce.htm;

National Conference of State Legislatures. http://www.ncsl.org; Trewhella, Matt. "5 Reasons Why Christians Should Not Obtain a State Marriage License." http://www.mercyseat.net/BROCHURES/marriage_license.htm.

Linda Pope Jones

CORPORAL PUNISHMENT

One of the most divisive debates in contemporary family sociology and child psychology centers on corporal punishment, known to most persons as spanking. Corporal punishment is the most widespread and well-documented form of family violence. In recent years, scholars as well theologians have debated the question of whether or not corporal punishment is an appropriate form of child discipline. This debate is particularly interesting in that it is relatively new and it taps into an area of firmly entrenched beliefs and values held by most Americans: that family is a private institution and that government should be minimally involved in guiding or mandating parenting practices. Furthermore, for most of American history, it was assumed that good parents used physical discipline and that an absence of physical punishment would be detrimental to the normal development of children. Indeed, the Society for the Prevention of Cruelty to Animals was established prior to any such organization formed on behalf of children's welfare. Both social as well as religious ideologies strongly legitimated the use of physical punishment in the home. The debate over corporal punishment is so volatile that the few scholars who dare study it empirically seldom have intellectual comrades. This is one area of social life in which even the most progressive-minded individuals find themselves in dissension with academia and perhaps personally conflicted. Indeed, one of the most prominent and widely recognized scholars in this area confronted quite a bit of resistance from publishers when attempting to market his book.

The scholarly study of corporal punishment is relatively new, with the vast majority of empirical studies conducted since the late 1950s. However, a few references to corporal punishment or harsh parenting appeared as early as the 1920s. Interestingly, in the 1960s, a popular magazine reported that there were more child deaths due to parental infliction than due to diseases. Despite this claim, many parental advice books make no mention of corporal punishment whatsoever, suggesting that the decision of whether or not to use it is a private one and must be decided by individuals. Culturally as well, the phenomenon is often either ignored or presumed normal and inevitable. Not surprisingly, most of these early works found that the vast majority of parents queried admitted to the use of physical punishment. Furthermore, in the early- to mid-1900s, the majority of child psychologists approved of or ignored corporal punishment. To be sure, the trend among early scholars and child experts was either to actively endorse or tolerate the use of corporal punishment by parents against children, at least on occasion. One notable exception to this was Dr. Benjamin Spock, who was perhaps the most well known pediatrician and parenting expert of the twentieth century. In his popular book, *Baby and Child Care,* he argued against the use of corporal punishment unless absolutely necessary. Spock later changed his position, arguing against the use of corporal punishment under all circumstances. Critics of Spock suggest that he led the trend toward more permissive parenting. Today, experts are divided on the issue, although awareness of the potentially harmful consequences of corporal punishment is higher today than ever before. Consequently, disapproval of corporal punishment seems to have grown somewhat among scholars and those who offer parenting advice, although even as late as the early 1990s relatively high levels of support have been found among general practitioners and pediatricians.

ATTITUDES TOWARD CORPORAL PUNISHMENT

The vast majority of American parents are supportive of the use of corporal punishment. This is peculiar in light of the purported overwhelming concern that Americans have about violence in society generally and certainly in relation to children and adolescents. In fact, parents who choose not to spank their children are in violation of a strong social norm and often encounter conflict with others. They may feel the need to justify their decision not to spank, whereas no justification for spanking is required.

Overall, corporal punishment is still commonly being used against American children. A number of Americans actually favor corporal punishment over other methods of child discipline. Most studies of the incidence of corporal punishment reveal that more than 90 percent of children and adolescents have experienced some form of physical punishment. What may be surprising, however, is that the use of corporal punishment is fairly common across the life course of a child, often beginning during infancy and continuing well into adolescence and even into young adulthood. Approximately three-quarters of American parents believe that spanking or slapping a 12-year-old child is necessary sometimes. Furthermore, studies of college students, for example, reveal that a significant proportion of them report having been slapped or hit by a parent in the recent past. One study found that one in four 17-year-olds is still being hit by a parent. The only significant decline is in the use of the most severe kinds of child discipline.

It should be noted, however, that attitudes and actions can be incongruent with regard to corporal punishment. Many Americans who do not verbally endorse corporal punishment do, in fact, spank or slap their children. On the other hand, some of those who endorse it may not use it. Interestingly, attitudes do not predict behavior for parents of toddlers. Almost all American parents of four-year-olds spank regardless of their approval or disapproval of corporal punishment. On the other hand, when looking at older children, attitudes are predictive of behavior. Parents of 16-year-olds who score high on approval of corporal punishment are more likely to use it. Personal experience with corporal punishment does seem to be a rather strong predictor of attitudes as well as actions. Individuals who were themselves spanked or slapped by a parent are more likely than others to indicate that they favor spanking. Furthermore, those who say that they were hit by a parent are in fact more likely to hit their own children, regardless of the children's age. Interestingly, in one study of parents who were hit but later chose not to hit or spank their own children, the influential variables seemed to be the educational level of the parents as well as their age at parenthood. The parents who decided to go against their upbringing—those who chose *not* to hit—were more highly educated and became parents at later ages.

All states give parents the right to use physical punishment against their children, regardless of the children's age. It may be surprising to learn that even spanking or hitting with an object such as a belt remains legal in the United States. More than 95 percent of parents of three-year-olds reported that they had been hit by their parents. Approximately 60 percent of parents admit to hitting their 10- to 12-year-old children. The lasting effect or mental imprint of having been physically punished is evident in the finding that 40 percent of adults over the age of 60 can recall being hit by their parents.

Little difference has been found between single-parent and two-parent families when it comes to the use of corporal punishment. It does appear that boys are hit more often than girls, although rates are not vastly discrepant. Adolescent boys are hit by both mothers and fathers, while adolescent girls are more often hit by mothers. There is evidence to show that mothers, in general, use corporal punishment more often than fathers, but this is generally assumed to be a consequence of the different amounts of time parents spend with children, with mothers spending considerably more time with children than fathers. Since it is known that men are more physically aggressive and more violent in all other areas of social life, it is assumed that if men spent as much time with children as women did, the use of corporal punishment by fathers would exceed that of mothers.

RELIGIOSITY, REGION, AND CORPORAL PUNISHMENT

American support for corporal punishment historically has always been high, and is often linked to religious or regional factors. Violence against children and babies is well documented and dates back to the biblical period. Historically, most forms of child punishment would today be considered severe child abuse. Parents were instructed to chastise and control errant children through such methods as swaddling, whipping, burning, drowning, castration, and abandonment. Puritans held a strict belief in original sin and parents were instructed to, in a very literal sense, beat the devil out of their children. Early American schools used corporal punishment so frequently that the birch rod became a symbol of education. In the not too distant past, there were even reports of special education teachers twisting and grabbing students' arms, hitting or banging their heads onto desks, and smearing hot sauce into their faces and mouths.

In the 1970s, it was found that Baptists were more likely to have experienced physical punishment at home than were persons from other denominations. In general, corporal punishment is more strongly supported by conservative or "fundamentalist" Protestants than by others. This association is explained by the emphasis on biblical literalism, biblical inerrancy, and original sin found among

ALTERNATIVES TO CORPORAL PUNISHMENT

Past studies have considered the effects of using various methods of discipline on child outcomes. For instance, the use of reasoning alone has proven to be just as effective in correcting disobedience as the use of reasoning combined with corporal punishment. Time-out is a type of punishment in which a child is removed from a volatile situation for a short period of time. The rationale underlying time-out is that removing someone from a reinforcing situation deters and discourages him or her from repeating the offense. Time-out is based on a contingency model of human behavior that suggests that some combination of removal of or provision of valued or devalued resources will shape behaviors. Parents and teachers may increase good behaviors and decrease bad behaviors by either giving the child something he or she values, such as praise, toys, or tokens, or by removing something important or by removing the child from a pleasurable or enjoyable experience.

It has been shown that mothers who use time-out without physical correction are just as effective in controlling their children as mothers who use time-out with physical enforcement. Long-term studies reveal that behavior problems improve if and when parents desist in the use of corporal punishment. Today, many parenting experts and family scholars recommend some combination of providing clear guidelines, role modeling, rewarding good behavior, and demonstrating love and affection to children as the most effective ways to elicit good behavior. Screaming, criticizing, and limiting recognition to bad behavior are all discouraged as they exacerbate behavior problems in children. In general, children whose parents give them prescriptive or affirmative instructions (telling children *what* to do rather than what *not* to do), praise them often, model appropriate behavior, and use calming reinforcements, such as time-out, are more well adjusted and better behaved than children whose parents rely on escalating methods such as yelling and spanking. Over time, children's noncompliance may result in the parents intensifying these methods, which increases the risk of physical or verbal abuse against the child.

---

these religious traditions. In addition, Christians from more conservative traditions often embrace a view of the family that is hierarchical—with children, as well as wives, subsumed under the headship of men. Fundamentalist Protestants and conservative Catholics are also more likely than others to support the use of corporal punishment in schools. Not surprisingly, it has also been found that conservative Protestants are, for the most part, not persuaded by social science research to modify their familial practices. On the contrary, conservatives may identify social science scholarship, as well as intellectual pursuits more generally, as antithetical to Christian beliefs and threatening to family life. Popular theologian and author, James Dobson, for example, has explicitly rejected the use of scientific inquiry to explore the appropriateness of various parenting practices. Dobson has also suggested that children suffer from an inherent predisposition toward selfishness and rebellion.

Attitudes toward corporal punishment have been found to vary regionally as well. In general, persons living in the Southeast are more likely to approve of corporal punishment, both at home and in schools. This is not surprising in light of other findings which reveal that Southerners hold more conservative attitudes in many areas, including gender roles, sexuality, race, and religion. In particular, the association between region and approval of corporal punishment has been linked to the predominance of religious conservatism and biblical literalism found in the southern region of the United States. In fact, a small number of states concentrated in what is commonly referred to as the Bible Belt, including Alabama, Mississippi, Tennessee, Georgia, and South Carolina, account for the majority of school spankings nationally. Interestingly, recent studies demonstrate that the most noteworthy aspect of regional variation in corporal punishment attitudes does not center on the South's approval of corporal punishment, but rather the rejection of corporal punishment found in the Northeast. In general, the Northeastern region has the least amount of legitimate, or culturally sanctioned, violence.

Southern support for corporal punishment has also been linked to lower levels of education, lower household incomes, and racial composition. It should be noted, however, that research in this area has resulted in a myriad of findings, some of which are complex and contradictory. For example, African American parents have been shown to express approval for corporal punishment at higher levels than whites, although some studies find that white parents are more likely than African American parents to use corporal punishment. In addition, some studies find little or no correlation between the use of corporal punishment and socioeconomic status, presumably because support for corporal punishment in the United States has been, and continues to be, extremely high due to a variety of social, cultural, and religious reasons.

In conclusion, it has been found that mothers spank more than fathers and younger parents more than older parents. Individuals who were spanked as children are more likely than others to spank their own children. Also, spouses involved in violent marriages are more likely to hit their children than spouses in nonabusive relationships. The relationship between social class and use of corporal punishment has been researched extensively and this research has produced mixed findings. Perhaps an accurate summary statement is that while some studies find greater approval and more usage of corporal punishment among lower income households, corporal punishment is so widely accepted and approved in American culture that it is commonly found among and across all social classes.

EFFECTS OF CORPORAL PUNISHMENT

The effects of corporal punishment are well documented and sobering. Studies reveal that individuals who were physically punished by parents or caregivers are more likely to be physically aggressive with others, including one's spouse; to severely attack one's siblings; to imagine or engage in masochistic sexual practices; to physically abuse one's children; to have depressive symptoms and suicidal thoughts; to become delinquent as a juvenile; and to have lower lifetime earnings. The more often one was subjected to corporal punishment during adolescence, the lower the chances of being in the top twenty percent of all wage-earners. It is worth reiterating that, contrary to conventional wisdom, a number of studies demonstrate that spanking children actually places them at greater risk for adjustment and behavior problems.

It has also been found that states in which teachers are permitted to hit children have a higher rate of student violence as well as a higher homicide rate. Nations that approve of the use of corporal punishment by teachers have higher infant murder rates than do other nations. This association is explained by using a so-called cultural spillover theory. That is, nations that strongly support corporal punishment in schools tend to have wide levels of support for the practice and consequently high rates of its usage at all ages and across varying circumstances and situations. Therefore, the likelihood that someone, a parent, teacher, day care worker, or clergy person, will use corporal punishment, even against an infant, is higher in such societies. Furthermore, the likelihood of corporal punishment resulting in death is obviously much higher for infants than for other age groups.

See also Child Abuse; Parenting Styles.

Further Reading: Bitensky, Susan H. *Corporal Punishment of Children: A Human Rights Violation.* Ardsley, NY: Transnational Publishers, 2006; Crary, Elizabeth. *Without Spanking or Spoiling: A Practical Approach to Toddler and Preschool Guidance.* Seattle, WA: Parenting Press, 1993; Gelles, Richard J., and Donileen Loseke. *Current Controversies in Family Violence.* Thousand Oaks, CA: Sage Publications, 1993; Hyman, Irwin A. *Reading, Writing, and the Hickory Stick. The Appalling Story of Physical and Psychological Abuse in American Schools.* Lexington, MA: Lexington Books, 1990; Spock, Benjamin. *Baby and Child Care.* New York: Simon and Schuster, 1996; Straus, Murray A. *Beating the Devil Out of Them: Corporal Punishment in American Families and its Effects on Children.* New Brunswick, NJ: Transaction Publishers, 2001; Straus, Murray A., Richard J. Gelles, and Suzanne K. Steinmetz. *Behind Closed Doors: Violence in the American Family.* New York, NY: Doubleday/Anchor, 1980; Straus, Murray A., and Richard J. Gelles. *Physical Violence in American Families: Risk Factors and Adaptations to Violence in 8,145 Families.* New Brunswick, NJ: Transaction Publishers, 1989; Wyckoff, Jerry L., and Barbara C. Unell. *Discipline Without Shouting or Spanking: Practical Solutions to the Most Common Preschool Behavior Problems.* Minnetonka, MN: Meadowbrook Press, 2002.

Susan Cody-Rydzewski

COSLEEPING

New parents have many decisions to make about caring for their infant children. Sleeping arrangements may not be on the top of their list of major decisions, but there is considerable controversy in the United States about the safest options when it comes to infant sleep. Most parents spend months creating a peaceful soothing nursery for their child. Some of these perfectly planned nurseries will end up as a sleeping haven for a child, but other nurseries will be utilized only as a tidy storage room for baby paraphernalia because the child actually sleeps in the parents' bed. The practice of an infant or child sharing a bed with one or both parents is called cosleeping. Cosleeping is also known as the "family bed," "bed sharing," and even "sleep sharing."

Through information provided to new parents by physicians and other health care providers, as well as print and online parenting magazines, most new parents are aware and concerned about the phenomenon of Sudden Infant Death Syndrome (SIDS), formerly known as crib death. In SIDS a seemingly healthy infant dies of unknown causes while sleeping. Cosleeping has been blamed for an increase in SIDS, though the supporting evidence for this assertion is sketchy. This supposed link has raised the stakes in the debate over the benefits and risks of cosleeping.

Parents who choose to cosleep with their babies may receive criticism from friends and family. This negative criticism has influenced some cosleeping parents to stop the practice and place the child in his or her own room. Cosleeping parents learn to be cautious about revealing their sleeping arrangements because of the negative opinions that others express. Many closeted cosleepers will admit to their sleeping arrangements if they find other cosleepers in their social setting. Some seek support at internet sites sympathetic to their parenting choices. Parents who choose to have their infants sleep with them, however, may just be following the patterns established by human ancestors.

BACKGROUND

Cosleeping has a long history in non-Western societies. In fact, a majority of the world's societies continue to embrace the practice. Ethnographic reports indicate that bed sharing is the preferred sleeping arrangement for mother-baby pairs, and approximately 90 percent of the world's population considers it a cultural norm. Estimates are that training children to sleep independently through the night is a relatively recent phenomenon, emerging in western societies approximately 200 years ago, but becoming the norm only in the last 100 years. Prior to that time, homes were very small (many had only one room), privacy was nonexistent, and family bed sharing was common, if not a necessity.

With children seen as a natural extension of the mother for the first few years of their lives, and with prolonged breastfeeding commonplace, the custom of cosleeping was widespread. James McKenna, anthropologist and cosleeping researcher, has suggested that cosleeping made sense initially because it increased the survival odds of the infant, serving to protect the health of both mother and baby. His data suggest that mothers and babies have coordinated sleep-wake cycles when they are bed sharing and that this helps both to sleep more restfully. Additionally, mothers are very aware of the baby's physical condition during the night, ready to respond if the child becomes ill or has other difficulties. Heart rate and breathing patterns also become synchronous between the two. SIDS deaths are virtually nonexistent in most of the traditional cosleeping societies.

Some of the controversy over cosleeping has come from the culturally accepted practice of separate sleeping in the United States, but also derives from different parenting strategies. Controversial in their own right, different parenting ethics or strategies are espoused by various pediatricians, child development specialists, and psychologists. Nearly all provide suggestions for sleeping options. Attachment parenting is a model of childrearing that has been closely linked with cosleeping. Originating from the work of John Bowlby about the positive outcomes of strong mother-child attachment, attachment parenting promotes using one's intuition to respond to the infant in the most effective way. In other words, parents should pay attention to the cues provided by the child, trust their judgment about what is best, and strive to know their child better than anyone else could. One of the controversies about attachment parenting is its assertion that parents should avoid separations from their infants and should not cede child care to anyone else, a task that is difficult in families that rely on the income earned by both parents.

Attachment parenting purists strive to be constantly present in their children's lives, with the goal of fostering emotionally stable and secure children. Cosleeping is one element of this attachment. Those who follow the attachment parenting model hope to provide consistent, attentive responses to an infant's needs. This responsiveness fosters in the child a sense of attachment to the stable caregiver, allowing that child to later demonstrate empathy and confidence at higher rates than among children who were not so closely attended. Among the proponents of the attachment parenting approach are William and Martha Sears. William Sears, a pediatrician, has written or cowritten more than 30 books designed to help parents with different aspects of parenting. The popularity of attachment parenting increased in the 1990s, perhaps as a result of the many contributions of Dr. Sears to popular parenting books, magazines, and child rearing advice segments in the mass media.

Many parents do not plan on a cosleeping arrangement. Parents usually have their new baby in their room for the first few weeks and then move him or her into a separate room. Having a baby in another room that wakes in the night for care requires someone, usually the mother, to get out of bed and care for the baby. By the time the baby is cared for and resettled in bed the mother is fully awake. Because this pattern is repeated several times a night while the infant is very young, the next morning the mother is exhausted. She may have a hard time starting the day knowing that at night the same thing is going to happen all over again. Mothers, especially nursing mothers, may decide to take the baby into bed to just lie down for a few minutes while the baby eats. They both fall asleep and if the baby wakes again the close proximity makes caring for the baby easier than going into another room. Some babies do sleep better being close to their parents. This allows the parents to sleep better as well. Parents who did not plan to cosleep or may not have coslept with previous children can find themselves with a child in their bed.

ADVANTAGES OF COSLEEPING

There are many advantages to cosleeping which families experience. They include attachment parenting, more restful sleep for the parents and babies, convenience for breastfeeding, and quick response to problems when they arise in the night. Attachment parenting is a popular strategy and cosleeping extends this technique into the nighttime, not just the daytime waking hours. Parents are readily available to respond to and care for their child's needs easier if the child is in the same room instead of in another location in the house. Dr. William Sears advises parents to be as available as possible to meet the needs of their infants, and with a few basic safety precautions this can include cosleeping.

Most babies and parents sleep better in a cosleeping environment. Babies feel safe and fall asleep easier in the arms of a parent. A mother is able to get more sleep if the baby is in her room because she is usually aware of the baby's wakefulness before the child cries out for assistance, does not always have to get out of bed, and need not go into another room to care for the baby's needs. Babies cry significantly less in a cosleeping environment compared to one where they are physically separated from their mothers. Parents who have toddlers sleeping with them can monitor a child who may wake in the middle of the night and try to leave the family room. Children can be soothed quickly when bad dreams occur and may not be quite as frightened because they are with their parents. Both mothers and fathers report that sharing a bed with their children is generally an enjoyable experience and leads to feeling more bonded to them.

Breastfeeding mothers tend to get more sleep if their baby is in bed or close to them. The world's leading breastfeeding organization, La Leche League International, recommends that cosleeping occurs, beginning at birth. Breastfed babies nurse more often than bottle-fed babies, so lactation consultants offer their clients cosleeping as a way to meet this need. Mothers are able to nurse right away before the baby is fully awake, thus decreasing the impact on both of their sleeping. Medical science suggests that the health benefits of breastfeeding for the child lead to a decrease in childhood illnesses as the mother's antibodies can help provide some immunity against common infections. Because breastfeeding is often seen as a critical step in establishing the mother-child bond, it is also a critical element of attachment parenting.

If the child is sleeping with the parents, any problems that might occur in the night will be quickly noticed. Parents will know right away if a child gets sick, spikes a fever, vomits, or even chokes and they can respond to the situation immediately. If a child is in another room, the parents may not realize he or she has had problems until the next morning. One highly controversial aspect of sleep choice involves the research of medical anthropologist James McKenna of the University of Notre Dame. McKenna's research suggests that SIDS rates are lower in cosleeping infants, when safety measures are taken, than in those infants who sleep independent of their parents. There is some research evidence that points to arousal difficulties as a risk factor for SIDS. This means that some infants sleep too soundly and may have difficulty awakening if they have trouble breathing. McKenna found that cosleeping babies spent less time in the deepest levels of sleep and therefore woke up more often. This would be beneficial for babies with a higher risk of SIDS. A cosleeping infant patterns its respiratory and central nervous system response after its mother's. Thus, their ability to rouse from sleep is aided by the presence of the parent.

Additionally, children with special needs may particularly benefit from cosleeping. A child with disabilities who needs nighttime care can be tended to and children with sleep disorders may experience better sleep. Studies show that babies pattern their breathing to the breathing of their parents, especially the mother's because the baby usually sleeps closer to the mother.

DISADVANTAGES OF COSLEEPING

While the advantages of cosleeping are many, particularly for breastfeeding mother-child pairs, there are also disadvantages to this arrangement and reasons for families not to cosleep. Among the organizations that have come out against cosleeping are the Consumer Product Safety Commission (CPSC) and the American Academy of Pediatrics (AAP). Both groups have expressed concern over the safety of the practice for infants. Media reports from the CPSC stress the dangers of cosleeping infants becoming trapped in bedding, between mattresses and bed frames, falling off of beds, and suffocating in waterbeds. Additionally, infants might be suffocated by a cosleeping parent accidentally lying on top of them, a phenomenon known as overlying. Because products for juveniles, such as baby furniture and cribs, must go through special testing, the assumption is that they are somehow safer than products available for general use.

The AAP has opposed cosleeping for similar reasons including a concern over SIDS. Instead, the AAP recommends that infants sleep in the same room as their parents, but in their own designated place such as a crib or a bassinet. Parents are encouraged to keep the infant in the same room with them until the infant is at least 6 months old. Among the experts supporting this stance have been Dr. Benjamin Spock and Dr. T. Berry Brazelton, both well know child care advisors. These authors encouraged parents to help their children sleep independently because cosleeping was thought to foster in the child an unhealthy dependency on the parents, as well as to create sleep difficulties and bad sleep habits in the children. A controversial figure in his own right, Dr. Richard Ferber has been a supporter of solo sleep, particularly as it relates to his method of helping children self-sooth at the time for sleep. The so-called cry it out method that he advocates has been well publicized and remains a hot topic of discussion among parents.

Cosleeping will not be beneficial if one of the parents is against the idea. Parenting decisions that are agreed upon by the couple are easier to implement. Some parenting experts have even suggested that cosleeping might be harmful to the marital relationship by decreasing spontaneous intimacy between the parents. Many critics, friends, family, and those new to cosleeping believe the sex lives of cosleeping parents are virtually nonexistent. Another argument against cosleeping acknowledges that some babies move around and make noises during sleep, particularly as they age, which can keep one or both parents from sleeping.

FUTURE OF COSLEEPING

Despite the official policy against cosleeping disseminated by the AAP, the medical organization devoted to child health and well-being, the practice remains controversial. As the AAP has encouraged more breastfeeding of infants, many mothers have rediscovered the convenience and utility of cosleeping with their infants. While the official AAP policy opposes cosleeping, many individual pediatricians take a less prohibitive position and may be unlikely to chastise the parents of healthy infants for participating in the family bed. This ambiguity has led parents to wonder which expert's advice is right for them.

Contrary to popular belief that the family bed causes stress on the partners' sexual relationship, marital intimacies are often strengthened in cosleepers. The family bed is not the only place a couple can have private time. Children can be moved to another room after they fall asleep or parents can make use of the other rooms in the home. Parents can plan date nights where the family car is not just used for transportation. While some cosleeping parents have difficultly adjusting, many say creativity is the key and oftentimes this helps spice up their relationship.

For parents who are concerned about the safety of a cosleeping child, placing the child in a separate bed or even separate room will allow the parents to sleep better. Babies can suffocate in thick bedding and waterbeds. They can get stuck in an open space somewhere on the bed and strangle themselves. Babies could get injured by falling off of the bed. There are potential accidents that can occur in a family bed, but if a family uses some safe-guarding techniques, accidents can be minimized. Drug and alcohol use could impair a parent's awareness of the child next to them, so they should not be used when cosleeping. Obese parents may find having the child sleep in a crib nearby a better arrangement due to fear of overlying. Big firm beds are ideal for cosleepers as they allow plenty of room for movement during the night and less chance of overlying. Parents who wish to cosleep but are afraid of the baby falling out of the bed can place their mattress on the floor. Even in a cosleeping arrangement, babies should always sleep on their backs to reduce the risk of SIDS.

Baby product manufacturers are responding to the questions that parents have about the appropriateness of cosleeping. Parents who are still concerned about sleeping with their baby can purchase things to help them feel more comfortable with a baby in their bed. Guardrails can help prevent a baby from falling off the bed. A three-sided baby bed that attaches to the parents' bed resembles a sidecar and allows the baby to be close to the parent without the fear of overlying. A popular brand, the Arms Reach Co-Sleeper, is heavily marketed in parenting materials.

Parents spend significant amounts of time reading guides on how to be better parents and learning the newest trends on child rearing. They try to learn all the pros and cons of the numerous proven techniques that result in a happy adjusted independent child. Many parents choose cosleeping with their children as a way to further strengthen the bond between each family member, whereas other parents believe that children will become too dependent if they share a room for a long period of time. Until a definitive link is established between infant health and sleep situation, the decision to cosleep is likely to remain controversial.

See also Breastfeeding or Formula Feeding; Midwifery and Medicalization; Parenting Styles; Transition to Parenthood.

Further Reading: Ask Dr. Sears, 2006. http://www.askdrsears.com; Attachment Parenting International. http://www.attachmentparenting.org; Aware Parenting Institute. http://www.awareparenting.com/comfort.htm; Ferber, Richard. *Solve Your Child's Sleep Problems: New, Revised and Expanded Edition.* New York: Fireside, 2006; Gordon, Jay, and Maria Goodavage. *Good Nights (The Happy Parents' Guide to the Family Bed).* New York: St. Martin's Press, 2002; Karp, Harvey. *The Happiest Baby on the Block.* New York: Bantam Dell, 2002; La Leche League International, Inc. *The Womanly Art of Breast Feeding,* 6th ed. Schaumberg, IL: La Leche League International, Inc., 1997; LaLeche League International. http://www.llli.org; MacGregor, Cynthia. *Mommy Rescue Guide: Getting Your Baby to Sleep.* Avon, MA: Adams Media, 2007; McKenna, James J. *Sleeping With Your Baby: A Parent's Guide to Cosleeping.* Washington, DC: Platypus Press, 2007; Mother-Baby Behavioral Sleep Laboratory. http://www.nd.edu/~jmckenn1/lab/mckenna.html; Nemours Foundation. http://www.kidshealth.org; Sears, William, M. D., and Martha Sears, R. N. *The Attachment Parenting Book.* New York: Little, Brown and Company, 2001; Task Force on Infant Positioning and SIDS, 1999. http://aappolicy.aappublications.org/cgi/content/full/pediatrics%3B105/3/650; Thevenin, T. *The Family Bed: An Age Old Concept in Childrearing.* Wayne, NJ: Avery Publishing Group, Inc., 1987; Young, J. "Babies and bedsharing . . . Cosleeping." *Midwifery Digest* 8 (1998): 364–369.

Taralyn Watson

COVENANT MARRIAGE

Beginning in the late 1990s several states enacted *covenant marriage* provisions that were aimed at elevating the status of marriage and making divorce harder to attain. This is an optional marriage contract that is completed in addition to the requirements for issuing a standard marriage license. In effect, when couples in those states with covenant marriage provisions elect a covenant marriage rider on their marriage licenses, they agree to give up their right to a quick, no-fault divorce and to follow certain provisions designed to increase the long-term stability of the marriage. In some ways covenant marriage is akin to prenuptial agreements in that couples are choosing to agree in advance on the rules that will govern their relationship. Unlike prenuptial agreements that have been used to specify the distribution of assets when a relationship ends, covenant marriage emphasizes the steps that partners will take to remain in their relationship, including premarital and relationship counseling and a waiting period should a divorce be seriously considered.

BACKGROUND

The idea of covenant marriage was first conceived of and presented in the Florida legislature in 1989. While the idea was discussed, the bill died in committee and was forgotten. Part of the problem for its cool reception may have been that it was targeted at strengthening marriage, rather than as a divorce preventative. In the Louisiana legislature covenant marriage was couched largely in terms of divorce reform legislation making the idea quite palatable and intriguing to southern conservatives. Introduced by state representative Tony Perkins, the bill was passed in June 1997 and the first covenant marriages were available August 15 of the same year. While it sounds like a covenant marriage would only be performed by a religious official, anyone who is licensed to wed couples in Louisiana can officiate at such a marriage ceremony.

Following the example of Louisiana, between 1997 and 2001, twenty-six states considered some form of covenant marriage laws. Only two states have followed Louisiana's lead: Arizona in 1998 and Arkansas in 2001. It is the responsibility of court clerks, who issue marriage licenses, to inform couples of the option of covenant marriage.

Definitions and Provisions

Covenant marriages follow certain rules. While the details vary slightly between each of the states, there are some common elements. First, partners agree to some type of premarital preparation or counseling. Some of this counseling includes information about the law itself and is designed to ensure that couples enter the agreement with full knowledge of what it might mean for their future together. Second, partners take an oath of lifelong commitment to marriage that is in addition to what they might say in the wedding vows. Third, the partners agree to accept limited grounds upon which a divorce may be granted, including a trial separation period. And fourth, they agree to seek marital counseling for a specified period if problems threaten the marriage or they contemplate divorce.

Part of the reason for the counseling about the law is to clarify for couples that no-fault divorce will not be an option for them unless they are willing to go to counseling and try a two-year separation period first. To divorce prior to that, they must demonstrate grounds to do so. Examples of grounds for divorce under covenant marriage provisions are adultery, abuse of the spouse or child (physical or sexual), conviction of a felony, incarceration or abandonment of at least a year, and addiction.

Characteristics of Covenant Marriage Choosers

Researchers at Louisiana State University have been interested in the effects of covenant marriage as well as the characteristics of persons choosing this option. They have conducted several different types of studies including content analysis of marriage license applications and interviews with marrying couples. Several clear findings have emerged from their research. Across all three states only a fraction of the couples who marry select the covenant marriage option. Those who do, however, tend to be more religious on average. They are also more likely to be from Southern Baptist or Nondenominational conservative Christian groups. They are more politically conservative as a group, but they do have fairly high levels of education. This led the researchers to estimate that engaged persons who were white, fundamentalist, and educated have a 25 percent chance of entering a covenant marriage.

Covenant marriage choosers are more traditional on issues of gender roles in the family, strongly agreeing with the statement that the husband is the head of the family. Most also saw divorce as a very serious problem nationally and agreed that society would be better off if divorce were harder to attain. They suggested that divorce was largely due to selfishness and a lack of family values. Not surprisingly, persons who had cohabited before marriage were very unlikely to choose the covenant marriage option.

PROPONENTS OF COVENANT MARRIAGE

Proponents of covenant marriage, many of whom are members of conservative Christian organizations, explain that a basic reason for the push toward covenant marriage laws is a concern for the welfare of children born to the union. They cite the sometimes dramatic decline in women and children's standard of living following divorce as support for the idea that two parents are better than one. Covenant marriage, by forcing partners to seek counseling, increases the likelihood that they will see the benefits of staying together, for themselves as well as for the good of the family. While not perfect, a two-parent family can insulate children from some of the difficult outcomes of a divorce. There is some evidence to suggest that couples who stay together for at least a year during difficult relationship times are more likely to see increases in their marital happiness and stay together.

Proponents also argue that too much individualism and too little familism are destroying the American family. Drawing on the ideas that marriage is about family goals and not individual desires, the practical aspects of marriage are highlighted. Covenant marriage is an attempt to legislate people's option in such a way that they can publicly choose familism over individualism. It reflects the sanctity of marriage through a public affirmation, the law, of its importance. Proponents also see the passage of covenant marriage provisions as a backlash against the proliferation of no-fault divorce and the doubling of the United States divorce rate since no-fault divorces became available. Ideally, then, covenant marriage will lead to a decrease in divorce.

Fred Lowery, a Baptist minister in Louisiana, has been a strong supporter of covenant marriage, providing guidance to the legislature when the statute was being constructed. Additionally, he has written materials to help couples who want to live a covenant marriage life stressing their commitment not only to each other, but to God and the institution of marriage.

CONCERNS WITH COVENANT MARRIAGE

Just as some religious leaders and groups support covenant marriage, others oppose it, going so far as to refuse to marry couples who want a covenant bond. Particularly strong in this camp are Catholics. This is most likely due to the fact that covenant marriage counseling and affidavits talk so much about divorce.

Concerns have also been voiced by some in the legal profession. Some legal scholars at Tulane University and elsewhere have expressed concern that such legislation would lead to three disturbing legal trends. The first is an increase in annulments (a declaration that says that a marriage was never legally valid) as couples try to skirt the two-year waiting period for divorce. The second is a return to fabricated reasons for divorce, such as were common in the days before no-fault divorce provisions, where couples might lie about negative aspects of their marriage so that a divorce would be granted. And third is an increase in migratory divorce, where couples go out-of-state and get a divorce in a state where covenant marriage is not recognized.

Additional criticisms from the legal arena suggest that it is an unconstitutional state support of religion. Given that the origin of the term covenant marriage is Biblical and the connotation has been a religious one, this suggests that the founding principles of the current legislation are religious and therefore in violation of the separation of church and state.

Some groups argue that covenant marriage leads to too much state involvement in marriage; that attempts are being made to govern how couples live their lives on a daily basis by limiting how they would get out of an unsatisfactory marriage. Marriage is redefined as the state sees fit, rather than how the participants would like it to proceed. On the other end of the argument is the idea that it infringes on the right to marry initially. If a person permitted to perform weddings won't marry you without the covenant marriage affidavit, then that limits your choices.

Finally, in opposition to the argument that covenant marriage protects women and children, Domestic Violence Groups and others have proposed that covenant marriage, with its waiting periods and required counseling sessions, is harmful to women and children. It keeps them in the abusive situation longer, and forces them to prove that abuse occurred.

FUTURE TRENDS

While the covenant marriage movement seems to have stalled in recent years, there is still a small but committed group working for its expansion. Perhaps there will be some changing statistics that will add fuel to the fire, though at the present time that does not seem very likely. Questions remain about the viability of these marriage licenses. If all covenant marriage offers is inconvenience as an obstacle to divorce, it doesn't really solve the problem of high divorce rates, it just prolongs the process. Family professionals hope to see other solutions in the works that better solve the problem of too-easy divorce. Most suggest that it is better to make marriage harder to enter so that couples would be better prepared, and have thoroughly considered their decision to wed.

Questions remain for researchers to explore. One is whether the persons who have opted for covenant marriage so far will stay together. Another asks that if they stay together, will it be because of the type of marriage that they selected, or did they select the marriage because they were persons who would have been more likely to stay together anyway?

Enacting laws on a wide scale that make it harder for couples to both get into and get out of marriages will bring divorce rates down. However, it seems unlikely that these measures would increase marital satisfaction or quality in any appreciable way. This is an area for future researchers to explore.

See also Adversarial and No-Fault Divorce; Divorce, as Problem, Symptom, or Solution; Religion and Families.

Further Reading: Hawkins, Alan J., Steven L. Nock, Julia C. Wilson, Laura Sanchez, and James D. Wright. "Attitudes about covenant marriage and divorce: Policy Implications from a 3-Stage Comparison." *Family Relations* 51 (2002): 166–175; Hawkins, Alan J., Lynn D. Wardle, and David O. Coolidge. *Revitalizing the Institution of Marriage for the 21st Century: An Agenda for Strengthening Marriage.* New York: Praeger, 2002; Lowery, Fred. *Covenant Marriage: Staying Together For Life.* West Monroe, LA: Howard Publishing Co., Inc., 2002; Nichols, Joel A. "Louisiana's Covenant Marriage Law: A First Step Toward a More Robust Pluralism in Marriage and Divorce Law?" *Emory Law Journal* 47 (1998): 929–930; Nock, Steven L., James D. Wright, and Laura Sanchez. "America's Divorce Problem." *Society* 36 (1999): 43–52.

Kimberly P. Brackett

CULTURE OF POVERTY

The so-called culture of poverty is a social theory developed to explain why some individuals and groups are poor. Historically, and presently, this approach has been used to explain the behaviors of persons in poverty and to make public policy decisions, often with harmful consequences. Competing approaches to examining poverty focus on conditions in society as a whole and the consequences of the social class system, rather than just the socialization that occurs in poor families and communities. While explanations for poverty that deal with the cultural messages transmitted in poor families tend to blame those in poverty for their own circumstances, other explanations for poverty tend to view the poor as victims of social forces or structural changes beyond their own control. Both schools of thought have adherents and each can contribute to a more complete understanding of poverty in American society.

Poverty, according to culture of poverty adherent Oscar Lewis, is both an adaptation and reaction of the poor to the conditions of poverty. The culture of poverty is a way of life and a set of learned behavioral traits that enable the poor to survive. The family is largely responsible for transmitting the traits to younger generations. These behavioral survival traits include an inability to control one's impulse, a focus on the present and lack of planning for the future, and the failure to defer gratification and plan for the future. While a focus on the present is an adaptive trait for someone whose future is bleak with little or no opportunity, living in the moment and little planning for the future are self-limiting behaviors in the long term and result in individuals becoming trapped in poverty.

ORIGINS OF THE CULTURE OF POVERTY

Some of the major concepts underlying the culture of poverty were first developed by the African American sociologist E. Franklin Frazier in his book, *The*

Negro Family in the United States, where he explores why African Americans did not develop the skills necessary for success. He found the problem to lie in behavioral traits that were counterproductive and trapped them in poverty. Frazier believed that the pathological nature of the African American family was a result of the social conditions present in larger society. He found that the family structure and cultural patterns that guided black families in Africa were totally destroyed by slavery, emancipation, and urbanization. These social conditions destroyed male dominance and encouraged the matriarchal organization of the family. Frazier argued that beginning with slavery and being reinforced by emancipation and urbanization, the family became matriarchal, and the position and authority of black males in the family was weakened. The matriarchal organization left the family dysfunctional and impacted the family well into the twentieth century. The outcome was a pathological family system resulting in poverty, illegitimacy, crime, and juvenile delinquency. Frazier posited that the problems of African Americans were a result of a cultural pathology, and the pathology was passed on through generations creating a self-perpetuating cycle of hopelessness.

It is believed that the poverty of African Americans is the result of social conditions that both influenced and reinforced individual traits that led to trapping people in poverty. Lewis (1966) found similar individual traits that trapped people in poverty when comparing a slave's way of life in the antebellum south with the families he was studying in Mexico, Puerto Rico, and New York. It was in Lewis's book, *Five Families: Mexican Case Studies in the Culture of Poverty*, where the term "culture of poverty" originally appeared. From this study, he wanted to see if the same behaviors he found in his study on Mexican families were also present in another group. In order to do a comparative analysis on families in poverty, he expanded his next study to 100 Puerto Rican families in four slum areas in San Juan, Puerto Rico plus their relatives in New York. The objective was to gain an understanding of urban life and develop new methods of studying the family.

Accordingly, the culture of poverty is useful because it shows that poverty is not a problem limited only to African Americans or other ethnic minorities, but is a way of life; a culture. It was concluded that even if physical poverty were eliminated it may not be enough to eliminate the culture of poverty. The culture of poverty is a whole way of life to which the poor become accustomed.

He concluded that the behavioral traits found among the poor went beyond regional differences and rural-urban distinctions to suggest that all poor were reacting and adapting to problems in a similar manner. The culture of poverty, then, is both a reaction and adaptation of the poor "to their marginal position in a class-stratified, highly individuated, capitalistic society." The poor person adapts with a list of 70 interconnected social, economic, and psychological traits that include, but are not limited to, the following: poor integration into society including involvement in major institutions such as political parties, welfare agencies, hospitals, department stores, museums, or art galleries; low wages, chronic underemployment or unemployment; little or no property ownership; absence of savings; production of very little wealth, and low levels of literacy and education.

APPLYING THE CULTURE OF POVERTY IN AMERICAN SOCIETY

The culture of poverty's focus on behavioral traits (*i.e.,* culture) makes it convenient for both public policy makers and professionals. For policy makers, an individual's behavior is the reason he or she is poor; therefore, if a policy can be written that could change a person's behavior then the person will no longer be poor. The reasoning that policy can change individual behavior can be seen in the changes in welfare policy starting in the 1960s.

Welfare services and policies originated with President Franklin Delano Roosevelt's Great Depression programs of the 1930s and were designed to help unemployed workers and their families. These programs became collectively known as welfare. One program in particular was the Social Security Act of 1935. From the Social Security Act developed Aid to Families with Dependent Children (AFDC) and for 61 years this federal program provided governmental aid to single mothers with children. In 1996, AFDC—the cash payment that most Americans think of when they hear the word "welfare"—was changed to Temporary Assistance for Needy Families (TANF) as part of the federal welfare reform legislation. One of the major incentives for the changes in TANF was to reduce the welfare rolls by putting a five-year limit on all welfare benefits. Advocates of the culture of poverty approach believe the poor are poor because of certain behavioral traits and choices. In other words, this approach would say the poor lack initiative in the labor market, leading to increases in rates of out-of-wedlock births, teen pregnancy, long-term unemployment, crime, and drug use. The hope of policy makers, and certainly that of TANF advocates, is that required employment would break the cycle of dependency by putting limits on welfare benefits and by teaching recipients a new life style.

Starting in the 1960s, welfare policy was largely shaped by the ideas of Daniel Patrick Moynihan. As the assistant secretary of labor for policy in the Kennedy administration, he believed that the government could use information from the social sciences to deal with social problems. Moynihan's ideas laid the foundation for the War on Poverty and his report was titled "The Negro Family: The Case for National Action." The report focused on female-headed households, matriarchy, economic dependency, unemployment, crime, and juvenile delinquency. His intention was to create an environment suitable to discussing poverty and developing policies that helped the black community.

The Moynihan Report, as it became known, was built on Moynihan's belief that "at the heart of the deterioration of the fabric of [African American] society is the deterioration of the [black] family." The report and his recommendations were based on the following characteristics of African American households: (a) nearly a quarter of marriages had dissolved, (b) nearly one quarter of births to African American women were illegitimate, (c) low rates of intact marriages, high rates of out-of-wedlock birth led to one fourth of families being headed by females, and (d) the breakdown in family structure had led to stark increases in welfare dependency. From these statistics Moynihan concluded that the direct cause of poverty was a family pathology created by female-dominant families, dysfunctional households, poor values, and a lack of aspirations that kept African Americans firmly rooted in poverty.

The report marks a change from the government's focus on changing laws to improving living conditions for African Americans. Moynihan felt that barriers such as discrimination that prevented African Americans from living as well as middle-class whites had been lifted, but the long-term effect of inequality was going to make it difficult for the majority of African Americans to take advantage of the new laws.

The report was an update to findings reported 30 years earlier by Frazier. Moynihan's goal had been to retest Frazier's predictions about the "intertwining effects of socioeconomic deprivation and family disorganization." For sociologists and psychologists, the report presented nothing new or startling and was a policy-oriented view of the problems that were affecting African Americans; however, publicly the report was controversial.

Moynihan's intentions were to help the black community, but his work was misunderstood. Three of the main criticisms consisted first of people who felt his work blamed the victim and portrayed the poor as responsible for their own misfortune. Second, press coverage primarily focused on the high number of children being born out of wedlock, which supported the views of racists. Third, by focusing on the unstable African American families, stable families that were not pathological felt it ruined the reputation of all African American families.

Today, the culture of poverty's easily understood and straightforward tenets have been applied not only to public policy but also in other areas, such as medicine and education. For example, physician Dr. Dale S. Benson offers advice to other physicians on how to provide health care to people living in poverty. He says, "the culture of poverty impacts everything patients in this socioeconomic group think and do. If what a poor patient says doesn't make sense it doesn't mean he/she is wrong. Physicians have to adjust their mental models and think in different cultural terms."

Educators use the culture of poverty to enable teachers to close the gap between the white middle class and their students who are living in poverty. The National Education Association (NEA) has developed a workshop called "A Framework for Understanding Poverty." The framework instructs educators on the so-called hidden rules present in every social class. The developers of the workshops believe that students living in poverty are unaware of the middle-class rules and educators are not knowledgeable about the rules of living in poverty. For example, the workshop teaches that for people living in poverty all of their energies are focused on finding food and keeping the lights on in the house, but for the middle class whose basic needs are easily met they focus on achievement. This workshop asserts that if educators understand the culture of poverty and understand the hidden rules of poverty, educators can instruct students on the cues and rules of the middle class and act as models for all the students.

QUESTIONING THE ASSUMPTIONS OF THE CULTURE OF POVERTY APPROACH

An alternative approach to understanding poverty deals with the institutional features of the social class system. Rather than an emphasis on lifestyle and lifestyle choices, the structural approach suggests that it is one's position in the social class system that enables or restricts access to key social resources including education and occupations. Poverty then is more the result of a knowledge base that is possessively maintained by those in power than the result of individual choices that poor persons make. Education is important as a source of jobs, but jobs are essential because they not only provide families with income to meet the needs of their members, but they also link them in important ways to the larger social structure. Adherents of the structural approach to poverty use terms like class privilege to indicate the advantages that are available to persons in the middle and upper levels of society. Family plays a key role in this system of privilege because it is family that passes along wealth and other valuable resources to future generations, thus maintaining their positive standing in society and helping to prevent a downward movement into poverty.

A structural approach to explaining the causes of poverty can be found in William Julius Wilson's book *The Truly Disadvantaged*. This book outlines how African American poverty is a result of economic changes that have disproportionately affected African Americans. Economic shifts away from manufacturing have disproportionately affected African Americans resulting in joblessness and subsequent poverty. Without a means to support their families, African America men are likely to turn to drugs and crime and less likely to stay with their families, resulting in the high rate out-of-wedlock births and single motherhood.

Persons who prefer a structural approach are critical of the culture of poverty's reliance on several key assumptions. The primary assumptions of the culture of poverty are: (1) one group's way of life is superior to another's, (2) the black family is pathological because of the loss of male dominance and the matriarchal nature of the family and (3) there are specific behavioral traits that the poor possess.

Way of Life

The idea that one group's culture, or way of life, is considered superior to another originated with Charles Darwin's survival of the fittest concept. This assumption leads to the following questions: What are superior survival skills? What can be defined as a better or more successful way of life? What are the markers of success—higher income, occupational success, education, relationships with extended family, or survival despite adversity? In answering these questions the culture of poverty considers the middle-class white emphasis on achievement as the superior survival skill, and the nuclear or conjugal family as the only appropriate way to organize the family. Proponents of the culture of poverty believe an emphasis on the nuclear family is the model that all families should aspire. The nuclear family is based on husband, wife, and children as the central organizing components of the family. A weakness of the approach is the belief that there is one superior model of the family that denies not only the richness of different groups' cultural heritages, but also the strength gained when ethnic families rely on family networks. Other ethnic groups that behave counter to the middle-class white norm are seen as deviant and disorganized.

African American and Latino families are seen as deviant because they are organized around the extended family. For middle-class whites, marriage joins two individuals, and they become the nuclear family; however, for African Americans two families are united through kinship ties that merge to form an extended support system. The strong extended ties can be traced back to tribal Africa. While middle-class white individuals define family values as chastity before marriage and child-bearing within marriage, African Americans define family values as commitment to the informal support system gained through networks of family, friendship, fictive kin, and church. The family offers an extended mutual-aid system that has for a long time been an important feature of the black family. The extended family offers financial aid in terms of food and transportation, emotional support through advice, counseling, visiting and companionship, and care for aging parents. The extended family, or kin networks, often live in close proximity and include frequent interactions, reciprocity of aid, and a feeling of closeness. Friendship networks can even take on the role of kin networks. All of these networks intersect at the black church, which holds networks together and redistributes resources.

The extended family is a key component not only for African Americans but also for Latino families. *Familism,* a key feature of Hispanic families, can be characterized by face-to-face interaction, supporting behaviors such as participation in relatively large kin networks, and engaging in high rates of visiting and exchange. Extended ties and networks include contacts with grandparents, aunts, uncles, and married sisters and brothers. Strong ties outside of the family link community members together through roles as co-parents (*compadres*) and godparents (*padrinos*). In comparison, whites maintain ties with fewer kin and the relationships are more likely to be long distance. Those who criticize the culture of poverty approach conclude that African American and Hispanic families are culturally different and middle-class white families are not superior.

Pathology

Frazier believed the black family to be pathological because of the loss of male dominance, and the matriarchal nature of the family. One of the main assumptions of the culture of poverty is that the loss of male dominance and move to a matriarchy has led to poverty. Does this assumption regarding the division of power in the African American family hold up under closer scrutiny? If the problem is lack of male dominance, then a cultural group that is male dominated should not be perceived as being pathological. However, Hispanic males are seen as domineering, and they are blamed for the plight of the Hispanic family.

Contrary to early reports, historical research has found that men played a dominant role in the family and slave families were not matriarchal in form. Families were listed in the planters' records by the husband's name, and the men were recognized as heads of the family. While there is plenty of evidence to support that the male slave played an active and leadership role in the family, it is difficult to ignore that there are long-term cultural and structural differences between black and white families. Many of the differences relate to the ways the African American family is organized. As early as the beginning of the nineteenth century, African Americans had higher rates of births outside of marriage, more females as head of the family, a higher divorce rate, and a greater tendency to remain single. These differences are related to three social conditions that are experienced differently by blacks and whites and include the marriage squeeze, labor-market success, and out-of-wedlock childbearing.

A long history of African American women working for pay has resulted in a more equal division of household labor and an increased likelihood of African American couples being dual-career compared to white middle class couples. These factors and a higher rate of single motherhood (due to cultural and structural differences between blacks and whites) do not translate into African American families being more matriarchal. Sociological research finds little evidence of African American families being matriarchal.

Rather than finding the problem to be matriarchy, it has been found that patriarchy is the problem with the Hispanic family. More specifically, family disorganization and poverty for Hispanics was due to hegemonic masculinity or machismo. The Hispanic male is seen as an individualist with rampant and out of control sexuality, who acts in a domineering manner, engages in too much drinking, and produces illegitimate children. Latino women are seen as too self-sacrificing, submissive, morally weak, and unable to protect themselves from their aggressive husbands. The combination of the aggressive male and passive female results in family violence and poverty.

Behavioral Traits

There are 70 psychological traits that the poor are believed to possess. Are these traits only found among the poor or are the poor more likely to have fewer safety nets and resources to protect them? It would be extremely difficult to identify specific traits demonstrated by only those in poverty. The signs of pathology noted by the culture of poverty school as afflicting African American and Latino families have also been present in white families, that is, increases in divorce rates, female-headed families, and out-of-wedlock births. White, Hispanic, and African American families have all seen dramatic changes in the last couple of decades, and these changes have affected all families no matter what their race, ethnicity, or social class standing.

Structural explanations would point toward the fact that individuals who are middle class have luxuries such as automatic bank deposits, bill due-date reminders, and low-interest credit cards. People who have more money are better sheltered from making a serious financial error and shortages in cash flow. For example, about 10 percent of households, many of them poor, do not use a bank. In the place of banks, the poor rely on check cashiers to process checks, and when they are in the need of emergency money they use payday loans or borrow from relatives and friends. Nontraditional financial institutions charge high fees and the poor do not have the financial protections that are available to the middle class. Many of the poor are hourly employees and a shortage of hours due to illness, injury, or market changes can create hardship. For financial emergencies, the middle class is protected by credit cards, sick leave, medical and disability insurance, retirement plans, and savings. Culture of poverty supporters would say that not placing one's money in a bank and the poor rate of savings is an example of the poor living for the moment, and their inability to plan for the future. Another approach would be to reason that the poor make a rational choice not to use banks. With little money to save plus the cost of maintaining a bank account (such as minimum balance fees), and with few banks located in poor areas the poor make a rational choice to keep cash on hand.

CONCLUSION

Today, the culture of poverty approach is most often represented by those who talk about persons making bad choices and being part of the underclass, groups persisting in poverty over several generations. The idea that persons become trapped in poverty as a result of their defective or dysfunctional upbringing was a popular stance for welfare reform proponents who suggested that AFDC payments become a way of life and an intergenerational pattern, despite evidence from those favoring the structural approach that less than 10 percent of current welfare recipients were reared in families that consistently received welfare payments. Some social scientists and media analysts continue to discuss urban poverty in cultural terms. Even comedian Bill Cosby cited a culture of poverty argument in chastising young blacks for their failure to rise above their circumstances.

While maintaining either a cultural or structural approach to explaining poverty is possible, these two approaches do not fully capture the complexity of poverty and family life. One example of a new approach to understanding poverty is Intersectionality Theory. Intersectionality Theory highlights how the family is experienced differently in different social classes, by different race and ethnic groups, and by women and men. Family lives are affected by class hierarchies (stratification), racial hierarchies, and gender hierarchies.

See also Deadbeat Parents; Poverty and Public Assistance.

Further Reading: Benson, Dale. "Providing Health Care to Human Beings Trapped in the Poverty Culture." *The Physician Executive* 26, no. 2 (2000): 28–32; Bertrand, Marianne, Sendhil Mullainathan, and Eldar Shafir. "Behavioral Economics and Marketing in Aid of Decision Making Among the Poor." *American Marketing Association* 25 (2006): 8–23; Cabaniss, Emily, and Jill Fuller. "Ethnicity, Race, and Poverty." *Race, Gender, and Class* 12 (2005): 142–162; Collins, Patricia Hill. *Black Feminist Thought: Knowledge, Consciousness, and the Politics of Empowerment*. Boston, MA: Unwin Hyman, 1990; Dickson, Lynda. "The Marriage and Family in Black America." *Journal of Black Studies* 23 (1993): 472–491; Eitzen, Stanley, and Maxine Baca Zinn. "Contemporary Family Policy: An Alternative Vision." *Michigan Family Review* 2 (1997): 7–24; Eitzen, Stanley, and Maxine Baca Zinn. "The Missing Safety Net and Families: A Progressive Critique of the New Welfare Legislation." *Journal of Sociology and Social Welfare* 27 (2000): 53–72; Fogel, Robert W., and Stanley Engerman. *Time on the Cross: The Economics of American Negro Slavery*. Boston, MA: Little Brown, 1974; Frazier, E. Franklin. *The Negro Family in the*

United States. Chicago: The University of Chicago Press, 1966; Lewis, Oscar. *La Vida: A Puerto Rican Family in the Culture of Poverty—San Juan and New York.* New York: Vintage Books, Random House, 1966; Lewis, Oscar. *A Study of Slum Culture: Backgrounds for La Vida.* New York: Random House, 1968; Long, Cindy. "Understanding Poverty." *NEA Today* 24, no. 7 (2006): 16–17; Moynihan, Daniel Patrick. "The Negro Family: The Case for National Action." In *The Moynihan Report and the Politics of Controversy.* Cambridge, MA: The M.I.T. Press, 1967; Pagnini, Deanna, and Philip Morgan. "Racial Differences in Marriage and Childbearing: Oral History Evidence from the South in the Early Twentieth Century." *The American Journal of Sociology* 101 (1996): 1694–1718; Rainwater, Lee, and William L. Yancey. "The Moynihan Report and the Politics of Controversy." In *The Moynihan Report and the Politics of Controversy.* Cambridge, MA: The M.I.T. Press, 1967; United States Department of Labor, Office of Policy Planning and Research. http://www.dol.gov/oasam/programs/history/webid-moynihan.htm; Vega, William. "Hispanic Families in the 1980s: A Decade of Research." *Journal of Marriage and Family* 52 (1990): 1015–1024; Wilson, William Julius. *The Truly Disadvantaged: The Inner City, the Underclass, and Public Policy.* Chicago: University of Chicago Press, 1990; Wilson, William Julius. *When Work Disappears: The World of the New Urban Poor.* New York: Vintage, 1997.

Christy Haines Flatt

D

DATING

In Western society, mate selection, or choosing a socially approved partner to marry, has been the responsibility of young people. The primary way in which mate selection proceeds in the United States and other Western countries is dating. Scholars and lay persons have debated whether dating is an adequate way to select one's mate. Particularly, they have asked whether dating is the best way to choose someone with whom to form a lifetime bond. Is there anything about the process of dating that adequately prepares one for marriage?

Dating as an activity is embedded in the framework of partner selection and teenage ritual. Dating is the process whereby young people are expected to select a suitable life time partner and to learn how to be involved in an intimate relationship. By dating a variety of potential partners, the young person would theoretically arrive at a greater knowledge of who would make the best marital partner, and would select that one perfect person. This romanticized notion assumes that rationality prevails in the dating arena. However, dating is also an activity that is subject to group norms and is a way to gain popularity and status. When young people are asked about the reasons why they date, few respond that it is to find a life partner. Most mention reasons like fun, companionship, sexual encounters, to fit in with the group, and because it is expected of them. The most frequently cited way in which young people meet their dating partners is through friends.

This disconnect between dating as mate selection and dating as a source of fun has always existed in American society but has become more pronounced in recent decades when young people are marrying at later ages, and a larger percentage of young people choose not to marry at all. While people do tend to marry later in today's society, they begin dating earlier in their lives. This contributes to why dating is done for reasons other than mate selection.

HISTORY OF DATING AS PREPARATION FOR MARRIAGE

History of Dating: Courtship

In the United States, dating has evolved over time. The first transition was from a fairly autonomous mate selection system in the colonial era to a more restrictive and formal system in the 1800s referred to as courtship. The second transition occurred in the era of industrialization, specifically in the first two decades of the 1900s. This move away from courtship resulted in behaviors that today we would call traditional dating. One of the cornerstones of modern dating, traditional or nontraditional, is that it occurs in those places where mate selection is predominantly, if not completely, under the control of young people rather than their parents. Dating continues to evolve as younger people participate today and daters use different terms, such as "hanging out" or "getting together" to describe their experiences.

Parental control was very strong in the colonial era, although it was the strongest in wealthy families with strong European ties. Persons of more modest economic means were likely to have enjoyed significant freedom in the selection of a mate. The nature of colonial life meant hard work, long hours, and little leisure. For young men the choice of a mate was more closely tied to the mate's ability to help out, to run the household efficiently, and to be a good wife rather than to his love for her. Love was expected to come after the marriage; not to be a basis for it. The arrival of single persons in America, through immigration or indentured servitude, made a formal system unwieldy because there often was no one to perform introductions or act as a chaperone. Nuclear families that had left kin behind in Europe faced a similar situation.

Following the colonial era and through the 1800s, what is commonly considered formal courtship was the norm, particularly among the middle class. At that time, there was a strong belief in separate roles for men and women in society, resulting from the presumption that the sexes were completely different in nature, spirituality, morality, temperament, and so forth. Consequently, there was a separation between males and females in daily activities. This meant that there would be fewer opportunities for chance meetings between potential partners, unlike in the colonial era where men and women often worked side-by-side in commercial endeavors. This necessitated formal introductions of the couple by a third party who was acquainted with both of them.

While general compatibility and mutual respect had been key criteria for marital partners in the colonial era, during the 1800s it was increasingly expected that the romantic love component would enter the relationship prior to marriage. The process of selecting a suitable spouse became quite formal, reflecting a trend toward formality that was present in society as a whole. This resulted in engagement announcements, formal exchanges of engagement tokens, and formalized wedding ceremonies. It was during this time that the white wedding gown first appeared in popular women's magazines.

The trend toward formal interactions was reflected in the expected behaviors of young people as well. Thus, formal introductions occurred. Accepting a young man's attentions was seen as a serious decision because it was expected to ultimately lead to marriage. As a result, a female had to like the male, or at least believe she would learn to like him, before agreeing to a first date. At this time, dates centered on the woman's family and it is likely that the young man had to plead his case for marriage to the family as well as to the young woman. Parents played an important role in planning activities and encouraging the couple. The involvement of parents also helped to prevent sexual intimacies from being a part of the dating relationship.

During the period of courtship, women had a great deal of power in mate selection. A woman had to give some indication that she was willing to have the man call on her before he would ask for permission. Mothers and daughters would make themselves available at social occasions and would decide from which gentlemen visits would be accepted. Many women announced the days on which they would be home to receive visitors, both male and female, and a formal system of calling cards was used to announce one's presence as a visitor. There was a lot of control of courtship by women partly because of the permission a woman could grant a visitor, but also because the activities generally occurred in the realm of women, the home. The parlor and front porch were popular places for young couples to share refreshments and conversation. These places were approved by the parents because they were not particularly private and parents could usually remain inconspicuously nearby to monitor the interaction and conversation of the couple.

Once a couple was engaged, they were given considerably more privacy. During this time, typically lasting two years, couples began to know each other well. While the visiting and courtship system was quite common for middle class young people, it presented problems for less wealthy families who did not have the extra room in which to allow a couple to get acquainted in semi-privacy. For these couples, courting began to occur in public places. For young people who worked in cities, public courting became commonplace because respectable girls would have lost their respectability if they entertained men in their private quarters, whether that was a dormitory, apartment, or boarding house.

History of Dating: Traditional Dating

Dating began about the time of World War I and by 1920 it had become the way to court a potential mate. The reasons for the shift to dating are diverse, but tend to revolve around two key changes that were happening in society at that time: industrialization, or the move to greater technology and a manufacturing economy, and urbanization, or the movement of people from farms to urban communities to live and work.

People moved to cities in large part because this was where the better jobs could be found. Living in an urban environment brought young men and women in closer contact with each other because of the proximity of residences and the likelihood that both would hold jobs. Living in a more densely populated area expanded the chances for meeting potential partners with whom one could interact. Generally these city jobs, mostly factory, skilled labor or service positions, compensated workers well with both money and leisure time. The result of these better-paying jobs and limited work days was the opportunity to meet and spend time with potential partners and to have money to spend on them.

Industrialization meant that most persons no longer worked from home. Women as well as men could be paid for work outside the home that they had formerly provided in the home for no compensation. Working away from home took young women out of the direct control of their parents and permitted them to interact daily with a wide variety of individuals, including single men. Women working for pay and the women's equality movement in the 1920s likely contributed to women's acceptance of dates and generally more brash behavior. More women were also being educated. The advent of free-access, public coeducational high schools also gave dating a push. Males and females had daily contact with each other and participated in classroom activities together.

The new technology of the industrial revolution spawned the widespread availability of two inventions that are critical for daters: the telephone and the automobile. The telephone was a way for a man to ask a woman on a date, have her accept, and arrange the details of the meeting. The telephone also allowed couples to communicate even when they might not be currently in the same location or able to spend time together. The automobile provided transportation to dating events such as dances, movies, or parties. Daters could travel farther from home and participate in a wider variety of activities. Additionally, the car afforded couples privacy for not only conversation but sexual intimacies.

History of Dating: Current Dating

Through the 1900s and to today, dating has continued to evolve and change. During the 1950s dating was characterized by a strict set of behaviors for both males and females. Couples were, however, permitted privacy and going steady, or dating only one partner for a length of time, was an indicator of one's commitment to the partner and intention to marry. A popular activity for daters was cruising, highlighting the importance of the automobile in dating activities. In the 1960s and 1970s dating became less formal, with mixers and informal gatherings being common places to meet and mingle.

Based on criteria from early courtship and dating rituals, current dating is very relaxed by comparison with few, if any, prohibitions. Formal introductions are not necessary and chaperones are an anomaly. Either partner may do the asking or paying, and intimacies are permitted by the partners as they deem appropriate. Dating occurs for a longer period in one's life now than in the past because people are waiting until they are older to marry or are choosing to remain single. In addition, many persons participating in dating today are divorced or widowed and may bring new criteria for partners, goals for dating, norms for behavior, and expectations to the dating scene.

Several trends have been happening in dating over recent decades. Dating begins at younger ages today, such as 13, compared with 16 in 1920. People have progressively had more dating partners through the last 100 years, have gotten into relationships sooner, and have experimented with sexual intercourse in dating relationships sooner. Some experts suggest that the focus of dating is no longer on looking for a mate, but on looking for someone with whom to have fun.

The language that couples use to talk about their dating relationships has also changed. Are these couples "seeing each other," "just talking," or "going out"? These different descriptions of dating make it difficult to determine the nature of the relationship. Each might have a slightly different level of sexual involvement or exclusivity, for example. In today's dating arena, participants often avoid the term "dating" because it sounds too formal or old fashioned. A phenomenon spurred by the increase in younger daters is group dating. In group dating a network of males and females often go places together as friends who may or may not develop romantic relationships among some of the group. Recent research on college women by the Center for Marriage and Families confirmed that the phenomenon of hanging out has made dating roles and expected behaviors ambiguous and difficult to navigate.

Given the interest in and the confusion over dating, a new industry has emerged to help daters navigate the process. Long a staple of late night radio talk show programs, dating advice has become mainstream through its inclusion as a topic in the popular *Dummies* and *Idiots* guides. Each is respectively penned by a noted dating advisors Joy Browne and Judith Kuriansky. As dating has moved into arenas beyond the traditional face-to-face meeting, many advice manuals for these alternative locales have emerged. Most have focused on the rapidly expanding area of online dating.

DATING IS GOOD PREPARATION FOR MARRIAGE

Dating is good preparation for marriage because dating is under the control of young people who are expected to eventually form permanent personal relationships. They need to learn how to relate to each other under many different circumstances and activities and dating can assist in this task. The freedom that is allowed daters today gives them ample opportunity to see how partners react in a variety of situations. Couples in committed dating relationships must work out disagreements and differing desires to keep their relationships intact, much as they would need to do in a marital relationship. With fewer interventions by outsiders and parents today, daters meet a variety of persons who expand their experiences. They can take advantage of a wide variety of personality types and relationship styles. Often these are dating partners that would not have received approval in the past because they are of a different race, ethnicity, age, or social class.

Because today young people date for longer periods of time before they marry than in the past, they have many more experiences to help prepare them for marriage. Because those outside of the relationship may make the assumption that the couple are eventually planning to marry, they will let the couple know how they feel, either positively or negatively, about the association.

In today's nontraditional dating, there is less pressure on either partner to perform a specified role. Either person may ask, pay, plan, drive, or initiate sexual contact. These patterns appear to be more common among persons who are dating after a divorce or who are not currently looking for a marital partner. The incidence of asking by women seems to be fairly high, although women do not always pay the expenses of the dates they initiate. Many women today may choose to pay their own way on a date, referred to as going "dutch treat," so they will not feel obliged to participate in sexual activities with the partner as part of the date script. Likewise, today's emphasis on group dating may shield young people from the traditional expectations of sexual intimacy on a date. Thus, couples must negotiate the nature of the dating experience just as they would ultimately have to construct a meaningful marriage in a society of diverse opinions on the topic.

FOLLOWING THE RULES OF DATING

First introduced onto the dating scene in 1996, *The Rules: Time-tested Secrets for Capturing the Heart of Mr. Right* by Ellen Fein and Sherrie Schneider was at once both embraced and vilified. Among the shots lobbed by critics was the notion that the book advocated tricking the man into marriage and that the techniques advocated by the authors would erase everything that the women's movement had fought for regarding women's relationship choices. In a word, the ideas were too old-fashioned. Women who took the advice of the authors to heart and found a partner argued that the success of finding a marriageable partner outweighed any stodgy techniques. Among the more than 30 pieces of advice aimed at women that are supplied by Fein and Schneider are:

1. Never call a man first. He needs to be the pursuer and chase the woman.
2. Never accept a date for Saturday night if the invitation is extended after Wednesday. A woman will seem more special if a man has to think ahead to see her.
3. Don't talk to the man first; he should approach the woman.
4. No sexual contact on the first date. The longer the couple waits for the physical to catch up to the emotional connection, the better.
5. Never date a married man.

DATING IS POOR PREPARATION FOR MARRIAGE

On the other hand, the skills that make one a good dater may not be the skills that make one a good marital partner. In dating, the popular dater is the one who dates many different persons and is considered a desirable partner by many suitors. Good daters are fun and entertaining. Likewise they may be romantic with their partners and good at establishing a special mood. Because dating partners generally see each other in the best light, when they have dressed in nice clothes, prepared for an activity, and are excited to be together, they may not see the real personality of the partner. The good marital partner is one who is faithful and is not participating in other romantic relationships. Likewise, marital partners see each other when times are both good and bad, thus they are not able to simply put on their best faces. There is a falsehood in dating that is linked to expected roles and a predictable progression of relationship activities. Couples often respond to each other based on preconceived ideas about what each partner's responsibilities are in a dating relationship.

Traditionally in heterosexual dating, men are to ask women out on a date, plan what the activities of the date will be, drive both participants to the activities of the date, and pay the financial cost for the dating activities. It is also considered the task of the male partner to initiate sexual contact. Women in a traditional dating situation are expected to let the partner know, through subtle hints and comments, that she would be willing to accept a date with him. Therefore, she has the responsibility to accept the date or decline it if she is not interested. In the event her decision is to decline, she is to do so tactfully so that the male's confidence is not shattered by the rejection. She is additionally responsible for looking nice and being typically feminine on the date. She is also responsible for setting the sexual limits, or determining how much sexual contact will occur on the date. Women usually follow the norms of their social group in this area. Persons outside of the couple also have a stake in who eventually marries whom. Those observing the dating couple may be more permissive of who the dating partner is if they think that the relationship is not a serious one, as compared with when the couple is serious. While both daters and observers may be more willing to accept a partner who differs on social characteristics such as age, race, ethnicity, religion, or social class when the association is a casual one, they may be less willing to accept differences in these areas in a marital partner.

THE DATING GAME

In some instances dating has been characterized as a game, with participants making carefully planned and researched strategic moves. The male works to impress the female and gain sexual favors while the woman works to limit her sexual favors and maintain her social position. This dating game is based on the assumption that, traditionally, males and females have wanted different things from dating relationships. Whereas women hoped that dating would lead to marriage and involved a romantic notion of the future with the partner, men wanted the company of the woman and the possible sexual relationships that dating might provide.

As with any game, dating has rules. Gendered rules have been a key component of the dating game from the beginning. While under the courtship system, women had significant control over the initiation, activities, and intimacies of getting to know a partner. This was in large part due to the location of the courting, her home. In the system of dating that emerged in the 1920s, the power and influence of women had declined in the area of mate selection. A woman had to wait to be asked out by a man. She might give subtle hints of her interest, but could not appear too eager. She rarely had anyone announcing her willingness to receive callers. Men, through the mechanism of asking, became the dominant partners in dating relationships because they had control over which women dated and which sat home waiting for a date. Additionally, dating took place in the world of men, the public sphere.

Men were responsible for asking for the date, planning the activities, paying for any expenses, and choosing the most popular partner that they could. An important resource for daters was money. Because men generally had more of it than did women, he could control what the couple did together. A man with money could date frequently and could expect to have the "best dates" accept his invitations. Some dating scripts also list making sexual advances as the man's responsibility. The primary tasks of the female partner in a traditional date situation were to accept dates selectively so that she would not appear too eager (or to decline graciously if that was her decision), let the partner know that care had been taken to look nice for the occasion, behave in a typically feminine manner, and set the sexual limits of the date. She must rebuff, at least in a token way, the sexual advances of the partner. This female role of sexual gatekeeper has been a theme throughout the history of dating. Some feminist authors have suggested that dating is legalized prostitution. In exchange for his financial investment in the date, the man expects sexual favors from his female partner.

Young people might find it necessary to put on a false face to the partner to get the desired outcome. Advice manuals of the past, as well as a few current ones, even suggest a specific number of dates that should occur before any sexual intimacies are permitted. For example, dating advice manuals of the 1950s and 1960s indicate that women should permit no kisses until after the third date. Intimate touching and intercourse would only be permitted after additional milestones had passed. The idea of engagement as a rite of passage to greater sexual intimacy has some support in the advice manuals as well. Both males and females were aware of when behaviors would be permitted and generally acted accordingly. By the early 1980s a majority of both males and females felt that kissing was appropriate on the first date and nearly all indicated it was acceptable by the fourth date. This idea of limiting the female's sexual expression to keep a male partner interested in the relationship is still being marketed to modern daters, most notably in the widely read *The Rules* series. Among those authors currently offering dating advice are Barbara DeAngelis, Susan Forward, and John Gray.

See also Arranged Marriage; Mate Selection Alternatives; Premarital Sexual Relationships; Preparation for Marriage.

Further Reading: Bailey, Beth. *From Front Porch to Back Seat: Courtship in Twentieth Century America*. Baltimore, MD: Johns Hopkins University Press, 1988; Browne, Joy. *Dating for Dummies*, 2nd ed. Hoboken, NJ: Wiley Publishing, Inc., 2006; DeAngelis, Barbara. *The Real Rules: How to Find the Right Man for the Real You*. New York: Dell Books, 1997; Fein, E., and S. Schneider. *The Rules: Time-Tested Secrets for Capturing the Heart of Mr. Right*. New York: Warner Books, 1996; Kuriansky, Judith. *Complete Idiot's Guide to Dating*, 3rd ed. Indianapolis, IN: Alpha Books, 2004; Laner, M. R. *Dating: Delights, Discontents and Dilemmas*. Salem, WI: Sheffield Publishing Co., 1992; Rothman, E. A. *Hands and Hearts: A History of Courtship in America*. New York: Basic Books, 1984.

Kimberly P. Brackett

DAY CARE

Parents—especially mothers—have historically been deemed responsible for the night-and-day care of younger children. Since prehistoric times when men went off to hunt and the women gathered, gave birth, and guarded young children, motherhood has been the primary function of womanhood. The world has changed and contemporary culture is now much more accepting of women working out of the home. According to the U.S. Department of Labor, as of 2006 women made up 46 percent of the total U.S. labor force. Women are no longer strangers to the workforce and a woman without a job is considered atypical. The previous truism that a woman's place is in the home has been invalidated. Now a new challenge arises for women who are expected to be wage earners as well as the primary caregivers for their young children. Some are opposed to the idea of a new mother returning to work and leaving her offspring in the care of relative strangers. For many, however, institutionalized care is the only option.

The previous convention of the stay-at-home mom has given way to that of the working mother. As a result, young children formerly raised at home are now spending significant portions of their time in child care centers, commonly known as day care. Although many see day care as a relatively new phenomenon, it has roots in nineteenth-century society. It was introduced primarily with the onset of the industrial revolution in the Western Hemisphere. However, day care existed in smaller and more elementary forms in both Europe and the United States even before the revolution. Advocates of day care see it as a necessity—without mothers free to earn wages families would slide into poverty. Naysayers believe that raising children in a nontraditional setting is detrimental to the development and eventual cognitive and social abilities of these children. Research supporting both viewpoints exists while other studies demonstrate no conclusive findings. The debate over institutionalized care and its purported benefit or detriment to children is currently being waged with no side being able to declare clear victory.

INSTITUTIONALIZED CARE OF CHILDREN

Child care is defined as the nonparental care of children. Day care is the nonparental care of children in an out-of-home facility or establishment. It is important to note that in many sociological studies institutionalized care is broadly defined as care provided by anyone else other than the mother. Child care includes the day care industry but also includes preschool and kindergarten institutions and orphanages. Preschool and kindergarten institutions are focused on the educational development of children while day care and orphanages concentrate on child well-being more than pedagogical activities. The current controversy over nonparental care focuses mainly on day care. Day care is primarily for the benefit of infants and toddlers.

In the United States, day care centers are regulated by each state and providers are required to obtain licenses. However, some providers can be exempt from licensing based on the number of children that will receive care. As a result of the existence of 50 different licensing processes and regulations, as well as the nonlicensing of certain providers, the United States has a veritable hodgepodge of laws and requirements for its day care centers. This has made research and conclusions about the effects of institutionalized care on young children often unreliable and conflicting.

DAY CARE HISTORY (EUROPE)

Day care emerged out of necessity during the industrial revolution. The industrial revolution was responsible for major technological and socioeconomic changes in Western countries during the eighteenth and nineteenth centuries. It was the triumph of the middle-class business owners and managers at the wide expense of the labor force. The mechanization of industry and advent of new coal and steam power forced many cottage industries out of business because the factories produced more products at a faster pace. Those families, thus disenfranchised, had to seek outside employment, often at the very factories and mills that had scuttled their own businesses. They found themselves in the predicament of what to do with infants and young toddlers while they labored. Slightly older children were not a problem because they often worked in the same factories as their parents.

In 1816 infant schools were started in Scotland in order to control street preschool-age children during the day. Infant schools were seen as a way to solve the urban infant care problems that resulted from industrialization and were established in England, the United States, and France. Currently infant schools still exist in the United Kingdom but have become more similar to the American kindergarten.

In France, crèches were established in the mid-1800s as a full-day institution geared toward the children of working mothers. It became a very popular model of care and spread as far as China and Belgium. Because the emphasis of crèches was merely on daily supervision of children and mostly unconcerned with their emotional well-being, crèches often resulted in large groups of children in unsanitary buildings being watched by untrained and poorly paid caregivers. Both crèches and infant schools were supported by local charities before being incorporated into state or local government funding.

DAY CARE HISTORY (UNITED STATES)

Before the arrival of the industrial revolution, colonial America continued a model of child care born in England—the apprenticeship model. Apprenticeship is the indenture of a child to a tradesman in order to learn a trade. It was mostly utilized by the poor and could even be considered a type of foster care. Young children, often barely older than toddlers, were sent to their master who often served as their father until they were old enough to be on their own or, if they were girls, until they married. Apprenticeship declined with the beginning of the industrial revolution and was almost obsolete by the Civil War.

The mid-nineteenth century saw the advent of the so-called cult of domesticity. This movement portrayed women only as tireless mothers and faithful

THE EXPERTS, AND THE MEDIA, WEIGH IN

Broadcast and print media outlets often report contentious studies that claim to expose the dangers or benefits of day care and further exacerbate the polemical issue. The aroused anger, anxiety, and worry among the nation's parents and caregivers further inflame this already heated debate.

Jay Belsky, professor of psychology at Birbeck College in London, has authored many articles purporting the dangers of child care and encourages the idea of extending maternity leave and enforcing part-time work for new parents. His paper, "Infant Day Care: Cause for Concern," published in 1986 terrified many parents and he has followed it up with the more recent "Development Risk (Still) Associated with Early Child Care." Belsky is a media favorite in child care research but many accuse him of chasing the spotlight by exaggerating results and using alarmist tactics. Sarah Friedman, a developmental psychologist with the National Institute of Child Health and Human Development, states that the results of the study do not warrant policy recommendations and that those results would limit new parents' time to work as economically dangerous. Linda Hirshman, a law professor and working mother, is an advocate of the working mother. She believes that women leaving the workforce to care for their children are hurting themselves and setting unhealthy examples for their children. Hirshman sees the college-educated woman ceasing to work because of offspring as a direct challenge to the idea of gender equality and causing women to lead lesser lives. There are several groups of mothers that are completely against Hirshman and see staying at home as a job. They feel that to be there for their children every day as an attentive mother is essential for the healthy emotional and intellectual growth of their children. In the aptly named "Mommy Wars" the battle is continually supplied by the fevered interests of television and radio stations, newspapers, and Internet sources.

Despite the warnings of naysayers and the support of advocates, institutionalized care for children is a modern reality. For over 200 years day care and its antecedents have filled a vital need for society during national emergencies and for individual families during times of economic stress. Despite its longevity, results assessments of the benefits and harms of institutionalized care remain mixed. What does appear clear is that the quality of the infant-mother attachment depends more on the responsiveness of the mother than on the amount of time spent in day care or even the quality of the day care setting. While day care appears to give a boost to the acquisition of cognitive skills to children who are from a deprived home setting, this effect appears to level out in later years. Children spending greater amounts of time in day care are sometimes considered by their observers to be more disobedient. Despite conflicting research and continuing parental concerns about the effect of institutionalized care on children, day care is a fact of life in contemporary society.

and supportive wives. Women were not expected to work unless it was in the home. The initial popularity of these beliefs hindered the creation of any new day care ventures. The 1850s also saw the emergence of the controversial Oneida Community. In the community, once children were weaned they became the responsibility of the whole community and were housed and raised communally. Parents were permitted to visit their children but if they were suspected of forming a special bond visitation was no longer allowed.

It was around this time that settlement houses were beginning to develop. These settlement houses included day nurseries for young children whose mothers were working. They closely resembled current conceptions of day care as they also allowed drop-off and even sick care, as well as the fact that caretakers occasionally made home visits.

Orphanages were previously mentioned as a form of child care. They were even further utilized beyond a day care setting when working-class families chose to put their child into an orphanage temporarily. This often occurred when the family was impoverished and financially unable to provide and care for their children. Parents would maintain contact with their children and the children would return home when financial situations improved.

The 1930s witnessed the devastating effects of the Great Depression, and the Works Progress Administration started an emergency day care system in an attempt to give jobs to unemployed teachers and make child care services available to poor families. Child care centers were built for children of migratory farm workers by the Farm Security Administration. In 1943 these centers became Lanham Act centers geared toward the children of mothers working in defense and war-related industries. Across America 3,102 centers attended to about 600,000 children during World War II in communities that were deemed sufficiently war-impacted. Many felt that this government support of mothers working outside the home was only justified in light of the current national emergency of war. As soon as the war ended federal funds were terminated and the only sites that survived had to receive other forms of local or state support.

Since the Second World War the influx of women into the workforce has steadily increased. With increasing numbers of single mothers, child care became a necessity rather than a choice. The Aid to Families with Dependent Children Act had been in place since 1935 (it began as the Aid to Dependent Children Act) but many challenged it because it provided little incentive for further job training and education, and some saw that the birth of more children prolonged the provided benefits. Mothers in the predicament of having young children, having no money, and having no husband were considered undeserving of these monetary allowances given by the government for them to stay at home with their children.

Policymakers and reformers decided it was time that individuals were assisted to secure their own future. As a response to this particular welfare reform, the Family Support Act was passed in 1988. The act emphasized a person's return to basic education and job training in order to receive benefits. Child care was guaranteed for mothers and fathers who were working or returning to school. The Family Support Act offered the first comprehensive support of child care by the federal government. However, many still remained concerned because the act offered child care primarily to keep parents in productive work or education activities, and did not heavily promote child development.

EFFECTS OF DAY CARE

Those against the institutionalized care of children believe that day care is harmful to the cognitive, behavioral, and social development of children. Certain studies have linked day care to an increase in aggression in children as well as a weakening of mother and child attachment. Promoters of day care point to other studies that have linked day care with an increase in language and cognitive skills. Most of these studies focus on infants and toddlers and the care they receive as these years are considered the most formative and the most developmentally significant.

These studies stress high-quality care as an indicator of positive results. The quality of care in a child care center is often based upon the child-to-caregiver ratio and education of the adult caregivers. When caregivers are responsible for fewer children, they can provide more individual care to each of them. A high-quality child care center features large amounts of caregiver-child verbal and social interaction as well as responsiveness to the child's needs.

Several studies have delved into the effects of institutionalized care on the mother-child relationship. The most comprehensive has been a study conducted by the National Institute of Human Health and Development Early Child Research Network. The study investigated claims that the time a child spends away from his or her mother in a day care center weakens the attachment between infant and mother. Some go as far as to say that young infants who experience this daily separation perceive it as a form of maternal rejection. However, the study concluded that mothers who do not see their children during the day often make a greater effort to spend more time with them at night and on the weekends. This increase in attention seems to almost make up for a marked absence during the day. The study's most conclusive finding is that the child's attachment is directly related to the sensitivity and responsiveness of his or her mother. The amount of time spent in, and the quality of, the child care is secondary. Less sensitive and unresponsive mothers were more likely to put their children in low-quality childcare. Therefore attachment already weakened by the mother's behavior is compounded by the addition of low-quality care. Conversely, it was shown that the effect of high-quality child care may have a moderating effect on a child whose mother is insensitive. It has been suggested that parental involvement (this includes fathers) plays a much bigger role in a child's development than does day care. It is the mother's interaction with the child and her utilization of time spent outside of day care that seems to decisively dictate the quality of attachment between parent and child.

Attempts to determine the effect day care has on the development of children's cognitive abilities and behavioral tendencies have always been at the forefront of child care research. It is at the end of early infancy, when a child is one or two years old, that speech develops and emerges. When a child is two years old his or her vocabulary is continually expanding and the use of grammar is introduced. Symbolic thought and language are in the early stages at this time, a precursor to the development of logic that will occur around seven years of age. Most studies examining the effect of institutionalized care concentrate on children between

15 and 36 months old because this is when critical linguistic and cognitive development occurs.

Several theories exist that alternately denounce and praise institutionalized care and its effects. One opinion is that children from low-income families with little opportunity for cognitive stimulation benefit more from high-quality care than do more advantaged children. The opposite of this hypothesis states that high-quality child care centers are substandard to the care well-off children receive in a home environment, and therefore do not provide any extra cognitive advancement opportunities. Some studies suggest that the higher-quality child care results in better acquisition of language and cognitive skills. Despite common fears that the more time children spend in day care the more deprived they become, there is no evidence that the amount of time spent in day care is related to poorer cognitive skills or decreased language development. In fact, when comparing the cognitive and language performances of children in maternal care with children in nonmaternal care, children in medium- and high-quality child care centers performed better. Despite any improved language and cognitive performance that may be apparent between one and three years of age, many question the sustainability of these advanced skills as the child becomes older. Some studies show these advanced skills dissipating through early school years and others claim they remain through to adulthood. In other words, the apparent increase or decrease of cognitive and language skill development, as a result of day care, may or may not become moot in later years due to time and other factors in early school education.

Researchers often question if the more time a child spends in a child care center the more they are likely to suffer from behavioral problems. This is a tricky effect to analyze because behavior analysis is considered to be very subjective. The term aggressive behavior is used most often but can have different meanings to different people. According to one study, time spent in child care had no relation to behavioral problems that warranted any clinical or professional care. Based on the reports of caregivers, teachers, and mothers, children in kindergarten who spent 30 hours or more in an institutionalized care setting were less cooperative and more disobedient. However, as with the strength or weakness of the mother-infant attachment, family influence played more of a role in a child's behavioral development than any amount of time spent in nonparental child care.

After reviewing a plethora of studies with conflicting and coinciding results, it is obvious that there is no definitive research on the effects of day care on child development. The studies that do exist have not provided conclusive answers. Several variables including the quality of the day care institution, the amount of time spent in day care, the age institutionalized care starts, and the quality of care a child receives at home from parents are all factors that determine a child care institution's benefit or detriment.

See also Child Care Policy; Family and Medical Leave Act (FMLA).

Further Reading: Clarke-Stewart, A., and V. Allhusen. *What We Know About Childcare.* Cambridge, MA: Harvard University Press, 2005; Cohen, Abby. A Brief History of Federal Financing for Child Care in the United States. *Financing Child Care* 6, no. 2 (1996).

http://www.futureofchildren.org; National Institute of Child Health and Human Development, NIH, DHHS. "The NICHD Study of Early Child Care and Youth Development (SECCYD): Findings for Children up to Age 4 1/2 Years (05-4318)." Washington, DC: U.S. Government Printing Office, 2006; NICHD Early Child Care Research Network. "The Effects of Infant Child Care on Infant-Mother Attachment Security: Results of the NICHD Study of Early Child Care." *Child Development* 68, no. 5 (1997): 860–879; NICHD Early Child Care Research Network. "The Relation of Child Care to Cognitive and Language Development." *Child Development* 71 (2000): 960–980;

Margeaux Corby

DEADBEAT PARENTS

A question that has appeared in recent years, largely as a result of the increases in divorce and nonmarital child bearing, is the question of whether child support enforcement leads to an increase in deadbeat parents. Over the last few decades, the United States has witnessed an increase in the number of parents, mainly fathers, who are not taking responsibility for their children. Many of these parents have come to our attention through the child support system. The child support system is fundamentally an economic phenomenon run by the various states with federal oversight and guidelines. Historically, its focus was on either recovering welfare money for the government or on preventing the government from having to expend money on single mothers and their children. However, in recent years, the focus has expanded to include ensuring the health and well-being of the nation's children. Along with this expanded focus has come an increase in the strict enforcement of child support obligations. Consequently, some parents who fail to comply with their child support obligations, for whatever reason, are at risk for fines and imprisonment and are labeled as so-called deadbeat parents. In fact, the Deadbeat Parents Punishment Act makes it a federal offense for a noncustodial parent to willfully fail to pay past-due support obligations for a child residing in another state.

Referring to these parents as deadbeats has spawned great debate regarding how we conduct child support in America. On one side of the debate are child advocates who suggest that we need to be more aggressive with our child support policies in an effort to reduce childhood poverty. On the other side are fathers' rights activists who argue that the current child support system is unjust in that it favors women in most actions that pertain to the child, leaving fathers out.

CHILD SUPPORT

Child support is the transfer of resources to a child living apart from a parent. The most common type of transfer is direct financial payment to the custodial parent on behalf of the child. However, child support can be indirect in the form of medical insurance and care, dental care, child care, or educational support.

The transfer of resources occurs at both the private or public level. Private child support is paid by the noncustodial parent to the custodial parent. The majority of custodial parents have some type of agreement or court award to receive financial and nonfinancial support from the noncustodial parent for their children. In most cases, these are legal agreements established by a court or other governmental entity, such as the local child support agency. Although the majority of custodial parents have legal agreements for child support, about 40 percent of custodial parents do not have such agreements or have informal agreements with the noncustodial parent. According to the U.S. Census Bureau, the three most-often cited reasons for the lack of child support agreements are: (1) custodial parents did not feel the need to go court or to get legal agreements; (2) the other parent provided what he or she could for support; and (3) the other parent could not afford to pay child support.

On the other hand, public child support is paid for by the state on behalf of a child living in poverty in the form of public assistance, such as Temporary Assistance to Needy Families (TANF), Food Stamps, Medicaid, or Women, Infants, and Children (WIC). Roughly, about one-third of all custodial parents receive some form of child-support-related assistance from the state. Historically, child support was a means for the state to receive reimbursement from noncustodial fathers for public child support expenditures. In the case of public child support, it is the government and not the custodial parent who is the direct beneficiary of the noncustodial parent's financial payment. In fact, some scholars and fathers' rights activists suggest that it is the reimbursement of public child support which has stimulated interest in stricter child support enforcement.

THE TRANSFORMATION OF CHILD SUPPORT IN AMERICA

Child support in its present form has not always existed. Initially child support was considered a civil matter. Since the arrival of settlers in America, child support has existed in some form, with parental responsibility at the heart of collections of aid. Child support has its foundations in the Elizabethan Poor Laws of 1601, sometimes referred to as the English Poor Laws. The English Poor Laws were a system of relief to the poor that was financed and administered at the local level (parishes). The poor were divided into three groups: able-bodied adults, children, and the elderly or non-able-bodied. The overseers of the poor relief system were to put the able-bodied to work, to give apprenticeships to poor children, and to provide "competent sums of money" to relieve the non-able-bodied. It is this system of assistance to the needy that British settlers brought with them to America.

Child Support in Colonial America

Colonial child support had a slow start. In colonial America, when a couple married, the wife's identity merged with that of her husband. Women did not have the right to hold property, therefore the husband controlled and managed all property. In return, the husband was obligated to provide for his wife and children. Fathers had a *nonenforceable* duty to support their children. Under the Poor Laws, child support was considered a civil matter. Although desertion was rare, when a man did desert his family, the local community would provide for the mother and child to prevent destitution. In return, local communities would attempt to recover from the father monies spent in support of the mother and child. The money collected from the father was put back into the poor relief system's reserves. However, near the end of the eighteenth century, as the population increased, there was an accompanying increase in the numbers of individuals needing assistance, which eventually caused a breakdown of the colonial poor relief system.

Child Support Enforcement and the Making of the Deadbeat Dad

The revolutionary changes brought about by the industrialization, or the movement to greater technology, and urbanization, or movement to the cities, of the nineteenth century encouraged courts to strengthen the child support system. During this period, divorce and child custody laws were transformed. For instance, child custody laws that had previously favored the fathers in divorce began to favor the mother, increasingly granting custody of the child to mothers. Therefore, when divorce and desertion rates increased, many mothers and their children became dependent on the state for subsistence. In response to this rise in the utilization of and dependency on public resources, states began to make child support a criminal matter by establishing a legally *enforceable* child support duty. State legislators passed desertion and nonsupport statutes that criminalized and punished fathers for their refusal to support their child, especially if the mother and child were recipients of public child support. Fathers who failed to comply with child support were either fined or imprisoned.

Despite states' efforts to improve child support enforcement and to reduce public child support expenditures, a sizable number of fathers and husbands fled the state to avoid their child support obligations, leaving a host of mothers and children destitute and dependent on public child support services. In the mid-twentieth century, the Uniform Reciprocal Enforcement of Support Act implemented federal guidelines that made fathers who moved from state to state to avoid child support still responsible for their children through both civil and criminal enforcement. Yet these guidelines caused confusion between states regarding the jurisdiction of child support; hence, some fathers could have multiple child support orders. Throughout the remainder of the twentieth century, state and federal child support enforcement programs continued to address interstate inconsistencies that provided irresponsible parents with a means of avoiding their child support obligations.

The Personal Responsibility and Work Opportunity Reconciliation Act (PRWORA) of 1996, known to most Americans as "welfare reform," emphasized parental responsibility for the financial support of their children as well as implemented more aggressive enforcement techniques, and additional provisions that unified state collection efforts. For instance, to reduce delay in establishing wage-withholding for parents who are delinquent in their child support payments, PRWORA requires employers to report all new hires to child support enforcement authorities. As a result, The National Directory of New Hires, a centralized electronic system, was developed to match all employees with parents who owe child support and are listed in the federal case registry. In fiscal year 1998, the National Directory of New Hires located 1.2 million parents who were delinquent in their child support payments; in fiscal year 1999, the directory identified an additional 2.8 million delinquent parents.

The most recent child support enforcement effort focused on curtailing deadbeat parents is the creation of the Deadbeat Parents Punishment Act (DPPA), which makes it a federal offense for a noncustodial parent to willfully fail to pay a past-due child support obligation, with respect to a child residing in another state. Under the DPPA, if the obligation remains unpaid for longer than one year or is greater than $5,000, then a misdemeanor charge may be considered. On the other hand, behaviors that constitute a felony offense are: (1) traveling in interstate or foreign commerce with the intent to evade a support obligation, if the obligation has remained unpaid for longer than one year or is greater than $5,000; or (2) willfully failing to pay a support obligation regarding a child residing in another state if the obligation has remained unpaid for longer than two years or is greater than $10,000. Maximum penalties for a misdemeanor are six months incarceration and/or a $5,000 fine. Maximum penalties for a felony offense are two years and/or a $250,000 fine.

The past few centuries have seen a noteworthy transformation in the child support system in the United States. Yet, there is scholarly and political debate about whether our current system works and if so, for whom.

POLITICS AND CHILD SUPPORT

The issue of child support is just one of many topics related to the changing family. Scholars and politicians continually debate whether the traditional family is in decline. On one side of the debate are those who think the family is in decline. Proponents of this perspective hail the traditional family, that is, a breadwinner husband, a stay-at-home wife and mother, and children, as the best environment for children. Along with this perspective comes terms such as "family values" or "families first" that are used to affirm and clarify the merits of the two-parent home. Thus, the federal government spends millions of dollars on marriage promotion programs that are mainly aimed at the poor. Some argue that if marriage promotion works, we will witness more stable families and a reduction in government spending on public child support related services.

On the other side of the debate are those who argue that the family is not in decline, but is changing in response to societal shifts. This perspective also contends that it is unlikely that American families will ever return to the traditional family. Therefore, terms such as "family values" and "families first" should be used in relation to all family types. If we accept all families, then more aggressive efforts will be made to support single-parent households and to assist in moving families out of the poverty trap.

CHILD ADVOCATES

Child advocates argue that the child support system has improved but suggest that more changes are needed to improve the health and well-being of children and to lift families out of poverty. For instance, the number of custodial parents receiving full private child support payments has increased over the last ten years, from 36.9 percent to 45.3 percent. In contrast, among custodial parents who live below the poverty line, only 35 percent received all the private child support that was due.

In terms of public child support-related services, advocates argue that these services rarely prevent poverty, and in fact, are a poverty trap. Public child support services provide meager, below-poverty-level benefits, reduce benefits when mothers earn more, and take away medical benefits when a mother leaves welfare. A strategy such as this promotes dependency and perpetuates the cycle of poverty.

However, child advocates note that closely related to the poverty trap is the child support enforcement trap. Specifically, advocates are concerned that custodial parents receiving public child support such as TANF are required to assign their right to private child support to the governmental welfare entity before cash assistance can be received. Moreover, custodial parents must pursue child support from the noncustodial parent, which is then diverted to the welfare assistance program instead of the custodial parent. Child support payments that are used to reimburse government public assistance costs deprive many poor children of much of the child support paid on their behalf. Even after the family leaves welfare and is struggling to avoid return, in some circumstances child support collections will go to repay government arrears before going to the family. What's more, child advocates note, if the amount of private child support paid equals or exceeds the public child support assistance, the family is moved off of TANF, the cash assistance part of the program.

Finally, the federal government through the Social Security Administration provides up to $4.1 billion in financial incentives to states that create child support and arrearage orders. Again, child advocates argue that this type of child support enforcement system is a trap that perpetuates the cycle of poverty and is more beneficial for the state and federal government than for children and families.

FATHERS' RIGHTS ACTIVISTS

Overall, fathers' rights activists find that the current child support system is a gender-biased system that discriminates against men. However, these activists' dissatisfaction with the child support system begins prior to the child support order, with the divorce proceedings. Many divorced men argue that awarding sole maternal custody denies a father equal rights. Yet, many fathers admit that they don't want the responsibility of caring for their children on a daily basis but do want to continue the parenting role and visit with their children regularly.

A second issue that concerns fathers' rights activists is that mothers are awarded unjust child support payments; that is, more money than is needed to care for the child. Furthermore, fathers seem to resent that they have no control in the manner in which support payments are spent. Even more, fathers who pay child support become angry when visitation with their children is limited, again blaming a gender-biased system for these problems.

Activists also take issue with the term "deadbeat dad." They contend that the concept of deadbeat dad carries the connotation of an affluent man who fails to meet his parental responsibility to provide for his children. However, some activists suggest that the majority of dads who are labeled as deadbeats do not fit this image. In fact, they argue, many fathers just are not financially able to provide for their children, yet the court awards child support payments that he is unable to afford. For instance, activists assert that men characterized as deadbeats are either (1) remarried and the second family is worse off financially than the original family because the father is supporting his biological children and several stepchildren; (2) living in poverty, homeless, or incarcerated; (3) fathers who are providing indirect support to the child and custodial parent such as repairing items around the custodial parent's house; (4) fathers who can't find their children because the mother has moved, but the mother has filed a case with the local child support enforcement entity; (5) fathers with high arrearages in relation to their current economic circumstance; and (6) fathers who are truly child support resistors, that is, deadbeat dads.

Finally, some activists claim that child support enforcement benefits all entities related to the divorce industry. They point out that the divorce and child support industry creates jobs for many. For example, family court judges earn $90,000 to $160,000 per year and each judge requires a staff, not to mention child support staff, social workers, private collections agencies, and attorneys. In addition, they note the availability of federal funding for the administration of child support enforcement programs under the Social Security Act. Federal funding incentives have led a number of for-profit and privately-held corporations to offer services to state and local child support agencies ranging from consultation to payment processing. Thus, fathers' rights activists argue that the current child support system actually tears families apart while benefiting government and child support related businesses.

See also Adversarial and No-Fault Divorce; Child Support and Parental Responsibility; Culture of Poverty; Divorce and Children; Fatherhood; Marriage Promotion; Poverty and Public Assistance.

Further Reading: Alliance for Non-custodial Parents Rights. http://www.ancpr.org/; Braver, Sanford L. *Divorced Dads: Shattering the Myth*. New York: Putnam Special Markets, 1998; Crowley, Jocelyn. *The Politics of Child Support in America*. New York: Cambridge University Press, 2003; Father's Rights. http://www.fathersrightsinc.com/; Mobilia, Marcia, and Joel Bulmil. *Deadbeat Dads: A National Child Support Scandal*. Westport, CT: Praeger, 1996.

Annice Yarber

DEVELOPMENTAL DISABILITY AND MARITAL STRESS

The typical American family struggles with the prospects of divorce, even when life appears relatively stable or normal. The union of two people is in part built out of compromise and negotiation. When persons marry, they expect a wonderful life together. How does the introduction of a child with a developmental disability influence the lives of the parents and subsequent family? Is it simply an added stressor or can it be an opportunity for personal growth and fulfillment?

BACKGROUND

A developmental disability is a severe, chronic disability of a person that (1) is attributable to a mental or physical impairment or a combination of mental and physical impairments; (2) is manifested before the person attains age 22; (3) is likely to continue indefinitely; (4) results in substantial functional limitation in three or more of the following areas of major life activity: self-care, receptive expressive language, learning, mobility, self-direction, capacity for independent living, and economic self-sufficiency; and (5) reflects the person's need for a combination and sequence of special interdisciplinary or generic care, treatment, or other services that are of lifelong or extended duration and are individually planned and coordinated.

Since the early 1970s, the emphasis in American politics has been to integrate those with disabilities into mainstream society. This began with the Rehabilitation Act of 1973. The last of that era's Civil Rights legislation, this act emphasized training people with disabilities to work. In 1990, the Americans with Disabilities Act expanded the rights of people with disabilities even further, addressing such things as access to services, access to buildings and other structures, accommodations for those disabled, including the use of communication devices, and many other actions. The act also made discrimination of any kind against people with disabilities a crime, as well as protecting family members of, and those that work with, people with disabilities. During this time subsequent lawsuits have closed long-standing state institutions that housed people with developmental disabilities. Social movements have emphasized "people first" movements, stressing that we must think of those with disabilities as human beings first and foremost. But have these changes influenced how people maintain their lives apart from protection under the law? Does the stigma attached to those with developmental disabilities have long-lasting consequences for parents and the stability of their families?

NEGATIVE EFFECTS ON MARRIED LIFE

Traditionally, the research on families or marital partners where there has been a child with developmental disabilities present has suggested that giving birth to a child with a developmental disability was a tragedy. As late as the 1980s, the term "baby doe" was used to identify babies born with a developmental disability that were then left unaided in the hospital until they died. The research often emotionally equated the birth of a child with a developmental disability with death. While this perspective is not as common within the literature today, it is still generally accepted that parents caring for a child with a developmental disability will have a more difficult time. Much of the literature addresses four key areas to reflect this view: (1) the parent of a child with a developmental disability will experience more stress than the typical parent; (2) parenting a child with a developmental disability is believed to lead to more time and energy parenting, as well as to more family routines and activities subject to frequent disruptions; (3) single mothers of a child with a developmental disability are more likely not to marry; and (4) married couples with a child with a developmental disability have a greater chance of divorce within a two-year period.

Another component that these partners and families experience is stigma. Stigma is a devalued attribute directed toward or identified with an individual or group of people. It can include a flaw of character or intelligence, as well as a flaw of the body. Typically, once a stigma is identified a person is then labeled with a master status, which is an identity that supersedes all other identities. It is what most people see or acknowledge first when they meet someone with a stigma. When coming into contact with someone who has cerebral palsy, we would notice the wheelchair, the slight disfigurement, and the inability to move or talk in a manner similar to the rest of the population. So we would treat that person first with those things in mind. With the typical person, most likely we would not take notice of those things because they would be viewed as normal. To have a child with a developmental disability would be to recognize that your child has this stigma, yet at the same time acknowledge that those around you will also look at you, the parent, differently. This creates some uneasiness, at least temporarily, as parents are forced to deal with a new identity associated with them.

As mentioned, the early research focused on the parental stress involved when a child with a developmental disability is present. This form of research is still found today. Much of that research found that parents of a child with disabilities were indeed more stressed than the parents of a child without a disability. Likewise, these same studies identified that the mother of the child with the developmental disability was more likely to have to quit her place of employment to focus on the needs of the child. Unable to afford the care from professional services, it was more cost-effective for one of the parents, in this case the mother, to leave work and take care of her child.

Parents suffer more from depression if they have a child with a developmental disability. As many as 20 percent of parents with a child having a developmental disability score above the clinical cut-off for depression (Feldman et al. 2007). The explanation for this has typically been that the parents are suffering due to the tragedy involved in their lives, and this does not match the expectations parents had when they thought of having a child.

There has been an alternative explanation that has carried some weight involving support groups. Because there is a wide array of disabilities categorized as developmental disabilities, parents have a difficult time finding others with similar children. There are not as many people around with which to compare notes, as well as to create a sense of camaraderie. This phenomenon has led to a belief that without such support-based relationships, parents experience more instability. Because people with developmental disabilities have the most stigma attached to them, this isolation for parents can be devastating.

Likewise, another aspect has to do with marriage or the likelihood of marriage after giving birth to a child with a developmental disability. Unmarried mothers who give birth to a child with a developmental disability are less likely to marry. The rationale for this outcome is that part of the union of marriage in the United States involves the contributions of children to marital stability. This is based on the Judeo-Christian belief that we are to populate the earth, as well as act as stewards in that endeavor. When a child has a developmental disability, there appears to be a disruption to the natural order; a disruption to the American Dream. The child is not only different, but he or she cannot contribute to the stewardship of earth.

Early research found that parents of a child with a developmental disability were more likely to divorce. New research suggests a slight change with a 10 percent greater likelihood that parents of a child with a disability will divorce within the first 12–18 months (Reichman et al. 2004). This outcome is explained by societal expectations as well as by the tendency that when life does not unfold as expected, it is not unusual for people to reassess their positions and seek change to form some kind of stability. Divorce would fall into this realm.

POSITIVE EFFECTS ON MARRIED LIFE

To focus entirely on the negatives is misleading. As research on people with disabilities has increased, findings have become more inconsistent and some even contradict research from the past. Some studies have demonstrated no significant differences in parental stress compared to other parents. In addition, socioeconomic status (SES) has been identified as contributing to problems within the relationships of parents with a child with a developmental disability as it does in any relationship. Lower SES contributes to lack of parental satisfaction and general malaise, which could also indicate depression.

There are identified positives for families with a developmentally disabled child. They include the lack or absence of stress and depression in families where a child has a developmental disability, the recognition of the common benefits found when a family member has a developmental disability, and the special benefits of having a family member that has a developmental disability.

First, there remain questions about whether parents or family members do in fact suffer from depression, as well as stress, when a child with a developmental disability is present. The key variable, as mentioned above, is SES. While many studies show that parents who have a child with a developmental disability suffer from more stress and more depression, the trends are less clear when one looks closely at SES. People that are in the lower economic classes suffer more stress and depression from their financial situation than from the developmental abilities of their children. Earlier, less-sophisticated studies ignored factors beyond the disability that could better explain the outcome. One such variable beyond SES is behavioral problems. When behavioral problems become the dependent variable, meanwhile holding constant other variables such as level of mental retardation, SES, and physical ability, there is a positive correlation with depression and stress of the parents.

Second, common benefits are typical for parents of a child with a developmental disability, regardless of the type of developmental disability. Common benefits include such things as increased sensitivity to people's needs, tolerance and a changed perspective on life. The rationale for these outcomes involves being exposed to a new world of existence. Many parents, especially those in the middle and upper classes, learn to understand the stigma attached to being different in a negative manner. They see that the world is not as easy as they once thought, and that not all people are created equal within societal norms and laws. To be different and therefore marginalized can come as a shock to these parents who may have never experienced nor acknowledged such phenomena. The result is that these parents tend to see many more people needing to be included within public policy; they recognize the shortcomings of the law.

Third, special benefits are connected intrinsically to the common benefits, and often times are talked about interchangeably. Special benefits are when parents, family members, and caregivers learn new things. This goes beyond seeing the world and others differently. This is a phenomenon where parents, family members, and caregivers learn the ins and outs of the social services business, recognize the politics involved with and against people with developmental disabilities, and develop the technical competency needed to assist people with developmental disabilities. They may learn sign language, about services available or not available to assist children with developmental disabilities, the necessity for wider bathroom stalls, the need for handicapped-accessible parking, how the brain works, how the body works, and about how much the medical field still is uncertain about specific developmental disabilities. In all, some parents, family members, and caregivers utilize this as an opportunity to expand their knowledge of life at a multitude of levels.

FUTURE PROSPECTS

One of the key areas within disability studies recently has been the distinction between impairment and disability. Impairment is defined as a physical condition that prohibits a person from participating in a type of activity. Disability, on the other hand, is defined as a social constraint placed on a person or persons who are defined differently from the majority within that population. So instead of seeing diversity of the human body, we place labels on these individuals that carry meanings that suggest they are not good enough to go to the same schools, date, marry, or have children in the same manner as the rest of the population is. The term "disability" continues to facilitate social outcomes that limit or remove the civil rights and liberties of those defined as having a disability. In this case, many marginalized groups have much in common with those defined as having disabilities. Nevertheless, the difference in these terms has allowed people with disabilities in general to recognize that like everyone in society, limitations are part of the human condition. This is an area to watch as families adjust to the changing roles, definitions, and expectations imposed by society.

See also Attention Deficit Hyperactivity Disorder (ADHD); Child Abuse; Family Roles; Marital Satisfaction, Parenting Styles.

Further Reading: Baumeister, Alfred A. *Mental Retardation: Appraisal, Education, and Rehabilitation.* Chicago: Aldine, 1968; Berry, Judy O., and Michael L. Hardman. *Lifespan*

Perspectives on the Family and Disability. Boston: Allyn and Bacon, 1998; Blacher, Jan, and Bruce L. Baker. "Positive Impact of Intellectual Disability on Families." *American Journal on Mental Retardation* 112 (2007): 330–348; Boyce, Glenna C., Brent C. Miller, Karl R. White, and Michael K. Godfrey. "Single Parenting in Families of Children with Disabilities." *Marriage and Family Review* 20 (1994): 389–409; Davis, Lennard J. *The Disability Studies Reader.* New York: Routledge, 2006; Edgarton, Robert B. *The Cloak of Competence: Stigma in the Lives of the Mentally Retarded.* Berkeley: University of California Press, 1967; Feldman, Maurice A., and Shannon E. Werner. "Collateral Effects of Behavioral Parent Training on Families of Children with Developmental Disabilities and Severe Behavior Disorders." *Behavioral Interventions* 17 (2002): 75–83; Feldman, Maurice A., L. McDonald, L. Serbin, D. Stack, M. L. Secco, and C. T. Yu. "Predictors of Depressive Symptoms in Primary Caregivers of Young Children with or At Risk for Developmental Delay." *Journal of Intellectual Disability Research* 51 (2007): 606–619; Francis, Leslie Pickering, and Anita Silvers. *Americans with Disabilities: Exploring Implications of the Law for Individuals and Institutions.* New York: Routledge, 2000; Goffman, Erving. *Stigma: Notes on Management of Spoiled Identity.* Englewood Cliffs, NJ: Prentice Hall, 1963; Hastings, Richard P., and Helen M. Taunt. "Positive Perceptions in Families of Children with Developmental Disabilities." *American Journal on Mental Retardation* 107 (2002): 116–127; Hayden, Mary F., and Brian H. Abery. *Challenges for a Service System in Transition: Ensuring Quality Community Experiences for Persons with Developmental Disabilities.* Baltimore, MD: Paul H. Brookes, 1994; Hegeman, Mary Theodore. *Developmental Disability: A Family Challenge.* New York: Paulist Press, 1984; Olsson, Malin B., and C. P. Hwang. "Depression in Mothers and Fathers Rearing Children with Intellectual Disabilities." *Journal of Intellectual Disability Research* 45 (2001): 535–545; Reichman, Nancy E., Hope Corman and Kelly Noonan. "Effects of Child Health on Parents' Relationship Status." *Demography* 41 (2004): 569–584; Risdal, Don, and George H. S. Singer. "Marital Adjustment in Parents of Children with Disabilities: A Historical Review and Meta-analysis." *Research and Practice for Persons with Severe Disabilities* 29 (2004): 95–103; Smith, J. David. *In Search of Better Angels.* Thousand Oaks, CA: Corwin Press, 2003; Stainton, Tim, and Hilde Besser. "The Positive Impact of Children with an Intellectual Disability on the Family." *Journal of Intellectual and Developmental Disability* 23 (1998): 57–70; Viesson, Marika. "Depression Symptoms and Emotional States in Parents of Disabled and Non-disabled Children." *Social Behavior and Personality* 27 (1999): 87–97.

David G. LoConto

DIVORCE AND CHILDREN

In any given year, about one million children discover that their parents are divorcing. Approximately 60 percent of all divorces in the United States involve children. Prior to the 1970s, social scientists believed, as did the general public, that for a person to have an adult life without added emotional and behavioral problems, they had to grow up living with their biological parents. Early studies seemed to substantiate this, showing that children were scarred by divorce and left with emotional insecurities that continued when they became adults.

Later research has not shown this blanket concept to be true. Research shows that out of the one million children of divorce created each year, about 750,000 to 800,000 will suffer no long-term effects as they transition into adulthood. These children are able to function in the same way as those children reared by two parents. Indeed, many of these children may end up better off than they would have if their parents had remained together (see the sidebar "Staying Together for the Children").

Even if the long-term effects of divorce are not universal, this still leaves the 20 to 25 percent who do suffer from these effects. Additionally, most of those who do not suffer long-term effects still have an emotional adjustment period of one to two years immediately following the separation and divorce of their parents. This is often the period with the most intense conflict between the parents and the period when younger children most often believe that their parents will come back together. While it should be noted that adolescents adapt emotionally more readily than younger children, this period is frequently marked by depression, sleep disturbances, and general feelings of insecurity and confusion for both older and younger children.

LONG-TERM EFFECTS

A variety of effects are noted among those children with adjustment problems to parental divorce. Compared as a whole with the general population of children, they are more likely to have emotional problems. It was commonly thought that during a divorce boys were more likely to experience symptomatic problems than girls. Studies have shown that they suffer equally but differently, probably due to gender socialization differences. Boys' emotional symptoms are external, such as angry, violent, impulsive, or oppositional behaviors. In contrast, girls' emotional reactions to divorce are most often internalized and can be expressed as depression, headaches, and changes in sleeping and eating habits. In the segment of children who do suffer long-term effects, these symptoms and others are more likely to be acute and more likely to carry over into adulthood.

Statistically, children of divorce are more likely to have emotional problems as children and adults. They are more likely to commit acts of juvenile delinquency, abuse drugs and alcohol, and have early or increased sexual activity as youths.

Educationally, children of divorce tend toward higher absentee rates from school and lower levels of academic performance. This makes them less likely to graduate from high school or to attend or graduate from college. All of these factors compound the likelihood that they will have lower earning potential as adults.

Difficulty making personal relationships is also noted among children of divorce. This can manifest itself generally as a reluctance to join organizations or even to have a religious affiliation. More personally, children of divorce are less likely as a whole to marry, but those who do marry are more likely to do so at an early age and are more likely to get divorced themselves. This has been seen to actually lead to a ripple effect across generations where even the grandchildren of divorce, not just the children, have a greater likelihood of divorce.

"STAYING TOGETHER FOR THE CHILDREN"

The concept of "staying together for the children" was born out of the popular belief of the need for two parents in the household. It was thought that a child had to grow up under the direct influence of both of their parents in order to mature socially and emotionally. Additionally, staying together for the sake of the children was generally considered to be noble and selfless. Parents were expected to sacrifice their personal happiness as a way of protecting their children from the stress of being part of a divorce.

During much of the twentieth century in the United States, divorce was stigmatized. It was discouraged by many religions and often viewed as deviant by the public. Because of this atmosphere, the existence of children in a marriage was often used as an excuse to not get a divorce. While on the decline as an idea, "staying together for the children" was common prior to the 1970s when divorce became more publicly acceptable.

However, for proper development, a child needs to grow up in a warm and loving environment that may not exist in a household racked by conflict. In these cases, the emotional well-being of children may be better if their parents divorce, at minimum reducing much of the daily discord and possibly even allowing the parents to find happier relationships elsewhere. "Staying together for the children" may do more harm than good in these situations.

PROCESSES OF DIVORCE EFFECTS

Many recent studies of the effects of divorce on children have stopped looking at the harmful effects and have started looking behind them to discover the actual processes that cause the harm. A survey of recent studies reveals several important factors. First, divorce is stressful for the parents and tends to upset both the quantity and the quality of parenting from both parents, but especially the parenting from the adult who no longer lives in the household. Parents tend to become so involved in the divorce process themselves that they are unable to prepare the children for it or to help them through it.

Second, any conflicts that led the parents to divorce are made worse by the divorce itself. This often leaves the children in the middle of an emotional "no man's land," unsure of whether they should pick a side. The choice is often made to side with one parent and to reject the other. This often leads to having less contact with one of their parents, even as an adult.

Third, divorce is likely just the first of a series of disruptive and stressful events for the child. A shortened list of events can include moving away from the house and friends they have always known, remembering what bed they are sleeping in each night based on custody schedules and—often most devastating for younger children—the possibility of one parent re-marrying.

The final process appears to be the most important: the decline in the child's household income after the divorce. Many of the basic insecurities and emotions that come out of divorce can be tempered by support from peers along with relatives and other adults. The decline in income often cannot be so easily rectified and represents lost opportunities in both the present and future of the child. Even some forms of emotional support such as therapeutic interventions are affected by the economic decline.

THE ECONOMIC FACTOR

Divorce has huge economic consequences for the family, although the change is not as great for men as it is for women and children. Men, often the former primary breadwinner in the family, generally see an improvement in their standard of living, while women and children see a decline. The three major reasons for this are interrelated, and are that women are more than four times as likely as men to get custody of the children, women are paid less on average than men, and only about two-thirds of divorces involving children have child support awarded by the court system. Even when alimony and child support are awarded, the payments tend to not be linked to cost of living allowances and one-quarter of the payments granted are not even paid.

Obviously, single-parent families typically have less household income than two-parent families, but the single-parent families are more likely to live in poverty. These families are more likely to be headed by women who were not the main source of income before the divorce. These women experience an average of a 30 percent drop in income in the first year.

The employment that is available to them may be restricted by their education and skill levels leading to lower-paying positions. These jobs are not as likely as higher-paying positions are to allow for the flexible hours and time off that are needed for child care and maintenance of the household. Often a large percentage of the salary goes to pay for the most basic child care while they work, and misfortunes as simple as a flat tire can be devastating for the family's finances. Educational and extracurricular activities for the children can become luxuries in these situations.

In these circumstances it is easy to see why divorce can make it difficult for a parent to provide physical and emotional support for his or her family. As a whole, the lower the income of the parent who is awarded custody of the children, the more likely those children are to experience problems.

MINIMIZING THE EFFECTS OF DIVORCE

Feelings of closeness and affection with the parents are one of the most important ways for the emotional effects of divorce to be minimized. Children who feel close to both parents make the best adjustment, as opposed to situations where the parents use the children as weapons against each other. The next-best situation is when children feel close to one parent—this is the most common pattern. Children who feel close to neither parent fare the worst.

Children react better if there is a second adult that they can count on for support. This person can act as a surrogate for the custodial parent, relieving some pressure on them, but they are more important as a confidant for the child. This allows the child to talk over their feelings and problems that may involve the custodial parent. This adult can be anyone in the child's life: a relative, a neighbor or a family friend, but the best choice is the parent with which they do not live, most often the father.

Unfortunately, only one out of six children who live apart from their fathers sees them as often as one time a week. Most divorced fathers stop seeing their children at all. The emerging trend of serial fatherhood plays a part in this. In this trend, the father maintains close contact with his children after divorce for the first one to two years. This close contact begins to fade as the father begins a relationship with another woman, with the father either having new children or taking over the role of father with the other woman's children from previous relationships. In either case, his level of contact with his previous children declines and may completely end. If the current relationship ends, this cycle can repeat itself.

Children react better if they experience little conflict from the divorce itself. Some research suggests that some of the emotional and behavioral problems are caused by exposure to parental conflict both before and after the divorce. Because of the emotional stress and anger associated with the divorce, children tend to do better if they live with the parent who is adjusting better to the divorce.

Quite often children do better if they live with the parent of the same sex. This is especially seen in boys who sometimes do not seem to manage as well if they are living with their mothers.

During and after the divorce, children should have consistent routines. Children crave consistency and structure to their lives. It should be understood that the parent's life transitions are also the child's transitions, so effort should be made to remember this and incorporate structure into the children's lives so that they feel secure.

People, even children, worry about money. In addition to the obvious economic consequences of the divorce, there are emotional consequences that can have a more immediate impact on children. These can range from embarrassment or disappointment over clothing and entertainment budgets to feelings of guilt or empathetic worry due to their perception of the parents' fears over finances. Feeling that the family has adequate money for its needs is an emotional relief to the child.

The most noticeable effect that carries over into adulthood is the difficulty that is experienced in relationships, including an increased likelihood of divorce. Adult children's difficulty in relationships often depends greatly on their mother's adjustment to the divorce. If the mother establishes stable, intimate relationships after divorce, an environment is created where the children learn to create intimate relationships themselves. The children experience the greatest difficulties if the mother did not re-marry, the mother remarried and then divorced again; or the mother interfered with the children's relationship with their father.

Additionally, the likelihood of divorce can go down if the adult child marries someone from a nondivorced family of orientation. The spouse and their parents can provide new role models of relationships for the adult child.

It is not the absence of the father that is at the root of the symptoms that affect children from divorced families. Instead, it is more often low income and the lowered standards of living and the lowered parental supervision that come with it. These same factors often affect children from two-parent families that have similar problems in their development. Child rearing, whether part of a two-parent family or as a single parent, is not easy. But with parental care and the support of others, children of divorce can grow up and prosper in healthy environments.

See also Adversarial and No-Fault Divorce; Child Support and Parental Responsibility; Deadbeat Parents; Divorce, as Problem, Symptom, or Solution.

Further Reading: Ahrons, Constance. *We're Still Family: What Grown Children Have to Say About Their Parents' Divorce.* New York: Harper Collins, 2004; Amato, Paul R., and Alan Booth. *A Generation at Risk: Growing Up in an Era of Family Upheaval.* Cambridge, MA: Harvard University Press, 2000; Emery, Robert E. *Marriage, Divorce and Children's Adjustment,* 2nd ed. Thousand Oaks, CA: Sage Publications, 1999; Furstenberg, Frank F., and Andrew Cherlin. *Divided Families: What Happens to Children When Parents Part.* Cambridge, MA: Harvard University Press, 1991; Hetherington, E. Mavis, and John Kelly. *For Better or Worse: Divorce Reconsidered.* New York: W. W. Norton and Company, 2002; Wallerstein, Judith S., Julia M. Lewis, and Sandra Blakeslee. *The Unexpected Legacy of Divorce: The 25 Year Landmark Study.* New York: Hyperion, 2001.

Donald Woolley

DIVORCE, AS PROBLEM, SYMPTOM, OR SOLUTION

The answer to the question of whether divorce in the United States is best viewed as a problem, symptom, or solution, often depends on who is answering. Different stakeholders are concerned with the quality of family life and the effects that divorce might have on individuals and the culture as a whole. Among the groups with a vested interest in divorce are politicians, religious groups, counselors, educators, and families themselves.

Persons viewing divorce as a problem tend to focus on statistics indicating a high likelihood of divorces for first marriages and direct much of their concern toward the effects of postdivorce circumstances on children. These stakeholders have been very successful at getting their message to a wide audience. Among those viewing divorce as a problem are clinical psychologist Judith Wallerstein, James Dobson of Focus on the Family, and the Institute for American Values.

Persons who indicate that divorce is a symptom, express the sentiment that modern society is too quick to seek easy solutions to problems and suggest that couples' expectations of marriage are too idealistic. Additionally, those who see divorce as a symptom of a larger problem argue that the moral standards and values of society as a whole are in decline. They also tend to focus on individualism, secularization, and instant gratification as responsible for the increases in divorce. Advocates for this approach include the Institute for American Values, Maggie Gallagher, and Barbara Dafoe Whitehead.

Persons who emphasize the solution elements of divorce often point to decreases in violence and anger between the former partners as the biggest benefit to divorce. Likewise they would suggest that divorce is a solution for persons who entered a marriage unwisely or who were unprepared to assume the responsibilities of a life-time commitment. Divorce is seen as a solution when the environment at home is one of constant tension and anger. Persons coming from this perspective tend to emphasize constructing a meaningful life after the divorce for both the couple and any children and include Constance Ahrons, the American Academy of Matrimonial Lawyers, and Mavis Hetherington.

BRIEF HISTORY OF DIVORCE

It seems that persons of all recent societies place value on a marriage-like or lasting union between a man and woman. As a result, most societies historically and presently have frowned upon the ending of such unions and have generally put barriers in the way of dissolving the relationships, although surviving documents indicate that divorces occurred at least as far in the past as ancient Mesopotamia. While the process is formal and legal in the United States and other westernized societies, at other historic periods and places the mechanism has been quite different. Ancient Greeks were unlikely to place a high premium on marriages for other than the legitimating of heirs and divorce was available provided the reasons a person was requesting a divorce were approved by a governmental official. In the later years of the Roman Empire a couple could simply agree to divorce and it would be done. In other societies, the husband was the only party who could petition for and receive a divorce.

For the most part the widespread acceptance of Christianity in the middle ages served to decrease the availability of divorce and to enact stringent limitations on the rare instances when it would be permitted. This pattern reflects the fact that marriage at the time was a religious sacrament and under the control of the church, rather than the civil authority. Annulment was the more available path to marital dissolution. In an annulment granted by the church, the marriage was declared null, as if it had never occurred. This stance regarding divorce remains a hallmark of Roman Catholicism. Even today, devout Catholics and clergy chastise those Catholic lawyers who facilitate divorce proceedings. Annulment is also a legal term that is used when a condition existed prior to the marriage that would have prevented the marriage from being legally permitted or recognized. Thus, in the eyes of the law, the marriage never existed.

Divorce has always been available in some capacity in the United States, although the ease with which one could attain divorce and the likelihood of social rejection for doing so has varied over time. The United States has a more liberal history of divorce than does Great Britain and other Western European countries, despite the reliance on English Common Law as the basis for American civil authority. The first recorded divorce in what is now the United States was granted in the Plymouth Colony in 1639 to a woman whose husband had committed bigamy (was married to two women simultaneously). Divorces were rare, however, in the colonial period. This is likely due to the influence of religious beliefs, but also to the economic necessity of partners working together to survive the sometimes harsh conditions of colonial life. A wife was sometimes referred to as a "help-meet" in colonial literature, reinforcing the role that she assumed in the success of the farm or family business.

While the United States was more liberal than many of the European countries regarding divorce, grounds for divorce had to be established before a divorce would be permitted. Traditional grounds for divorce included adultery, cruelty, nonsupport, desertion, incarceration, and so forth. It was not until 1970 that any state statutes permitted divorce simply because the partners were incompatible. The bold move by California of instituting the first so-called no-fault divorce laws paved the way for partners to divorce for other than traditional grounds. By 1985, when South Dakota became the last state to permit no-fault divorce, all states had some provisions for these divorces, although a few states (such as New York) required a mandatory waiting period before such a divorce could occur. No-fault divorce meant that neither partner had committed a crime against the other, thus the traditional grounds for divorce had not been met. Under no-fault divorce, couples agreed that they could no longer be married and would like to have their legal marital contract dissolved.

DIVORCE AND THE INTERNET

The Internet has been blamed for ending more than a few marriages due to chat room infatuations that lead to affairs. However, there is another link between the Internet and divorce. Resources for divorce information and divorcing couples have flooded the Internet. Among the active sites are: preventingdivorce.com, divorcereform.org, divorceinfo.com, and divorceonline.com. Most provide a supportive community and others provide practical advice for those contemplating or experiencing divorce. There are even sites that will help couples select a lawyer to use for the divorce proceedings.

DIVORCE STATISTICS

Divorce is measured by using several different statistics. One of the most widely used is the crude divorce rate. This tells the number of divorces in a given year per 1000 population. This rate was 4.2 for the year 1998. This statistic makes divorce look fairly uncommon and is not very useful because it includes all persons in society, whether married or not. Another measure of divorce, which academics feel is a more accurate way to measure divorce, is known as the refined divorce rate. It considers the number of divorces in a given year divided by the number of married women in the population. By focusing on married couples (women) it includes only those persons who are eligible to divorce. In the United States for the year 2004 the refined divorce rate was 17.7. This statistic allows for more comparisons between countries and periods to determine meaningful differences in divorce.

A statistic often quoted in the discussions of divorce is that 50 percent of marriages will end in divorce. This statistic is rather misleading, if not wholly inaccurate, because it is very difficult to predict what will happen over the duration of a marriage. In an average year in the United States there are about 2.4 million marriages and 1.2 million divorces. It is from these data that the 50 percent figure is derived. However, experts who take into account the factors that lead to divorce for given social groups and historical eras put the likelihood of marriages beginning today and subsequently ending in divorce at around 40 percent.

For women who are college-educated and have family incomes over $30,000 the likelihood of divorce decreases to around 25 percent. Race and ethnicity play a part in the likelihood of getting a divorce as well. After ten years of marriage, 32 percent of non-Hispanic white women's first marriages end in divorce, compared with 34 percent of Hispanic women's first marriages, approximately 50 percent of black women's first marriages, and 20 percent of Asian women's first marriages. Current dissolution rates for first marriages indicate that approximately 20 percent of first marriages end within five years.

For the past 100 years there has been a generally upward trend in divorce in the United States. A slight decrease in divorce occurred during the early years of the 1930s. The economic troubles of the Great Depression likely influenced the divorce rate, but economic recessions since that time have not showed the same pattern regarding divorce. While divorce declined in the 1930s, it spiked dramatically in the second half of the 1940s. This change has been attributed to the effects of World War II. It seems reasonable that some partners found others during the time they were apart, women discovered independence through their work in the war effort, or persons were changed by the separation so that they were no longer compatible. Another probable explanation for the spike was that marriages contracted hastily before or during the war were no longer appealing to the partners when the war was over.

Despite the changes brought about in the era immediately following World War II, the time of most rapid increase in divorce was from the early 1960s to 1980, when the divorce rate more than doubled. Factors that have been proposed to account for the increase in divorce include the Second Wave of Feminism (also known as the Modern Women's Movement), an increase in women attending college and perceiving options outside of married life, increases in the accessibility and effectiveness of birth control, increases in opportunities for cohabitation (living together without being married), and the introduction of no-fault divorce statutes. During the most recent 20 year span, the divorce rate has declined from its all time high, but continues to be high when compared with the rates of divorce in other countries. Among the factors related to the recent decrease in divorce is that persons are waiting until later to marry for the first time. Early marriages, particularly among those under age 20, have a much higher chance of ending in divorce.

DIVORCE AS PROBLEM

While divorce rates in the United States have been stable or declining for 20 years, Americans express an overwhelming anxiety about the state of marriage. The rate of divorce peaked around 1980, but persons from all across the political spectrum propose that divorce is a serious problem in the United States today. Persons who see divorce as a problem come from the perspective that current divorce rates are unnaturally high and that society should work to reduce

KEY MOMENTS IN THE HISTORY OF DIVORCE

529 Byzantine emperor Justinian, no doubt influenced by his Christian beliefs, issues a strict anti-divorce decree.

1439 Marriage is declared a sacrament by the Roman Catholic Church. It is therefore indissoluble for any reason.

1529–1534 When the Catholic Church refuses to grant King Henry VIII a divorce, he breaks away to form the Church of England. He then marries Anne Boleyn.

1857 A divorce court is established through the British Parliament's Act of 1857. The U.S. would eventually follow this model.

1936 King Edward VIII of Britain abdicates his throne to marry twice-divorced American Wallis Simpson.

1949 South Carolina is the last of the states to give its citizens permission to divorce.

1957 The television courtroom drama *Divorce Court* begins.

1967 The number one song for four weeks on the country music charts is Tammy Wynette's "D-I-V-O-R-C-E."

1970 California starts a trend that will carry into all other states by enacting the first no-fault divorce laws.

1997 Covenant Marriage, a voluntary marriage provision that makes divorce harder to attain, is enacted in Louisiana.

them. There is a long history stemming from religious prohibitions and middle class morality, suggesting that divorce is a problem.

Divorce is defined as a problem because of the trauma of the breakup as well as the after-effects for both the partners who divorce and any children that are involved. Divorce is a problem for couples through both psychological and financial costs. Divorce is seen by many, including the divorcing partners, as a failure of the couple. They experience guilt, loss of self esteem, and anger. Divorced people are more likely to commit suicide than are married people.

Additionally, divorce has financial consequences for couples. Many times they sell their jointly held assets to divide the results equally. Because males provide on average more than 60 percent of household income, women may face a difficult decline in standard of living following divorce. Research suggests that more than 25 percent of divorced women experience at least some time in poverty during the five years following the divorce. Financial concerns are perhaps heightened for women because they are more likely to receive custody of and be caring for children than are their former husbands. This situation leads to an increase in the numbers of single parent families in society.

Society's concern with the effects of divorce on children has been a recent phenomenon, but has been a politically useful tack. The presence of children does little to prevent parents from divorcing; it only seems to delay it. Each year more than one million children are involved in the divorce of their parents. For those advocates who see a two-parent home as essential for rearing well adjusted children, divorce creates additional problems by creating single parent families.

Divorce decreases the economic and social resources available to children. In terms of economics, children reared by only one parent are far more likely to live in poverty than those reared in a two-parent home. There is less disposable income available to splurge on leisure activities or academic endeavors. Among the potential social consequences of divorce are problems in school, marrying at a young age or never marrying, and abusing alcohol or drugs. Children may experience depression and have less chance to be equally bonded with both parents. Usually it is the father who misses out on the experiences of the child's life. Some older studies of the consequences of divorce for children pointed to divorce as a factor in children's delinquency, truancy, and difficulty with peer relations. Judith Wallerstein has been particularly vocal about the long term consequences of divorce for children, including the increased chance that their marriages are more likely to end in divorce than those of children whose parents did not divorce.

Those most likely to view divorce as a problem in society are groups that desire to strengthen marriage as an institution. Marriage is viewed by many as the only acceptable way to live an adult life and the only situation in which to rear children. It is in the context of a nuclear family that children learn the skills that will enable them to be successful and productive members of society. One of the primary concerns of those who oppose divorce is that the option of divorce weakens the institution of marriage. In other words, as more couples divorce, the decision to get a divorce is more acceptable.

Religious organizations, such as Focus on The Family, have been critical of divorce for not only the negative consequences for adults, children, and society, but for issues of morality as well. Given Christian ideals that marriage is a sacrament before God lasting a lifetime, the only reasonable ending for a marriage is the death of one of the partners. There are, therefore, moral or religious consequences for the violation of holy law by divorcing. One of the most intriguing questions researchers are currently exploring with regard to divorce is how persons who hold some of the most conservative views on divorce have divorce rates higher than the national average. Born again Christians and Baptists had divorce rates of 27 and 29 percent, respectively, in a study by the religion-motivated Barna Research Group. The conservative religious right opposes divorce, but the Southern Bible belt states have the highest rates. The Catholic Church has been a harsh critic of divorce and lobbied hard to keep divorce options out of countries around the world.

DIVORCE AS SYMPTOM

Divorce is a symptom of the pressure that Americans put on the marital relationship to be all things to the partners. The romantic notion of marriage that says marriage to that one perfect person will make all of your dreams come true may be partly responsible for the high rates of divorce. Asking one person to be your everything is putting a lot of faith in and pressure on that one individual. While partners are expected to marry for life, they are given very little preparation, other than what they have witnessed in the marriages of their parents and other adults, about how to make a marriage work. Divorce is a symptom of the inadequate preparation for marriage that exists in our society. To combat this, clergy and counselors have developed programs for persons contemplating marriage in attempts to strengthen marriages. One popular program is known by the acronym PREPARE.

Pamela Paul has suggested that because cultural notions of marriage have changed very little over time, while society has changed a great deal, Americans are particularly likely to find that marriage is not meeting their needs. She suggests that several trends in society today are largely responsible for why marriages are likely to end in divorce. Among these trends are (1) people are living twice as long as they did 100 years ago, (2) the most intensive active parenting takes only about 20 years, so the couple likely has 40 or more years without children in the home, (3) persons are likely to have multiple careers over their lifetimes, so change becomes normative, (4) persons who marry today have grown up in a time in which the stigma of divorce has decreased and they may have personally experienced divorce as a young person and (5) the increased likelihood that both spouses are employed frees women to explore nonfamilial roles and to experience economic independence from their husbands. Given these changing circumstances of social life, Paul suggests that it may be unrealistic for spouses chosen while people are in their twenties to be appropriate partners at other life stages.

The Family Research Council has argued that divorce occurs because people are misguided about the purpose of marriage. Marriage is the institution in which children are to be reared and that is the primary function of marriage. It is not for the fulfillment of the couple, but rather for the fulfillment of procreation that marriage is intended to provide.

The phrase "divorce culture" reflects the notion that in today's world divorce might be seen as a rather common, even expected, occurrence. The cavalier attitude Americans display toward divorce, argue the critics, makes the harmful effects of divorce seem small. Thus, divorce might be chosen even when a couple has not seriously tried to resolve any difficulties. This choice locates the desire of the individual above the good of the family group. This is particularly criticized when children are involved. Divorce, then, is a sign of selfishness and individuality. Others would argue that it is the no-fault divorce provisions themselves that make divorce quick and easy and thus permit Americans to have a selfish attitude toward marriage. If no-fault divorces were not an option and couples had to go through the court system to end their marriages, they would work harder to keep them together and resolve any difficulties.

Organizations such as the Institute for American Values and the National Marriage Project routinely suggest that the increases in divorce and continuing high divorce rates are the result of a loosening of the moral code in the United States and an increase in individuality. The freedoms that Americans have to conduct personal relationships today have consequences for the individuals and the whole society. One area of concern is the prevalence of media images that depict divorce positively and marriage negatively. Additionally, a more secular society, one that is less apt to follow all aspects of religious teachings, has been blamed for an increase in divorce. Likewise, they suggest that removing the stigma from divorce has meant there is less social pressure to stay in a marriage.

One of the behaviors related to an increase in divorce and a questioning of morality is cohabitation. Cohabitation, living with a partner in a marriage-like relationship without being married, has increased dramatically in the last 30 years. There are now around 5.5 million households of heterosexual cohabitors in the U.S. In some communities as many as 60 percent of couples marrying in a given year are currently cohabiting at the time they apply for the marriage license. Research suggests that despite the common rationale for cohabitation, testing the relationship for compatibility, persons who cohabit before marriage are more likely to divorce than those who do not live together first.

DIVORCE AS SOLUTION

For partners who do not grow together in terms of interests and expectations, married life can be stifling. Divorce permits those couples in unhappy unions to end their relationships and start anew. While ending a marriage is a difficult, even traumatic, life transition, it does permit persons to make meaningful life changes and experience a renewal in their lives. This notion of being renewed after severing ties from an unsatisfactory relationship has been particularly likely to be mentioned by women after a divorce. In some communities, a woman's female friends might even throw her a liberation party to celebrate her newly single status.

Despite the potential for some women to experience financial difficulties after divorce, when dealing with their children divorced women are often calmer and more effective parents than when they were in the conflicted marriage. Women also tend to have decreased tension and fewer bouts of depression when single. Clearly for women (and children) who were victims of abuse during a marriage, divorce is a solution to the daily threat to their safety.

Children who experience high levels of conflict or even violence in their families enjoy an increase in well-being after a divorce has occurred. Most children from divorced families, even those without a violent past, live good lives after overcoming some initial difficulties. Staying together for the sake of the children, while a politically provocative idea, does not seem to have the desire outcomes. In fact, Constance Ahrons has indicated that a good divorce is much better for kids than a bad marriage because they see a healthier way to interact that validates the feelings of the partners and permits them to strive for greater happiness in their lives. Divorce may even lead to better parenting because the time with the children is coordinated and special. Partners no longer have to disagree about the problems of the marriage, but can work on the most effective way to parent the children that they share. Positive outcomes are particularly likely when parents and children attend special classes on how to build their skills in dealing with family issues.

Persons who view divorce as a solution tend to point to studies that argue that not only can children be reared successfully in arrangements other than a traditional two-parent family, but that adults can also find fulfillment in situations other than marriage. Those taking this view would not suggest that divorce or its consequences are easy; it is a highly stressful transition. However, it does permit adults a second chance at happiness and permits children to escape from a dysfunctional home life. In fact, Stephanie Coontz argues that we have made the traditional two-parent family look so good in our nostalgic yearning for the past that even the most functional of families would have difficulty living up to the expectations.

Perhaps it is the unrealistic expectations of married life that push some people to marry in the first place. While there are no overt penalties for singlehood nor current laws in the United States that indicate that one must be married by a certain age, there may be social pressure to demonstrate adult status by marrying. For these persons, marriage may not meet with their expectations, they may have married the wrong person, or they may have married too early. Research consistently shows that persons who are teenagers when they marry have far higher rates of divorce than do persons who wait until they are slightly older to marry. For these persons divorce may be a solution to a decision made when they were not yet mature. Likewise, persons who marry due to a premarital conception have higher rates of divorce than those whose children are conceived after the wedding.

Divorce may be characterized as a problem, symptom, or solution. At the present time, popular conceptions of divorce have given more support to the notion of divorce as a problem to be solved. It is a problem of both long-term and short-term consequences. It is a problem of individuals, as well as society. It is also a symptom of how much we might value personal relationships. We value them so highly that we want them to be all things to all persons and feel betrayed when they are not. Perhaps it is a symptom of the freedoms that U.S. society permits its citizens. Divorce is also a solution for those situations and times in which no other options seem to work, or when staying in the marriage might have devastating emotional or physical consequences for the participants.

See also Adversarial and No-Fault Divorce; Benefits of Marriage; Covenant Marriage; Divorce and Children; Marital Satisfaction; Prenuptial Agreements; Religion and Families; Remarriage.

Further Reading: Ahrons, Constance. *The Good Divorce: Keeping Your Family Together When Your Marriage Comes Apart.* New York: Harper Collins, 1994; Coontz, Stephanie. *The Way We Never Were: American Families and the Nostalgia Trap.* New York: Harper Collins, 1992; Hetherington, E. Mavis, and John Kelly. *For Better or For Worse: Divorce Reconsidered.* New York: W. W. Norton and Company, 2002; Paul, Pamela. *The Starter Marriage and the Future of Matrimony.* New York: Villard, 2002; Swallow, Wendy. *Breaking Apart: A Memoir of Divorce.* New York: Hyperion, 2001; Tesler, Pauline, and Peggy Thompson. 2006. *Collaborative Divorce: The Revolutionary New Way to Restructure Your Family, Resolve Legal Issues, and Move on With Your Life.* Los Angeles: Regan Books, 2006; Wallerstein, Judith, Julia Lewis, and Sandra Blakeslee. *The Unexpected Legacy of Divorce.* New York: Hyperion, 2000.

Kimberly P. Brackett

DOMESTIC PARTNERSHIPS

Over the last 25 years, numerous legal options have emerged for same-sex and opposite-sex couples wishing to legitimize their intimate unions in ways other than through heterosexual legal marriage. Four of these options are civil unions, same-sex marriages, reciprocal beneficiaries, and licensed domestic partnerships.

LEGAL OPTIONS

Civil Unions

Three states (Vermont in 2000, Connecticut in 2005, and New Jersey in 2007) have implemented *civil union* legislation. In all three states, only same-sex couples are eligible to enter into a civil union; with the exception of sexual orientation, they must also meet the eligibility requirements for legal marriage. At the state level, civil unions are the functional equivalent of legal marriage, in that they provide to couples all of the benefits and protections of marriage afforded to spouses. Due to the federal Defense of Marriage Act signed into law by President Bill Clinton in 1996, which defines marriage as consisting of the legal union of one man and one woman, these couples do not enjoy any of the benefits or protections at the federal level afforded to the legally married. Furthermore, while nonresidents are eligible to form civil unions in these three states, only in New Jersey do they receive any legal acknowledgment, benefits, or protections associated with their unions (Vermont and Connecticut do not grant legal acknowledgment to civil unions contracted elsewhere; nor does any state without civil union legislation).

Legally dissolving a civil union involves the same process as dissolving a marriage, in that one partner must file for divorce. In Vermont, for example, at least one partner must reside in the state for a minimum of six months prior to filing for dissolution, and that partner must reside in Vermont for at least one year prior to the hearing date for final dissolution of the civil union. If a couple that entered into a civil union either relocates to or are residents of another state, and they wish to legally dissolve their union, the lack of acknowledgement of civil unions in other states means that a legal divorce is difficult, if not impossible, to obtain. Indeed, two couples who entered into civil unions in Vermont currently are struggling to dissolve their unions in other states (one in Connecticut, initially heard before the court in 2002, and one in Texas, initially heard before the court in 2003). In both cases, decisions as to whether the unions may be legally dissolved in these states are yet to be rendered.

Same-Sex Marriage

Another legal option made available in 2004 only to couples residing in Massachusetts is *same-sex marriage*. Currently, Massachusetts is the only state in the United States that permits same-sex couples to legally marry. Furthermore, the federal Defense of Marriage Act dictates that states are not required to legally recognize the same-sex marriages contracted in any other state, and no other state legally acknowledges the same-sex marriages contracted in Massachusetts. New Jersey, however, legally translates these marriages, in addition to the legal same-sex marriages contracted in other countries (same-sex marriage was legalized in the Netherlands in 2001, Belgium in 2003, Canada and Spain in 2005, and South Africa in 2006), into civil unions if the couples relocate there, and provides to these couples all of the state-level benefits and protections of legal marriage. Similar to civil unions, same-sex marriage in Massachusetts grants to couples all of the benefits and protections afforded to the legally married at the state level, but these couples do not enjoy any of the benefits or protections afforded to the legally married at the federal level as a result of the Defense of Marriage Act. Furthermore, because no other state legally acknowledges the same-sex marriages contracted in Massachusetts, couples may be prohibited from divorcing if they relocate to another state.

Reciprocal Beneficiaries

A third legal option, available only in the State of Hawaii, is *reciprocal beneficiaries*. According to Hawaii's Reciprocal Beneficiaries Law, implemented in 1997, same-sex couples, as well as unmarried relatives and friends of heterosexual and homosexual individuals legally barred from marrying each other, are eligible to register with the Hawaii Department of Health as reciprocal beneficiaries. Hawaii's policy is unique because it extends eligibility to those not in an intimate union. The law grants some of the benefits of marriage to reciprocal beneficiaries, including property rights, protection under the state's domestic violence laws, the ability to visit a beneficiary in the hospital and to make medical decisions for him or her, to sue for the wrongful death of a beneficiary, and to inherit property without a will. Because individuals in reciprocal beneficiaries are legally single, dissolving the relationship legally simply involves informing the Hawaii Department of Health of its termination.

Licensed Domestic Partnerships

A fourth legal option is *licensed domestic partnerships*. These partnerships were first instituted in Berkeley, California in 1984, and were originally intended to grant public acknowledgement to the unions of same-sex couples. Local government officials at that time determined that unmarried opposite-sex couples also needed legal acknowledgement of their unions, particularly with regard to protecting the so-called weaker party in the relationship upon the dissolution of it; thus, eligibility for participation in licensed domestic partnerships was extended to them as well. Since then, two states (California in 1999 and Maine in 2004) and the District of Columbia (in 2002) have implemented domestic partnership ordinances, as have 11 counties and 55 cities. An analysis of the domestic partnership records provided by most locales (some do not release this information due to confidentiality concerns) indicates that most licensed couples are in same-sex unions.

Domestic partnership ordinances typically define partners as two financially interdependent adults who live together and share an intimate bond, but are not related by blood or law. Couples wishing to license their cohabiting unions complete an affidavit attesting that they are not already biologically or legally related to each other or legally married to someone else, that they agree to be mutually responsible for each other's welfare, and that they will notify the local government records office if there is a change in the status of the relationship, either by dissolution or by legal marriage. Along with a fee, the affidavit is then submitted to the local records office or, in some locales, may be notarized to register the partnership. To dissolve a licensed partnership, one partner simply must inform the office where the partnership was registered. Within six months after this notification, an individual in most locales may then register another domestic partnership.

As stated above, the first state to implement a domestic partnership ordinance was California in 1999; in that state, both same-sex and opposite-sex couples are eligible to become licensed partners, although the age-eligibility requirements differ. Specifically, both partners in a same-sex couple must be at least 18 years of age to become licensed partners. One partner in an opposite-sex couple, however, must be at least 62 years of age and meet eligibility requirements for old-age benefits under the Social Security Act. These differing eligibility requirements were implemented to encourage legal marriage among opposite-sex couples, while also recognizing that remarrying after the death of a spouse imposes financial costs in terms of reductions in Social Security benefits to those remarrying as opposed to remaining single. Upon implementation of the legislation, licensed domestic partners in California received a number of tangible benefits that the legally married enjoyed; since 2005, essentially all state-level rights and responsibilities of marriage were extended to licensed partners.

In the State of Maine, both opposite- and same-sex couples are eligible to register as licensed domestic partners, with the same age-eligibility requirements (both partners must be at least 18 years of age). To become licensed, both partners must be residents of Maine for at least one year. Licensed partners in Maine also enjoy limited benefits, including protection under the state's domestic violence laws, the right to inherit property from a partner without a will, making funeral and burial arrangements for a partner, entitlement to be named the partner's guardian in the event he or she becomes incapacitated, and to make decisions regarding organ or tissue donation for a deceased partner.

According to the District of Columbia's domestic partnership ordinance, both opposite-sex and same-sex couples are eligible, and there are no differentiating age-eligibility requirements. Only district government employees first employed after October 1, 1987, however, are eligible to participate. While a handful of benefits were initially included in the legislation upon its implementation, the Domestic Partners Equality Amendment Act of 2006 dictates that licensed partners must be treated similarly to how spouses are treated in nearly all cases concerning rights and protections.

Three of the 11 counties and five of the 55 cities that have implemented domestic partnership ordinances restrict eligibility to same-sex couples. Furthermore, in 13 locales, both partners must be either residents of the city or county or couples must include at least one partner who is an employee of the city or county. Thus, couples throughout the United States may become licensed domestic partners in many locales, although they do not reside there. Their home city or county will not acknowledge their licensed status, however, and they will receive no benefits or protections as a function of being licensed partners. Most locales, however, do not offer any tangible benefits or protections to licensed partners anyway, regardless of where the couple resides. The benefits granted by the handful of counties and cities that do provide them include health insurance coverage for a partner, visitation rights in hospitals and correctional facilities, and bereavement leave.

Current Controversies. Those most concerned with the implementation of policies legitimizing various coupling options are divided along ideological lines to form two competing camps. The pro-marriage camp consists of those promoting legal marriage as the sole form of public acknowledgement of intimate unions. Individuals and organizations in this camp may be divided further into two classes: one that promotes heterosexual marriage and desires the exclusion of legal recognition of all other types of unions based on religious beliefs (referred to here as the "religiously-oriented"), and one fearing that the institution of marriage, along with its beneficial aspects to men, women, children, and society, are threatened by legally acknowledging other forms of relationships (referred to here as the "family decline-oriented"). Specifically, those motivated by religious arguments assert that only heterosexual relationships within the context of legal marriage are natural or ordained by God, and that recognition of same-sex unions and nonmarital forms of heterosexual unions undermines the inherent value of legal marriage and violates the will of God. They view marriage as much more than simply a civil contract; rather, it is a holy sacrament. Those motivated by concerns over family decline assert that there are tangible and emotional benefits to marriage that accrue only to individuals residing within the context of legal marriage, and that all of society benefits from the well-being these individuals enjoy. Those in this class are concerned that legal acknowledgement of other forms of coupling undermines marriage as the so-called gold standard, and that couples will be less likely to aspire to marriage as a result, leading to a host of social ills.

The other side involved in this debate, referred to here as the pro-inclusivity camp, advocates for legal recognition of both marital and nonmarital relationships. They assert that legal marriage for many couples is either unavailable or undesirable as an option to legitimizing a union. They argue that other forms of legitimization must be made available to these couples as a civil rights issue. Advocates of inclusivity argue that the well-being of men, women, children, and society would be advanced by the implementation of policies promoting their choices and protecting their interests, whereas denying them either the opportunity to legitimize their unions or forcing them into an all-or-nothing situation, where they must either marry and receive benefits and protections, or do not marry and receive no benefits or protections, harms the individuals in these families as well as the well-being of society.

The success of both the pro-marriage and the pro-inclusivity camps in promoting their views is mixed. As stated above, an increasing number of locales are implementing legislation that grants acknowledgement to various forms of coupling. At the same time, however, an increasing number of states have implemented their own Defense of Marriage Acts or amended their state constitutions to define marriage as consisting of the legal union of one man and one woman. Currently, only ten states do not have a version of this act or a substantively similar constitutional amendment.

Clearly, the most controversial issue surrounding the implementation of policies legitimizing various methods of coupling concerns public acknowledgment of same-sex unions. States in particular have struggled with determining what type of acknowledgment to provide, if any, and what terminology should be employed to grant this acknowledgment (e.g., civil unions, licensed partnerships). As noted above, only the State of Massachusetts has made legal marriage available to resident same-sex couples. Other states have attempted to strike a compromise in this debate by implementing very similar legislation, but referring to it as something other than legal marriage. The result of the compromise, however, is that parties on both sides of the debate are left dissatisfied. Pro-marriage advocates are alarmed that the unions of same-sex couples are receiving any acknowledgement all; for many same-sex couples and their advocates, however, anything short of legal marriage is simply not enough, as marriage enjoys a cultural aura and subsequent social support that is bolstered by history and religion, and that does not exist in any other form of coupling.

It is important to note that even homosexual individuals and organizations promoting their civil rights and well-being are divided on the issue of whether marriage should be extended legally to same-sex couples. Some argue for equal legal treatment between same-sex and opposite-sex couples, whereas others argue that legal marriage has never been an institution in which spouses, especially wives, enjoy equality and the benefits and protections of marriage that have been traditionally enjoyed by husbands. It appears, however, that most organizations serving as advocates for homosexual individuals and their intimate unions are fighting for access to legal marriage.

While receiving much less public attention, heterosexual licensed domestic partnerships are also a source of controversy. Those promoting heterosexual legal marriage on the basis of family decline concerns argue that opposite-sex couples are engaging in a rational-choice approach to coupling, looking to attain the benefits of marriage while attempting to avoid its costs and obligations. For example, they assert that cohabiting couples, licensed and otherwise, wish to enjoy the financial benefits of marriage by sharing household expenses, while also maintaining financial independence from their partners. Similarly, they are looking to attain the companionship found in marriage while also desirous of more emotional independence from their partners than spouses have from each other. Those in the family decline camp assert that by licensing heterosexual cohabitation, and thereby encouraging couples to cohabit rather than marry, legal marriage is losing its social status as the ultimate method of coupling in society, and is being redefined as simply one of several equally valid and valued coupling options. The repercussions, they argue, are significant: adults reduce their sense of commitment and are less likely to fulfill their obligations to others, leading to less security for both adults and children.

Advocates of licensed domestic partnerships, however, assert that emotional commitment and the sense of obligation to partners and children do not differ among licensed partners or the legally married. Instead, marriage is associated with baggage that may be avoided in licensed partnerships without undermining the quality of or obligations in intimate unions. For example, in legal marriage, spouses are responsible for each other's debts, whereas in licensed domestic partnerships, because the partners are legally single, the financial well-being of one partner is protected from the financial problems of the other partner. Because the partners reside together, the economic well-being of both partners and any children residing with them is protected. Similarly, marriage for some is associated with the oppression of women. Some women in licensed domestic partnerships believe that they are able to avoid what they see as the patriarchal nature of marriage by becoming licensed partners instead. As a result, they assert that they have attained equitable relationships that would not be possible in legal marriage.

In summary, civil unions, same-sex marriage, reciprocal beneficiaries, and licensed domestic partnerships provide some, but not all, of the legal benefits and protections of heterosexual marriage. As a result, these options are not, to date, the legal equivalent of marriage. Furthermore, these couples do not enjoy the social or cultural support promoting the maintenance of their unions that the legally married enjoy. If indeed individuals in families engaging in nonheterosexual or nonmarital forms of coupling experience lower levels of well-being, (and to date, research has not been conducted exploring this issue), the reasons should not be surprising.

See also Common Law Marriages; Fictive Kin; Nonmarital Cohabitation; Same-Sex Marriage.

Further Reading: Human Rights Campaign. "HRC: Domestic Partners. http://www.hrc.org/Template.cfm?Section=Domesticpartners1&Template=/TaggedPage/TaggedPageDisplay.cfm&TPLID=23&ContentID=103; Human Rights Campaign. "HRC: Civil Unions." http://www.hrc.org/Template.cfm?Section=Civil unions1&Template=/Tagged Page/Tagged PageDisplay.cfm&TPLID=23&ContentID=21804; Human Rights Campaign. "Massachusetts Marriage/Relationship Recognition Law." http://www.hrc.org/Template.cfm?Section=Center&CONTENTID=27640&TEMPLATE=/ContentManagement/ContentDisplay.cfm; Pinello, D. R. *America's Struggle for Same-sex Marriage*. New York: Cambridge University Press, 2006; Popenoe, D. *State of Our Unions: The Social Health of Marriage in America, 1999*. New Brunswick N.J.: The National Marriage Project, 1999; Willetts, M. C. "An Exploratory Investigation of Heterosexual Licensed Domestic Partners." *Journal of Marriage and Family* 65 (2003): 939–952; Willliams, H. K., and R. E. Bowen. "Marriage, Same-sex Unions, and Domestic Partnerships." *The Georgetown Journal of Gender and Law* 1 (2000): 337–359.

Marion C. Willetts

DOMESTIC VIOLENCE BEHAVIORS AND CAUSES

Domestic violence, also known as intimate partner violence, is a significant concern in society today. It is estimated that 9 million couples, or 1 in 6 marriages, experience some form of intimate partner violence, with 21 percent of all violent crimes committed against women perpetrated by a romantic partner (Strong, DeVault, and Cohen 2001). Although violence against women in intimate relationships has existed for centuries, it has only widely become acknowledged as problematic since the latter half of the twentieth century. Many credit this increased awareness to social and political movements such the second wave of feminism, also known as the modern women's movement, that have argued for equality and basic rights regardless of gender. Also, in association with an increase in activity in the academic, medical, social, and political communities legislation has been enacted for the purposes of domestic violence protection, prevention, and education.

Policies such as the 1994 Violence Against Women Act (VAWA) help to empower women through the funding of prevention and intervention programs. Despite the fact that social change has been credited with spurring protective legislation and social awareness concerning intimate partner violence, many claim that there has been a limited social understanding of the experiences of women in violent relationships, and there remains a victim-blaming bias in the ways we've responded to domestic violence as a society.

As an aside, it is thoroughly acknowledged that women are not the only victims of domestic violence because this is a social problem that victimizes men as well. However, research shows that the vast majority of reported domestic abuse victims in our society are female. Additionally, the injuries suffered by females tend to be more severe than those suffered by males. Therefore, we will focus on domestic violence as it affects women primarily.

ABUSE BEHAVIORS

Overall, behaviors associated with intimate partner violence are usually categorized into the following groups: physical abuse, emotional abuse, sexual abuse, and financial abuse. While all are harmful, when there are limited resources in a community leaders must choose where to direct these resources so as to do the most good. The most visible category is physical abuse, which has received the most attention from research and advocacy groups. This does not, however, imply that it is the most harmful or important abuse behavior. The following definitions of abusive behaviors have been taken from the National Center for Injury Prevention and Control and will be described here in greater detail.

Physical Abuse

Physical violence is defined as the intentional use of physical force with the potential for causing death, disability, injury, or harm. Physical violence includes, but is not limited to, scratching, pushing, shoving, throwing, grabbing, biting, choking, shaking, slapping, punching, burning, use of a weapon, and use of restraints or one's body, size, or strength against another person. Consequences associated with physical abuse are severe and far reaching, resulting in death in extreme cases. This is what most persons stereotypically picture when they hear the phrase "battered wife."

Emotional Abuse

Psychological or emotional violence involves trauma to the victim caused by acts, threats of acts, or coercive tactics. This can include, but is not limited to, humiliating the victim, controlling what the victim can and cannot do, withholding information, deliberately doing something to make the victim feel diminished or embarrassed, isolating the victim from friends and family, threatening or terrorizing, and denying access to basic resources. Scholars have reported that as many as 80 to 90 percent of women will experience psychological maltreatment at some point in an intimate relationship (Neufeld et al. 1999). The consequences of such abuse have been found to have devastating impacts on survivors as well. In fact, due to the devastating consequences of emotional abuse, many survivors report that they would rather be physically hit than emotionally abused by an intimate partner.

Sexual Abuse

The National Center for Injury Prevention and Control, a subgroup of the Centers for Disease Control and Prevention, defines and divides sexual abuse into three categories: (1) the use of physical force to compel a person to engage in a sexual act against his or her will, whether or not the act is completed; (2) an attempted or completed sex act involving a person who is unable to understand the nature or condition of the act, to decline participation, or to communicate unwillingness to engage in the sexual act (e.g., because of illness, disability, the influence of alcohol or other drugs, or because of intimidation/pressure); and (3) abusive sexual contact. Studies show that between 10 and 14 percent of wives have been forced into sexual activity by their partners (Strong, DeVault, and Cohen 2001). It is often difficult for women who are sexually abused by an intimate partner to seek help because it is often the case that sexual activity within relationships, whether voluntary or coerced, is not recognized as abusive. Although this has gotten better through more research and media attention given to sexual abuse in intimate relationships, it is still often very difficult for a victim to seek help or to receive the validation needed to overcome such traumatic experiences.

Financial Abuse

Financial abuse is usually characterized by an abuser withholding funds, stealing assets, stealing property, or compromising a partner's financial liberties. It can be difficult for the victim to seek relationship alternatives in situations where financial abuse is present, as the victim is often totally dependent on the abuser to provide for basic needs. This is especially true when children are involved. With this lack of resources available to the victim, there is also an increased risk of homelessness for the women and children impacted by violent relationships; an issue that will be discussed in further detail later.

COMMON COUPLE VIOLENCE VERSUS INTIMATE TERRORISM

Among the issues that have made it difficult over time to get the needed attention for domestic violence is the wide range of behaviors that fall under the umbrella of abuse. For many years there was a stereotypical image of a battered woman who was the victim of abusive beatings. However, recent thinking about domestic abuse has expanded to be more inclusive of a variety of unwanted violent acts. Intimate partner violence takes many forms, and involves many behaviors that are detrimental to the victim. In addition, some theoretical and methodological considerations in relation to intimate partner violence must be examined. Based on the work of Michael Johnson (1995), several theoretical distinctions have been made regarding domestic abuse. These categories originally arose during a comparison of domestic violence victims sample groups gathered from the general population and those from shelters. They also differ in areas related to power dynamics and behavioral characteristics, as well as on overall outcomes for victims. Johnson terms them as common couple violence and as intimate terrorism.

Common Couple Violence

Common couple violence is considered the most common type of violence that occurs in relationships, and is a less dangerous form of intimate partner violence. In situations where violence is present, conflict usually arises from a mutual disagreement between the partners and is considerably equally perpetrated among partners, although women are more likely to be injured during violent episodes. It is important to recognize that both partners can be violent in this scenario. This form of violence rarely escalates over time, and is more likely to be identified through surveys of the general population.

Intimate Terrorism

Intimate terrorism, also referred to as patriarchal terrorism, on the other hand, is very severe and can be highly lethal in nature. In situations where intimate terrorism is present, the abuser usually demonstrates power and control in order to dominate their partner. Conflict in these relationships is usually one-sided and can be very severe. In these forms of relationships, conflict usually escalates over time and increases in both frequency and intensity. Intimate terrorism is frequently characterized by a physical or emotional domination of the victim, and often involves social isolation, financial dependence, emotional degradation, and is characterized by feelings of fear and hopelessness of the victim.

Finally, Johnson reported that victims of intimate terrorism are more likely to be identified through research that focuses on specific samples, such as that taken in shelter settings.

While Johnson's work has been credited with uncovering a broad range of domestic violence types, there is some concern with defining domestic violence in this way. For example, the use of common couple violence suggests that all partners participate and it must then be normal to do so. If we assume that it is a normal part of relationships, that changes how society is willing to respond. There is a concern that a partner's requests for help may not be taken seriously if she were violent against her spouse. This could set up a situation in which only victims of intimate terrorism may be seen as worthy of assistance by shelters and other agencies. A victim of common couple violence, then, may be blamed for putting herself in a situation in which she and the partner resorted to violence.

WHY DOESN'T SHE JUST LEAVE?

A common question that arises in relation to domestic violence is *why doesn't she just leave? Surely women don't enjoy to be treated this way, so why don't abused women get out?* Many feel that if a victim of domestic violence *really* wanted to leave the relationship, she would just move on. However, as will be discussed further here, the circumstances that often surround domestic violence, especially situations where intimate terrorism are present, tend to be very complex, and choosing to just leave can be much more difficult, if not more lethal, than most people may realize. The suggestion that she should just leave blames any future abuse on her decision to stay, thus the victim blaming becomes acute.

BARRIERS TO SEEKING HELP

Due to various social barriers, many abused women don't perceive their decision to remain in a violent relationship as a choice at all because few, if any, reasonable alternatives may be available to her. Common barriers that exist for victimized women include: social isolation, financial dependence, fear of repercussions, pressure to keep the family together, and a lack of appropriate community response. Advocates for the victims of domestic abuse debate which of these exerts the biggest pressure on women to stay in abusive situations.

Social Isolation

As previously stated in the discussion of Johnson's concept of intimate terrorism, social isolation is a common factor found in most cases of domestic abuse. It is quite common in situations of intimate terrorism, because isolating one from the external support system enables the abuser to maintain power and control through forcing dependency of the victim on the abuser. This can include instances in which the victim is moved, often repeatedly, from place to place to ensure a lack of social contacts such as friends and family and external support such as community resources. In our individualistic society, this isolation is especially problematic because of cultural norms regarding the right to privacy of the family. The practice of purposeful isolation usually involves limiting access to friends, family, coworkers, or forbidding outside employment altogether. Increasing isolation of the victim greatly decreases the perceived and actual availability of support in situations of abuse. Therefore, escape from abusive relationships can become very difficult. In fact, isolation increases the likelihood that a woman will live with an abusive partner from 12 to 25 percent (Bosch and Schumm 2004).

Financial Dependence

Studies show that domestic violence is more likely to occur in situations where couples are less educated and live in poor economic conditions. Poverty, which is directly correlated with lowered levels of education, is also a strong predictor of domestic violence. In fact, among all couples, a top cause of conflict is related to economic stress and strain. In addition, a woman living in poverty is also more likely to be financially dependent on her abuser, especially if she is unable to work. Therefore, for many women, the reality is that if she chooses to leave her abuser, the alternative is an inability to provide for her children and herself, or experiencing homelessness.

Fear of Repercussion

Many women remain in violent relationships because they are afraid to leave because the abuser has threatened severe violence, or he has threatened to kill the woman or her children. This fear may be quite valid because most of the severe acts of violence tend to be perpetrated against women who have left or attempted to leave a violent relationship. Furthermore, a woman is more likely to be murdered during the first six months following her exit from an abusive relationship than at any other time in her life, and at least 67 percent of female homicide victims had a history of physical abuse by an intimate partner (NCVC 2004).

Many women who exit abusive relationships are stalked by their abuser. Stalking is an issue of significant concern because it often results in psychological problems including anxiety, insomnia, fear, depression, loss of work time, and the need for legal protective orders. Furthermore, the risk of homicide for stalked women is substantial; 76 percent of women who are murdered were stalked by their killer during the year prior to their death (NCVC 2004).

Pressure to Keep the Family Together

Societal norms and values concerning the family often create pressure for women to keep their families together. Therefore, if a woman, especially a married woman, is in an abusive relationship she may find it difficult to separate her family. Many women believe that if their children are not being directly physically assaulted, they are being protected from the abuse. This is seldom the case because most children are much more aware of domestic violence than their parents realize. Furthermore, many women have been raised to believe that the outcomes of raising children in a single-parent home would be a far worse alternative to the abuse. Also, many abused women receive messages from friends, family members, or members their religious community that steps must be taken to ensure the family is kept together, regardless of the presence of abuse. This not only places women and children at risk, but also places responsibility for the family health on the abused women.

Lack of Appropriate Community Response

Another barrier that domestic violence victims face is a lack of appropriate community response. Often, the seriousness of abuse situations is underestimated, or blame is placed on the victim. Survivors of abuse often report that they experienced being mocked, blamed, or completely ignored by law enforcement. It is also common for abuse victims to not report the abuse because they feel hopeless about the situation; like it wouldn't make a difference or things would only worsen. Thus, abused women may be abandoned by the system, and left in a more dangerous situation with a perpetrator who has been agitated by her attempts to seek help.

In addition, a common concern experienced by abused mothers is that she will lose her children if she attempts to sever ties with the abuser. This concern is valid because there are many documented cases of women losing custody of the children to an abuser, especially when domestic violence is present. A common misconception in society seems to be that mothers are favored for custody within the court system. However, on an increasing number of occasions, we see abused women losing custody of their children on the basis of an inappropriate judicial response to domestic violence.

For example, Parental Alienation Syndrome (PAS) is a scientifically invalid condition in which a woman is accused of making up accusations of violence and abuse with the expressed purpose of alienating her children from the abuser. Although PAS has been debunked and deemed as so-called junk science, it still remains one of the most widely used arguments in our legal system today to award primary child custody to abuse perpetrators.

LEARNED HELPLESSNESS?

A commonly taught principal on college campuses today regarding domestic violence victims is that of learned helplessness. The theory, originally derived from Seligman's experiments with dogs, has been applied to abused women and was commonly accepted as an explanation regarding why she might not leave an abusive situation. In developing her concept of battered woman syndrome, psychologist Lenore Walker drew heavily on this idea. The argument is that a victim who has been repeatedly worn down both physically and emotionally by an abuser will reach a psychological state where she no longer perceives that she is able to or worthy enough to escape her situation. Consequently, she loses her will to leave the relationship. Therefore, learned helplessness focuses a great deal on the psychological condition of victims, who commonly report having feelings of low self-esteem, depression, self-blame, and passivity and guilt, as well as experiences of repeated victimization, including those during childhood and adulthood.

In contrast, many argue that learned helplessness fails to take into account the fact that women often remain in relationships for rational reasons, such as those discussed previously, and not for psychopathological reasons. In addition, many criticize the approach that learned helplessness takes to domestic violence victimization in that it places the primary reasoning behind and responsibility for abusive relationships on women. This constitutes just another form of blaming the victim. Those who are skeptical of the learned helplessness argument suggest that domestic violence should be viewed in terms of the context of the situation and the resources, or lack thereof, available to the victim, including the social response to domestic violence, as opposed to the characteristics of the victim.

WHAT RESOURCES ARE AVAILABLE?

In many communities, domestic violence organizations exist in some capacity. Common services provided by these groups may include: adult victim counseling, child counseling, legal assistance, voucher plans (for necessities such as food, clothing and furniture), shelter services and protection if deemed necessary, transitional housing for women and children, safety planning, and coordination or participation in community activism on behalf of domestic violence victims.

Many online educational resources exist pertaining to domestic violence as well. Some focus exclusively on the victim by providing information on abuse signs and symptoms, safety planning and tips, building healthy relationships, and prevention by providing information on local community resources. Such resources can be found through the Department of Health and Human Services, the Centers for Disease Control and Prevention, Womenshealth.gov, or MEDLINEplus.

Other services, such as the cell phone program, include those sponsored by the National Coalition Against Domestic Violence. The cell phone program is a national program that accepts donations of old cell phones to provide means of emergency communication for domestic abuse victims in need of immediate help. In addition, the National Domestic Violence Hotline (1-800-799-SAFE) exists for anyone who may be in need of help or advice pertaining to domestic abuse. It is advisable that anyone who suspects that they, or someone they know, may be in an unhealthy or abusive relationship seek the guidance of one of the above listed organizations. Taking a step that is as simple as making a phone call can save a life.

Finally, national movements such as Take Back the Night exist to provide individuals and communities with the opportunity to be empowered through providing a voice to victims to be heard and to live lives that are free from violence and abuse.

CONCLUDING REMARKS

A common critique pertaining to research on and response to domestic violence lies in that most approaches to this social problem are oriented from a victim blaming perspective. Even in discussing this topic here, which focuses on the awareness of such a bias, domestic violence must still be approached largely from this perspective. This emphasis on the role of the victim is very difficult to avoid because a substantial portion of what we know about domestic violence comes from examination of the victim's choices as opposed to those of the perpetrator. This perspective is also not an inherent flaw because understanding the issues facing domestic violence victims is critical to providing assistance and increasing awareness. However, caution must be taken when examining abuse from this perspective if we are to avoid placing primary responsibility for the occurrence and continuation of domestic violence on one partner (i.e., the victim). This is critical because it is through an examination of this social problem from multiple perspectives that we will be better equipped to address ending domestic violence as a responsibility of society as a whole.

See also Addiction and Family; Battered Woman Syndrome; Child Abuse; Domestic Violence Interventions; Mandatory Arrest Laws; Religion, Women, and Domestic Violence.

Further Reading: Bosch, Kathy, and Walter R. Schumm. "Accessibility to Resources: Helping Rural Women in Abusive Partner Relationships Become Free from Abuse." *Journal of Sex and Marital Therapy* 30 (2004): 357–370; Family Shelter Service. "On Learned Helplessness." http://www.familyshelterservice.org/pdf/survivor.pdf; Johnson, M. P. "Patriarchal Terrorism and Common Couple Violence: Two Forms of Violence against Women." *Journal of Marriage and Family* 57 (1995): 283–294; Johnson, M. P., and K. J. Ferraro. "Research on Domestic Violence in the 1990s: Making Distinctions." *Journal of Marriage and Family* 62 (2000): 948–963; The Leadership Council. "On Parental Alienation Syndrome," 2005. http://www.leadershipcouncil.org/1/pas/faq.htm; The National Center for Victims of Crime. "Stalking Fact Sheet." http://www.ncvc.org/Src (accessed May 15, 2008); The National Domestic Violence Hotline. http://www.ndvh.org; Neufeld, B. "SAFE Questions: Overcoming the Barriers to Detecting Domestic Violence." *American Family Physician* 53 (1996): 2575–2581; Strong, B., C. DeVault, B. W. Sayad, and T. F. Cohen. *The Marriage and Family Experience*, 8th ed. Belmont, CA: Wadsworth, Thomson Learning Inc., 2001; Take Back the Night. http://www.takebackthenight.org; U.S. Department of Health and Human Services. "Preventing Violence against Women," 2001. http://www.hhs.gov/news/press/2001pres/01fsdomviolence.html; U.S. Department of Health and Human Services Office on Women's Health. "Violence against Women." http://www.womenshealth.gov/violence/index.cfm.

Rachel Birmingham

DOMESTIC VIOLENCE INTERVENTIONS

Interventions in domestic violence refer to the ways in which the situation can be altered to change the course of action. In other words, an intervention is the means by which persons outside of the coupled relationship or agencies respond to domestic violence in such a way as to keep the abuse from continuing. Sometimes, it is only the victim who is able to intervene because others are unaware that the abuse is occurring. There are many factors that make intervening in domestic violence situations difficult. Not only is there the expectation of privacy in one's family life, but society still has far to go to fully assist victims and offenders.

INTRODUCTION

For decades, domestic abuse has been one of those taboo subjects that no one wants to talk about. People know it exists, but when confronted with the effects of domestic abuse they prefer to look the other way. However, after many years of society directly and indirectly telling families that what happens in the home stays in the home, the societal and familial consequences of domestic abuse are coming to light. Domestic abuse takes many forms and has many consequences for the physical and emotional well-being of individuals. Most of the time when people hear the term domestic abuse they automatically think of abuse between persons in a marital relationship.

Violence between partners in a marital relationship, referred to as spouse abuse, is only one aspect of domestic violence. In fact research suggests that other intimate relationships such as cohabitation as well as homosexual partnerships are even more prone to abuse than are marriages. Thus the term domestic violence or interpersonal violence is more accurate to describe the phenomenon than is the traditional term spouse abuse. Domestic violence also encompasses child abuse, sibling abuse, and elder abuse. Each facet of domestic abuse harms the society, the family, and the individuals involved. The causes of each form of domestic abuse might vary, but the end conclusion and its resulting consequences are quite similar.

The controversies surrounding abuse between intimate partners have varied little over time. However, the media attention domestic violence receives varies by the latest trend, hot topic, heinous domestic crime, or celebrity escapade. When domestic violence is prominent in the media, such as with the recent case of Laci Peterson, questions of prevention and intervention abound. While more media attention is paid to abuse cases currently than in previous years, no recent case has captured American's attention quite like the O. J. Simpson case. When individuals in society take a position on the intervention issues, they become separated by their differing views on five key controversies concerning spouse abuse: (1) divorce is the best solution for abused spouses, (2) arrest deters the behavior from occurring in the future, (3) government should or should not intervene in private family matters, (4) mandatory arrest should be universal policy, and (5) the shelter movement is the most effective solution.

BACKGROUND

Throughout history, women have generally been subjected to harsher living and working conditions than men. Surviving in the early days after the establishment of the United States not only meant carving out a living for herself and her family, but often meant enduring the physical punishments of first a father and later a husband. Those same physical punishments that women of the past endured are now defined by today's criteria as spouse abuse. The women subjected to spouse abuse in the early days of American society had nowhere to run. Likewise they may have expected the abuse in light of their lower social standing compared to men. There were no advocacy programs, shelters, or counseling groups from which to get help or advice. The privacy of the family was sacred ground not to be trespassed upon. Those who saw the plight of the women and children in society, and aimed to make changes, often became victims themselves. It wasn't until the battered women's movement, also known as the domestic violence movement, began that change started to take place. As an offshoot of the women's equality movement, originating in the 1960s, domestic violence awareness began to have positive effects. Society's views concerning domestic abuse began to be more concerned with victims' safety and causes of abuse, most notably a patriarchal model that assigns all power to men, were identified. Publicly recognized shelters were first opened for abused women at this time. Arizona's Rainbow Retreat and California's Haven House were two of the first. They began treating women who were victims of spouse abuse by alcoholic partners.

After people started acknowledging spouse abuse as a social issue, one that had been happening in their own backyards for years, strong opinions clashed and social policies developed. The public and the government agreed that spouse abuse could have serious repercussions if not addressed efficiently. Over the years, opinions and domestic abuse policies have changed, but the heart of the issue remains—love should not hurt. A relationship between two consenting adults should not cause harm, and any relationship that causes physical or emotional distress is not a healthy relationship. However, it is hard to determine when a relationship is unhealthy because people outside of the home cannot tell just by looking if someone is an abuser or not. Abusers do not wear signs around their necks or have a scarlet letter of some sort emblazoned upon them. An abusive spouse could be a relative, a friend, or a neighbor. The media also plays a part in how domestic violence is defined. Society interprets the severity of the issue based on the amount of media coverage the offense generates. The more detailed and graphic the media coverage, the more we understand that society disapproves of domestic violence. The media is further powerful as a mechanism to transmit information about prevention and intervention. This is important because spouse abuse takes several different forms and is defined by different behaviors.

Categories of Spouse Abuse

The Centers for Disease Control and Prevention (CDC) cite four types of spouse abuse: physical violence, sexual violence, threats of violence, and psychological or emotional violence. According to the CDC website, physical violence includes any physical show of force toward a partner that intentionally inflicts harm. Sexual violence is divided by the CDC into three categories: rape, a sexual encounter with a mentally or physically incapacitated individual, or contact with an individual that is both sexual in nature and abusive. It is any sexual encounter in which the victim does not or can not consent. Threats are tactics of intimidation that may involve weapons or other shows of force, but do not culminate in physical abuse. It could involve a partner indicating the abuses that would be perpetrated on the partner if she were not to follow his wishes.

Sociologists have done considerable research on domestic violence and categorize spouse abuse as originating in the following ways. From the structural functional perspective of society, sociologists explain that spouse abuse is a method used by abusers to sustain what they consider to be the proper functioning of the family. The abuser functions as the authoritarian head of the household. Gender roles are emphasized under the structural functional perspective because the threat of the abuse creates a sense of fear that causes the female victim to want to please the male abuser in order to avoid punishment. Men and women are thought to best fulfill the goals of family life when they conform to a traditional model of breadwinner husband and house-manager wife. Deviations from the pattern create role difficulties. Conflict perspective adherents argue that abuse is used to re-gain power. A relationship between two people that is not egalitarian usually consists of one individual exerting control or influence over the other individual. However, when the dependent person attempts to gain some influence or control, the independent person—the abuser—uses abuse to force the other person back to dependent status. The power struggle between the two individuals is cyclic and, therefore, creates a cycle of abuse that is hard to escape. From the symbolic interaction approach, spouse abuse can be a result of miscommunication or misinterpretation of the messages being passed between two people. Every message a person sends and receives contains numerous meanings, both verbal and nonverbal. If the meanings in the messages are not the same for both of the individuals involved, one person may construe a message negatively. Therefore, when an individual is misunderstood, frustration mounts and can lead to an outburst of violence.

Relevant Domestic Abuse Statistics

While the differing explanations for abuse and the different categories of behavior may make it hard to know what intervention tactics would be the most effective, the data below indicate that something must be done. The likelihood of victimization, as well as the costs to society, families, the economy, and individuals demands that interventions at least be attempted.

The National Center for Injury Prevention and Control, under the umbrella of the Centers for Disease Control and Prevention (CDC), refers to spouse abuse as Intimate Partner Violence (IPV). The rates of IPV are hard to determine because intimate partner violence is defined differently in different areas and, importantly, not all instances of IPV are reported. For example, the best estimates indicate that only about 20 percent of sexual assaults or rapes, 25 percent of physical assaults, and 50 percent of stalking directed toward women are reported. Even fewer incidents of IPV against men are reported.

In the category of physical abuse, nearly 5.3 million incidents of IPV occur each year among U.S. women ages 18 and older. Fortunately, most assaults are relatively minor and consist of pushing, grabbing, shoving, slapping, and hitting. IPV accounted for 20 percent of the nonfatal violence against women in the year 2001. There are, however, nearly 2 million injuries and 1,300 deaths nationwide every year as a result of IPV. A national study found that 29 percent of women and 22 percent of men had experienced physical, sexual, or psychological IPV during their lifetime. Up to 8 percent of pregnant women are abused at least once during pregnancy.

A particularly concerning aspect of physical abuse is intimate partner homicide. From the years 1976 to 2002, approximately 11 percent of homicide victims were killed by an intimate partner, however the total numbers of victims did decrease some over time. The decrease was higher for male victims than for female victims who remain far more likely to be murdered by an intimate partner. For the year 2002, of those victims of intimate partner homicide, 76 percent were female. Firearms are the predominant weapon used. In the cases of intimate partner violence resulting in homicide it is not the first occurrence of violence between the partners. Forty-four percent of women murdered by their intimate partners had visited an emergency department within 2 years of the homicide. Of these women, 93 percent had at least one injury visit.

Sexual abuse also affects women more often than men. Every year in the United States there are about 1.5 million women and more than 800,000 men who are raped or physically assaulted by their partner. This translates into a victimization rate of about 47 intimate partner assaults per 1,000 women and 32 per 1,000 men. Stalking rates also reflect this gender difference with estimates of more than 1 million women and 371,000 men stalked by intimate partners each year. Previous literature suggests that women who have separated from their abusive partners often remain at risk of violence.

Therefore, even though the facts about IPV are disturbing, what is even more troubling is the likelihood that IPV in the United States is worse than the official measures can uncover. This underreporting has lead to a strong push by advocates to educate the public. One of the best avenues is through the media. Thus, when domestic violence cases make the news, they are often followed with facts about the frequency of domestic violence and information about how to get help if one is in a similar position. Ideally, this recognition in a public forum of the problem of domestic violence would make a victim less embarrassed to reveal the abuse. Furthermore, letting the victim know some of the wide-ranging causes of the problem can be helpful.

CAUSAL INFLUENCES

The causes of spouse abuse are many and are not all-inclusive. A lot of people in today's society have the misconception that abusers must have psychological problems in order to be abusers. However, there are many other factors that either cause or create an environment conducive to spouse abuse. The abuse of alcohol and drugs reduces inhibitions and heightens the abuser's awareness of personal insecurities, lowering inhibitions and resulting in an abuser verbally or physically attacking the victim.

If an individual has been a victim of prior abuse, that person is more likely to become an abuser. As contrary as it seems, being a victim teaches a person that that is how relationships work. If abuse is all an individual has known throughout life, then abuse is normative to that person. Low self-esteem and feelings of inadequacy have also been linked to a greater tendency to abuse compared with persons of higher self-esteem. When an individual has a poor self-concept and low self-esteem, he or she tends to think everyone around them shares the same opinion about him or her. After prolonged exposure to negative opinions, an individual may become violent as a way of venting the built-up pressure and anxiety caused by low self-esteem. Abuse is also used as a method to gain control or power over another individual. A person who has a poor-self concept, low self-esteem, or been a victim of prior abuse may have a stronger need for control and power because it is the ability to gain power and control that validates the abuser. This cyclic pattern is difficult to break.

Furthermore, environmental stressors such as the family ideal, work, finances, and even health issues can cause significant amounts of stress. Society's focus on the ideal family creates stress when an individual realizes that he or she is not living up to the standard of the modern family by not making enough money, not having the right possessions, or requiring a two-income household to get by. Also, pressure from a boss at work may cause tension that adds to the build-up of stress. An unplanned pregnancy that would add to financial stress may be an additional factor. These stressors may create a volatile home life where abuse is the outlet for a massive release of pent-up stresses. Because the causes of abuse are many, it follows that the consequences of abuse are just as numerous and likely compound over time.

COMPOUND EFFECTS

Abuse is not an action that happens and then is forgotten. Every act of abuse leaves its mark. Repeated abuse lowers the self-esteem of the abused spouse. As a result of the lowered self-esteem, the abused spouse may seek comfort in activities such as drug use, alcohol consumption, and promiscuity. Spouse abuse may also cause depression that can lead to neglect of children who may be present in the home. The abused spouse may also begin to live a lie by presenting a false front of happiness to the outside world to keep others from knowing her internal conflict. The abused spouse may even deny the abuse when confronted about it. Avoiding the abuse becomes a means of self-preservation for the victim. The victim may even fear the discovery of the abuse by her peers more than the abuse itself. After an individual's self-esteem has declined due to the abuse, the idea of others thinking badly of the victim causes more distress. Therefore, the abused spouse might withdraw from friends and family to keep the lie a secret.

By witnessing the abuse of a parent and being subjected to negative attitudes and perceptions on a daily basis, children in the home learn negative relationship skills and values. They are also likely to be victimized themselves, if not directly through a personal attack against them, perhaps as a bystander injured by an errant attack with fist or object. If a child grows up with abusive role models then that child might believe that abuse is acceptable and could become either the abuser or the abused. Statistics show that children who witness abuse are more likely to become abusers than are children who did not witness abuse in their formative years. The lasting effects on children who witness abuse are behavioral changes and learning problems. These children do not know how to control or express their emotions in a constructive and nonthreatening manner. Therefore, they act out or withdraw from group activities. Many children from abusive homes are hyper-vigilant and easily distracted because they feel the need to constantly be on the lookout for any sign of a threat. Spouse abuse does not only affect the partners in the relationship, it affects everyone within the family and is why solutions for spouse abuse are needed.

DOMESTIC VIOLENCE IN THE MEDIA

Because it is everywhere and readily captures the public's attention, the media have a unique opportunity to influence society. With regard to domestic violence, however, some critics contend that the media focuses only on the most sensational and unusual cases rather than the experiences of "every woman." In the recent past, several prominent domestic violence cases have received considerable media attention. They are illustrative, however, of how a chance for advocacy is lost when sensationalism takes over. Two of the more sensationalized domestic violence cases in recent years are the cases of Laci Peterson and Nicole Brown Simpson.

According to www.courttv.com, Laci Peterson was a pregnant 27-year-old in Modesto, CA. While no one can confirm that she and husband Scott had a history of abuse, she was reported missing with few leads. Her husband, Scott Peterson, was initially questioned by police and suspicions seemed to be directed toward him. As evidence emerged, it was revealed that he was having an affair with another woman. While there were receipts to corroborate his alibi, there were no witnesses and a neighbor saw him removing something heavy from his home about the time of Laci's disappearance. When the body of a woman and baby washed onto the beach nearly four months after Laci was reported missing, DNA testing confirmed it was the missing woman and child. Peterson was arrested. He had $10,000 in cash on his person. Peterson was later convicted on two counts of murder and sentenced to death by lethal injection.

The O. J. Simpson case is discussed in several ways. One questions the role of race in the criminal justice system. Another considers how social class of defendant matters in acquittal. A third deals with domestic violence. In the Simpson case, the victims Ronald Goldman and Nicole Brown Simpson, the former wife of the defendant, were found murdered outside of her condominium in 1994. This was two years after her divorce to Simpson, who was described as abusive. In a recorded 911 call introduced at the trial, there was evidence that Simpson was stalking his former wife. While Simpson was acquitted in the criminal proceedings, in a civil trial brought by the victims' families he was found liable for their deaths and order to pay more than $33 million to the families. The Brown family established the Nicole Brown Charitable Foundation to assist victims of domestic violence.

INTERVENTIONS

Solutions and interventions are controversial in themselves. Solutions to spouse abuse have been hard to create because the same solution will not work for every situation. Among the proposed solutions are divorce from the abuser, arrest of the abuser (sometimes mandatory), government policies and programs, and the shelter movement.

Divorce

People argue that divorce is the best solution for abused spouses because then a victim is removed from the situation. It does decrease the daily contact between victim and offender, providing a hope that both can move on to nonabusive relationships. One of the concerning aspects of this approach is that it may remove the spouse from daily contact with the abuser but does little to prevent the pattern from being repeated with another victim. It is passing the problem to the next unlucky person. While on the surface divorce seems reasonable for a given woman in an abusive marriage, that conclusion is not always accurate. Divorce is only a reasonable solution when the abused spouse has income available that allows her to leave. This situation does not happen very often. Most often by the time the abused woman leaves the home, she has been a victim for so long that she has no outside resources and has become a prisoner within the home. In extreme cases, the victim may not even have a purse or keys to a vehicle because the abuser gains his power from the victim's lack of control and helplessness. Money is the means to escape and if a victim doesn't have money, then divorce is not a very real possibility. Additionally, she may feel incapable of supporting herself with few if any marketable skills with which to acquire a job.

Another argument against divorce comes from the conservative religious camp and suggests that couples can overcome the abuse and its negative effects on the family by prayer and worship. With God's help the family can be maintained and divorce is unnecessary. Often divorce is seen as the greater evil to persons from this perspective. Conservatives of all faiths are concerned that divorce would result in single parent-families and they tout the benefits to children when two parents are in the home.

In cases where a break-up does not involve counseling for both victim and offender, there is a legitimate concern about the victim's future safety. If the abuser feels that there is unfinished business in the relationship, he may stalk the victim. Given that some states permit one person to file and receive a divorce without the consent of the other this is a legitimate concern. Many women are particularly likely to be victimized when they are attempting to leave, and divorce is a clear marker of the leaving.

Arrest of Offender

Arrests of offenders have been popular for some time. However, historical evidence suggests that many police officers were unlikely to do so. Individuals that support arresting the abuser have contended that arrest offers a chance to rehabilitate the abuser. There is little evidence to support that this occurs. As more persons are jailed for drug and other offenses, the prison population has swelled and the resources for rehabilitation are very limited. Removing the abuser from the situation and sentencing him to jail time very rarely is effective at reducing violence. Most often the abuser has a tendency to become more abusive after incarceration because of the experiences associated with the prison system.

For some groups, arrest does seem to lessen the behavior. For employed men who have a lot to lose by being arrested or labeled an abuser, the rates of abuse do go down after an arrest. For men who are unemployed however, arrest significantly increases abuse. One of the positive things that abuse does is to serve as a visible display that the community takes domestic violence seriously. In those jurisdictions where district attorneys are required to prosecute these offenders, the arrest can have valuable symbolic value.

One of the issues that has made many domestic violence advocates the most distressed is that when convictions for domestic violence do occur, the sentences are usually comparatively light. In some municipalities there are stiffer penalties for animal cruelty than for domestic violence.

Government Policies and Programs

Governments have a vested interest in ensuring the safety of the citizenry. With regard to domestic violence, government programs have been largely focused on education, with the emphasis on spotting the signs of domestic violence and reporting the abuse to the proper authorities. Due to its greater resources, however, the government can provide support to programs that assist victims, record statistics, and provide counseling. The money from these federal sources is far greater than what is available to most nonprofit organizations through donations or grants. Governments might also wield influence to publicize the problem and increase awareness, thus influencing social norms of acceptability or unacceptability for behaviors. Government has a vested interest in reducing the rates of domestic violence because of the costs to the nation as a whole. The CDC estimates indicate that domestic violence cost $8.3 billion in 2003. This figure included the costs of medical care, mental health services, and loss of economic productivity, particularly through time off of work.

Among the sticking points of critics of government policies is the contention that they may violate the traditional expectation of family privacy. Relationship matters are held to be personal matters and government policies make them public. While most individuals today view domestic violence as unacceptable, there are still those who believe that marriage and what goes on within the family behind closed doors is private. At what point does spouse abuse override the privacy of the family? This concept in itself contributes to the controversies of mandatory arrest laws and the shelter movement.

Mandatory Arrest

Mandatory arrest laws require that a police officer make an arrest in a domestic violence case if he or she witnesses any evidence that abuse has occurred. The idea originated in Minneapolis where an intervention program was designed to remove offenders from the home for at least a minimum amount of time. While the principle of protecting the victim from immediate future abuse is a good one, there may be later consequences for her. Also, the victims have been known to come right down to the police station and bail out the offenders.

Mandatory arrest laws have lead to a backlog of court cases in some municipalities, overburdening scarce resources. This is more likely to be true where no-drop clauses mean all domestic violence arrests must be prosecuted.

Critics of mandatory arrest contend that it is a government-instituted policy that disregards the sanctity of the family by making decisions for the family that may or may not be beneficial to all of the individuals involved. By arresting the abuser, who is most often the breadwinner of the family, the government institution is breaking the financial backbone of the family when mandatory arrests are enforced. If the abused spouse does not work or her income is a supplemental income, the family may suffer financial strain. Occasionally both partners are arrested on domestic violence charges due the requirement to arrest and the inability of law enforcement officers to determine a victim and offender. If the situation involves common couple violence and she defends herself, she may be charged with abuse. This leaves any children in the home without supervision, at least temporarily, so they may be sent into state custody through the foster care system or sent to live with relatives.

Shelter Movement

The shelter movement also violates the private sector of the home by offering abused spouses and children a place to go for a safe haven. Therefore, some family advocates have suggested that they harm the family by removing even the tenuous stability of the abusive home. One of the most common criticisms against shelters is that they are only a temporary solution. When a woman returns home to abusive partner to give him one more chance the violence may intensify. Shelters can be expensive to operate and are constantly in need of donations. They rely largely on volunteer staff, but do usually have some paid staff for continuity.

The shelter movement was one of the first attempts to improve the lot of abused women and to ensure their safety. As such, they have a loyal following and strong advocacy tradition. With the creation of domestic violence shelters, abuse victims regained a small amount of control over their and their children's lives. Abuse victims did not have to wait until they squirreled away enough money to be able to run in the middle of the night; shelters made it possible to just leave and not look back. Shelters that have excellent resources are able to provide both personal and legal counsel to abused women. They are generally successful at seeking and acquiring restraining orders and helping victims get back on their feet if they leave their abusers.

One of the most disconcerting things about the shelter movement is that it has not yet been able to fully meet demand. There are shelters in more than 1400 counties in the United States; however, this is less than half of the 3000 counties in the country, leaving some women with extremely limited options for leaving an abusive situation.

FUTURE DIRECTIONS

The controversies over various interventions show that domestic violence is still misunderstood and misrepresented in the culture. Given the broad effects of abuse, workable solutions are needed. Future policies and programs targeting domestic violence will likely place an increased emphasis on prevention. One of the government-sponsored programs of the CDC takes this approach. While the interventions are still needed, the hope is that prevention will decrease the need for additional interventions in the future. The current emphasis on prevention targets young people encouraging and empowering them to create healthy relationships and patterns of interaction. One of the elements involves strategies for dating that help weed out potential abusers and focus on respect. Additionally, men and women can model good relationship patterns for young people through mentoring youth, thereby reinforcing the idea that violence is not acceptable.

See also Battered Woman Syndrome; Child Abuse; Domestic Violence Behaviors and Causes; Mandatory Arrest Laws; Religion, Women, and Domestic Violence; Sibling Violence and Abuse.

Further Reading: Buzawa, Eve S., and Carl G. Buzawa. *Domestic Violence: The Criminal Justice Response,* 3rd ed. Thousand Oaks, CA: Sage, 2003; Family Violence Prevention Fund. http://www.endabuse.org; Feminist Majority Foundation: Working for Women's Equality. http://www.feminist.org/911/crisis.html; Flowers, R. Barri. *Domestic Crimes, Family Violence and Child Abuse: A Study of Contemporary American Society.* Jefferson, NC: McFarland and Company, 2000; Jones, Ann. *Next Time She'll Be Dead: Battering and How to Stop It.* New York: Beacon Press, 2000; Kelly, Kristin A. *Domestic Violence and the Politics of Privacy.* Ithaca, NY: Cornell University Press, 2003; LaViolette, Alyce D., and Ola W. Barnett. *It Could Happen to Anyone: Why Battered Women Stay.* Thousand Oaks, CA: Sage, 2000; Mills, Linda G. *Insult to Injury: Rethinking Our Responses to Intimate Abuse.* Princeton, NJ: Princeton University Press, 2003; National Coalition Against Domestic Violence. http://www.ncadv.org; National Network to End Domestic Violence. http://www.nnedv.org; National Sexual Violence Resource Center. http://www.nsvrc.org; NOW: National Organization of Women. http://www.now.org/issues/violence/; Stop Family Violence. http://www.stopfamilyviolence.org.

Amanda Singletary

E

ELDER ABUSE

Elder abuse is a very serious issue that affects families and society. Elder abuse involves the acts of commission (abuse) and omission (neglect) as do other definitions of domestic violence. Unlike spouse and child abuse, which were defined as key social issues in the 1960s, elder abuse did not surface as a social problem until the late 1970s in congressional hearings examining the status of aging in the United States. The awareness generated through government and the media brought attention to the phenomenon. There are many questions about the prevalence of elder abuse and the vulnerability of certain categories of elders to abuse.

One thing that makes elder abuse difficult to discuss is that it is difficult to measure. Because domestic issues remain largely private, the true prevalence of elder abuse is not known. The best estimates, based on national samples and state data, indicate that about five percent of persons over 65 will be abused in some way. It seems that spouse abuse is the most common abuse of those past retirement age, although abuse by adult children does contribute to the problem. Given the dependencies that most aged persons have, their reliance on others sets the stage for exploitation. Elders are potential victims whether they are being cared for in their own homes by family or at a nursing home by paid staff. There is evidence to suggest that as today's elders are more likely to have retirement accounts and pension plans, their likelihood of being a victim of financial abuse is increasing.

WHAT IS ELDER ABUSE?

Elder abuse is the sometimes intentional, but often times unintentional, mistreatment of a person over the age of 65. Elder abuse involves several aspects including financial, physical, and emotional abuse. A special subcategory of physical abuse is sexual abuse. An inclusive definition of elder abuse would also consider neglect and self-neglect as additional aspects. Abuse of elders can lead to a worsening of the elder's health or even to death. Questions surround the causes of elder abuse as well as the ways that treatment and prevention should be approached. The different categories of abuse do not affect all elders in the same way.

TYPES OF ELDER ABUSE

Physical Abuse

Physical abuse can be any of the following: pushing, kicking, slapping, choking, beating, punching, pinching, throwing, hitting, paddling, shoving, inappropriate restraints, assaulting, or harming with hand or objects. This force can lead to pain, injury, impairment, and disease of an elderly person. Given that humans get weaker and frailer as they age, abuse of elderly persons is particularly likely to result in injury. Additionally, these persons are less likely to be strong enough to defend themselves from attack and may even be confined to a wheel chair or bed due to their physical conditions. For the oldest old persons, age 85 and over, the consequences of physical beatings can be severe. The physical indicators of abuse are dehydration, malnourishment, sprains, dislocations, bite marks, internal injuries, unexplained bruises and burns, welts, skull fractures, lacerations, black eyes, and abrasions. Older persons, due to dementia or other memory-impairing conditions, may be unable to explain how their injuries occurred, making them a safe victim because they may find it difficult to get assistance or intervention from law enforcement.

Sexual Abuse

Sexual abuse is any sexual activity performed on an elder without consent. Sexual abuse can be sexual intercourse, anal intercourse, or oral sex. Other sexual behaviors, however, can also be termed abuse if the elder is not a willing participate or is unable to provide consent. These activities include displaying ones genitals or making the elder display theirs, watching while the elder does sexual things, or making the elder watch while the perpetrator does sexual things. It can even include watching pornography, taking pictures, and sex talk. The most likely perpetrator of sexual abuse is a family member. This is because the elder has trust in the family member and lets them get close without knowing that they want to do harm. It is also possible for an elder to be abused in a nursing home or for an outside caregiver to be the perpetrator of sexual abuse, but these cases are more limited. An elder with a severe disability is more likely to be abused because of dependency on the help of the nursing home staff or outside caregiver. Indicators of sexual abuse include: genital or urinary irritation, frequent infections, vaginal or anal bleeding, bruising on the inner thighs, sexually transmitted diseases, depression, conversation regularly is of a sexual nature, severe agitation when being bathed or dressed, agitation during medical examination, and sudden confusion. Depending on the circumstances, sexual abuse can involve both physical and emotional elements.

Emotional Abuse

The elder is distressed, upset, depressed, experiencing withdrawal, and in emotional pain in this nonverbal or verbal situation. When elders are emotionally abused they become unresponsive, fearful, lack social interests, and evade others. Emotional abuse is equally likely to be perpetrated by a family member, nursing home staff and outside caregivers. Elders may be particularly prone to emotional abuse because they question their role in the family and society. Many persons perceive that as they age they are more of a burden on the family and have a harder time fitting in. They may feel that they deserve any treatment they receive because they can not keep up mentally and physically with the younger generations. Some common types of emotional abuse include ignoring the elder, harassment and intimidation, insults and yelling, embarrassing or humiliating the elder, odd forms of punishment, and blaming. Also included are isolation from others or activities, and not attending to the elder when necessary.

Financial Abuse

Financial abuse is the improper or illegal use of an elder's money and property. The financial abuser can be anyone, but is most likely a family member as they have more direct access to aged family members' resources. For various practical reasons, including fear of money management, tax savings, and inheritance, among others, elders may ask family members to tend to their financial concerns. Sometimes this takes the form of a power of attorney where the family member is the legal guardian of the older person's estate and authorized to act as his or her agent. Other times the arrangement is informal, and the older person just asks someone else to keep their bank accounts and take care of daily financial transactions. Government estimates indicate that approximately five million elders are victims of financial abuse each year, with most cases going unreported.

A dishonest person can take advantage of the elder, misinforming them about their assets, or using the money for their own needs. They may even get the elder to give their consent to such things through threatening them, or constantly harassing the elder about his or her financial status. Elders can be financially abused in many different ways. They include exploitation and fraud by both primary and secondary contacts, signature forging, embezzling, and theft of property. Certain areas of fraud have targeted older persons and include home repair fraud, insurance fraud, medical fraud, telemarketing, and confidence games. Another egregious component is nursing home theft. Considering that most very old people are females, who often have fewer funds available at retirement than do males and often relied on their husbands to manage their funds prior to his death, the costs of financial abuse can be very high.

Neglect

Neglect of the elder can occur when the elder is in isolation, has been abandoned, or a caregiver refuses to provide the elder with essential needs, including physical and emotional needs. Just as neglect is the most frequent type of child abuse, neglect is considered the most common type of elder abuse. Self-neglect has also been a problem with elders. This can occur when an elder neglects his own needs. There are two types of neglect, active and passive. Active neglect is defined as refusal or failure to fulfill the needs of the elder. This would be intentional neglect. Passive neglect is also failing to fulfill an elder's needs, but this type is unintentional. It has been known to occur in nursing homes that do not have the most qualified staff or the resources to meet the needs of the elder residents. Neglect is also done by family members and by outside caregivers. Examples of neglect include denial of needs such as food and water, lack of assistance with food and water (if required), improper supervision, inappropriate clothing for the type of weather, or inadequate help with bathing or other hygiene practices. Other examples are lack of access to the toilet, lack of diaper changing, strong smell of urine or feces, and physically restraining the elder without medical cause. Finally, refusing to seek required medical care for the elder is a type of neglect.

BRIEF HISTORY

Elder abuse first appeared on the public radar in the 1970s. However, many professionals did not care about abuse of the elderly at the time, but were more concerned with child abuse and abuse against women. Consequently, elder abuse was not taken very seriously. There was inadequate knowledge about the scope of the issue and what to do for such situations. There were few ways that family professionals could intervene in such cases. In the late 1970s Congress began to hear of "granny battering" and became interested in this issue. As groups began to testify in congress in defense of older Americans, the tide began to turn. In 1989 the Older Americans Act was proposed. While there was not a lot of money available to assist in stopping elder abuse, it was recognized as a problem and over time more and more people became interested in this issue. The media helped to spread the word about elder abuse, getting the attention of medical professionals and the criminal justice system. Researchers began to attend to the issue as well. However, the extent of the problem remains hidden. The best estimates indicate that for every abuse case reported, there are about five more that are not reported.

CONTROVERSIES IN ELDER ABUSE

While it is generally accepted that abuse is a problem in the culture that needs to be eradicated, the paths to decreased violence are often contradictory. Often experts suggest that one cannot end abuse without knowing the causes of abuse. Elder abuse shares some links with domestic violence causes in general, but because of the intergenerational nature of the abuse, there are some important differences. Another area of controversy involves whether gender plays a role in the status of both victim and perpetrator. Other questions remain as to the best course of action when dealing with older persons who have been abused and the role that the state plays in providing assistance to them.

Contributing Factors in Elder Abuse

There have been wide-ranging suggestions as to the factors that contribute to elder abuse. Not only have the ideas of "violence as a way of life" in American society been blamed, but the cultural belief in the value of youth and devaluing of elderly, referred to as ageism, have been touted as a contributing factor. It seems likely that there are factors both within the culture as a whole and in the personal interactions of families that make abuse more likely to occur. Among the explanations in the literature are caregiver stress, victim disability, social isolation, perpetrator deviance, and victim-perpetrator dependency.

Situational factors can make caring for an elder particularly difficult. The caregiver may have emotional, psychological, financial and mental problems of her own. These can become compounded when caring for an elderly person. A family member caring for an older relative may experience financial problems due to the material needs of the elder or missing work to care for the elder. The caregiving is particularly likely to compound any financial problems that were already there, leading to increasing stress for the carer. If the physical space is inadequate for the caring tasks, any poor housing conditions can become more concerning. Additionally, caregiving is stressful work and many caregivers will feel overburdened after an extended time in the role. It is quite hard if persons are caring for more than one dependent at a time, such as caring for one's child and aging parent simultaneously. The more dependent on a caregiver the elder person is, the more the stress for the person caring for the elder.

Some of the dependencies that exist between an abusive caregiver and victimized elder relate to the tactics and responses developed in family life that can carry over into adulthood. For example, a history of psychological or mental health problems, physical abuse, or poor communication or relationships in a family may continue. There may also be personality problems and difficult behavior displayed by the elder that compounds the problem.

Abuse in an institutional setting such as a nursing home might occur because an elder is cared for in an institution that lacks proper resources. This might refer to the physical structure of the facility, but also includes a lack of training for the staff, inadequate staffing relative to need, and stressful work conditions. It is important to remember that there is a component of today's society that argues the elderly are not important. They can no longer contribute to the economy and become costly. This approach suggests that elders feel unimportant as they age, less critical in the operations of community life. The removal of older members from society and into nursing homes marginalizes elders, making them ripe for exploitation.

While each of these approaches may contribute to the abuse of any given elder, there is no definitive statement about which is the most powerful in explaining the phenomenon. Another variable in the abuse model is the gender of the victim and perpetrator.

Gender Issues in Elderly Abuse

Are elders at differential risk of abuse by gender? Because the population of elderly is comprised of more women than men, due to women's greater life expectancy, women have a higher chance of becoming a victim. Not only are there more women, but in general women have less power in society. Research on violent crime shows that women are more likely the victims of assaults perpetrated by family members and acquaintances than those by strangers. Does this pattern hold for elders?

One of the critical elements in elder abuse seems to be dementia. Those elders with dementia and related problems are more likely to be victimized. In three out of four cases where the wife abused her husband, he was suffering from severe dementia. In those cases where the son was the abuser the man also suffered from mild dementia. Dementia featured less prominently in the cases of men being psychologically abused. Daughters, fathers, and sons all abused mothers with severe dementia. For most of the elderly women who are abused, it is generally by someone they live with. Regardless of sex, the worse the health of the elder is the more likely that the elder will be abused. Overall, women are abused more than men. This is partly because women live longer but they suffer from different health issues. Elder women's health deteriorates more over the years, which makes them more prone to being abused.

Males and females are not equally likely to abuse elders. As the ones primarily responsible for caregiving, females have a greater likelihood of abusing elders. This is a point that has been quite controversial, due to the assumption that males are more likely to use violence than females and that women are more nurturing than men. While female relatives outnumber male relatives as abusers, it is wives who constitute the majority of abusers. In some studies males have been found to be more likely to neglect an elder than are women. It is more likely that men financially abuse elders, and women physically abuse elders.

HELP FOR THE ELDERLY

The type of help proposed to counteract and decrease elder abuse depends on which of the explanations for abuse is applied. When the abuse is thought to be the result of caregiver stress, which is often associated with neglect, the abuse may be ameliorated by reducing how dependent the victim is on the caregiver. One way to assist is to bring services into the home so that the caregiver does not have to do everything. Meals-on-wheels, respite care, skilled nursing care, housekeeping services, and so forth have all been proposed as strategies to reduce caregiver stress. Another component in reducing stress is the use of adult day care. Skill building and counseling for the caregiver have also been recommended.

ELDER ABUSE IN OTHER SOCIETIES

Elder abuse is not limited to the United States, but has been defined as a problem in other societies including: South Africa, Australia, Greece, Hong Kong, Finland, Israel, India, Poland, Ireland, and Norway. Many countries do not have a consistent definition for elder abuse nor do they research its prevalence and societal impacts. The least-common type of abuse reported in other countries is physical abuse. Some definitions ruled out self-neglect as a type of abuse. Physical abuse is very rare in some countries because the culture espouses keeping harmony rather than using violence. Thus, abuse is culturally specific to the values and morals of the society. Some countries have few health care institutions available for the elderly. Failure to define behaviors as abuse may result from economic issues in different countries. They may not have adequate resources to take proper care of the elderly population that has increased as a result of longer life expectancy and lower mortality rates.

Three themes related to elder abuse that many countries have in common are dependency, economic conditions and cultural change. Each of these can contribute to the likelihood of elder abuse. Dependency is a problem due to more responsibilities and demands placed on caregivers. Economic conditions are a problem because of unemployment, reductions in incomes, reductions of programs and services, and cutbacks of government assistance. Cultural change is a problem because of different traditions, industrialization, and new technologies. Differing values are also a problem because the elder may still believe in doing things the way they were brought up, but their adult children may have a different way of doing things, creating conflict between elders and their family. In order to assist elders and prevent abuse, countries should first define and address the problem at hand. Second they have to understand the problem, know why it occurs, and want to end it. And lastly they have to get assistance from the government, economy, and media so that it will be taken seriously.

If the abuse or mistreatment has more to do with the dependency, emotional or financial, between the perpetrator and the elder, which is often linked to physical abuse, the strategies change. Successful interventions might include mental health services, alcohol or drug treatment, job placement, housing assistance, or even vocational training. Sometimes emergency intervention is necessary and courts may have to assign a guardian for the elderly person.

The National Center on Elder Abuse, part of the Administration on Aging of the U.S. Department of Health and Human Services, has been active in providing assistance to both caregivers and elders. It educates and advocates for better circumstances for senior citizens and is among the many groups focusing on elder abuse. It may be hard for an elderly person to come forward and ask for help after abuse because they may not be able to do so, or may be afraid they will get hurt even worse. They can also have feelings of embarrassment, being ashamed of their victimization and expecting that no one will believe in them.

There is a lot that can be done to help. Abuse reporting hotlines are available to help caregivers and the elderly. Volunteer work at nursing homes can help identify problems or just be a friendly face who can listen to elders' concerns. One group called Beyond Existing was formed for victims of elder abuse. This group determines the exact abuse problem, talks over the problem with the elder, lets the elder meet others that were in their position, and helps them plan for the future. Finally, there is also help for elders through physicians, nurses, social workers, and case management workers.

As a public health issue, elder abuse is not expected to end but to increase. Elders are treated by health care professionals, social workers, and case management workers to make sure their needs are met. Health care professionals indicate that elder abuse adds to a health care system already experiencing problems. Nurses play a very important role in the detection and resolution of elder abuse. They work as individuals or in a team setting to assess elder mistreatment. If any degree of abuse is present, the most important goal of the nurse is to maintain the safety of the elder and possibly remove him from that care setting. It is also the nurse's job to teach the caregiver proper caring procedures for an elderly person because they may lack the proper knowledge needed to care for an elder.

Physicians have an ethical and, in most states, a legal role in the recognition of and intervening in suspected cases of elder mistreatment. To be fully successful, physicians should be aware of legal issues, ethical issues, communication needs and have a solid base in principals of geriatric care. Physicians must be able to detect mistreatment bruises from normal bruises. The presence of physical abuse marks and the stated causes of them must be documented. If a physician suspects mistreatment, she is expected to report it. It is also the responsibility of the physician to interview the elder to assess the elder's relationship with the caregiver. Social workers also have an important role in assessing elder abuse. Their main goal is to investigate any allegations of harm being done to an elder.

CONCLUSION

Elder abuse is a very serious issue that society and families must examine and end. Today, there are a large number of elders that are dependent upon others for daily care; however, as U.S. society continues to age that number will only increase. To ensure that the aged are properly cared for caregivers need support and training from a variety of sources and settings. Institutions should be monitored to ensure that they have all the proper resources to care for elderly patients, including a well-educated staff that is not over-burdened. The government plays a role through monitoring and legal regulation. Health care professionals should properly assess mistreatment of the elderly and get help right away.

See also Children as Caregivers; Elder Care.

Further Reading: Aitken, Lynda, and Gabriele Griffin. *Gender Issues in Elder Abuse.* London: Sage, 1996; Anetzberger, Georgia J. *The Clinical Management of Elder Abuse.* New York: The Haworth Press, 2003; Biggs, Simon, Chris Phillipson, and Paul Kingston. *Elder Abuse In Perspective.* Buckingham: Open University Press, 1995; Bonnie, Richard J., and Robert B. Wallace. *Elder Mistreatment: Abuse, Neglect, and Exploitation in an Aging America.* Washington, D.C.: The National Academic Press, 2003; Brownwell,

Patricia J., and Stuart Bruchey. *Family Crimes Against the Elderly: Elder Abuse and the Criminal Justice System.* New York: Garland Publishing, 1998; Garcia, Juanita L., and Jordan I. Kosberg. *Elder Abuse: International and Cross-Cultural Perspectives.* New York: The Haworth Press, 1995; Hoffman, Allan M., and Randal W. Summers. *Elder Abuse: A Public Health Perspective.* Washington, DC: American Public Health Association, 2006; Kakar, Suman. *Domestic Abuse: Public Policy/Criminal Justice Approaches Towards Child, Spousal and Elderly Abuse.* San Francisco: Austin and Winfield, 1998; Payne, Brian K. *Crime and Elder Abuse: An Integrated Perspective.* Springfield, IL: Charles C. Thomas, 2005; Pillemer, Karl A., and Rosalie S. Wolf. *Helping Elderly Victims: The Reality of Elder Abuse.* New York: Columbia University Press, 1989.

Lasita Rudolph

ELDER CARE

At both ends of the life course, infancy and old age, the question of care is paramount. Not only do discussions revolve around the quality of care available to assist with the needs of these groups, but costs and moral obligations compound the debate. Just as young parents must decide whether to place a child in day care or find an alternative so that the child may be cared for at home, adult children and their aging parents must decide how best to care for the aged. Is home care by a family member or skilled nursing care in an institutional setting most appropriate? Often families agonize over the decision of how to care for their loved one. Many times, financial limitations determine the options more than does personal preference.

BACKGROUND

Even though the nuclear family has been the norm in American society, caring for ill and elderly kin in one's home was common. Few options existed until the early twentieth century when nurses, who were concerned about the health and care of elder citizens, began to operate elder care facilities. Accelerated by the Great Depression, they opened their homes at a time when the elderly had few other choices but to accept their care. Nurses could use the meager income that elderly residents could provide from federal Old Age Assistance (OAA) funds. Thus nursing homes began as a for-profit enterprise. Nurses were the first professionals to begin research in the area of aging.

At the founding of the United States, there were few options to care for the elderly aside from their own wealth, or the generosity of their children. Those who had neither were usually at the mercy of the poorhouses or almshouses that generally were responsible for all those who had no means of support, not just the frail elderly. By the early 1800s many young folks were moving west to seek their fortunes, often leaving older relatives behind to fend for themselves. In the mid- to late-1800s residential homes for the elderly began to appear. These were largely the result of benevolent societies such as the Masons and the Knights of Columbus. These voluntary and charitable residences were unlikely to provide medical care, but were simply a place to live. Some may have had separate hospital areas where ill persons were housed. Some of the wealthier elderly began to live in so-called rest houses, which were often several rooms for rent in private homes. By the end of the nineteenth century, more options were emerging for elders. However, care in an institutional setting would not emerge en masse until the 1950s, largely as a result of changes to Social Security programs. In 1954, for example, a national survey found 9,000 nursing homes housing about 270,000 residents.

Elder care today has changed in response to the needs of patients, as well as to their desires. There are many different levels of care that are available, and families often find that they need to research them thoroughly to determine which is the most appropriate for their elder relative. Aside from care by a family member, or care in the elder's own home, options include adult day care, assisted living, continuous care communities, independent living, and nursing homes. Adult day care provides respite care. This means the regular caregiver can use services to take a break from the rigors of caring. In independent living, residents live in a community setting where all of the maintenance is performed for them. Lots of amenities and the ability to furnish one's residence as he desires make these attractive for healthy elders. There is generally no medical staff on site, however. Very similar to independent living is the continuous care community. These are sometimes touted as the most luxurious option for retirement living because of the desirable amenities. These communities provide, for a fee, the health care support and assistance that will change with the needs of the resident. Assisted living facilities provide significant support with the tasks of daily living, changing the services as needed by the resident. There is 24-hour security and support staff presence, food service, daily task assistance, and personal support like assistance in dressing, bathing, and so forth. In nursing home care, there is medical assistance available on site, more direct supervision of daily activities, personal support, and end of life care.

CAREGIVER STRESS

Caring for a loved one is stressful. The literature suggests that the arrangement works best when there is at least some time for the caregiver and patient to be away from each other. This is where adult day care and other caregiver support tools can be particularly helpful. There are positive aspects to taking care of a loved one at home, usually because of the relationship between the caregiver and the elder. The satisfaction the caregiver feels, knowing that she is taking care of and helping the loved one, can help reduce the stress of the task and can improve her outlook on the role. People with higher rates of positive aspects of caregiving report less depression and more feelings of fulfillment. When the patient is mentally sharp and the relationship between caregiver and patient is close, the caregiving is viewed more positively. Likewise, the attitude one has going into the caregiving task is important in determining the attitude toward the task later. A difference between the races has been found for positive aspects of caregiving. African Americans report higher positive affect toward caregiving and lower anxiety. They also have comparatively lower socioeconomic status.

Older caregivers tend to view the caregiving more positively than do younger caregivers, who might see the task as a burden or interruption of their lives. Caregivers are particularly concerned with the quality of life that they can provide for their patients. When they feel that the loved one's quality of life is deteriorating, they may be more likely to see alternatives to home care.

THE GENDER OF CAREGIVING

Women do more than their share of caregiving. Today men contribute to caregiving more than ever before, but women are still in the primary caregiver role. Estimates are that more than 70 percent of caregivers are women. This disproportionate burden on women might be the result of their socialization. Gender role attitudes are learned early in life and often indicate a gender-based division of labor in families. The most likely provider of care is a spouse. However, when that person becomes unable to provide care, an adult daughter is usually tapped to fulfill the tasks. The order of care providers reflects this gendered expectation: daughter, daughter-in-law, son, younger female relative, younger male relative, and then female nonrelative.

Not only do daughters perform more health care, they do it earlier in life and for longer periods of time than do men. Men usually provide financial and maintenance assistance, not direct personal care. Spouses are the most dependable caregivers and because women generally live longer than men, this usually means that wives are doing the bulk of the caring. Spouses generally provide care until the spouse dies or their own health deteriorates significantly. They report seeing the caring as part of the marriage contract. Spouses feel less role conflict and burden in taking care of the partner than do other family members.

NURSING HOME ISSUES

Often the decision to use a nursing home is seen as a last resort. Much of this comes from the stigma of being in an institutional setting. There are circumstances, however, in which a nursing home can be the most beneficial option. While most assume that care outside the home is chosen because the elder relative requires a level of care that can no longer be provided by family, there may be other factors that make nursing home care and similar supportive options attractive. Unlike with other housing options, true nursing homes admit residents only with a physician's order. Nursing home is used here to refer to both assisted living and nursing home type care settings, what is more generally termed institutional care.

Many elderly people do not want to impose on their families and want to remain independent as long as they can. When they can no longer live independently the family is faced with the choice to care for the loved one at home or employ some type of residential facility, such as a nursing home. In some cases, particularly where there are few financial resources, a nursing home may be the most cost-effective option. Most residents have their care paid for by federal or state subsidies such as Medicare or Medicaid. While this may necessitate the surrender of all the elder's assets to the nursing facility, it may be the best long-term option.

Many of the benefits of nursing home care relate to the tasks of daily living that may become increasingly challenging as persons age. Included would be assistance with dressing, bathing, toileting, and other hygienic self-care. Additionally, for patients who are infirm, changing positions on a routine schedule and diapering can be hard for families, but more easily managed with a trained staff. Other daily living tasks that nursing homes provide include food service and assistance with feeding, if needed. They also do laundry for residents and provide housekeeping services in their rooms or apartments.

Among the factors that are comforting to residents and family members are 24-hour security and trained staff caregivers. Additionally, social and recreational activities are available to provide leisure and enjoyment for residents. Given that the oldest and sickest elderly are likely to be in nursing care, the provision of medical supervision, including physician and other health care provider visits, is of benefit to the residents and families. Assistance is just a call button away and someone can respond rapidly should an emergency occur.

Socially, many residents of institutional care are very satisfied with the situation. In a nursing home there are staff and other residents with whom to interact, rather than just one caregiver. Communal living creates a bond with the other residents who have for the most part had similar life experiences. This socially stimulating situation provides a daily activity schedule and residents are encouraged to participate in it as they are able, thereby providing benefits to physical and psychological health. Even watching television is often done in a group context, thus encouraging interaction and shielding the elder from depression and loneliness.

There is a long standing fear that nursing homes and other institutional settings are simply warehousing the elderly and they do not take care of the elder as well as family members would. This stereotype leads to stress over the decision and fear of additional harm occurring as a consequence of the living situation. Most persons have a fear of institutionalization and prefer to stay in a familiar setting. Staying at home might also provide the elder with a sense of independence. Occasional reports of abuse of nursing home residents also make families and elders leery of such settings. While the abuse in these places draws media attention, elders are more likely to be abused by a family member at home than by a staff member at an institution.

HOME CARE ISSUES

Reciprocity, giving back to those who have given to you, plays a role whether consciously or unconsciously in the decision to care for an older relative at home. When one is a child, parents provide care; as parents age, children provide care. This creates a sense of being responsible for the care of one's elders. This can lead to guilt when factors limit the amount of care that a child can reasonably provide. This obligation is also mirrored in societal expectations that nursing care is a last resort.

Home care works best when there are multiple people in the family who can help provide it, including household maintenance, transportation, stimulation, and direct physical care. Loved ones who are in poor health necessitate more of a commitment on the part of caregivers. Caregiving involves much more than just providing medical assistance. Family roles and relationships may become altered in the process: economic difficulties, curtailed work and social activities, and exacerbation of family conflicts can all change the interaction dynamics in a family. It is, however, becoming increasingly possible for family caregivers to acquire the needed support to care for the elder at home. When care is directed from home, family can set up who the additional caregivers are, when they provide care, and under what circumstances. This sense of control can be positive for the family and the elderly relative.

It is sometimes less expensive to care for an elderly family member at home than in an institutional setting. Particularly if funds have been established for such purposes, family members can stretch the budget by performing tasks themselves rather than hiring them out. There may, however, need to be actual physical changes to the home to accommodate adequate care for the elder. The costs of remodeling may be prohibitive.

Having the elder at home makes it easier to interact with that person on a daily basis and monitor their health. This is much more convenient than having to arrange a time to travel to another location to visit and interact. Additionally, more family bonding can occur in the home compared with institutional setting. From the standpoint of the elder, it is a comfortable situation because they can retain more of their personal belongings and may not have to consolidate items like persons in institutional care must do.

A benefit of home care that is sometimes overlooked is the ongoing contact that the elder has with the community. Rather than being forced to conform to a totally different routine, as occurs in some institutional settings, home care permits the elder to remain an enmeshed participant in the social life of the family and community. This occurs through continuing to see the same health care providers, attending the same church, visiting the same recreational facilities, and so forth.

FUTURE DIRECTIONS

There are many issues that will continue to influence the way that families make the decision about institutional care compared to home care. Among the most critical are the changing demographic patterns of the society. As the U.S. population continues to age there will be more concern about having enough spaces for all those who wish to or need to reside in nursing homes. For persons who are older but still highly functional, having some decision-making ability over their own health is expected. One of the concepts that will likely be discussed more in the coming years is aging in place. Growing older without having to move to secure necessary support services as one's needs change can be beneficial. Advocates (such as the National Aging in Place Council) suggest that efforts should be made to support older persons remaining active participants in their communities and experiencing fulfilling interactions by living independently as long as their health permits them to do so. An intergenerational environment is the likely outcome. This approach is particularly supportive of those of low to moderate incomes because they experience more financial constraints in the selection of care options.

More institutional facilities recognize this desire for independence and long-term participation in a residential community. Subsequently, they may offer a variety of services to provide long-term options for clients as they move from lower levels of care need to higher levels. For persons who are fortunate to be financially prepared for retirement and longevity expenses, the option of assisted living and other nursing home alternatives is attractive, suggesting that these types of facilities will be increasingly popular because residents are usually active participants in making the decision to live there.

As today's elders age, they are in fact living longer than past generations due to increased nutrition, medical knowledge, and positive lifestyle choices. This means there are more so-called oldest old (persons 85 years and older) who are likely to have several medical issues with which they are contending and require more complex chronic disease management. As family size has decreased, the persons who can share the burden of caregiving, both financially and directly, are fewer in number, requiring a greater commitment from those providing care. Likewise, the continuing high rates of women's employment suggest that there will be fewer traditional caregivers available to assume in-home care giving. Increased mobility for the population means that older people may not live in the same general locale as their potential family caregivers, giving more support to the idea that institutional care will increase as a percentage of all care for elders. Just because nursing and other institutional care is likely to increase, that does not mean that the decision about how to best care for elders will become any easier for families. Social pressures still suggest that the preferable pattern is for family to provide care as long as it is possible to do so.

See also Changing Fertility Patterns; Children as Caregivers; Elder Abuse; Grandparenthood.

Further Reading: AARP. http://www.aarp.org; Baumhover, Lorin A., and S. Colleen Beall. *Abuse, Neglect, and Exploitation of Older Persons.* Baltimore, MD: Health Professions Press, 1996; Berg-Weger, Marla. *Caring for Elderly Parents.* New York: Garland Publishing, 1996; Caplan, Arthur L., and Rosalie A. Kane. *Everyday Ethics: Resolving Dilemmas in Nursing Home Life.* New York: Springer Publishing Company, 1990; The Caregiver Initiative. Johnson and Johnson. http://www.strengthforcaring.com; Digregorio, Charlotte. *Everything You Need to Know about Nursing Homes.* Portland, OR: Civetta Press, 2005; National Aging in Place Council. http://www.naipc.org.

Kimberly P. Brackett

EMPLOYED MOTHERS

Maternal employment has been the subject of considerable debate for many years. Women's labor force participation rates have been steadily increasing since before the turn of the twentieth century. In fact, over the past 100 years, the number of women who are employed for pay, or seeking paid employment, has increased from about 4 million in 1890 to almost 63 million in 2001. Furthermore, between 1980 and 2000, the paid labor force participation rate for mothers of school-aged children increased from 64 to 79 percent. For mothers of preschool children, the rate increased from 47 to about 65 percent. In 2005, over half of married mothers with children under the age of one were in the paid labor force. The percentage of mothers who return to work within one year after their child's birth has dropped slightly since the late 1990s, however. This has led some to suggest that there may be an increase of so-called neotraditional families—families in which women opt out of the labor force and in which spouses prefer traditional gender roles. Evidence seems to suggest that this opting out may be the result of a weak labor market more than a genuine change in gender role ideologies or a concern with family well-being. Labor force participation among women who must work—single parents and those with low levels of education—has continued to grow.

There is a popular misconception that women, especially wives, primarily worked inside the home until the second wave of the women's movement in the 1960s. This myth is largely based on American nostalgia surrounding the period after World War II, in which women were encouraged to leave their jobs to make room for men and return to the home in fulfillment of their natural roles as wives and mothers. It should be made clear, however, that this return to homemaking and domesticity represented a reversal from previous, longstanding patterns.

In preindustrial America, almost everyone, including children, worked. Survival in agrarian economies depends on a stable and predictable supply of food; thus, all members of society must contribute, in some way, to food production. While some tasks were associated more with women than with men, there was considerable overlap in roles and most work, including parenting, was performed by both women and men. Industrialization and urbanization led to an initial segregation of gender roles and of work. Men, single women, and women of color were expected to enter into the new paid jobs while affluent, married women were expected to perform unpaid labor at home. This division of gender roles was supported by a belief system known as the "ideology of separate spheres," which posits that work and family are separate domains and that each is better suited to the strengths and skills of either men or women. In summary, expectations for women and mothers vary according to current economic demands. Women's employment is dependent on various social-context variables, including available opportunities for women, economic constraints more generally (on men and women), as well as the perceived rewards and costs of the homemaking role.

Despite economic and social changes, this ideology has remained deeply embedded in the culture and minds of most Americans. It appears that many continue to believe that women's natural place is at home. Even among dual-earner couples, it is more common for husbands to describe themselves as primary providers and for husbands and wives to describe wives as secondary providers or to describe their earnings as supplementary. Generally speaking, most couples consider housework and childcare to be the province of women. As such, the domestic burden carried by wives results in a reinforcing cycle in which women's contributions to the paid labor force are severely compromised, and their commitment to it perceived as weak. In other words, if women perform more housework, they are less able to contribute to their jobs or careers. This inability to contribute may be perceived as an unwillingness to contribute and thus a lack of professional commitment.

Both the family and the workplace are so-called greedy institutions, demanding a great deal of time and energy from individuals. In fact, in the United States the full-time work week is quite a bit longer than in many western European countries. Furthermore, individuals often find that these domains require the most from them during the same period of their lives. That is, the demands of work and family peak around the same time. Thus, many women and men feel that it is difficult to balance the demands of career, marriage, and family. This is particularly true of women because they are expected to be the "kinkeepers"—maintaining a happy marriage, a stable and successful family, routines, rituals, and extended family ties. Not surprisingly, balance may be most difficult to achieve among dual-earner couples with preschoolers. To help achieve balance, one spouse, typically the wife, may choose to limit the time spent in the paid work force. Other strategies include seeking more flexible work schedules, although historically in the United States flexible options in the workplace have been scant. Some spouses may opt to work from home. However, studies have shown that women who work from home contribute more to housework than do men who work from home. Another consequence of the inability to balance work and family is a lack of leisure time, especially for wives. In one study, it was found that while husbands tend to relax in the evenings or enjoy a personal hobby, wives tend to be focused on housework and childcare.

Because a belief in separate spheres remains firmly entrenched in American ideals, employed women, and especially mothers, often find that they not only confront conflicting role expectations but also social disapproval. Approval for working mothers seems to be on the increase, however. A 2001 survey of women found that over 90 percent of them agreed that a woman can be successful at both career and motherhood.

Today, a majority of mothers are employed. This trend has prompted a significant amount of negative attention, especially from social and religious conservatives. The primary concern seems to revolve around the potentially negative effects of maternal employment on child development and on family relationships more generally. The current ideal and expectation for so-called intensive mothering requires that women be available and receptive to their children's needs for most, if not all, hours of the day, every day of the week. There is no comparable expectation for fathers. Good fathering is normally defined as stable providing; thus, there is no contradiction between the roles of father and employee. For women, however, employment presents a challenge, at least ideologically, to the mothering role because good mothering is not equated with providing. In fact, commitment to paid work is typically viewed as posing a threat to successful mothering. Women who wish to pursue both a career and motherhood may feel that they must choose between two opposing, mutually exclusive alternatives. The cultural contradiction of being a working mother has negative economic and professional ramifications for women. It has been found that not only does being married reduce the chances that a woman will be promoted, but being a mother does so as well. Women with preschool-aged children have lower rates of promotion than do other women, whereas the opposite is true for men. Motherhood has a definite negative impact on lifetime earnings—this is known as the motherhood penalty. This penalty has not declined significantly over the years.

Many of the concerns surrounding mothers' employment are unfounded; there is little, if any, empirical support for them. The primary concern surrounds the effects of maternal employment on the well-being of children. Furthermore, this seems to have been prompted by a larger concern with the rise of women's equality, threats to the masculine gender role, especially men's role as providers, and what some believe are the long-term, negative effects of the feminist movement. For the most part, Americans are accepting of mothers' employment if and when it is absolutely necessary to provide for basic necessities. Attitudes become more intolerant, however, of mothers who have careers and work for personal fulfillment. In fact, in recent years, there have been several instances of highly publicized cases in which children were harmed while under the supervision of a paid caregiver, such as a nanny. In such instances, it was the employed mother, not the hired caregiver or the employed father, who was held responsible for the child's well-being. Rarely, if ever, are fathers implicated in such cases.

A number of research studies have examined the question of what effect, if any, maternal employment has on child well-being. Among mothers who work outside the home during their child's first year of life, some negative outcomes have been found. However, many factors, such as the type and quality of child care, home environment, spousal attitudes toward women's employment, and gender role ideology need to be considered as well. After careful consideration of many of the studies examining the effects of women's employment on child outcomes, some have concluded that, in and of itself, maternal employment has little, if any, negative impact on child development or on child-parent relationships. In fact, some studies find that children benefit from maternal employment or from high quality child care. Interestingly, a number of studies indicate that parents today spend as much or more time with children than in the past. For instance, it has been shown that in 1975 married mothers spent about 47 hours per week with their children whereas in 2000 they spent 51 hours per week with them. This increase seems to be the result of a decrease in time spent on personal care, housework, and marital intimacy.

Regardless of the child care arrangement, employed mothers may feel as if they are being asked to juggle and manage multiple roles—to do it all. The idea of the "supermom" is that of a woman who successfully manages a marriage, a family, and a career with time left over for herself. The reality is quite different from the image, however. Working mothers often report feeling overwhelmed with the kind and quantity of responsibilities they maintain. Not only are mothers expected to manage and execute tangible tasks such as meal preparation and transportation, but also psychological tasks such as planning and preparing for family routines. While husbands may serve as occasional pinch hitters, wives typically have an executive function, meaning that it is ultimately their responsibility to see that the household runs efficiently. Furthermore, the demands of the household are continuous and unrelenting; thus, household executives are never off duty.

While women have made a substantial entry into the public sphere of paid work, men have not made a comparable entry into the private sphere of unpaid work. Even among dual-earner couples, wives perform the majority of unpaid labor in and around the home; this extra shift of work for employed wives has been referred to as the "second shift" or "double day." Ironically, just being married seems to increase the amount of housework that women perform, as single mothers spend less time in housework than do married mothers. Because of the uneven distribution of household labor and childcare, there is a considerable leisure gap between mothers and fathers; that is, mothers have much less free and discretionary time than do fathers. Employed mothers often report feelings of physical and psychological exhaustion. Affluent couples may decide to hire outside help to assist with childcare, household chores, or both. However, research indicates that it is still wives who initiate and coordinate such services. Other couples may rely on older children to assist with housework. This may be more common among single-parent households. Over 40 percent of children have been in some sort of nonrelative childcare arrangement by the time they enter school. About 40 percent of children age 12–14 and 8 percent of those age 5–11 whose mothers were employed were in unsupervised self-care arrangements. Self-care is more common among white upper-middle and middle-class families. Lower income, single-parent, and Latino families are much more likely to involve extended family members in the care of children.

Encouragingly, husbands' contributions to unpaid work have increased somewhat over the past 20 years or so. Husbands' involvement in household labor and parenting varies somewhat by race or ethnicity. African American couples, for example, are characterized by greater sharing and more egalitarianism. This may be due to higher rates of labor force participation among women of color as well as more cultural approval for a communal approach to parenting. Participation in housework is generally related to the relative earnings of spouses. That is, husbands of wives who earn a significant share of the total family income generally perform more housework than do husbands of wives who earn very little. Ironically, men may actually do less housework if and when they become unemployed. This may be an attempt to reclaim or hold onto an already threatened masculine identity.

See also Family and Medical Leave Act (FMLA); Family Roles; Housework Allocation; Marital Power; Marital Satisfaction; Mommy Track; Motherhood, Opportunity Costs; Stay at Home Dads.

Further Reading: Blair-Loy, Mary. *Competing Devotions: Career and Family among Women Executives.* Cambridge, MA: Harvard University Press, 2003; Crittenden, Ann. *The Price* of Motherhood: Why the Most Important Job in the World is Still the Least Valued. New York: Henry Holt and Company, 2001; Galinsky, Ellen. *Ask the Children: The Breakthrough Study that Reveals How to Succeed at Work and Parenting.* New York: HarperCollins, 1999; Hays, Sharon. *The Cultural Contradictions of Motherhood.* New Haven: Yale University Press, 1996; Hesse-Biber, Sharlene, and Gregg Lee Carter. *Working Women in America: Split Dreams.* New York: Oxford University Press, 2000; Hochschild, Arlie Russell. *The Time Bind: When Work Becomes Home and Home Becomes Work.* New York: Henry Holt and Company, 1997; Landry, Bart. *Black Working Wives: Pioneers of the American Family Revolution.* Berkeley: University of California Press, 2000; Padavic, Irene, and Reskin, Barbara. *Women and Men at Work.* Thousand Oaks, CA: Pine Forge Press, 2002; Williams, Joan. *Unbending Gender: Why Family and Work Conflict and What To Do About It.* New York: Oxford University Press, 2000.

Susan Cody-Rydzewski

EXTRAMARITAL SEXUAL RELATIONSHIPS

Extramarital sexual relationships, known to some as the forbidden sexual relationship, affairs, cheating, or infidelity, are relationships that involve sexual contact with someone other than the spouse. According to historical evidence there has always been and probably always will be marital infidelity. Opinion polls routinely find that more than three-quarters of American adults disapprove of extramarital relationships, indicating a strong cultural prohibition on participation. In an open marriage, however, an extramarital sexual relationship is acceptable to both partners despite not being accepted by social custom. Controversy surrounding extramarital sexual relationships in part depends on whether one views the practice as harmful or helpful to a marriage. While affairs are often anecdotally cited as a reason for divorce, sexual infidelity is not a primary factor in marital breakups.

BACKGROUND

The biblical proscription of "thou shalt not commit adultery" entreats Christians to be sexually faithful in marriage. Even though most Americans are taught that adultery is unacceptable, it occurs nonetheless, and more commonly among the male population. Reports in the United States alone show the percentage of married men and women who have had at least one incidence of extramarital sexual relations ranges from 13 to 50 percent or even higher. The debates about extramarital sexual relationships center on a person's perception of, and beliefs toward, extramarital sexual relationships as well as the legal status of these relationships.

Gender certainly plays a role in the differences in participation rates and responses to these relationships, with males more interested and likely to participate in them. According to a recent National Opinion Research Center (NORC) study based on a representative sample of the U.S. population, approximately 25 percent of married men and 15 percent of married women reported having engaged in extramarital sex at least once. Some traditions believe it is the nature of the man and is expected. They are not emotionally committed, whereas females are more emotionally involved, searching for a committed long-term relationship. Males are more likely to have an outside sexual relationship at an early stage of marriage whereas females are most likely older when becoming involved in an extramarital sexual relationship. Studies show that the older the woman gets, the more likely she is to participate. Additionally, women are more likely than men to end an existing relationship (perhaps even through divorce) before becoming involved in a new one.

Looking at extramarital relationships from an evolutionary gender perspective, researchers can rationalize the male involvement in an extramarital sexual relationship. To be successful in the biological reproductive process, the male has to produce as many offspring as possible to avoid being a genetic dead end. Therefore, the evolutionary model suggests that men are genetically programmed to cheat. On the other hand, the female should be the long-term committed partner in the relationship that produces offspring. She will have no more children by being promiscuous than by being faithful. Researchers Oliver and Hyde suggest that because she needs help rearing very young children and providing for her own needs, she seeks a partner who will be stable with her for at least some time. Men receive positive reinforcement for engaging in extramarital sexual relationships while women receive reinforcement for keeping their sexual activity confined to a loving, committed relationship involving a single partner.

REASONS FOR INVOLVEMENT

When looking at the different reasons for why males and females become involved in extramarital sexual relationships, most married men say they enter into the relationship for one reason—simple pleasure. For females, getting involved in a relationship is often done for commitment and love. The spouses' willingness to stray and opportunity to do so are major factors to consider in determining involvement in an extramarital sexual relationship. Some relationships can be short-term, others long-term. There can be long-term effects on the family as a result of the extramarital affair. Not only can the marriage be damaged, the children can be damaged also. An affair can cause mistrust in the marriage, something that can linger for years and may never be repaired. Among other things to worry about, the uninvolved spouse runs the risk of contracting a sexually transmitted disease. For many spouses the concern about contracting HIV/AIDS means that the anger over the affair in the marriage intensifies.

While extramarital sexual relationships are generally unacceptable, and a large majority of people disapprove, affairs still happen. Research suggests that when husbands and wives become involved in these relationships, they are looking for satisfaction that is missing in the marriage. A wife who feels emotionally detached from her husband feels alone and unwanted. Searching for the attention lacking in her relationship with her husband, she finds it in someone else. Research suggests that the motivation for women to stray is to establish an emotional connection rather than a desire for sexual gratification. For the husband, having an affair is primarily for sexual satisfaction. It is not necessarily that he wants to leave his wife for another woman but he wants to try something new and different. The new relationship is exciting because they may not see each other often and it has a forbidden quality. Couples may seek outside relationships due to the frequency and quality of sexual intercourse in the marriage. Most couples who have sexual affairs report feeling as if something was missing in their sex lives, so they turn to someone else. Many felt that the marriage was boring and all the excitement that was once there was gone.

OPEN MARRIAGES

Although society disapproves of extramarital relationships, some couples hold attitudes that permit partners in addition to the spouse. These couples permit, and even encourage, extramarital sexual encounters. Open marriage refers to an honest and open relationship between two people, based on the equal freedom and identity of both partners. It involves a verbal, intellectual, and emotional commitment to the right of each to grow as an individual within the marriage. An open marriage occurs when a married couple has a mutual understanding that each may be involved in a relationship outside the marriage without viewing this situation as adultery. While both open marriages and extramarital sexual relationships involve a sexual relationship outside the marriage, the former has the approval of the spouse and the latter does not. For most American couples, the idea of one's partner having a sexual relationship with someone else is hurtful and damaging.

Open marriages, where both partners agree that participating in an extramarital relationship is acceptable, are based in the idea that either partner may explore their sexual interests. Individuals condone the behavior; society at large does not. Because society disapproves of open marriages, couples are more likely to hide these relationships from their family, friends, and the people they work with daily. "Openly" married spouses describe engaging in extramarital sexual relationships as a key to maintaining their marital satisfaction, while other advocates view it as an opportunity for personal growth within a marriage. Generally, couples who participate in open marriage are not religious because the behavior opposes the principles presented in the Bible and practiced through tradition. Open marriages are specified by the terms polyamory and swinging.

STYLES OF OPEN MARRIAGES

There are different styles of open marriages. These are distinctions between open marriages based on the motive for participating and in the nature of the extramarital relationships. Couples whose extramarital relationship is based in love and emotional involvement with the nonmarital partner are experiencing a polyamorous style of open marriage. Couples whose extramarital relationship deals with sexual gratification and friendship are experiencing a swinging style relationship.

POLYAMORY

Polyamory refers to marriages in which one or both spouses retain the option to sexually love others in addition to their spouse. According to Rubin, "Polyamorists are more committed to emotional fulfillment and family building than recreational swinging" (Rubin 2001). Polyamorists follow the philosophy and practice of loving more than one person at the same time. In other words, you can't help with whom you fall in love and you may love several people at the same time. Polyamory is about a stable relationship, commitment, and an emotional attachment, unlike the uncommitted sexual gratification pleasure of swinging. People of this ilk have formed and organized their own society to promote the polyamorous lifestyle.

Organized on June 6, 1996 in Washington, D.C., the Polyamory Society was created to bring positive social change for the institution of marriage. The objective of the Polyamory Society is to educate those who are not yet part of the society about the rules of polyamorist relationships. Another objective of the society is the social and economic support for polyamorists and polyfamilies. They are involved in the creation of a day where the families come together and celebrate and honor families and friends for their support. Classic polygyny, or one man with multiple wives, as practiced by fundamentalist Mormon groups in the United States would fall under the category polyamory.

According to the Polyamory Society, polyamorists believe that extramarital sex is not the problem when falling in love with someone other than your spouse; it is the lying and betrayal. They also say that sex can be something positive if it is done with honesty, trust, and responsibility for one's actions. Because these persons feel that love has no boundaries or limits, polyamorists can get help from the outside lover to meet the needs of his or her partner. The need can range from sex to going to a movie or just hanging out together.

Jealousy is something that often occurs in the polyamorous relationships. Looking at it positively, polyamorists do not see jealousy as an emotional reaction that is impossible to overcome but, rather, as a feeling of joy from knowing the one you love is loved by someone else. It is the belief of the Polyamorist Society that they represent family values. For example, the more parents a child has to take care of him, the less likely he is to feel abandoned if someone leaves. In other societies this lifestyle is condemned and disapproved.

Polyamory is not the answer if one is having relationship problems or wants a quick fix to a bad marriage. Neither is swinging, sometimes confused with polyamory.

SWINGING

While the two alternative relationship patterns have a lot in common, swinging is a marriage arrangement in which couples exchange partners in order to engage in recreational sex. It is also known as wife swapping or spouse swapping. Some might think of it as cheating but it is not. It is in the open because all parties involved are aware of what is going on. Couples openly agree to participate and discuss this relationship.

In the late 1960s and early 1970s swinging gained media and research attention as one of several alternative lifestyles. It was estimated that during that time, approximately 2 percent of the adults in the United Stated had participated at least once in swinging. It was also at this time in Berkeley, CA that the first swinging club was opened. The Sexual Freedom League later formed an umbrella organization called North American Swing Club Association (NASCA) to provide information regarding the lifestyle of swingers.

People who are classified as swingers come from all economic levels, races, nationalities, and job classifications. The great majority of swingers, however, are Caucasian and of middle- to upper-middle socioeconomic class. Those who participate in swinging suggest that it helps them to see their mate as an individual and not as a possession. Sometimes couples get bored in the marriage so they look somewhere else to put a spark back into their life and into the marriage. Experiencing jealousy is common in swinging, just as it is in polyamory. This is a normal feeling, a feeling of hurt knowing that instead of reassuring you of the love and commitment your partner has for you, he or she looks somewhere else for a sexual experience. If a marriage is already in trouble, then swinging may not be the lifestyle to choose. Although it may not save a bad marriage, it may very well strengthen a good one.

Interestingly, swingers often advertise for partners. Through newspapers and magazines couples advertise for partners of the same lifestyle. Psychologist Shelley Peabody found that sometimes it is not just sex that a coupled partner is looking for; they might search for intimacy as well. Combining the two, sex and intimacy, is a way to increase the number of one's friends as well as the number of sex partners. However, it is believed that when the friend aspects develop more fully, the sex aspects decrease.

HEALTH RELATED DANGERS OF OPEN MARRIAGES

Extramarital sexual relationship in marriages can lead to increased health concerns, especially regarding the spread of sexually transmitted diseases. Thirty-three percent of male swingers and 10 percent of female swingers feared catching a sexually transmitted disease (Jenks 1998). In another study, sexually transmitted diseases topped the list of disadvantages of swinging, and 58 percent of swingers expressed some fear of catching HIV/AIDS. Sexually transmitted diseases like HPV (human papilloma virus) and herpes are transmitted from partners who don't know that they are infected with the diseases because there might be no signs or symptoms. The safest way to stop the spread of sexually transmitted infections without giving up the relationship is to practice safe sex.

A TRADITION OF MONOGAMY

Monogamy refers to the marriage of one man to one woman and this has been the preferred pattern of social life in Western society for centuries. Religious and legal prescriptions support the one man, one woman doctrine. Not only are the couple to be practical helpers for each other, but they are to be each other's sole source of sexual satisfaction, an idea referenced at several points in the traditional Christian marriage vows. Prohibitions on adultery and sex outside of marriage have a strong tradition in Judeo-Christian teaching and in legal statutes.

When looking at extramarital sexual relationships from a Christian perspective, many faith traditions say everything God created is good when it is used properly, including sex. He gave humans the capacity to enjoy sex so he made it a vital part of us, wanting it to be as rewarding and pleasurable as possible. Christians are admonished to make careful and wise choices, so when choosing a partner, be selective. This is the person to whom one will be bound for the rest of their lives.

The Bible teaches that sex outside the marriage is wrong. The marriage is between the man and the woman and their needs, not those of the couple and their external lovers. In the Bible Ephesians 5:31 says of marriage that, "the two shall become one flesh." This being true, man should be of one woman and woman should be of one man. Christian teachings stress that when two people are joined together they are joined physically; sharing multiple partners dilutes one's soul by allowing bits and pieces of oneself to spread socially. Also, Christianity addresses the health issues regarding how this relationship can affect the entire family.

LEGAL ASPECTS

While extramarital sexual encounters do not generally lead to one's arrest, there can be legal consequences. Most notable among them is that adultery is traditionally among the grounds for divorce under the fault-based divorce model. While most divorces today are filed as no-fault divorces, where the reason for the divorce need only be the couple's inability to get along, some persons still pursue a traditional divorce. They may petition for divorce based on the partner's infidelity. In a case such as this, the alimony payments from a husband to his former wife represent his reparations for the commission of the crime of adultery against the spouse; they are the punishment inflicted upon him for violating the marital contract. Because adultery was worthy of inclusion in the law as grounds for divorce, as a society we must think it harms marriages and should be discouraged. Another legal issue to consider in extramarital relationships is paternity. While illegitimacy was traditionally viewed more negatively than it is today, the assignment of paternity matters as it has financial obligations for the male even if he is not legally married to the mother of the child.

AFTER EXTRAMARITAL SEXUAL RELATIONSHIPS

When one partner discovers that the other has been having an affair, there are many questions that arise. One may ask: Are there problems in our marriage? Did I drive him or her to someone else? Are we not satisfying each other? Moreover, upon discovery of the affair, the partners may ask if they will we ever be able to regain the trust that had been broken. Many times the couples say that they cannot love and trust the partner again because doubt or suspicion will always be there. Depending on the persons involved, the circumstances surrounding the affair, and whether there was trust there to begin with, the trust can be regained. Because adultery accounts for only a small percentage of the reasons for divorce, it is clear that many persons try to work through this obstacle with the help of marital counseling.

Therapists suggest that the following are required in rebuilding the marriage. The spouse responsible for the affair must sincerely apologize, and should try not to be defensive about his or her behavior. He or she must listen to the offended spouse, allowing the spouse to scream and yell, and to get all the feelings in the open. Care must be taken not to allow it to become physical. The responsible spouse needs to be patient and allow time to try and rebuild trust, as trust rebuilding does not happen over night. The responsible spouse needs to help in rebuilding the trust by not giving the other reason for suspicion. The offended spouse needs to decide if the marriage is really worth fighting for or if too much damage has been done. The couple should consider ongoing counseling. Therapist Douglas Snyder maintains that sexual infidelity is the most difficult relationship issue to treat.

Unfortunately couples experience relationship betrayals. Psychotherapists at the University of Colorado examined annual evidence of extramarital sexual relationships and found that approximately 2 to 4 percent of all married men and women had engaged in an extramarital relationship in the past year (Treas and Giesen 2000). With today's technology, having an extramarital relationship can be done with just the click of a button. Cyberspace relationships, or online affairs, are easy to initiate and have increased in number. A person can meet a partner online in a chat room and chat as long as he or she wants. Knowing that they may never get to meet the actual person, participants may not provide accurate information. One or both parties might lie about their age, occupation, attractiveness, marital status, and so forth. Despite the format and lack of physical contact between the participants, even when this affair is discovered it can destroy a marriage. Because cyberspace relationships are anonymous and so easy to initiate, researchers have yet to determine how much participation is occurring.

CONCLUSION

There are different levels of concealment and consent of extramarital sex. In a clandestine affair, neither spouse is aware of the other's involvement and would disapprove if they did. In an ambiguous affair the noninvolved spouse is aware of the extramarital sex but does not confront the partner. The partner may experience pain over the affair but is likely to stay in the marriage rather than seek a divorce. A last type of affair, consensual sexual relationship, is when both spouses know and approve of the outside relationship. Each spouse may at some point participate in this type relationship.

Today's data on extramarital sexual relationships suggests spouses are torn between the commitment and sexual exclusivity of marriage and desire for outside sexual relationships. However, when most couples decide to get married it is with the intent to avoid outside sexual relationships. Fidelity in a marriage means being committed to the partner and to the relationship.

Despite a loosening of sexual standards in regard to premarital sexual encounters, Americans as a group still disapprove of extramarital sexual relationships. Despite the benefits that some who participate attribute to these encounters, this type of relationship seems destined to remain on the fringes. Both socially and personally, participants pay a price for their choices. Even though this type of relationship may be accepted by the partners that are involved, it may never be accepted by society.

See also Marital Satisfaction; Plural Marriage.

Further Reading: Cloud 9 Social-Networking site. http://www.cloud9social.com; Frinz, Iris, and Frinz Steven. *Secret Sex: Real People Talk About Outside Relationships They Hide from Their Partners*. New York: St. Martin's Press, 2003; Jenks, Richard J. "Swinging: A Review of the Literature." *Archives of Sexual Behavior* 27 (1998): 507–520; McCullough, Derek, and Hall, David S. "Polyamory-What it Is and What it Isn't." *Electronic Journal of Human Sexuality* 6 (2003). http://www.ejhs.org/volume6/polamory.htm; North American Mission Board. "Extramarital Sex: A Christian Perspective," 2007. http://www.namb.net; Oliver, Mary Beth, and Janet Shibley Hyde. "Gender Differences in Sexuality: A Meta-analysis." *Psychological Bulletin* 114 (1993): 29–52; The Polyamory Society, Inc. http://www.polyamorysociety.org; Rubin, Roger H. "Alternative Lifestyles Revisited, or Whatever Happened to Swingers, Group Marriages, and Communes?" *Journal of Family Issues* 22 (2001): 711–726; Sprechcer, Susan, Pamela C. Regan, and Kathleen McKinney. "Beliefs about the Outcomes of Extramarital Relationships as a Function of the Gender of the 'Cheating Spouse.'" *Sex Roles* 38 (1998): 301–311; Treas, J., and D. Giesen. "Sexual Infidelity among Married and Cohabiting Americans." *Journal of Marriage and the Family* 62 (2000): 48–60; Whisman, Mark A., and Tina Pittman Wagers. "Assessing Relationship Betrayals." *Journal of Clinical Psychology* 61 (2005): 1383–1391; Winking, Jeffery, Hillard Kaplan, Michael Gurven, and Stacey Rucas. "Why Do Men Marry and Why Do They Stray?" *Proceeding: Biological Sciences* 274, no. 1618 (2007): 1643–1649.

Linda J. Rudolph

FAMILY AND MEDICAL LEAVE ACT (FMLA)

The Family and Medical Leave Act was passed in 1993 to help employees balance the responsibilities of work and family. By 1984, 42.1 percent of all women were in the workforce. The traditional family, comprised of a breadwinner father and a homemaker mother, was no longer the norm. Women were not just choosing to work; many needed to work to help support their families. However, the workplace had not adjusted to help employees balance work and family. Many women and men were losing their jobs because they took time off to care for a newborn baby or a sick child.

THE DEVELOPMENT OF THE LAW

Soon enough, the United States government took notice of this problem and the Parental and Disability Leave Act was introduced in Congress in 1984 by Republican Howard Berman. The bill requested 18 weeks of unpaid leave upon the birth, adoption, or serious illness of a child, along with six months short-term disability leave, with no job loss, for employees in workplaces that had at least five workers. If an employer failed to allow employees these rights, employees could file a right of action in civil court against their employers. The bill also would commission a study on wage replacement for individuals taking leave. The name of the bill was subsequently changed to the Parental and Medical Leave Act in 1985, and then to the Family and Medical Leave Act (FMLA) in 1987.

Many of the earlier witnesses who testified to Congress in favor of the FMLA represented women's groups, who saw the bill as a way to reduce gender inequality. Even though the FMLA was a bill to support both parents, women's groups acknowledged that women were the ones most likely to be taking care of children. Yet the message of gender equality was silenced early in the bill's life when Representative Pat Schroeder stated about the bill, "Here people want to play like it is women's legislation. Well, I mean, it's parents' legislation. All these children have fathers too." From this point on, the FMLA was characterized as gender-neutral legislation that would help both mothers and fathers take care of newborns or sick children.

The biggest opponent to the FMLA was small business. In fact, small business interests all but took over the conversation about the FMLA in 1987. Witnesses testifying on the behalf of powerful groups such as the Chamber of Commerce argued against a government mandate that would force businesses to allow workers time off work for the care of infants or sick family members. Small business groups believed that the cost of the FMLA to businesses would be twofold. First, they argued that they would spend a great deal of money trying to replace workers who take time off and to hire personnel to deal with the paperwork usually involved with new government policies. Second, small business representatives believed that replacement workers who were less experienced and less dedicated to their jobs would not be as productive as regular employees.

On the other hand, groups that represented workers, such as unions, women's groups, and the elderly, as well as state and local government officials, argued in support of the FMLA. They believed that the FMLA set a minimum standard that would protect workers who took time off for family concerns from unjust firings or demotions.

Although small business interests could not stop the bill from being enacted, many changes were made to the bill from its beginnings to its passage. The small business lobby influenced a change in the proposed bill that reduced the number of weeks off of work allowed to 12 per year, and increased the firm size that must adhere to the bill to 50 employees.

The House and Senate first passed the FMLA in 1990, but then-President George Bush vetoed it twice before he was defeated in the 1992 presidential election. By this time, the small business community no longer saw family leave as a threat to its interests after many changes to the bill. President Bill Clinton signed the Family and Medical Leave Act on February 3, 1993. The final version of the act allows women and men to take time off for family-related concerns. Individuals who have been employed more than 12 months with a company that employs at least 50 people may take up to 12 weeks of unpaid leave per year. Employers must permit leave to care for newborn or newly adopted children, to care for ill children or parents, for recovery for their own serious illnesses, and for maternity leave.

Under the Family and Medical Leave Act of 1993, individuals are allowed leave under the guidelines mentioned, but must give 30 days notice or as close to 30 days as possible if that amount of time is not feasible. Employers may request certification from the employee's health care provider. Additionally, workers have the right to return to the same or similar position and must not be treated differently upon return to work. However, if the employee or an immediate family member of the employee becomes seriously ill and does not return to work, the employee is responsible for repaying his or her share of health care benefits upon employer request. Workers are also allowed a period of time to become requalified for the job if the employee's qualifications were not maintained as a direct result of taking leave. Finally, employers must continue paying their share of health benefit premiums; however, employees must continue to pay their share if they were obligated to do so before the leave.

RESEARCH AFTER FMLA

On the surface, the FMLA appears to support the roles of both men and women in the workplace. Women should not lose their jobs due to a maternity leave. Men are able to spend time with newborn children without penalty. Because the policy is relatively new, little research has looked at its results and what actually predicts leave taking. However, studies that have been performed highlight the strengths and weaknesses of the law.

Studies have found that women are more likely to take leave for others (children, elderly parents, etc.), while men are more likely to take leave for themselves ("sick days"). They also discovered that women and whites are more likely to take leave and that married women who report needing leave take leave more often than married men. Having children, belonging to a union, caring for an ill family member, and working 25 or more hours per week were associated with taking longer leaves for women. Having children decreased leave length for men. Women were also more likely to say that they needed a leave but did not take it. Men working in a company with 50 or more employees, caring for a baby, caring for an ill family member, working 25 or more hours per week, being a salaried employee, and over 38 years old were also more likely to take leave than other men. Certain states also seem to be more generous and allow more time off for family issues. The more time a woman's home state allowed for leaves, the more likely she was to take leave following the birth of a child or within the first three months of birth.

There has also been research on employee attitudes toward leave takers, although the results are mixed. Men felt that their employers would look down upon them for taking leave. Although leaves are allowed, men often felt discouraged to take leaves and pressured to stay at work, a reflection of the gendered norms of the workplace. A study of one company covered by the FMLA revealed that none of the men (10) with young children had taken advantage of the FMLA. Although 14 women had taken leave, most women and men in the company believed they would be perceived as uncommitted to their work. Workers felt that if they took leave, they would not have a job when they returned to work. In these studies, both men and women felt the pressure to stay at work, but women were taking more and longer leaves. This reflects notions that women see responsibility for caregiving as primarily theirs because they feel the task would not be completed otherwise.

On the other hand, government-funded research revealed that employee attitudes toward leave have been favorable thus far, with 72.6 percent of respondents somewhat or very satisfied with the FMLA. The majority of those who have taken leave report few worries about losing their positions, find leave easy to arrange, and have few complaints about the amount of time taken off. If women are the leave takers, and caregiving is seen as an essential characteristic of women, it is not surprising that leave takers (women) do not have trouble arranging their time off.

FUTURE DIRECTIONS

Very few changes to the FMLA have been adopted since the law was passed in 1993. In January 2008, Congress approved a change to the law that requires employees to call their employers before requesting family leave. Before this, employees could take two days off before requesting that their time off fall under FMLA. Additionally, FMLA has been extended to military families, who can take up to 26 weeks off of work to care for a sick family member who is a member of the armed forces. Although there has been a proposal to allow employers to discuss employees' health with their health care professionals, because employers fear abuse of the law, this has not yet been added to the law. Questions about how this could be reconciled with federal health care privacy statutes remain.

While employers are still arguing that the FMLA gives workers too much time off, the post-FMLA research suggests the law has not done enough. Women's groups note that the FMLA has not helped married women involve their husbands in childrearing. Some critics believe that this is because family leave is unpaid. If married couples are starting a family, and, with the wage gap, men are likely to be making more money than their wives, men are going to be less likely to take leave. Others say that the cultural and workplace constraints limit men's leave taking. If Americans accept women as natural nurturers, women are going to take more time off, and employers may reflect cultural beliefs by discouraging married men from taking leave.

DID YOU KNOW?

The United States and Australia are the only Western nations that do not provide paid maternity leave to citizens. On the other hand, Sweden provides paid maternity *and* paternity leave, where couples can split up to 16 months of a leave at 80 percent of their salaries or wages.

Unpaid leave is also discouraging for single parents and the poor. Families with lower incomes are less likely to take advantage of leave. There is also a gray area when it comes to gay and lesbian couples. Because most states do not recognize their marriages, the majority of gay and lesbian couples are unable to take advantage of the FMLA. Thus, critics have noted that the FMLA is most usable for married, middle-class, heterosexual couples. The provisions of the FMLA reflect a traditional family structure and do not help the balance of work and family for those living in nontraditional families. Critics believe that paid family leave for both men and women would alleviate many of these problems.

See also Child Care Policy; Day Care; Employed Mothers; Mommy Track.

Further Reading: Commission on Leave. *A Workable Balance: Report to Congress on Family and Medical Leave Policies*. Washington, D.C.: GPO, 1996; Gornick, Janet C., and Marcia K. Meyers. *Families that Work*. New York: Russell Sage Foundation, 2003; Gowan, Mary A., and Raymond A. Zimmerman. "The Family and Medical Leave of 1993: Employee Rights and responsibilities, Employer Rights and Responsibilities." *Employee Responsibilities and Rights Journal* 9 (1996): 57–71; Han, Wen Jui, and Jane Waldfogel. "Parental Leave: The Impact of Recent Legislation on Parents' Leave Taking." *Demography* 40 (2003): 191–200; Marks, Michelle Rose. "Party Politics and Family Policy." *Journal of Family Issues* 18 (1997): 55–70; Marks, Michelle Rose. *Business, Labor, Gender, and the State: The Shaping of the Family and Medical Leave Act of 1993*. Akron, OH: University of Akron Press, 1995; Prohaska, Ariane. *The Gendered Division of Leave Taking*. Akron, OH: University of Akron Press, 2006; U.S. Census Bureau, *Statistical Abstract of the United States*; U.S. Congress House of Representatives. Committee on Education and Labor. *Family and Medical Leave Act of 1987,* 100th Cong., 1st sess., February 25, 1987, March 5, 1987; U.S. Congress House of Representatives. Committee on Post Office and Civil Service. *Parental and Disability Leave Act of 1985*. 99th Cong., 1st sess., October 17, 1985; U.S. Department of Labor. *The Family and Medical Leave Act*. http://www.dol.gov/esa/whd/fmla/ (accessed February 2008); Waldfogel, Jane. "Family and Medical Leave: Evidence from the 2000 Surveys." *Monthly Labor Review*124 (2001): 17–23; Wright, David W., and Earl Wysong. "Family Friendly Workplace Benefits: Policy Mirage, Organizational Contexts, and Worker Power." *Critical Sociology* 24 (1998): 244–276.

Ariane Prohaska

FAMILY ROLES

As the family form undertaken by the majority of the United States population has shifted in the last several decades, many people have begun to question the state of families and the roles being fulfilled by their members. Today, considerable controversy surrounds family roles. Questions emphasize whether the family roles performed both historically and currently among more traditional couples are healthier or more functional than the family roles of more egalitarian couples.

Each member of a family fulfills one or more roles to accomplish the tasks of family life. Thus, a husband generally has certain expectations regarding his place in the family and the duties he should perform. The same is true of a wife, who has her own expectations about her place and duties within the family. Arlie Hochschild referred to this as "gender ideology," saying that every man and woman has one and that it consistently impacts how each feels and behaves within the family. In addition, individuals have gender ideologies for their partners, expressed as opinions regarding the other's proper roles and responsibilities. These ideologies are shaped by often-conflicting forces that include individual personality, societal pressure, influence of parents or other role models, and life experience.

The term *family roles* is relatively new. As husband and wife roles have historically been divided between the sexes, family roles have traditionally been synonymous with gender roles. Gender roles may be defined as the tasks, behaviors, rights, and responsibilities sanctioned by society and deemed appropriate for males and females. Gender roles in this context are usually assumed to be opposite one another and to have strict boundaries. This is expressed through the femininity-masculinity dichotomy. Therefore, a so-called real man would never present characteristics belonging to a woman, and a lady should never take on any characteristic considered manly. But as society changes, gender roles are becoming more fluid. As people are beginning to accept that men and women may share tasks and responsibilities without compromising their individual identities the term gender roles is being replaced with the idea of family roles.

FAMILY ROLE CATEGORIES

Within the current lexicon surrounding family roles, husband-wife partnerships are typically lumped into two major models: traditional or egalitarian.

The Traditional Model

Traditional marriages are described as nuclear families (mother, father, and children in one household with no other family members present) in which the mother cares for the home and the father works outside of it. In this mother-as-homemaker and father-as-breadwinner model, male and female spheres are completely separated and partners view their roles as complementary. The woman is responsible for all home-care tasks, with the exception of some chores deemed man's work, such as repairs or yard upkeep, and child rearing. She does not earn a wage. She is expected to put the needs of her husband and children before her own and to be an emotional support for her husband who, in return, supports her financially.

The man shoulders the entire economic burden of the household. He is expected to work hard and earn enough money to give his dependents a comfortable lifestyle. Not upholding this requirement is detrimental to his place in society and to his self-esteem as a man. As the head of the household, he has the majority of decision-making power and all others are expected to defer to him. The traditional model is the idealized family form in United States society. For proponents of traditional marriage, any other family form is considered deviant, unhealthy, and dysfunctional.

The Egalitarian Model

In egalitarian marriages, partners view themselves as having more equal roles. However, this does not mean that everything in these marriages is evenly divided. Rather than necessitating an exact division of tasks and responsibilities, though this is possible, egalitarianism indicates a feeling of equity between mates. This means spouses feel they have achieved a balance in their relationship that is fair to both partners. Rather than assigning chores and responsibilities based on gender, egalitarian couples might divide tasks based on areas of interest, competence, or expertise. A spouse who is good at managing money could take over bill-paying duties, while one who is a good cook might prepare most meals. The responsible party for either task could be the husband or the wife.

Also characteristic of these relationships is a balance of decision-making power and an equal value placed on meeting the wants and needs of both individuals. The number of people who consider egalitarian marriage the best model has grown considerably in the last several decades, and this form's popularity is expected to continue to expand.

The general categories of traditional and egalitarian marriages are at opposite ends of a spectrum along which family roles usually fall. The controversy surrounding family roles arises when people label one or the other end of the spectrum as better or right. Proponents on each side of the controversy present various arguments as to why one model is healthier or more functional than the other. Those of the traditionalist viewpoint have included Talcott Parsons, Dan Quayle, Pat Buchanan, and James Dobson. Advocates for egalitarian partnerships have included Stephanie Coontz, Arlie Hochschild, Pepper Schwartz, and Jessie Bernard.

A BRIEF HISTORY OF CHANGING FAMILY ROLES

The main thrust for the shift in family dynamics and role expectations was the Industrial Revolution. This movement, which began for the United States in the early 1800s and ended around 1910, revolutionized the way North Americans related to work, society, and family. Three distinct stages of society are often identified in relation to this unprecedented upheaval of human life: preindustrial, industrial, and postindustrial.

Preindustrial Times

The preindustrial age can be described as all human history prior to the Industrial Revolution, but it is often taken more specifically as beginning with hunting and gathering societies. Within this era, the United States is a special case. Although native inhabitants lived for centuries in hunting and gathering tribes or bands in North America, the predominantly European peoples who colonized the land were agriculturalists. Thus, the literature on United States family forms often ignores Native American family structures and begins with the family models presented by European farmers.

Consequently, beginning with the colonial period and spanning the centuries until the Industrial Revolution, the locus of economic productivity in North America was the family. Husbands, wives, and children were generally self-sufficient in meeting survival needs, both physical and emotional. Everyone worked for the good of the group, and while men's work tended to focus in the fields and women's in the home, both sexes pitched in with tasks in the other's realm. Both male and female labor was crucial for life, and each sex valued the other's contributions. A system of exchange was enjoyed by family members where each worked and produced in order to advance the survival of all. In this way, rather than based on romance, marriage was an economic contract between two individuals or those individuals and their families.

Although nuclear families predominated, the full traditional model did not exist at this time. Women held a subordinate position in society as their husbands' helpers, but their labor within the home was well-valued. In addition to producing vital materials and providing services, many wives also participated in the cottage industry. This involved the household production of goods, such as candles or cloth, which could be traded within the community. Thus, in pre-industrial times women's domesticity and work were merged.

Industrial Times

The dawning of the Industrial Revolution in North America brought extraordinary change within society. As everything around them transformed, families had to adapt and the familial landscape was radically altered as a result. The nexus for this was the advent of the mass production of goods that were previously produced within individual households. As wage work within factories took over, people came to depend on it as a means for survival.

Although many women worked in factories, especially in the beginning, eventually the idea of separate spheres emerged. Under this ideal, men became responsible for the instrumental role of tending to their families' financial needs. Women took over the expressive role, tending to the emotional, social, and moral needs of their families. Because of this, husbands' and wives' roles were divided between work and home respectively, with clearly delineated boundaries between them. Men were given the duties of social production, or the work of making goods or providing services for a wage, and women took up the work of social reproduction, or the duty of caring for family and home. These separate spheres marked the heyday of the traditional family. During this time, more families accurately fit the description of this model than had ever previously or since. Found among the majority of middle- and upper-class families, though rarely in working- or lower-class families, the traditional family became so idealized that people seemed to forget that it had only recently come into functional existence.

As husbands became responsible for the financial well-being of households, they were thrust into what is known as the good provider role. The ideology of this role connected a man's self-worth to how well he could provide for his family. Men were considered tireless machines of production whose most vital function was to bring wages into the home. Finding a well-paying job was crucial, and any male who could not support his family financially was labeled as less than a man.

Women, in turn, became subject to the Cult of True Womanhood. This ideology, put forth by the media, ministry, and other authority figures, emerged to justify the position of women in the home. Women were told the best service they could do themselves, their families, and their communities was to uphold the four virtues of True Womanhood—piety, purity, submissiveness, and domesticity—and that they would find true fulfillment and happiness in doing so. By endowing women with such high morality, society tried to disguise their true place of subordination to men.

Much later, in the 1970s, a different ideology arose with the same goal. During World War II, the domestic labor shortage from the deployment of men to war in Europe and the Pacific changed the lives of countless women forever as they left their homes to fill empty manufacturing, service, and other positions across the nation. While society encouraged this for the duration of the war, when the soldiers returned women were expected to give their positions back to men and return to the home. When many were reluctant to do so, an ideal that Betty Friedan called the feminine mystique was used to encourage them to return to domesticity and subordination. This ideology told women that their true identities were those of wife and mother and that they would find satisfaction only in those roles and not in the world of paid labor.

Postindustrial Times

In contemporary North America, the postindustrial era has brought another wave of change affecting all aspects of society, including the shape of families. The crux of this transfiguration is the shift from a manufacturing to a service economy. Under this service economy, the value of men's labor has suffered. Many in manufacturing industries have lost and continue to lose their jobs and find their skill sets do not allow them access to well-paying positions in the new economy. Also, service industry work is generally lower-paying than manufacturing for both sexes, and the potential money to be made by working has decreased. Adding increased unemployment and underemployment characteristic of this service economy to higher goods costs and the unchecked consumerism that has also developed creates a reality in which dual incomes seem necessary for a family's survival. Therefore, the traditional model, with only the husband employed, is rarely a feasible or sufficient lifestyle in the United States today.

But even if it were, research has shown that the majority of women would prefer to stay in the labor force rather than returning to or entering a homemaking role. The number of women holding jobs has steadily increased since the 1950s, with the majority of women earning an income today. Coinciding with this has been an increasing number of women completing higher education, which often encourages them to use their talents and skills in paid labor in addition to being part of a family at home. Despite this, women's increase in outside work has not been balanced by an equal increase in men's work inside the home.

In this postindustrial era, the egalitarian relationship model has gained many active participants and others attempting some form of it. Although the shift to egalitarianism has often been led by a woman's desire for equality, research has found that a number of men have discarded traditional ideals to seek more equitable relationships. Many men today report that they like for their wives to work, and that they enjoy and want to share more household and parenting tasks.

DEBATING FAMILY ROLES

Arguments for the Traditional Model

The 1950s, commonly called The Golden Age of Family, has become an almost mythical era in the minds of many Americans. Large numbers of people, even those who were born much later, look back on this period with nostalgia. This decade symbolizes a simpler time, the so-called good old days, when the family was an institution of stability, comfort, and reprieve. For some, these qualities are indivisibly linked with the traditional model of separate family roles for males and females. These individuals often feel that the blending of home and work responsibilities for both sexes has created confusion about expectations. They say consequently that neither home nor work is being given adequate attention in many households.

When making the case that traditionalism is the best model, advocates cite varying arguments. One is the conception proposed by structural functionalism that traditional family roles provide stability, not only for individual families, but for society in general. According to structural functionalists, such as Talcott Parsons, gender stratification arose as ancient men and women undertook the tasks for which they were most suited. In these societies, due to the limitations of child care, it was functional for women to focus their energies in or around the dwelling. Men, who were not constrained by pregnancy or nursing infants, were free to travel to meet their function of acquiring meat or making war. Structural functionalists feel that the separate spheres continue to be a stabilizing force today. They propose that rigid family roles create harmony between the sexes because expectations for husbands and wives are clear under this system. Men and women both know the responsibilities and tasks that they must fulfill to perpetuate their own survival and that of their loved ones. Advocates of this view decry the blending of roles under egalitarianism, citing this change as a major contributor to the high divorce rate in the United States.

In relation, some traditionalists argue that women's entrance into the labor force has been a driving factor behind rising divorce. Popular among some politicians is the idea that the movement of wives and mothers out of the home has left a void of morality and cohesion in its wake. The absence of a full-time, homemaking wife has been blamed for marital dissatisfaction, juvenile delinquency, children's low academic achievement, teenage pregnancy, and a number of other social ills. Proponents of this view reiterate the problem of unclear family role expectations as leading to divorce. They feel that when one of the sexes takes on the tasks of the other, confusion and marital tension result.

One issue associated with rising tension and discord due to women's work is that some husbands feel less masculine when their wives take jobs outside the home. This feeling is compounded when the woman's employment is economically necessary for the household's endurance, and it is often heightened when their wives earn more than they do. Due to the strong connection between identity, self-esteem, and being good providers found within several generations of American men, it can be difficult for a husband to feel good about himself or his marriage if his wife works. Additionally, in some cases, a husband may become violent toward his family, leading his wife to seek divorce. Therefore, some traditionalists might contend, the potential negative consequences of wives' work outweigh the possible positive economic impact.

The solution proposed by some traditional model advocates is the return of the family wage economy, under which a husband alone could earn enough money to support a family, and the exodus of wives from the paid labor force. A few have cited a correlation between increases in women's employment and the current necessity for two-earners in most households. The Family Research Council, for example, has blamed women's work for the earnings power drop among male workers, as well as the emergence of a household consumption rate that cannot be sustained by a single income.

An assertion most often made by religious (notably Christian) denominations, organizations, and individuals is that traditional family roles are sanctioned by God. The creation story, found in Genesis, the first book of the Bible, is given as evidence for this. Following the belief that Eve, the first woman, was created from the rib of Adam, the first man, these advocates validate males' superior position in society. According to the Bible, Eve was made as a companion to Adam, to care for, follow, and support him, and to bear his children. Thus, traditional role supporters, such as Marabel Morgan, claim it is natural and within God's plan for a wife to serve her husband and defer to him on all things. Likewise, God intends for men to be sole providers for their wives and children.

A final contention supported by empirical research is that working women who are also wives or mothers can face negative psychological effects, such as stress and depression, from the burden of multiple roles. Supporting this are a number of studies conducted in the 1980s and 1990s that discovered high stress levels in dual-earner households, especially for wives. This research found a correlation between women's efforts to fulfill work and family duties simultaneously and the high stress they reported experiencing. Upon repeated publication of such findings, the idea of work-family conflict began to appear in the literature and media surrounding family life.

A few variables have been found to add to the anxiety or depression of working wives. The first is if the woman holds traditional values about her role in family and society. When a woman must enter the labor force due to economic necessity when she feels it is wrong to do so, she faces increased guilt and anxiety. She may also resent her husband for his inability to properly provide for her. Likewise, when the husband is a traditionalist, he may react negatively to her working outside the home, thus contributing to her guilt and stress.

Working wives also face added strain when their husbands do not support their work by taking over more home and child care responsibilities. The result is the so-called second-shift phenomenon, first identified by Arlie Hochschild, in which women work their first shift for an outside employer and then begin their second shift upon returning home. Men, in general, are not subject to this dual demand on their time and energy, and often feel they have fulfilled their duties by attending to the first shift only. Many women try to fully accomplish the requirements of both shifts and experience significant stress when they cannot.

Traditionalists, therefore, propose a return to divided family roles to improve the psychological health of married individuals. Overall, some feel the modern egalitarian family model puts avoidable pressure on both women and men in the form of less leisure time, increased parenting conflicts, and an elevation of general stress due to a more harried lifestyle. They claim that by reinstating the separate spheres spouses could better attend to all the tasks and responsibilities of life and would ultimately be more satisfied.

TRADITIONAL FOR WHOM? SOCIAL GROUPS WHO NEVER FIT THE IDEAL

Although many supporters present traditional family roles as applicable to all demographic categories of the past, overall this model was a phenomenon of the Caucasian middle and upper classes. Specifically, the traditional paradigm was one rarely realized by African Americans. African American women, in general, have always worked outside the home, first within the slavery system and later in paid labor. African American men have continuously faced outright and institutionalized racism barring their access to well-compensated employment. As a result their wives' wages have been necessary for family survival. Therefore, African American women often do not share the personal and cultural gender ideologies which cause Caucasian women guilt over dividing energy between work and home. Instead, African American women are more likely to view working as just another integral component of their family role.

Another demographic group whose majority experience has never been that of the father-breadwinner and mother-homemaker is the working class. Working-class women, a large number of whom have been African American, have rarely had the option of staying at home. Far from being averse to hiring females, during the Industrial Revolution factories regularly recruited women from the lower class. Moving from the home production of goods and services to manufacturing jobs, many less fortunate girls, wives, and mothers had to learn to combine home and work responsibilities to take care of themselves and their families. This effort continues for many today as the working class is hit hard by the shifting economy and the rising cost of living.

Finally, homosexual partnerships by the very nature of the relationship have never been traditional. The basis for traditional roles is a legal marriage contract between a man and a woman. Homosexual couples are deficient on both counts of this requirement because they are composed of either two men or two women, and to date the United States as a whole does not allow them to legally marry.

Arguments for the Egalitarian Model

While traditional model advocates argue that rigid family roles are more stable, healthy, and functional, egalitarian model advocates provide evidence contesting these claims. Many refute the assertion that the father-breadwinner mother homemaker-structure is the traditional American way of life. Researchers, such as Stephanie Coontz, say that the 1950s family was more myth than reality, and that the family roles that became popular during that decade were an anomaly within U.S. history. For these supporters, traditionalism is but one of several possible models that individual families might follow, any of which could be stable, healthy, or functional for the particular people involved. However, those on this side of the debate often offer the egalitarian model as the most promising standard, citing many arguments as to why this structure might be better than the others, especially the traditional model.

Refuting the allegation that equal roles and women's paid work create discord and instability for marriages, egalitarian supporters suggest that traditional roles are a source of spousal conflict. They claim that troubles may arise if a husband becomes domineering to the point of abuse, taking his authority as head of the household to the extreme, or if a wife feels her complementary role is not valued by her husband. Traditional family roles can also be problematic if one spouse, usually the wife, feels that they are imposed upon him or her. Studies have shown marriages in which one spouse holds traditional ideals while the other holds egalitarian ideals to be the most subject to conflict, dissatisfaction, and eventual divorce. A possible basis for a homemaking wife's distress is the lack of power in her subordinate position. More equitable roles can reverse wives' feelings of despair by giving them more decision-making authority and marital power, which in turn could lead fewer of them to seek divorce.

Considering traditionalists' claim that women's entrance into the workforce was a major contributor to increasing divorce, egalitarian advocates assert that the reverse correlation is true. Rather than seeing a woman's increased labor participation as a cause of marital unhappiness, egalitarian advocates say that increases in women in the workforce was a symptom of preexisting discord at home. In their view, women used paid work as an opportunity to escape unhappy situations at home or to build economic and social resources they would need to survive after a divorce.

Another argument presented by egalitarian supporters is that more equitable roles bring spouses together, not tear them apart. Egalitarian partners view one another as equals. They place value on sharing decision making, working together in the home, and being involved in the varied aspects of one another's lives outside the marriage. Due to the increased contact these couples have when reaching decisions, working together on tasks, or being together in leisure, they are better able to communicate, have more to talk about, are more empathetic toward one another, and are better able to avoid or overcome dissatisfaction than are traditional couples.

While their opponents feel that women find true satisfaction only in homemaking, egalitarianists say that a woman whose station is the home is subject to great dissatisfaction. Many researchers, including Jessie Bernard, have reported that marriage in general is more beneficial, physically and psychologically, for a husband than for a wife. Some also argue that this disproportion can be exacerbated when the wife stays at home. Although traditionalists feel a woman will find happiness and fulfillment in the home, a number of egalitarian role advocates argue that it can make for a lonely and unrewarding existence. Studies have shown that paid work, especially a career, is often a source of self-esteem, purposefulness, and identity for women. Employment can also be a venue for social connections and mental growth. Those who stay at home are cut off from these employment benefits.

Another issue affecting homemakers' feelings of self-worth is the sense that the roles they fulfill in the home are devalued by their loved ones and society. While a husband may put in 40 to 50 hours weekly in the workplace, a homemaking wife is on the clock 24 hours a day, seven days a week. However, some husbands have a tendency to downplay the demanding nature and importance of their wives' responsibilities because they "get to stay home all day." Feeling that her husband does not value what she does can have negative psychological consequences for a wife. Whether or not they have supportive husbands, homemakers generally face devaluation by society. For several decades homemaking has been portrayed and perceived as nearly effortless. Because caring for the home and children are viewed as natural actions for a woman, homemaking is considered a simple occupation. Thus, the impression continues today that women who stay at home have it easier than those who do not. This can lead homemakers to question their true usefulness and place in society. In sum, some egalitarian claimants feel that being a homemaker severely limits a woman in life goals and accomplishments, denies her a social network, and causes her feelings of loneliness, isolation, devaluation, and distress.

While traditionalists' claim that the strain of multiple roles causes stress and depression in working wives, women in egalitarian relationships experience these states less than do those in traditional arrangements. Many wives who are free to work have reported contentment with doing so. A lot of women are exhilarated by the various sides of themselves they engage when meeting the demands of being an employee, wife, and mother. Large numbers also enjoy the more balanced responsibilities and marital power they gain in egalitarian relationships. Increased marital satisfaction for spouses, especially wives, has been linked to a husband's greater participation in housework and childrearing, actions often found in egalitarian marriages.

In addition to the benefits egalitarian roles may have for women, advocates of this model point to positive psychological results for men as well. Studies find that husbands who are active in the home report greater happiness, less stress, and better sex lives than their traditional counterparts. In addition, for a number of men having a working wife eases the pressure associated with being a provider. Sharing the financial burden gives men a sense of improved well-being and more time to pursue personal interests. Finally, being more involved at home can help fathers have closer relationships with their children and gain more pleasure from the parenting experience.

THE FUTURE OF FAMILY ROLES

Family forms are not static. As long as society evolves, families will change and adapt. At no point in history has every U.S. family been defined by the same expectations, demands, or roles, nor will they ever be. Variation is an undeniable characteristic of the American familial landscape. Despite this, people will likely continue to lobby for the greater functionality of one family model over another, whether traditional, egalitarian, or some structure that has yet to be labeled. However, within the heated debate over whether traditional or egalitarian roles are better, some make the more neutral argument that the most satisfied couples are those who agree on expectations and negotiate roles, be they equal or complementary, with their marriages' best interests at heart.

See also African American Fathers; Cohabitation, Effects on Marriage; Developmental Disability and Marital Stress; Employed Mothers; Housework Allocation; Marital Power; Marital Satisfaction; Marriage Promotion; Preparation for Marriage; Religion and Families; Stay at Home Dads.

Further Reading: Bernard, Jessie. *The Future of Marriage,* 2nd ed. New Haven, CT: Yale University Press, 1982; Carlson, Allan C. "Love is not Enough: Toward the Recovery of a Family Economics." The Family Research Council. http://www.frc.org (accessed September 2007); Coontz, Stephanie. *Marriage, a History: From Obedience to Intimacy or How Love Conquered Marriage.* New York: Penguin Group, 2005; Coontz, Stephanie. *The Way We Never Were: American Families and the Nostalgia Trap.* New York: Basic Books, 2000; Dobson, James C. *Marriage Under Fire: Why We Must Win This Battle.* Colorado Springs, CO: WaterBrook Multnomah Publishing Group, 2007; Hochschild, Arlie. *The Second Shift.* New York: Penguin Books, 2003; Landry, Bart. *Black Working Wives: Pioneers of the American Family Revolution.* Berkeley: University of California Press, 2000; Lindsey, Linda L. *Gender Roles: A Sociological Perspective,* 3rd ed. Upper Saddle River, NJ: Prentice Hall, 1997; Popenoe, David. *Disturbing the Nest: Family Change and Decline in Modern Societies.* Piscataway, NJ: Transaction Publishers, 1988; Schwarz, Pepper. *Peer Marriage.* New York: The Free Press, 1994; Steil, Janice M. *Marital Equality: Its Relationship to the Well-Being of Husbands and Wives.* Thousand Oaks, CA: SAGE Publications, 1997; Warren, Elizabeth. *The Two-Income Trap: Why Middle-Class Parents are Going Broke.* New York: Basic Books, 2004.

Nicole D. Garrett

FATHERHOOD

In current American society mothers often receive both the praise and criticism when it comes to rearing children. They also receive the most research attention, but scholars are beginning to more fully explore the role that fathers play in the lives of their children and in children's growth and development. As a brief history of fatherhood in the United States suggests, there are multiple ways in which fathers can positively and negatively impact the lives of their children. The fatherhood role and definitions of good fathering have changed over historical periods, with dramatic effects on fathers' interactions with their children. Currently, some fathers have embraced an expanded fatherhood role encapsulating more than just physical presence while others have maintained a more traditional fatherhood role as financial provider, an idea with roots in the Victorian era.

It should be noted that there is tremendous variability in the behavior and notions of fatherhood throughout history. Historical resources are often limited to white middle-class sources, so the portrait of changing roles of fatherhood presented here is bound by these same limitations.

SOCIAL HISTORY OF FATHERHOOD ROLES

Colonial Period: Father as Primary Parent

The fatherhood role has changed dramatically over time. Contrary to many current parenting and gender roles, fathers played the primary role in the home in the colonial period. In the seventeenth and eighteenth centuries, fathers were immensely involved in the lives of their children. Fathers were in charge of the moral and religious education of their children, teaching them to read and write if they were literate themselves, and even playing a large role in the courtship and marriage process, including approving or disapproving of a potential match and providing part of the family property for the couple's future. At the time, men were understood as having a greater aptitude for intelligence, reason, and moral character than women. Women were seen as intellectually and morally inferior to men because of the perception that women had weak powers of rational thinking that would make them more easily misled by passions and affections and that women were more likely to indulge and spoil children, so men held the power in domestic affairs.

Children spent a great deal of time with their fathers and often developed closer relationships to them than to their mothers. Because of the perceived moral superiority of men, they were in charge of the moral supervision of their children and monitored their behavior. Work was typically carried out at home, so it was normal for both male and female young children to spend much of the day with their father and often assist him on the farm or in his shop. Personal correspondence letters show that children, especially sons, were closer to their fathers than to their mothers. Sons who were away wrote to the family often through the father, asking only to be "remembered" by their mother. Sons were seen as continuing the father's legacy and good name into the future, so fathers took responsibility for their successes and failures.

Mothers did play a role in parenting. Daughters were more likely than sons to spend longer amounts of time with their mother and develop a closer relationship. Daughters would often do household tasks with their mother, preparing for their future roles as wives and mothers. Mothers were also in charge of taking care of infants and breastfeeding them. However, once they were weaned off of breastfeeding, children were more likely to be looked after by their fathers.

Fathers in the colonial period were largely seen as the primary parent. The moral and intellectual superiority attributed to men made them the best candidates to be a role models and supervisors of the moral conduct of their children. The importance placed upon fathers as parents is demonstrated by the fact that in the event of a marital separation, fathers were typically awarded the overall rights of child custody.

Victorian Era: Separate Spheres Separating Fathers from Family

The nineteenth century experienced rapid change on many levels. One of the most fundamental changes during this period was the increasing separation of work and home. With industrialization, men had to leave the home for income-producing work. Previously, most working activity occurred at home, especially on farms. This transition to work outside the home led to separate spheres of domain for women and men. The female domain became the home while "the world," or everything outside of the home, became the domain of men. Women became the primary parents in charge of rearing children. Not coincidentally, the cultural conception of female character changed as well. Women were no longer seen as morally inferior, and instead were now seen as pure and virtuous, which made them especially qualified to care for the children.

A new emphasis in fatherhood emerged in this new economy—that of *father as provider*. In this period, the main role of fathers was to provide for the economic needs of the family. This was not always easy to do in nineteenth century America because of limited opportunities. Failure to provide for his family affected a man's sense of self-worth. On the other hand, success as a provider could lead to more time spent at work, and limit, to an even greater degree, how much time men could spend with their families. This, of course, affected the relationships of fathers to their children. Contrary to the colonial period, children were more likely to be closer to their mothers than their fathers.

Men became part-time parents, and the fatherhood role emphasizing interaction with children became less prominent. Men had to leave home for long periods of time during the day to work, and thus could only spend limited amounts of time with their children. Fathers would still play with children and interact with them to some extent when they were home, including providing discipline. They would also provide advice and guidance to their sons regarding occupations.

Because of the sacrifices men made to work outside the home and bear the risks associated with the world outside the home, fathers expected respect, affection, and deference from their families when they came home. The world was associated with disorder, temptations, and vice, whereas the home was seen as pure and innocent. Many of the characteristics leading to success in the outside world were too harsh for the purity and sacredness of the home. Men had competing cultural messages regarding the way they were supposed to behave in work settings versus in the home. All of these developments led to a pattern of more limited fathering and an increased domestic role for women. Consequently, nineteenth century child custody patterns increasingly shifted toward entrusting children to their mothers rather than their fathers.

Modern Era: Slowly Shifting Fatherhood Roles

Just as the shift toward more limited fathering was related to changes in the types of employment for men, shifting fatherhood roles in the modern era are related to changes in the rates and types of employment for women. During the Great Depression and World War II, women found themselves in a position in which they were encouraged to work outside of the home. During the Depression, it was difficult to find employment, so the family often welcomed any opportunity for one of their members to work. During World War II, as men left to fight in the war, there was a demand for female labor to fill the positions left vacant when men went overseas. Even married women, often with children under 14 years old, became employed for pay.

The cultural myth is that once the war ended, men went back to their jobs and women went happily back to the home. However, the reality is that not only did most women not leave the workforce, but the rates of female employment actually increased after the end of World War II, which was a period of great prosperity and consumerism. People who had suffered through the difficulties of the Depression now wanted to buy all of the luxuries and material goods they previously could not afford. Despite postwar inflation driving prices up, they wanted to engage in the consumerism of the era. Women could work to help families afford these goods. Men typically were still the main breadwinners of the family, but a single income could no longer suffice if a family wanted to keep up with this consumerism. Soon, women were working for reasons other than just the support of the family's consumer habits. Many found working outside the home fulfilling, and as the number of single mothers rose, many had to work to support their family without the income of a husband. Despite these structural realities, the cultural message continued to suggest that the ideal family would have a breadwinning husband and a homemaker wife and mother who was not employed.

An important characteristic of female workers is that many of these women were married with small children. Many women outsourced child care through family members or child care facilities. Fulfillment of gender roles became less clear as women wanted a larger part in the outside world. It became increasingly difficult for middle-class families to live off of one income, that of the father, and still maintain their standard of living. Consequently, the father as the provider ideal diminished somewhat as mothers played a larger role in providing for the family. Although there is evidence of a second shift, in which women take care of family and household responsibilities after they have put in their time at work, some fathers are slowly increasing their roles as parents. Cultural patterns, although with some vestiges of norms from the Victorian Era, are shifting to recognize and even to accept that women are sharing in the economic productivity of the family and encouraging men to take on more household and parenting responsibilities.

However, increased fathering is still more of a voluntary role than a cultural prescription. Because child care can also be outsourced to daycare facilities, nannies, and the like, fathers do not necessarily experience the same pressure to provide more child care with the employment of their wives as mothers did in the Victorian Era when their husbands left the home to work. There is a subset of fathers who have wholeheartedly embraced an expanding role of fatherhood. They spend more time with their children and are more involved in their daily activities, such as helping with homework, time spent in leisure together, going shopping together, going to religious services or church-related events together, and talking about achievements and problems with each other. These fathers often have more egalitarian gender roles and believe in sharing the responsibilities of children, household, and finances with their wives. On the other hand, with the increasing incidence of divorce and single parenthood, there has also been an increasing trend of absent fathers. These fathers may be absent from both the home as well as from involvement in the lives of their children. However, the men's liberation movement and the Fatherhood Foundation encourage men to shed the oppressive cultural attitudes that prohibit them from becoming good fathers. They provide goals and models for fatherhood today.

FATHER ABSENCE AND ITS EFFECTS

These historical trends summarized above have influenced the roles that fathers play in their children's lives today. There is both an increasing trend of a subset of fathers playing larger roles in the lives of their children and in the household and another increasing trend of a subset of men who are absent fathers. With increasing divorce and nonmarital childbirth in recent decades, as well as child custody typically being awarded to mothers, fathers are increasingly absent from the home. It may become more difficult for fathers who do not reside in the same household as their children to play a larger role in their children's lives on a daily basis because they may have to contend with financial, distance, and time issues when trying to visit their children.

Father absence, typically measured in terms of fathers not residing in the same household as the child, has a myriad of negative consequences for children. Children with absent fathers tend to have lower academic achievement, to be held back a grade, and to be suspended from school. In terms of higher education, they are more likely to drop out of high school, less likely to attend college, and more likely to drop out if they do attend college. There are also numerous social consequences for children with absent fathers. They are more likely to experience problems such as insecurity, immaturity, and disobedience. Children without fathers residing in the household are more likely to run away from home and to get into trouble with the police. Children with absent fathers also have higher rates of early sexual activity and teenage pregnancy, and they are more likely to lack steady employment. Clearly, having an absent father can lead to negative ramifications affecting the life chances of children in many ways.

There are, of course, financial ramifications for children with absent fathers as well. Although some fathers pay adequate child support, a large subset of fathers pay nothing or very little. This phenomenon of many fathers not providing much money for child support, combined with lower overall earnings of women in the labor market compared with men, produces difficult situations for single mothers trying to support their children, which can affect the life chances of children in many ways. Single-mother households are more likely to be living in poverty than two-parent households, which often leads children to attend schools with fewer resources. Lack of child support payments have been linked to lower grades for children and increased behavior problems at school. Having an absent father reduces the chances of children going to college, which has many ramifications on future earnings. In short, the absence of fathers from the household can lead to many negative psychological and financial consequences, which can reduce the life chances of children.

FATHER PRESENCE AS A MORE MEANINGFUL MEASURE

The primary measure of a father's contribution to the lives of his children has often been whether he financially provided for them and lived in the same residence with them and their mother. Father *residence* has often become synonymous with father *presence*. The assumption in most research studies of fatherhood has been that fathers who live with their children are always better fathers than those who reside apart from their children. However, this assumption may not necessarily reflect reality. Noted fatherhood researcher Michael E. Lamb suggests that a broader and more inclusive conception of fatherhood will provide greater insight into the fatherhood role.

Researchers are beginning to define father presence in more meaningful terms than residence in the same household as his children. It is a reasonable scenario that a father may be present in the household, but he may not be present to his children. He could be emotionally unavailable and uninvolved, which can have devastating effects on children. It is also a reasonable scenario that children may maintain a close relationship with a father who is present in their lives despite not being present in their household. Some nonresident fathers are still able to spend a large amount of time with their children. Fathers may be an integral and influential part of a child's life without having to live with that child. Thus, an important development in research on the effects of father presence on children is the use of more meaningful measures of father presence than merely residence in the household.

There have been a number of ways researchers have begun to redefine father presence beyond residence in the household. Some studies have examined father presence in terms of father involvement such as spending time with children, helping with everyday activities such as homework, supervision or monitoring of the children's behavior, as well as satisfaction with children's relationships with their fathers and in terms of closeness to fathers. Adolescents who are more satisfied with their relationship with their fathers are likely to have fewer symptoms of depression, greater well-being, and higher self-esteem. Fatherhood researcher Paul Amato found that closeness to the father is related to children's better academic performance and fewer externalizing and internalizing problem behaviors.

In addition to measuring father presence in more meaningful ways, it is also important to take into account whether or not fathers reside with their children. If we take, for example, the more meaningful measure of closeness to the father as defining father presence, and it is still significant after taking into account father nonresidence, then that shows that these new ways of measuring father presence may be more important for children's outcomes than father nonresidence. This has been done in a recent study that found that children who are closer to their fathers engage in significantly fewer delinquent activities than those who are not as close to their fathers, even after controlling for whether or not the father resided in the household with his children. Thus, children who were still close to their nonresident fathers were better off in terms of committing fewer delinquent behaviors, which can have a positive impact on their life chances. This phenomenon demonstrates the importance of defining father presence in more meaningful terms than merely father-child residence.

CONCLUSION

Finally, when thinking about fathering, we need to remember that fathers learn their role from their culture, including their own fathers. The changing roles of fathers over time have lead to much debate about the way to perform the role of father today. Noted fatherhood researcher, Frank Furstenberg, has suggested that fathers are viewed in two opposing ways, as either "good dads" or "bad dads." He identifies the growing divergence of the behaviors of fathers who are present in their children's lives and those who are absent (not merely nonresident). Due to the positive impact that present fathers can have on the lives of their children, it is important for more fathers to embrace the expanded fatherhood role that fosters the father-child relationship and can have enormous effects on the life chances of children.

See also African American Fathers; Deadbeat Parents; Marriage Promotion; Parenting Styles; Stay at Home Dads.

Further Reading: Coltrane, Scott. *Family Man: Fatherhood, Housework, and Gender Equity.* New York: Oxford University Press, 1996; Demos, John. *Past, Present, and Personal: The Family and the Life Course of American History.* New York: Oxford University Press, 1986; Fatherhood Foundation. http://www.fathersonline.org/; Furstenberg, Frank. "Good Dads—Bad Dads: Two Faces of Fatherhood." In *The Changing American Family and Public Policy,* ed. Andrew J. Cherlin. Washington, D.C.: Urban Institute Press, 1988; Marsiglio, William, Paul Amato, Randal D. Day, and Michael E. Lamb. "Scholarship on Fatherhood in the 1990s and Beyond." *Journal of Marriage and the Family* 62, no. 4 (2000): 1173–1191; United States Department of Health and Human Services. "Fatherhood Reports." http://aspe.os.dhhs.gov/_/topic/subtopic.cfm?subtopic=376; Whyte, Paul. "An Introduction to Men's Liberation." http://www.gelworks.com.au/MENDOCUM.NSF/504ca249c786e20f85256284006da7ab/befd776247d76f99ca2566430043201b!OpenDocument.

Patricia A. Thomas

FICTIVE KIN

Throughout history the kinship group has been necessary for survival. Kinship is defined as a form of social organization that ties individuals to others by marriage or descent. In tribal societies the tribal elders set laws and the kinship group defended themselves from outsiders, provided order, helped the less fortunate, and recruited outside members through marriage. Today, the functions of the kinship group have been replaced by the state that makes the laws, protects its members from enemies, and provides for the poor. Fictive kin extends the functions of the kinship group to describe a relationship that consists of non-relatives, has many characteristics of kin relationships, and is based on religious rituals or close friendship ties. Other terms for fictive kin include pseudo-kin, quasi-kin, or social families.

FICTIVE KIN THROUGH HISTORY

Dating back to the seventeenth and eighteenth centuries in Northwest Europe, colonial America, and early twentieth century America unrelated nonblood relatives can be found living together. In Northwest Europe, particularly England, as far back as perhaps the fifteenth century servants or apprentices lived in the homes of persons to whom they were not related. This pattern continued in Colonial America. In Northwest Europe and Colonial America these servants or apprentices were considered a part of the household, lived as members of the family, and even participated in meals. Social class or money was not a limitation for having servants in the household or sending children to work in another household. A peasant would send out his own children to work as a servant and bring in other young men and women to work the land or as an apprentice with craftsman such as a butcher, baker, mason, or other skilled tradesman. One of the arguments for why families of the time were so large is that they expected to cede at least some of their children to others to care for because apprenticeships beginning by the age of 10 were not unheard of.

Unrelated individuals can be found living together in the urbanizing America of the late 1800s and early 1900s, though the apprentice system had largely dissolved by this time. As America urbanized, become more industrial, and jobs moved from the small towns and farms to the growing cities, unmarried young adults moved to the new urban areas. During this time wages were low, the United States was experiencing an influx of immigrants creating a housing shortage and driving up the cost of rent. Furthermore, modern convenience technologies such as refrigerators, microwaves, and inexpensive fast food did not exist and food preparation was a time-consuming process. The expense of setting up a household and the time it took to complete chores made establishing a household as a young adult an expensive if not impossible undertaking. In order to compensate for the economic shortfalls, most young adults became either a boarder or lodger in someone's home. A boarder is someone who stays in a nonrelative's home and eats food (room and board), and a lodger is someone who only rents a room and meets other daily needs elsewhere. Other options included boarding houses, where large numbers of young people would pay for room and board in the same physical space. The family that took in these young people benefited because the money contributed by the boarder replaced the income that was lost when a child moved out of the home.

FICTIVE KIN CROSS-CULTURALLY

In addition to the historical presence of fictive kin relationships, fictive kin relationships can be found worldwide. Fictive kin relationships can be found in Spanish-speaking countries, Asia, Africa, and the Caribbean. Anthropologists completed the first study on nonblood relationships based on the Catholic ritual of baptism. The practice, known as *compadrazgo*, consists of a godparent being appointed to oversee the well-being of the child. The godparent is appointed at baptism and is to instruct the child in spiritual matters, also providing material and emotional support. *Compadrazgo* exists throughout Latin America, is supported by Catholic doctrine and ritual, and is required under Canon Law. Anthropologists have documented customs similar to *compadrazgo* in Spain, eastern Turkey, Hungary, Yugoslavia, Greece, Sri Lanka, and Belgium.

Not all fictive kin relationships are tied to religious traditions. *Ddharmaatmyor* of rural Bangladesh have a kinship structure that ties together diverse groups. Muslims may have fictive kin ties to Hindus, or an upper-class individual may develop a relationship with a member of the lower class. The ties are both among and between these groups. The fictive kin relationships may include godmother, godfather, godbrother, godsister, or friend and offer social and economic advantages. A couple without children may have a godchild or a poor family may establish a fictive kin relationship with a wealthier family who will exchange financial support for taking care of them in their old age. There are endless forms and ways fictive kin relationships are organized, but many of the fictive kin relationships replace the functions of the family, such as providing spiritual growth, social control, financial, and social support.

THE LANGUAGE OF FICTIVE KIN RELATIONSHIPS

Fictive kin relationships have a historical and cross-cultural significance, and evidence of the importance of these relationships can be found in language. Language showing familiarity without legal and biological ties can be found among African Americans, Hispanic Americans, European Americans, Japanese Americans, Haitian immigrants, and gays and lesbians. The use of family terms for nonfamily members is a verbal way of showing closeness, and reinforces to the individuals involved and others the significance of the relationship. A woman using the term "sis" to address another woman does so in order to signify an additional level of closeness.

African Americans, especially poor African Americans, rely heavily on aid from family members and extended friendship networks. The friendship networks are built, reinforced, and held together through the black church. A set of terms has developed that represents these extended networks. The terms used by African Americans include "play mother, sister, brother," and so on, "like a second mother," "godmother," or "godfather," "church mother, aunt, or uncle," or "going for brothers." These terms signify to the participants and observers of such relationships that the relationship has family-like feelings and functions, even if the participants are not linked by traditional family means.

Hispanic Americans have a similar group of terms including "*compadrazgo*," "*la familia*," "*hijos de crianza*," "*comadre*" and "*copadre*" while European Americans use "godparent," "adopted daughter," "aunt," "sister," "uncle," and so forth. Gay families use the term "quasi-kin," the Japanese use "brother by religion" or *oyabun-kobun,* and Yoruba and Haitian immigrants use *kouzin.*

THE FUTURE OF FICTIVE KIN RELATIONSHIPS

One battleground for the study of fictive kin relationships is whether these types of kin relationships will increase or decline in importance. Fictive kin relationships have served many purposes and can be found in a number of historical time periods, in different countries, and in a variety of cultural and ethnic groups. For example, in one of the most extensive studies of modern fictive kin relationships, Carol Stack reported that these relationships were crucial in providing emotional and financial support for inner-city black women. Of particular importance were the child care and financial support functions that older women provided to younger single women with children.

What about the future role that fictive kin are likely to play in the lives of families? Will fictive kin become less or more important as society changes? In traditional communities kinship groups regulated marriage, fulfilled religious and ceremonial functions, and satisfied social and economic needs. As societies move to become more modern, secular, and urban, the family may no longer be able to meet these needs. It is well documented that more competing forces and alternative ideas are present in modern society compared to premodern society. According to a study of 21 rural Mexican communities, fictive kin relationships played the biggest roll in the organization of the communities that were in the transition to modernization. One future possibility is that fictive kin relationships will continue to play a crucial roll in those communities that are transitioning to a more modern state. Once modernization occurs, however, the family may be replaced by domestic groups, governmental agencies, and occupational and social associations. In this scenario fictive kin relationships would become less important over time as formal institutions more directly govern the lives of individuals.

The opposing argument suggests that social change may increase the need for fictive kin. The American family has changed dramatically over the last 50 years. Among the most notable changes is increasing ethnic diversity that exposes all of society to different cultural norms and family organizations that they may wish to adopt. Demographic changes have a strong potential to necessitate fictive kin arrangements. As declines in fertility and mortality rates continue, the result is people have smaller families and live longer. With more generations alive at one time, this results in the family tree becoming more vertical, thus sibling type relationships might be sought outside of the biological family.

Among the factors that have been proposed for the present rates of social family formation in the United States is high geographic mobility. With more persons moving away from their families of orientation for work or educational opportunities, family members are increasingly dispersed over a wide distance and have less physical contact and ability to help with crises that arise. As rates of marriage remain low, one should remember that people who are single, divorced, or never married are less likely to maintain family relationships, but often form very close and supportive friendships.

Divorce and remarriage create complex living arrangements where there are few standards for postdivorce familial ties. As divorce rates remain historically high, questions over dissolved kinship become important. While no longer ones in-laws, the affective and practical bond may remain between former partners' families. In remarriage, children in particular may adopt the parents of their new step-parent as grandparents, even using the familial language to classify the relationship.

All of the family change indicated above has created complex living arrangements with few rules and norms. With all of these changes, alternative family forms will continue to be present, will increase in importance, and take the place of the traditional family. Clearly families of choice have come to fulfill some of the myriad functions that biological families have played over time.

See also Biological Privilege; Common Law Marriage; Domestic Partnerships; International Adoption; Nonmarital Cohabitation; Pet Death and the Family; Plural Marriage; Transracial Adoption.

Further Reading: Demos, John. *A Little Commonwealth.* New York: Oxford University Press, 1970; Ebaugh, Helen Rose, and Mary Curry. "Fictive Kin as Social Capital in New Immigrant Communities." *Sociological Perspectives* 43 (2000): 189–209; Hajnal, John. "Two Kinds of Preindustrial Household Formation System." *Population and Development Review* 8 (1982): 449–494; Ibsen, Charles, and Patricia Klobus. "Fictive Kin Term Use and Social Relationships: Alternative Interpretations." *Journal of Marriage and Family* 34 (1972): 615–620; Johnson, Colleen. "Perspectives on American Kinship in the Later 1990s." *Journal of Marriage and Family* 62 (2000): 623–639; Liebow, Elliot. *Tally's Corner.* Boston: Brown and Company, 1967; Stack, Carol B. *All Our Kin: Strategies for Survival in a Black Community.* New York: Harper and Row, 1974.

Christy Haines Flatt

FOSTER CARE

Defining foster care is a challenge in itself. The most often stated definition for foster care is "care given outside a child's natural home for more than 24 hours when the child's home is not available to him or her excluding children at camps, in hospitals, or on weekend visits" (Stone 1970). This definition implies that the parents cannot provide adequate care for some serious reason. The essential element of foster care is childrearing responsibility shared with the child welfare agency, the original parents, as well as the foster parents, the child care staff, and social workers. Foster care also has an expectation that it is of a limited duration; it is not a permanent method of childrearing but a temporary solution to a crisis in the home.

A simpler definition for foster care is simply "a generic term for children living in out-of-home care" (Curtis, Dale, and Kendall 1997). Historically, foster care was referred to as boarding out, implying that foster parents were almost always nonrelatives. These persons were reimbursed the expenses of caring for dependent children residing in their household on the assumption that the arrangement was a temporary one. The four basic types of foster care in the United States are: family (nonrelative) foster care, kinship (relative) care, therapeutic foster care, and residential group care.

A thorough examination of the child welfare system, or foster care, in America finds that problems in foster care are similar to the issues that need to be addressed in the larger society as well. These issues include race, class, gender, government funding or lack thereof, acceptance of people with mental and physical disabilities, among other issues.

The foster care system is imperfect because it has to deal with a myriad of complex social problems. When one is dealing with imperfection, it would be impossible to create a perfect system. Our foster care system works with the worst aspects of social problems within our society. As a result, a social worker's job is not easy. A child welfare worker, during the course of a typical workday, could have to remove a child from a family that has physically, emotionally, or sexually abused the child, and then turn around and go to another house and attempt to find a solution for a child who has severe physical or emotional disabilities. Social workers are constrained by laws that limit what they can do. While they are thought to be the last line of defense in the care of a lost child, they rarely have adequate resources and community support to protect children who are in the direst situations.

Roughly 500,000 children are in foster care in America. African American children make up two-thirds of the foster care population and stay in foster care longer than the average child. About 30 percent of children in foster care have emotional, behavioral or developmental problems and the average age of a child in foster care is 10.1 years old.

The number of children in out-of-home care is enormous. According to the Child Welfare League of America (CWLA), in 2006 the national mean per state was 9,993 and the national median was 6,803. California had 92,344 children in foster care, the largest total in any state. Wyoming had the fewest children in foster care with 1,209.

Any attempt for a state to create a better foster care environment must first recognize the number of the children in foster care and then budget accordingly for an adequate caseload per social worker. The Child Welfare League of America has set up recommended caseload standards for each state to follow. The CWLA recommends that one social worker should have at most 12 to 15 children that are in foster family care. The CWLA also recommends one supervisor for every 5 social workers. Additionally, there are guidelines suggesting that more than 12 initial assessments or investigations per month would be too much for one social worker.

Many states have strains on their budgets, which cause these recommendations to go unfulfilled. Instead the state follows the guidelines that they have already established, which are likely to be less stringent than the CWLA recommendations. There is very little uniformity in foster care among the states. Our system of federalism as well as budgetary constraints in each state strain the uniformity in the child welfare process; therefore varying standards of care among each state are bound to occur. In a way, each state is its own laboratory of experiments working to design a child welfare system that is responsive to each child within the budget limitations that each state has to work with.

BACKGROUND

English colonists arriving in the United States brought the Poor Law System with them. Long after the American Revolution, the well-established tradition continued to inform poverty practices. During the beginning of the nineteenth century, adults and children were cared for with very little or no distinction. Almshouses were gaining in popularity for the care of both the children and the elderly in large cities. Almshouses were privately funded (usually through churches) houses that cared primarily for the poor and destitute.

Agencies that cared for destitute children tended to spring up from two sources. The first of these was from public bodies that would act as representatives for the community as a whole. The second was from private donations and was exercised by benevolent individuals or associations. In 1853 Charles Loring Brace began the free foster home movement. Brace was concerned at the large numbers of homeless children in the streets and wanted to find families for them in the United States. He started advertising all across the country and would send children in groups of 20 to 40 in trains to their new destinations. Reverend Brace's work lead to the creation of the Children's Aid Society, as well as provided a framework for the establishment of a permanent foster care system in the United States.

In 1868 Massachusetts became the first state to pay for children to board in private family homes. In 1885 Pennsylvania became the first state in the United States to pass a licensing law. This law made it a misdemeanor for a couple to care for two or more unrelated children unless they were licensed to do so by the state. In 1910 Henry Chapin circulated statistics showing that orphanages sickened and killed large numbers of children. It was Chapin's belief that a poor home is better than a good institution. However, it wasn't until 1950 that the number of children in foster care outnumbered the number of children in institutions. In 1935 Aid to Dependent Children (ADC), which later became Aid to Families with Dependent Children (AFDC) was established through the Social Security Act of 1935. What AFDC and other antipoverty programs did was give financially struggling families an alternative to placing their children in institutions or losing them forever. The program was later expanded in the 1960s and with that expansion federal funding for foster care was added.

While foster care has come a long way in the United States, there are still a host of problems that are present within the current system. Many of these problems are still vestiges of our old child welfare system. However, there are also new problems that social workers are just now beginning to see and researchers are just now beginning to understand. With all these problems there will still be a long history that will be written about foster care.

FOSTER CARE VALUES

Foster care can be based on eight values. The first five values are described below. Maternal deprivation in the early years of life has an adverse effect on personality development, and later difficulties of the individual can be traced to a breakdown in this early relationship. This value shows the focus on child development at an early age and the need of social workers to become more engaged early with children from troubled homes.

The second value maintains that the parent-child relationship is of vital importance; all efforts must be made to restore it. No child should be deprived of his natural parents for economic reasons alone. If, for some extreme reason, a child's own parents cannot take care of him or her, another family is the best place for him or her. The child's own extended family is preferable to complete strangers.

The fourth and fifth values speak to the role of the foster parents in the foster care process. The fourth value maintains that the rights and interests of the child take priority over those of the parents in any plans affecting him or her. Natural parents and foster parents are to be understood as individuals with their own needs, but these needs cannot be permitted to affect the future of the child. If a child cannot be returned to his or her own family, whatever the reasons, the goal is to afford the child the needed security and feeling of belonging within the foster home by making arrangements permanent, preferably through legal adoption.

In addition to these five values some scholars acknowledge three other values for foster care. One value maintains that there should be a responsibility assumed by every community for seeing that a continuum of care and service is provided for children who must live outside their homes. No child should be lost because referrals are not made or adequate services are not available. Another value sets the goal for all children at minimal reasonable parenting, and this may not necessarily be tied to middle-class childrearing patterns. The final value is that criteria for evaluating foster parents should focus on their parenting abilities and their capacity to share these abilities with parents and agencies.

These values have helped to shape laws in the states and helped to define ways in dealing in a foster care relationship. However, these values are not without debate. For example, how can one define what is in the best interests of the child? Is the best interest of the child going back to his natural parents? What if there is a history of abuse and domestic violence? These are all questions that have no easy answers. While one may be able to say that these values, in an ideal situation, may be good values, as was mentioned earlier, the foster care situation is not an ideal situation.

Another thing to consider about these values is that different decision makers may interpret these values differently. For example, what constitutes an extreme reason for taking a child away from his natural parents? What one person views as an extreme reason may be different than what another person views as an extreme reason. Another example would be what constitutes good parenting? Is spanking good parenting? Some may consider it to be so, while others may not. While the values may be perfectly reasonable, the interpretation of those values can turn into something that may be unreasonable.

THE FOSTER FAMILY

Research has indicated that "children who are placed in group homes are more likely to experience emotional disturbance and behavioral problems than those who are placed with families" (Perry 2006). According to Perry this is because the foster family will provide a less disruptive environment for a youth than a group home because a family environment is more structured to his or her normal life. Most social workers want to put children in the least disruptive environment possible in order for them to either keep or regain stability in their life.

So how can a foster family do this? There are five things that a foster family must do in order to be successful, which are communication, integration, flexibility, compassion, and patience. How a child reacts to a new environment will be based on the amount of success the parents, social workers, educational administrators, and other members of the community react to the child based on these five factors.

It is important that before the child even reaches the foster family's home that there is an open line of communication between all the people involved in the child's life. This includes the foster parents, the child's caseworker, the school administrators of where the child is moving, and the relatives of the child if possible. The caseworker is the person who needs to start the communication line but it is the responsibility of everybody involved, and especially the foster parents, to maintain that communication line through the child's stay with their family.

Successful communication leads to the next step, which is successful integration. This integration process can take several forms based on the child's background and emotional experiences. One also has to be careful in this process because if there is a possibility, as is in most cases, that the child will go back to a natural parent then the integration must be flexible to make sure that the child can re-establish those ties to the natural parents. What a successful foster family must do is to treat the foster child as if he or she was a member of their immediate family. They must realize, however, that this child's needs may be different than their own children's (if they have children), so the structure the foster child lives under could possibly be different than the structure their natural child lives under. This also needs to be explained to the natural children or other foster children in the household before the foster child comes to live with them.

Once they arrive and are put in school the communication line must hold firm to make sure that the teachers understand the child's problems and the best ways to address those problems. Parents and teachers need to make sure that they have adequate records from the child's past schools and they need to speak regularly to see how the child is integrating into the classroom, such as with making friends, doing schoolwork, and getting involved in extracurricular activities. The administrators at the school also need to be made aware of any special medications or learning disabilities the child has in order to set acceptable guidelines for the child to follow and create the best learning environment possible.

A foster family has to be flexible. Children coming into their care will come with a wide range of social problems. These parents must be flexible enough to know that you cannot deal with a child who has been sexually abused in the same way you deal with a child who has lost both of his or her parents in a car accident. The school system also must be flexible enough to work with the parents and social workers in order to make the child's transition as smooth as possible.

The last two factors are interrelated: compassion and patience. If a foster family has compassion they can begin to understand the problems the child is facing and work to find him the help he needs. However, they must also be patient and realize that there are going to be bumps in the road. The process for a child whose social network has been severely disrupted is not short but a journey that the family will have to take with him or her throughout the child's entire stay.

AGING OUT

Aging out refers to children who reach adulthood while in the foster care system. Each year there are 20,000 children that age out of the foster care program, and many of these children are still in need of support or services. Imagine a child who has just turned 18 and has just been told to go out in the world with little to no social network. Imagining this leads a person to wonder not how a child learns to survive but how a child who is aged out is able to maintain his or her mental sanity. The unfortunate fact is that many of these children have a hard time coping with going out in the world without a social network. Only two percent of children who have aged out of foster care obtain a four-year college degree. Thirty percent of these children are without adequate health care and 25 percent of these children have been homeless at some point in their life (Child Welfare League of America 2007).

These numbers for youths transitioning out of foster care are dramatic. It also causes one to pause and to ask, what are the options? A system that can keep the children in foster homes a few more years in order to ease into the transition away from the foster care system would probably be one avenue that needs to be examined. Also, scholarships for children in foster care for college or job training may be another area that might be beneficial in assisting the transition from foster care to adult hood. Encouraging adoption may be another step in helping children to find a permanent family.

However, while the ideas above may ameliorate a crisis, it still does not get to the root of the social problems that are causing children to get placed in foster care. There needs to be an increased emphasis not only on what happens to children after they get out of foster care, but also preventing them from getting into foster care. Foster care is the intersection where all social problems meet and in order to stop children from entering the system society has to confront the social and structural problems within the country that created this intersection.

FUTURE PROSPECTS

The future of foster care is complex because it is not a uniform system. Each state has its own idea about how the system should be working. While there are certain values that all foster care agencies try to maintain, who interprets those values is a big issue and each state and even each judge can vary on those interpretations. Also, the state and federal funding that is devoted to foster care is unstable and prone to budget cuts. The future of foster care is also going to be based on how well society handles other social problems. If society confronts the challenges of poverty, homelessness, health care, and so forth, then the future of foster care may be optimistic. However, if society does not confront these challenges then the future may not be as bright.

So what can we predict about the future of foster care in the United States? We know already that there is a strong correlation between race, poverty, and entry into the foster care system. With the growing ranks of minorities in the United States, especially minorities from Central and South America, it could be possible that minorities will come to dominate the ranks of children in foster care even more than they do presently.

Immigration also brings about a whole host of questions about the legal status of immigrants in the U.S. How the states handle the children of immigrants could often depend on citizenship status. This classification of children who may be undocumented will probably lead to a host of other issues within the foster care realm. Not least among the issues could be a language barrier between the child and available foster families.

No discussion about foster care can be complete without discussing the Personal Responsibility and Workforce Opportunity Reconciliation Act of 1996 (PRWORA) also called welfare reform. The goals of welfare reform were to promote two parent families and work among single mothers. However, an unintended consequence of this reform may have been an increase in the children who enter foster care. In 1984, 2.5 percent of children under the age of 18 lived in families where neither parent was present. There was an almost 60 percent increase from 1984 to 1998 where 4.2 percent of children lived in families where neither parent was present. While only a portion of this increase can be attributed to the federal welfare reform that was passed in 1996, there were many states that experimented with various elements of welfare reform beforehand. The increase in children in foster care from various welfare reform initiatives could lead to a decline in child well-being within the country, especially among poor families.

The challenges facing social workers all across the country are not going to get any easier. In order for foster care to improve, the system has to be more flexible, but at the same time more structured, focused on prevention, address aging out, and less prone to budget instability at the federal and state levels. Policy makers are going to have to become aware of the dilemmas that social workers face on an everyday basis and create laws accordingly. Foster care is a complicated system and one that will have huge social implications for children well into the twenty-first century.

See also Biological Privilege; Child Abuse; Child Support and Parental Responsibility; Gay Parent Adoption; Grandparents as Caregivers; Juvenile Delinquency; Poverty and Public Assistance.

Further Reading: Administration for Children and Families. 2007. "Trends in Foster Care and Adoption." http://www.acf.hhs.gov/programs/cb/stats_research/afcars/trends.htm; Adoption History Project. 2007. "Timeline of Adoption History." Eugene Oregon, University of Oregon. http://www.uoregon.edu/~adoption/timeline.html; American Academy of Child and Adolescent Psychiatry. "Facts for Families: Foster Care." http://www.

aacap.org/cs/root/facts_for_families/foster_care; Bernstein, Nina. *The Lost Children of Wilder: The Epic Struggle to Change Foster Care.* New York: Vintage Books, 2001; Brown A. W., and B. Bailey-Etta. "An out of Home Care System in Crisis: Implications for African-American Children in the Foster Care System." *Child Welfare* 76 (1997): 65–83; Children's Defense Fund. http://childrensdefense.org; Child Welfare Information Gateway. http://childwelfare.org; Child Welfare League of America. http://cwla.org; Child Welfare League of America. *CWLA Standards of Excellence for Family Foster Care,* Washington D.C., 1995; Child Welfare League of America. *CWLA Standards of Excellence for Services for Abused or Neglected Children and Their Families.* Washington D.C., 1999; Child Welfare League of America. *Special Tabulation of the Adoption and Foster Care Analysis Reporting System.* Washington D.C., 2006. http://ndas.cwla.org/data_stats/access/predefined/Report.asp?PageMode=1&%20ReportID=379&%20GUID={4859F5C2-DD74-4AF0-AD55-8360140347E3}#Table; Child Welfare League of America. *Quick Facts about Foster Care.* Washington D.C., 2007. http://www.cwla.org/programs/fostercare/factsheet.htm; Courtney, M. E., R. P. Barth, J. D. Berrick, D. Brooks, B. Needell, and L. Park. "Race and Child Welfare Services: Past research and future directions." *Child Welfare* 76 (1996): 99–137; Curtis, Patrick A., G. Dale, and J. Kendall. *The Foster Care Crisis Translating Research into Policy Practice* Lincoln, NE: University of Nebraska Press, 1997; Folks, Homer. *The Care of Destitute, Neglected, and Delinquent Children.* London: Macmillan Company, 1978; Foster Care Month. http://fostercaremonth.org; George, R. M., F. H. Wulczyn, and A. W. Harden. *Foster Care Dynamics 1983–1993: California, Illinois, Michigan.* Chicago: University of Chicago Press 1995; Jagannathan, R., M. Camasso, and S. McLanahan. "Welfare Reform and Child Fostering: Pinpointing Affected Child Populations." *Social Science Quarterly* 86 (2005): 1081–1103; Lindsey, D. *The Welfare of Children.* New York: Oxford University Press, 1994; Meisels, Joseph, and Martin Loeb, "Foster Care and Adoption: Unanswered Questions About Foster Care" *The Social Service Review* 30, no. 3 (1956): 239–246; National Association of Former Foster Care Children of America. http://www.naffcca.org; National Foster Parent Association. http://www.nfpainc.org; National Foster Parent Association. *History of Foster Care in the United States.* Washington D.C., 2007. http://www.nfpainc.org/content/index.asp?page=67&nmenu=3; Perry, Brea. "Understanding Social Network Disruption: The Case for Youth in Foster Care." *Social Problems* 53, no. 3 (2006): 371–391; Pew Commission on Children in Foster Care. http://pewfostercare.org; Stone, Helen D. *Foster Care in Question: A National Reassessment By Twenty-One Experts.* New York: Child Welfare League of America Inc., 1970.

Derrick Shapley

G

GAY PARENT ADOPTION

Gay parent adoption or same-sex adoption refers to the adoption of children by individuals who prefer romantic partners of the same sex—gays and lesbians. Same-sex adoption is portrayed by the media as being a potentially good thing but with potentially detrimental side-effects, most notably for the adopted children themselves. This type of adoption is generally made to look as if it could be done but should not be for the sake of the children involved. With groups such as the religious Right, fundamentalist Christian denominations, and private religiously-affiliated adoption agencies backing the opposition to adoption by gays and lesbians, and the American Civil Liberties Union, the Human Rights Campaign, and various LGBT (lesbian gay bisexual transgender)-friendly groups of the liberal Left making up the proponents, the battle over same-sex adoption is well-defined and entrenched in a deep and long-standing debate. That battle begins with the media and its portrayal of gay parent adoptions versus the agencies and advocacy groups and their perspective on placing children in the homes and care of homosexual individuals.

BACKGROUND

Adoption remained for a long time a rather homogeneous action, with the placement of children in the homes of middle-class, married couples. Over the course of the last three decades, adoption went through a metamorphic change, from being merely a source for married, middle-class couples to create families to being a pathway for a number of diverse and sometimes marginal populations to establish families of their own. According to the Adoption and Foster Care

Analysis and Reporting System, 127,000 children in the public child welfare system were waiting to be adopted in late 1999. As of 1999, the average age of children awaiting placement in adoptive homes was between 7 and 8 years of age. Many of these children who were awaiting adoption spent more than 36 consecutive months in foster care. That same year, only 46,000 children were adopted from public welfare agencies. Those that were adopted ranged in age from infants to teenagers and differed in race from Latino to Caucasian to African American. The adoptive parents were also diverse: 31 percent were single women, 2 percent were single men, and 1 percent were unmarried couples. Among these adoptive parents was also a select group of gay and lesbian individuals and partners. In the early 1990s the term gayby boom (like baby boom) was coined to recognize the increasing visibility of gay and lesbian partners having and adopting children.

According to Ada White, the Child Welfare League of America (CWLA) director of Adoption Services, there are many agencies that do make placements with gay or lesbian parents, but they do not necessarily talk about these adopters. Agencies are not specifically tracking such adoptions and don't intend to track them. Consequently, the practice of adoption with many of these agencies is that they may place these children in homosexual homes but are not willing to make it public knowledge that they are doing so. The adoption of children by homosexual parents is often done so that others' knowledge of its occurrence remains minimal. The practices of adoption vary greatly from state to state and region to region and even from judge to judge. The Human Rights Campaign (HRC), the nation's largest gay and lesbian advocacy organization, has conducted research to determine that 21 states and the District of Columbia allow gay adoption. This wouldn't be the case if the religious Right had its way. It is suggested that the ability for gay and lesbian individuals to adopt would become much more limited, with a minimal number of states being welcoming of gay adoption.

LAWS

New Jersey was the first state to specify that sexual orientation and marital status could not be used against couples seeking to adopt. New Jersey also allows second-parent adoption, a legal procedure in which a coparent can adopt the biological or adopted child of his or her partner. New York soon followed, granting second-parent adoptions statewide and forbidding discrimination in adoption proceedings. California joined the party by enacting new domestic partnership legislation that legalized second-parent adoptions. On the opposite end of the spectrum, there are a number of states that exclude gays and lesbians from adopting either as primary or as secondary adoptive parents. Florida stands out among the states in that gay adoption has been banned since 1977. Utah prohibits adoption by any unmarried couple or individual, regardless of sexual orientation. While Mississippi does not actually ban gay and lesbian individuals from adoption, same-sex couples are absolutely prohibited from adopting. The laws regarding same-sex adoption within most states aren't even actually on the books, and are similar to accepted or nonaccepted practices within each respective state, based more on tradition than on legal precedent.

After the turn of the millennium, there has been an increase in the number of children within the child welfare system in need of homes and a growing acceptance of nontraditional families looking to adopt them. However, among the opposition, with groups such as the religiously-based Focus on the Family and the judges who support them, there is a strong sentiment that placing children in the care of gay and lesbian individuals or partners is not in the best interest of the children involved in the respective cases. In April of 2001, researchers Judith Stacey and Timothy Biblarz of the University of Southern California published their findings in the prestigious journal *American Sociological Review*. The duo examined 21 studies regarding the effects of gay parenting. Their meta-analysis concluded: "There were subtle differences in gender behavior and preferences. Lesbian mothers reported that their children, specifically their daughters, were less likely to conform to gender norms in dress, play or behavior; more likely to aspire to nontraditional occupations, such as doctors or lawyers. They also discovered that children of gay and lesbian parents are no more likely to identify themselves as gay or lesbian than the children of heterosexual parents" (Stacey and Biblarz 2001). The latter part of their summary corresponds to what one might consider to be a fear among a majority of adoption agencies and judges—that by placing children in homosexual-parented homes, the children are thus in danger of so-called coming out as homosexuals themselves. This suggests that the environment of a homosexual family is instrumental in the child becoming gay. This argument is considered a fallacy on all levels by the liberal Left and by more and more of the general public as a biological origin model of sexual orientation gains support. Another facet of the Right's argument regarding the placement of children in homosexual-parented homes is that being raised by these individuals will have psychologically detrimental effects on the children. Stacey and Biblarz found that children of homosexual parents show no difference in levels of self-esteem, anxiety, depression, behavior problems, or social performance but do show a higher level of affection, responsiveness, and concern for younger children, as well as seeming to exhibit impressive psychological strength.

Stacey and Biblarz also report that gay parents were found to be more likely to share child care and household duties. In addition to this, the children of gay partners reported closer relationships to the parent who was not their primary caregiver than did the children of heterosexual couples. The fact that this study shows an increase in affection and higher psychological strength is just part of the positive effects that gay adoption can have on children. However, in opposition to the findings of Stacey and Biblarz, there are a great many arguments made against gay and lesbian adoptions including: "Feeling that only heterosexual couples should adopt.... people continue to believe that a two-parent (mother/father) household is best. Homosexuality is morally wrong, which is predominantly a personal opinion and not necessarily a fact.... gays and lesbians may abuse their children" (Stacey and Biblarz 2001). This argument has become known as the so-called best interest argument.

The American Psychological Association (APA) has proven to be a proponent of same-sex adoption, as long as it is in the best interest of the children. In their

Resolution on Sexual Orientation, Parents, and Children, from July 2004, they noted that in the 2000 U.S. Census, 33 percent of female same-sex couple households and 22 percent of male same-sex couple households reported at least one child under the age of 18 living in the home. There are a number of concerns regarding this idea of a minor living in a homosexual-parented household. First, these concerns are in contradiction to the APA statement that homosexuality is not a psychological disorder. Second, there is no scientific basis for concluding that lesbian mothers or gay fathers are unfit parents based solely on their sexual orientation, as many provide stable and supportive households much like their heterosexual counterparts. The APA's Resolution entailed 13 statements, including one which explicitly reads "The APA supports policy and legislation that promotes safe, secure, and nurturing environments for all children. The APA has a long-established policy to deplore 'all public and private discrimination against gay men and lesbians' and urges 'the repeal of all discriminatory legislation against lesbians and gay men.'"(Paige 2005)

The proponents of same-sex adoption argue in favor of the practice on the basis that both past and present research regarding gay parenting shows that there is no difference in the health and success of the children of lesbian and gay parents compared with the children of their heterosexual counterparts. There was no definitive indication of a disadvantage of children of gay and lesbian parents on the basis of the parents' sexual orientation. Home environments with gay or lesbian parents are just as likely to provide solid foundations of comfort and compassionate understanding as the homes of heterosexual couples. Data such as these supported the decision by the American Academy of Pediatrics to issue a policy statement endorsing adoption by same-sex couples.

In the opposition's corner, the article "Does the Sexual Orientation of Parents Matter?" from *American Sociological Review* argues that homosexual parents do not act in the best interest of the child (see Stacey and Biblarz 2001). A number of scholars, theorists, and researchers have posted the claim that gay parents subject children to unnecessary and increased risks. One notable suggestion is that children of gay parents are more likely to suffer confusion over their own gender and sexual identities, thus becoming more likely to claim a homosexual status farther in maturity. There are also claims from the opposition that homosexual parents are more likely to molest their children, as well as that these children are more likely to lose a parent to AIDS, substance abuse, or suicide, as well as to suffer from depression or other emotional disturbances. Arguments like these abound in the opposition's court arguments regarding the placement of children with gay or lesbian parents, as well as the transfer of custody from lesbian or gay parents to heterosexual couples. While somewhat narrowly focused, this is still one of the most widely-used arguments against gay and lesbian parents throughout the court system in the United States.

AGENCIES

Regardless of the position within the argument of whether gay parents should be permitted to adopt, there is still a distinct difference in how each side is portrayed via the media and the Internet in the form of advocacy groups' websites. Agencies reside on both sides of the issue of same-sex adoption. The Evan B. Donaldson Adoption Institute has done extensive work in improving the knowledge of the public in the area of adoption and even more precisely in same-sex adoption. Recently, the Institute published a national survey entitled "Adoption by Lesbians and Gays: A National Survey of Adoption Agency Policies, Practices, and Attitudes." Drawing on a number of surveys and studies, the Institute gives a plethora of statistics regarding the acceptance and placement of children into homosexual homes. Among the findings from the Institute study are: (1) lesbians and gays are adopting regularly, in notable and growing numbers, at both public and private agencies nationwide; (2) assuming that those responding are representative (and the results show that they are), 60 percent of U.S. adoption agencies accept applications from homosexuals; (3) about two in five of all agencies in the country have placed children with adoptive parents who they know to be gay or lesbian; (4) the most likely agencies to place children with homosexuals are public, secular private, Jewish-and Lutheran-affiliated agencies, and those focusing on special needs and international adoption. In addition to the specific findings, the study's results led to several major conclusions on the levels of policy and practice: (1) for lesbians and gay men, the opportunities for becoming adoptive mothers and fathers is significantly greater than is generally portrayed in the media or perceived by the public; (2) although a large and growing number of agencies work with or are willing to work with homosexual clients, they often are unsure about whether to or how to reach out to them; (3) because so many homosexuals are becoming adoptive parents, it is important for the sake of their children that agencies develop preplacement and postplacement services designed to support these parents.

In addition to the various types of programs that the adoption agencies utilize, ranging from special needs to international adoptions or a mixture of both, there is also a definite difference in the overall acceptance of adoption applications from homosexuals on the basis of the agency's religious affiliation. While Jewish-affiliated agencies were almost universally willing to work with LGBT clients, as were the majority of public agencies, private nonreligious and Lutheran-affiliated agencies, only samples of Methodist and Catholic agencies were willing to consider applications from homosexuals. Twenty percent of all agencies responding to the study acknowledged that they had rejected an application from homosexual applicants on at least one occasion.

Not all of the agencies surveyed through the Donaldson Institute survey actually responded to the questions presented to them. Of those who willingly responded, an estimated two-thirds of the agencies had actual policies in effect on adoption by gays and lesbians. Of those, an estimated 33.6 percent reported a nondenominational policy, 20 percent responded that placement decisions were guided by the children's country of origin, and another 20 percent said that religious beliefs were at the core of rejecting the homosexual applications. More than one-third of the responding agencies reported in follow-up phone calls that they did not work with homosexual prospective adoptive parents. On the opposite side of the situation, an estimated two in five, or 39 percent, of all agencies had placed at least one child with a homosexual adoptive parent between 1999 and 2000. Due to the fact that fewer than half of all agencies collect information on the sexual orientation of potential adoptive parents and do not actively track the statistics regarding the placement of children with adoptive parents who are homosexual, the Donaldson Institute was forced to estimate the number of such placements made. One adoption placement with a homosexual client per year was counted for statistical purposes. Based on these assumptions, there were an estimated 1,206 placements with homosexual parents (or roughly 1.3 percent of the total placements). This number is actually much higher in reality.

One aspect not yet discussed is the input of the birth parents in the proceedings of the adoption of their child. The Donaldson Institute delved into this issue and released the following findings: (1) about one-quarter of respondents said that prospective birth parents have objected to the placing of their child with gays or lesbians, or have specifically requested that their child not be placed with homosexuals. At that time, nearly 15 percent of all agencies said birth parents had requested or chosen lesbian or gay prospective adoptive parents for their child on at least one occasion; (2) Although most agencies worked with lesbians and gays, only 19 percent sought them to be adoptive parents and the vast majority of these (86.6 percent) relied on word-of-mouth for recruitment. Outreach efforts were made most often at agencies already willing to work with homosexuals (41.7 percent of Jewish-affiliated, 29.9 percent of private, nonreligiously affiliated, and 20 percent of public); (3) Similarly, adoption agencies focused on children with special needs were the most likely to make outreach efforts (32.1 percent) to gays and lesbians, followed by international-focused agencies (19.7 percent); (4) nearly half (48 percent) indicated an interest in receiving training to work with lesbian and gay prospective parents. Most likely to be interested were agencies already working with them; public, nonreligiously affiliated, Jewish-and Lutheran-affiliated agencies. Additionally, special needs programs and those with mixed needs were more likely to be interested in training than were those focusing on international and domestic infant adoptions.

There seems to be a growing interest and flexibility toward the idea that homosexual prospective parents may be a viable option for the placement of children into homes to ultimately give them a more stable and nurturing environment than one would find in child welfare systems. However, religious affiliation of the agency remains an important and prominent issue. Over half of the agencies held no religious affiliation (55.38 percent), while the rest represented a variety of faiths, the largest of which was Catholic-affiliated at 14.8 percent, with various other denominations reporting 5 percent or less. As one can see, with as many placements as are being made, it is clear that somewhere along the line the individuals who work in these agencies do actually want to place these children in good, stable, nurturing homes. However, a number of the agencies to which this survey was sent declined to participate. Their reasons for declining ranged from: (1) agency does not make adoption placements (36.7 percent); (2) agency does not work with homosexual clients (34.1 percent); (3) interested but agency director too busy (13.3 percent); (4) no reason given or not interested in the study (12.5 percent); (5) incomplete data from returned survey (3.0 percent). While there is still 0.4 percent missing from this data set, it does give some pretty startling ideas about the various agencies' reactions to this survey.

At the time of this survey, only Florida, Mississippi, and Utah had statutory bans on or prohibitive barriers to homosexual adoption. One of the more shocking discoveries of the Donaldson Institute research is that 17 adoption directors from other states incorrectly reported that lesbians and gays were barred from adopting children in their states; another 31 respondents were unsure of the states' law on adoption by homosexuals. This is slightly alarming, considering the work that has been done to include homosexuals in the adoption process, and yet it would seem that they are being excluded yet again but this time by ignorance. Despite being somewhat unaware of their states' legislation on homosexual adoption, there was a clear distribution of policy acceptance levels regarding homosexual adoption. According to the Donaldson Institute research, about 20 percent of all respondents said that their agencies, on one or more occasions, had rejected applications from gay or lesbian individuals or couples. The reasons for the rejections were as follows: (1) unrealistic expectations, (2) psychological problems, (3) questionable motives for adopting, (4) relationship problems, (5) placement with homosexuals violates agency policy, (6) applicant' lifestyle incompatible with adoption, (7) placement with homosexuals prohibited by country of origin, (8) sexual orientation of applicant incompatible with adoption, (9) lack of adequate social support, (10) financial problems, (11) placement with homosexuals violates community standards, and (12) medical problems with the applicant.

FUTURE DIRECTIONS

Generally, the presentation of gays and lesbians as adoptive parents has been biased by the group doing the presenting. Conservative media outlets and family values camps such as the Family Research Council predictably argue that the best home for a child is with two heterosexual married parents. These groups cite well-used arguments against homosexuality in general, such as the so-called unnaturalness of choosing a same sex partner and fears of deviant sexual choices, as evidence for why homosexuals should be excluded from the pool of adoptive parents. Increasingly, however, because there are many more children awaiting adoption than homes into which they can easily be placed, gay and lesbian individuals and couples may represent an untapped market. Anecdotal evidence suggests that not only have gays and lesbians been more willing to adopt special needs children, sometimes because those were the only children agencies would make available to them, but the outcomes are more positive than many critics predicted. As pressure mounts on states to solve some of the child welfare problems in the foster care system, an additional group of potential loving parents may be seen as a beneficial resource. For most, the best interests of the child means that the child is always better off in a permanent home setting than a temporary foster care setting.

Additionally, the opinions of the general public toward LGBT issues and individuals have become more accepting and positive over time. With increased media coverage, same-sex adoption and LGBT issues as a whole have gained a great deal of attention over the last two decades, with no real end in sight. With questions about homosexual marriage being debated across the country, the next step in the American dream is children. Consequently, we can anticipate more debate in the coming years about the characteristics of desirable adoptive parents.

See also Foster Care; International Adoption; Same-Sex Marriage; Transracial Adoption.

Further Reading: American Psychological Association. http://www.apa.org; Drescher, Jack and Deborah Glazer. *Gay and Lesbian Parenting.* Binghamton, NY: The Haworth Medical Press, 2001; Evan B. Donaldson Adoption Institute. "Adoption by Lesbians and Gays: A National Survey of Adoption Agency Policies, Practices, and Attitudes." 2002. http://www.adoptioninstitute.org; Family Research Council. http://www.frc.org; Kreisher, Kristen. "Gay Adoption." *Children's Voice Magazine* 17 (January/February 2002). http://www.cwla.org/articles/cv0201gayadopt.htm; Mallon, Gerald P. *Lesbian and Gay Foster and Adoptive Parents: Recruiting, Assessing, and Supporting an Untapped Resource for Children and Youth.* Washington, DC: Child Welfare League of America Inc., 2006; Paige, R. U. Proceedings of the American Psychological Association, Incorporated, for the legislative year 2004. Minutes of the meeting of the Council of Representatives July 28 and 30, 2004, Honolulu, HI, 2005. http://www.apa.org/governance/; Sember, Brette McWhorter. *Gay and Lesbian Parenting Choices: From Adopting or Using a Surrogate to Choosing the Perfect Father.* Franklin Lakes, NJ: The Career Press Inc., 2006; Stacey, Judith, and Timothy J. Biblarz. "(How) Does the Sexual Orientation of Parents Matter?" *American Sociological Review* 66, no. 2, (2001): 159–183.

Jeffery Jones

GRANDPARENTHOOD

At the beginning of the twentieth century, many people did not live long enough to reach grandparenthood. If longevity prevailed, grandchildren were born well into the latter part of the grandparent's life. In current times, grandparenthood typically occurs in mid-life and is now commonplace primarily due to the increase in life expectancy. Many more people are experiencing grandparenthood and for greater lengths of time. In fact, it is not extraordinary for someone to spend half of his or her life as a grandparent. It may not be shocking, then, to learn that about 50 percent of grandparents are under age 60. Some are even part of five-generation families. The greater likelihood that grandparenting will be a part of one's family life has led to questions about the role that grandparents should assume in the family.

BACKGROUND

Grandparenthood is a time when at least three generations of a family are present. For most of us, we think of older men and women in their late 60s when we think of grandma and grandpa, but because some parents do not delay childbearing, grandparenthood can occur as early as the mid-30s. It is estimated that over three-fourths of those aged 65 and over are grandparents and many get to see their grandchildren on a regular basis. Grandparents can share their love, understanding and knowledge with their grandchildren and have been shown to contribute to the well-being of grandchildren.

Many people remain active well into their 70s and 80s and may know the joys of being a part of their grandchildren and great-grandchildren's lives. For a percentage of grandparents, grandchildren are the center of their world because they have taken on the primary responsibility for their grandchildren. On the other hand, some grandparents may be estranged from their grandchildren due to family conflicts. Typically, parents determine the interaction that grandparents have with grandchildren when they are younger but do not determine the relationship when the grandchildren are older. Family size may also influence grandparent-grandchild relationships.

Grandparents have an important symbolism in our culture. They are the link to previous generations and may be the oldest living relative in a family. For some, they are the matriarchs and patriarchs of their families and communities and are role models and mentors to those around them. They also pass down family stories and traditions. In many cases, grandparents are the only contact young people have with older individuals. For some, grandparenthood is a time when they pass along their wisdom to younger generations, especially grandchildren. Grandparenthood can be a time where the older generation imparts the family history, educates or otherwise prepares grandchildren for the future.

For the grandparents who are fortunate enough to retire, they can enjoy a life without schedules or a workplace for one-third of their lives. They can take in the world around them and appreciate it. Some choose to give back to their communities and volunteer in the local government or programs such as grandparent fostering. Becoming a grandparent in later life can add a new dimension to retirement. It can be a fulfilling role for both the grandparent and the grandchild. Most grandparents idealize their new role and this can lead to a detrimental experience if they are unaware of their boundaries. Also, there can be conflict between grandparent and parent when parenting styles differ. In fact, there are two primary factors that influence the amount of time spent with a grandchild: the geographic location of the grandparent to the grandchild and the relationship with the parent.

STEREOTYPES

While popular conception does not typically show any negativity, becoming a grandparent may have its drawbacks. In a society that does not value becoming older, becoming a grandparent can signify being elderly. That is why becoming a grandparent in your 30s is viewed as off-time and nonnormative. Delight in being a grandparent can be overshadowed by the societal image of an old lady with gray hair, sitting in a rocking chair, knitting after she had just baked some cookies.

There can also be some resentment of the expectations that grandparenthood entails. A stereotype exists of grandparents where it is believed that much of their time is devoted to caring for and servicing their grandchildren's needs. As discussed earlier, some grandparents may be too involved in their grandchild's life, to the point of impeding the parents. On the other hand, some grandparents feel that there is an unspoken and undeniable requirement to baby-sit their grandchildren. Some research has shown that grandparenthood and the expectations that come along with this status are not supported by all grandparents and that many are unwilling to take this status as assumed.

Certainly grandparenthood has changed over the years, but the images and expectations surrounding the status of grandparents are slow to evolve. For example, grandparenthood is occurring in mid-life, and the status is not as tied to old age as it was in the past. Partly this is due to life enhancements that lessen the ill effects of the aging process. In addition, there is huge diversity in the ways in which people enact the grandparent role. One major reason there is so much diversity is due to the age of onset of this new status. A younger grandparent may still be in the workforce versus an older grandparent who may be retired. Yet the stereotypical images that are associated with this status have not changed. Because some grandparents may still be in the workforce when they become a grandparent, this may hinder their availability to be on-call to baby-sit. Moreover, because many contemporary families are in dual-earner households, grandmothers are more likely to be working. Many factors such as these can influence one's style of grandparenting, and in turn impact the grandparent-grandchild relationship.

FACTORS THAT INFLUENCE GRANDPARENTING STYLES

There are a number of grandparenting styles and meanings associated with grandparenting. In the 1960s five different grandparenting styles were identified that are still important today: reservoir of family wisdom, formal, surrogate parent, fun seeker, and distant figure. The *reservoir of family wisdom* is when the grandparent expects the parent to seek advice from them. They also have certain skills and resources that could benefit the parent. The *formal* grandparent creates a clear line between parenting and grandparenting. They are active in the grandchild's life but do not take on parenting, nor do they give advice. The *surrogate parent* is when a grandparent takes on caring for the grandchild during the time in which the parent is working. The *fun seeker* has a fun and casual relationship with the grandchild. There is an emphasis on a mutually beneficial relationship. The *distant figure* is the grandparent who does not have contact with the grandchild outside of special occasions. These styles of grandparenting have been found to be associated with age. *Formal* grandparents have been found to be older while *distant figures* and *fun seekers* are usually younger.

The reduction in the average size of families, the increasing ease in which to be geographically mobile, increasing rates of divorce, and more single-parent homes have all complicated grandparenthood, especially as it relates to contact and interaction with grandchildren. Technological breakthroughs and wider access to mass transit have served to alleviate some of these confounds; however, grandparenthood has changed considerably relative to the early-twentieth century largely due to these aforementioned trends. Other changes over time may not seem as obvious. For example, grandparents today are probably healthier than ever before due to the increase in health awareness. We can expect to see grandparents and grandchildren acting in ways that we do not stereotypically think about. It is not atypical to witness grandparents mountain-biking with their grandchildren. Indeed, grandparents today are wealthier, healthier and more active than those of previous generations.

Gender also impacts grandparenting. Grandfathers play more of an instrumental role in grandchildren's lives by providing advice while grandmothers emphasize an expressive approach to grandparenting through expressions of love and caring. Indeed, most stereotypes of grandparents focus on grandmothers. Grandmothers describe their relationships with grandchildren as close, warm, and fun. Because women have stronger bonds with family, adult daughters and mothers tend to have the closest relationship. Furthermore, while grandmothers and grandfathers both report closer relationships with granddaughters, grandmothers and granddaughters tend to be the closest. In the African American community, grandmothers play an important role in caregiving of grandchildren, great-grandchildren and fictive kin—people considered family without necessarily being blood-related. According to studies, African American grandmothers have been a major influence in stabilizing black families and socializing children since the days of slavery.

Another factor that contributes to the diversity of grandparenthood is the changing structures of families. Divorce and remarriage have changed the ways in which grandparents may be viewed and how their roles may be enacted. Divorce can create a stronger bond for the custodial grandparent-grandchild relationship while weakening the noncustodial grandparent-grandchild relationship. Because mothers tend to receive custody it is the maternal grandparents who benefit from divorce while paternal grandparents have a harder time sustaining a relationship. Blended families may make a grandparent's role unclear. Research has shown that in blended families paternal grandmothers are more likely to maintain relationships with daughters-in-laws and the new family members than are maternal grandmothers to maintain relationships with sons-in-law.

Grandparents can be providers of useful advice for their children to utilize in raising their own children. Grandparents must, however, be careful to wait until they are asked for this advice. Grandparents can be the ones to help bring together the family and keep communications open. At the same time, grandparents must face the fact that their children may have a different parenting style than they did and should respect their child's decisions on how to raise their grandchild. Grandparenting is different than parenting, and some grandparents welcome the opportunity to be the fun grandparent while others may not be able to take a backseat as an authority figure, especially when they wholeheartedly disagree with their child's choices.

GRANDPARENTS AND TECHNOLOGY

One of the interesting changes in the lives of grandparents has been the increases in technology such as the Internet. There are many organizations and web sites that are devoted to helping grandparents get the most out of their role in the family. Some of the well-known sites include: AARP.org, Grandparenting.com, Grandboomers.com, Grandparentsmagazine.net, Grandparents.com, Grandkidsandme.com, Grandtimes.com, Grandparentvisitationblog.com, WholeFamily.com: Senior Center Section. In addition to readily available information on grandparenting, today's grandparents may find that geographic distance is not as great a barrier to establishing a strong grandparent-grandchild bond as it would have been in the past. With email, web-cams, and photo sites among the technology readily available to a majority of American families, older Americans have sought computer training to keep up with the younger generations. Some senior citizen centers across the country have instituted courses on using these new technologies and have made computers available for the use of their members.

GRANDPARENTS RAISING GRANDCHILDREN

According to the U.S. Bureau of Census, in 2000 over 6 percent of children under the age of 18 live with a grandparent. At least one-third of these families are known as skipped generation families where neither parent is living in the household. The growth in skipped generation families has been attributed to incarceration of parents, child abuse and neglect, a rise in single parent households, divorce, parent drug use, crime, AIDS, physical and mental illness, and teen pregnancy.

There are a myriad of reasons why the parent is unwilling or unable to raise their child and a grandparent takes on this responsibility. Even when a grandparent is willing to take on the responsibility of being the primary caregiver of their grandchild, financial and health problems may complicate the situation. Also, social isolation may occur due to the fact that these grandparents are different than their counterparts because they are taking on the nonnormative life transition of becoming a parent to their grandchild at a time when their peers are enjoying a child-free lifestyle. Grandparents face many challenges when caring solely for their grandchildren, such as adding their grandchildren to health insurance policies, enrolling them in school, and finding affordable housing. These issues can be even more difficult when the grandparent does not have legal custody of the grandchild.

Four categories have been discovered that are affected by being a caregiver to grandchildren: changes in lifestyle, changes in relationship with spouse, changes in relationships with family, and changes in relationships with friends. They emerged from 114 in-depth interviews with grandparent caregivers. For surrogate grandparents, there was a decline in privacy, less time available for oneself, less money, less time spent and attention given to spouse, less time for leisure activities, less time spent with friends, and not enough time to get everything done that is needed to get done because of the time required to take care of their grandchildren. The surrogate grandparents also reported feelings of increased concern about things, feeling emotionally strained, feeling more physically tired, having to continuously change plans and routines, and having greater purpose for living since they became caregivers to their grandchildren.

The structure of the family and the resources available to the grandparent may either help to alleviate or cause more problems. Studies have found that family structure, the marital status and gender of the grandparent, and whether the parents are present in the home influence what problems arise. In 1997, over half of grandparent-headed households had both grandparents in the home, 6 percent were grandfather-only and the remainder were grandmother-only homes. Overall, grandparent households are usually composed of younger, better educated, working, and healthier grandparents. Only 15 percent of grandmothers and 21 percent of grandfathers are age 65 and older (Bryson and Casper 1999).

There are many different problems and challenges that can arise for surrogate grandparents as primary caregivers to their grandchildren. First of all, health problems are exacerbated by taking on this new role. Grandparents who raise their grandchildren usually also have financial strain due to the fact that many have a low-income status. Also, younger grandparents may have to quit their jobs or change their hours in order to provide child care. Retired grandparents who live off of a limited amount of money to begin with now have to make sacrifices, such as not shopping for themselves or selling off items to take care of the grandchild. Furthermore, many grandparents feel isolated when they take on the new role because they spend less time with family and friends to be able to take care of their grandchildren. For example, grandparents who are active in their churches may not be able to spend as much time there as they would like due to the everyday responsibilities of having to take care of a child. Also, they may not be able to connect with friends any longer because their friends may grandparent differently. The family structure and the resources available to the surrogate grandparents are extremely important factors in how successful and happy a grandparent is in enacting the role of surrogate parent as a grandparent.

Social support can help alleviate the stress that is incurred by surrogate grandparents. Researchers have found that grandparents are better able to cope with becoming surrogate parents to their grandchildren when they have the resources to alleviate the stress associated with taking on this nonnormative transition. Stress for the grandparent is negatively correlated with happiness and generativity (the desire to help the younger generation), but social support was found to help alleviate these negative associations. Stress is not the only problem that surrogate grandparents face when they become the primary caregiver to their grandchildren.

Grandparent Visitation Rights

For a majority of grandparents there is no question about whether they can visit with their grandchildren. Commonly, grandparents enjoy going on trips with grandchildren, provide needed day care, and in some cases become the primary caregivers. But some grandparents may be denied access to their grandchildren by the parents or legal guardians. This may be due to conflict between the parents and grandparents; the grandparents' child may have died or lost custody in a divorce and the other parent may refuse visitation.

The laws regarding visitation rights for grandparents vary by state. None of the states automatically give visitation rights to grandparents so they must research the laws in the state in which the child lives in order to determine their course of action. Before 2000, all of the states gave grandparents the ability to go to court to request visitation. In 2000, there was an influential case in Washington State that changed grandparents' visitation rights. The case decided that the broad visitation rights, which could be extended to nonrelatives, impeded on parental rights. In the last decade, many states have ruled that visitation rights have been too broad and may violate a parent's right in deciding who may be active in the child's life. In those states, grandparents must work with the parent for visitation. In states that still allow a grandparent to petition for visitation, grandparents must prove that they should have the right to visit with their grandchild and the courts must find it in the best interest of the child.

The most recent case in Hawaii has made visitation rights for grandparents more difficult to obtain. The courts decided that the grandparents had to prove that harm would come to the child if the parent's wishes were upheld. This means that grandparents must present evidence that the decision that the parents make regarding their child will bring harm to the child, otherwise the parent has the right to make decisions.

As of 2007, the highest courts of 23 states have looked into their visitation laws. The visitation laws have been reworked to give greater power to the parents' decisions on visitation. All in all, grandparents' visitation rights have dramatically changed in the last decade. There are still possibilities for grandparents to fight for visitation under certain situations. For example, grandparents have been given visitation rights when a parent has died or been incarcerated, have been raising their grandchildren for a certain amount of time in which they were suddenly cut off from seeing their grandchildren, or where the courts deem that the grandchildren's well-being would be compromised if they were disconnected from their grandparents.

There are arguments for and against grandparent visitation rights. People who advocate for grandparent visitation rights feel that grandparents can provide stability for a grandchild after a family crisis such as divorce or death of a parent. Also, it can be traumatic for a grandchild who has developed a relationship with the grandparents to be suddenly cut off from them. Furthermore, they point out that a divorce, incarceration, or death of a parent should not automatically grant the surviving parent the right to disunite a beneficial relationship between the grandchild and grandparent. On the other hand, there are people who oppose grandparent visitation rights. They feel that states should not interfere with a parent's child-rearing rights. In addition, there may be good reason why the parent has deemed it inappropriate for the grandchild to visit with the grandparent. For example, the grandparents may have been abusive to the parents and so they do not want them around their children, or in the case of lesbian and gay parents, the grandparents may not agree with their lifestyle and the grandchildren may be caught in the middle. Moreover, the grandparents may not be respecting the parents' parenting style or may be bad-mouthing them to the grandchild. Lastly, these advocates feel that the mere fact of the court being involved can cause havoc to the grandchild's home life.

The American Association of Retired Persons (AARP), a nonprofit organization for persons over the age of 50, recommends trying to work out issues between grandparents and parents before it escalates to a battle in courts since it is costly, time consuming, and can rip families further apart. In tough situations a less hostile and less costly solution may be mediation. A mediator helps both parties compromise where each may have to give a little to get a little. If mediation does not work, grandparents may then contact a family lawyer in the state in which the grandchild lives to explore what the visitation laws and rulings on grandparents visitation rights are in that jurisdiction.

See also Changing Fertility Patterns; Children as Caregivers; Elder Care; Grandparents as Caregivers.

Further Reading: Bryson, Ken, and Lynne M. Casper. "Coresident Grandparents and Grandchildren." *US Census Bureau: US Department of Commerce Economic and Statistics Administration* (1999): 1–10; Falk, Ursula A., and Gerhard Falk. *Grandparents: A New Look at the Supporting Generation.* Amherst, NY: Prometheus Books, 2002; Hayslip, Bert, and Robin Goldberg-Glen. *Grandparents Raising Grandchildren: Theoretical, Empirical, and Clinical Perspectives.* New York: Springer Publishing Company, 2000; Jendrek, Margaret P. "Grandparents Who Parent Their Grandchildren: Effects on Lifestyle." *Journal of Marriage and the Family* 55, no. 3 (1993): 609–621; Landry-Meyer, Laura, Jean M. Gerard and Jacqueline R. Guzell. "Caregiver Stress among Grandparents Raising Grandchildren: The Functional Role of Social Support." *Marriage and Family Review* 37, nos. 1/2 (2005): 171–190; Minkler, Meredith, and Kathleen M. Roe. "Grandparents as Surrogate Parents." *Generations* 20, no. 1 (1996): 34–39; Neugarten, B., and K. Weinstein. "The Changing American Grandparent." *Journal of Marriage and the Family* 26, no. 2 (1964): 199–204; Smith Ruiz, Dorothy. *Amazing Grace: African American Grandmothers as Caregivers and Conveyors of Traditional Values.* Westport, CT: Praeger Publishers, 2004; Szinovacz, Maximiliane E. *Handbook on Grandparenthood.* Westport, CT: Greenwood Press, 1998; U.S. Census Bureau. "QT-P18. Marital Status by Sex, Unmarried-Partner Households, and Grandparents as Caregivers: 2000." http://factfinder.census.gov/home/saff/main.html; Westman, Jack C. "Grandparenthood." In *Parenthood in America: Undervalued, Underpaid, Under Siege,* ed. Jack C. Westman. Madison: The University of Wisconsin Press, 2001.

Orli Zaprir

GRANDPARENTS AS CAREGIVERS

Grandparents play a variety of roles in the lives of their grandchildren. From playmate to confidante, as grandparents live longer and enjoy better health as they age, they have increased opportunities for contact with their grandchildren. One of the trends changing the nature of grandparent-grandchild relationships, however, is when grandparents routinely provide basic care for their grandchildren, sometimes called surrogate parenting. From serving as substitute caregivers while parents work to rearing their grandchildren on their own grandparents are finding that sometimes parenting tasks do not end when their children leave the home. There are both positive and negative consequences for the care that grandparents provide, and questions remain as to whether this is the best option for both the grandparents and the children for which they care.

BACKGROUND

Over the last decade, there has been a 40 percent increase in the number of grandchildren being cared for full time by their grandparents according to the United States Census Bureau. Currently in the United States, more than 3.6 million grandchildren under 18 years of age (around 6 percent on all minor children) are being cared for by their grandparents. There are many reasons why this arrangement occurs.

For children who are not yet of school age and in need of day care, staying with the grandparent while the parents are working may be an economical option. However, grandparents may themselves be employed and this may put a strain on their resources and time available for work. Some grandmothers may be reluctant to refuse this task due to the cultural expectation that grandparents will provide baby-sitting. The expectation for child care assistance seems to be one of the few cultural norms of grandparenting, which overall is a rather free-form role where participants set their own goals and objectives. This lack of standardization is likely due to the widely varying ages at which persons enter the role, gender differences, and personal experiences of having been a grandchild.

While some research has focused on this routine care by grandparents, more research attention has been given to situations in which the grandparents are the primary caregivers for the grandchild and the consequences of such arrangements. In this scenario, the household is marked by a so-called skipped generation, where neither biological parent is present in the home. Major reasons that grandparents care for grandchildren in this way are the result of unfortunate circumstances that families experience. For example, the parent of the grandchild might have been involved with drugs, suffered mental illness, experienced extreme financial strain, be incarcerated, have died, or the child has suffered abuse or neglect from the parent. There are positive and negative consequences for both grandchild and grandparent.

NEGATIVE ASPECTS

Researchers are beginning to explore the negative effects that caring for one's grandchildren in the capacity of parent have on the grandparent and on the grandchild. Among the areas that are of concern are the grandparent's health, financial status, mental health and role expectations, and legal right to care for grandchildren.

VARIATIONS IN GRANDPARENTING

The age, race, and gender of the caregiving grandparent play a significant role in the way a grandchild will be raised. According to Thomas et al. (2000), a grandparent that is under the age of 65 that has a more relaxed, playful relationship with their grandchildren are said to be fun seekers. For those grandparents over the age of 65, their grand-parenting was said to be more formal. It could be concluded that the younger the grandparent is, the easier it might be to raise the grandchild with less of a generation gap.

An interesting fact in regards to race is that African American grandparents have reported greater levels of both fulfillment and aggravation with the relationships with their grandchildren than their Caucasian counterparts. It seems that African American grandmothers have more support from their friends and other family members than the Caucasian grandmothers, perhaps due to the fact that more African American families experience grandmother care. African American grandparents represent 12 percent of those who care for their grandchildren while Caucasian grandparents represent four percent. Hispanic grandparents, with the exception of Cuban Americans, are likely to be involved on an everyday basis with their grandchildren.

With regard to gender, grandmothers cared more for the grandchildren than did the grandfathers. The grandfather's role was to offer advice and take responsibility for the grandchild but they note receiving less emotional fulfillment than do the grandmothers. Grandfathers' advice would center on future jobs, education, and financial decisions. Grandmothers would advise their grandchildren on more personal decisions in understanding life, love, and relationships. The grandmothers reported a stronger motherly bond when grandparenting. Finally, it should be noted that women's greater life expectancy compared with men means that they will spend more years of their lives in the grandparent role.

Health Concerns

Grandparents arrive at the point of parenting their grandchildren by many paths, nearly all of which have produced significant stress in the family prior to the parenting task. Among the stressful situations that necessitate grandparents stepping into the parent role are AIDS, divorce, teen pregnancy, mental illness, and so on. The stress of caring for the grandchild can be a huge burden for the grandparent—impacting the grandparents' health. Some studies have suggested that some grandparents are afraid to admit to health problems for fear of their grandchildren being removed from their custody.

Health costs are most noticeable when grandparents are older at the time they begin caring for grandchildren. The fatigue of caring for very young children may take a toll on older grandparents, causing them to feel overtired and more vulnerable to illnesses in general. It is true that children get sick; the presence of children in the home increases the likelihood that grandparents will get more colds and other communicable diseases. The need to care for children may push grandparents to delay needed health care. Having to pick up the grandchild, help with homework, or working more hours to financially support the child, if necessary and possible, can interfere with obtaining needed healthcare.

Focusing on the aging grandparent's health, stress over the obligation of caring for the child can manifest itself in physical ailments. Lack of leisure time, leading to more stress, can further harm the health of the grandparent. If a grandparent has worked for 40 years or more, it will be time for them to retire and retirement is affected by having to care for the grandchild on a fulltime basis. A delayed retirement is detrimental to the health of an aging person, particularly exposing him or her to more chances for on-the-job injury, and can cause more stress which could lead to more health problems.

Financial Concerns

Being both a grandparent and the sole caregiver for a grandchild means more financial stress as well. They may have planned and saved for retirement or wanted to travel and live abroad, but now they are caring for the grandchild. Depleting the savings account, taking out loans, going bankrupt or living a lifestyle of financial worry are all consequences of becoming a new parent. Most persons who have planned for retirement have enough saved to cover their projected expenses, not the additional expenses accrued during childrearing. Because children often become more expensive as they enter the teen years, as the grandparent is aging the financial burden may be increasing.

Particularly if the grandparent has already retired, it may be quite difficult to find work to supplement with extra money; indeed grandparents sometimes have to rely solely on outside sources, such as public assistance programs, to help with the financial burden of caring for their grandchildren. According to the American Association of Retired Persons (AARP), grandparents can turn to government or private agencies to assist in the time of financial stress. The AARP suggests that the grandchild might be able to file for their own social security or receive money from the state's Temporary Assistance for Needy Families (TANF) program. But this program is as its title states: temporary. The grandparent might qualify for food stamps or be able to inquire with the Internal Revenue Service about a tax credit or exemption for the grandchild.

Another financial strain may come from the grandparent's home. Will it be big enough to accommodate this new family arrangement? As persons retire they often downsize into smaller residences to make their upkeep tasks fewer as they age. Again, The AARP has a suggestion, recommending that the grandparent seek out special housing for grandfamilies. Or, the grandparents can take out a reverse mortgage, which only applies to those 62 years or older. This would provide some money for support of the grandchild out of the equity in one's home. As long as they live in that house, the money does not have to be paid back until they move, or die. But the debt is passed on or if the money is paid back it will leave less of a buffer for the grandchild to inherit.

Another issue of finances relates to the working grandparent. For many grandparents who have retired, the rehiring of the elderly is a major concern in the United States. Although there are laws providing protection against age discrimination, many cases go unreported. As a result, many retired grandparents are unable to return to work to earn sufficient income to support the addition of the grandchild. Even those fortunate to return to work full-time will face issues that add to their already overtaxed new situation. Some of these concerns include, but are not limited to, the following. Will the company provide time off for the new employee (the grandparent) to attend to the grandchild's school or medical affairs? Will the grandparent (the new employee) be able to have access to medical insurance that covers the grandchild? Will the grandparent (the new employee) be paid a wage sufficient to support the newly structured family?

Emotional Concerns

Of added concern is the emotional toll this arrangement will have on both the grandparents and the grandchild. Often grandparents were put under more emotional stress due to the behavioral or physical health problems of the grandchild. Many grandbabies that were born addicted to a drug cry excessively or need special attention for their care. The combination of less sleep, more worry, and concern for the grandchild who has an addiction or other chronic problem adds a significant level of stress to the caregiving.

However, another emotional issue the grandchild may deal with is trying to understand why he or she no longer lives with the parent. For particularly young children who may not fully grasp the situation, grandparents may have to be extra-reassuring about the stability of their home. Likewise, grandparents may be grieving over the situation with their own child and have a hard time providing the emotional support to the grandchild. If there is high emotional attachment between the grandparent and grandchild, sometimes when a grandparent is significantly aged, the grandchild may be particularly concerned about the longevity of the caregiver.

In one sample of African American grandmothers, a group very likely to be caring for grandchildren, 36 percent admitted to more strain on their mental health. Depression and anxiety were the most commonly reported mental health symptoms for those grandparents raising their grandchildren. With so much pressure to emotionally, financially, and educationally care for the grandchild one could only expect higher levels of stress. In the same study, African American grandparents whose grandchildren were the offspring of drug-addicted parents reported that 86 percent felt depressed and 72 percent suffered from anxiety frequently.

Another emotional concern involves how closely the situation fulfills the expected role of the grandparent. Culturally, there is no clear set of roles for grandparents, but generally grandparents are exempted from the routine care of grandchildren, often preferring a friendship-type relationship. By definition, parenting is not about friendship so some grandparents feel deprived of that experience; most never expected to be fully responsible for the care of their grandchildren. Middle-class society has created a role for grandparents in which they tell stories about the past exploits of the family, host holiday functions, travel extensively, and generally enjoy their golden years. The reality for many is quite different. Contrary to the belief, some grandparents now have new expectations and play new roles in society.

Grandparents who become primary caregivers migrate from the role of grandparent to full-time parent at 50 or 60 years old. Once the grandparent becomes the primary caregiver for the grandchild, there are many problems that may surface. For example, because grandparents are much older than the grandchild, the grandchild may feel a strong sense of a generation gap in being raised by people who are not as close to them in age as their parents. The children are not alone in feeling isolated. Grandparents rearing their grandchildren may experience a loss of friends and other important social relationships because they are not doing the same things that others their age are doing. In particular, their parenting responsibilities may keep them from participating in social activities with others of their cohort, thus decreasing their available support network.

Legal Concerns

The generational differences between the grandchild and grandparents may also create legal problems. For the grandparent who desires custody of the grandchild, the law has generally not been supportive. There are good legal reasons to assign custody to grandparents. Notable among them would be so that important decisions regarding health care or schooling for the grandchild can be made by the grandparent. The establishment of legal guardianship also helps with tax and inheritance benefits and application for public assistance. This shift from grandparent to caregiver needs to be addressed on a number of legal fronts to ensure that the rights of both parties are preserved.

POSITIVE ASPECTS

Becoming parents again with grandchildren doesn't have to be a negative event for most grandparents. Becoming a parent again can have a direct impact on mental health. For grandparents it can give a sense of renewal and provide them with an opportunity to do things differently than they may have done with their own children. It also allows for a connection with the past family history and many report improved life contentment and drive for satisfaction after parenting grandchildren.

Raising grandchildren can be a wonderful experience, and there are positive aspects relating to one's health and caring for a young grandchild. Some studies have found that some grandmothers lost weight when they began caring for their grandchildren due to increased levels of physical activity and some ceased smoking for the sake of the grandchild's health. One study reported that 28 percent of African American grandmothers felt more joy and self-esteem regarding their mental health when they were caring for their grandchildren. They worried less for the safety and well being of the grandchild when the child was not in the care of a negligent biological parent.

The idea that grandchildren keep one young does seem to be occurring. With increased levels of activity, both physical and mental, grandparents can see an overall increase in their health status. A positive aspect for grandparents is that they experience their grandchild more directly. This may increase the closeness between them and form a different kind of bond than had they not resided together. Additionally the grandparent can impart to the child the positive aspects of the skipped generation, which can be particularly important if the child's parent is deceased. Both child and grandparent may come to appreciate and respect the cohort differences between their age groups. A generation gap does not have to be viewed negatively. Of note, is the benefit to society when a child that might otherwise have been placed in foster care is parented by a family member biologically related to him.

FUTURE PROSPECTS

Given the increases in parenting by grandparents, one can expect the trend to continue. As a consequence, websites and books have begun to be widely available that may assist the grandparent who has begun parenting again. Just as parenting is a complex activity with many different styles, researchers are just beginning to understand the ways in which Americans do grandparenting. As a topic for exploration, grandparenting is new and unique. As more evidence emerges, we can expect that more benefits, particularly when the grandparents are younger and have more financial resources, will likely emerge.

See also Changing Fertility Patterns; Children as Caregivers; Foster Care; Grandparenthood.

Further Reading: AARP. www.AARP.org; All Family Resources. www.familymanagement.com; Berman, Eleanor. *Grandparenting ABC's: A Beginners Handbook.* New York: Perigee, 1998; Edwards, O. "Teachers' Perceptions of the Emotional and Behavioral Functioning of Children Raised by Grandparents." *Psychology in the Schools* 43 (2006): 565–572; Fay, Jim. *Grandparenting with Love and Logic: Practical Solutions to Today's Grandparenting Challenges.* Golden, CO: Love and Logic Press, 1998; The Foundation for Grandparenting. www.grandparenting.org; Grandparents Raising Grandchildren. www.raisingyourgrandchildren.com; Kornhaber, Arthur. *The Grandparent Guide: The Definitive Guide to Coping with the Challenges of Modern Grandparenting.* New York: Contemporary Books, 2002; Thomas, J., L. Sperry, and M. Yarborough. "Grandparents as Parents: Research Findings and Policy Recommendations." *Child Psychiatry and Human Development* 31 (2000): 3–22.

Tera Rebekah Scott